Praise for *The Family Legacy*

What I love about Brian's work is that he restores the Mystery to our ancient art, activating the imaginative function and widening the scope of our interpretive gaze. More than merely explaining and categorizing complex family dynamics, this work is an invitation to gaze deeply into the matrix of our first relationships and discover how Psyche weaves and interweaves through them all.
                                Jason Holley, Astrologer and Psychotherapist

I have known Brian Clark for nearly 30 years. Between 1995 and 2012 Brian taught regularly for our astrological program in Switzerland. His vast, encompassing knowledge as well as his experience on family issues and their impact on our lives has motivated my own work. This book allows the reader to participate in his work and inspires individual reflection and research.
                                Verena Bachmann, Psychotherapist and Astrologer

A fascinating, deeply researched and well informed book about the family legacy and its continued influence in our lives. Brian Clark has immense experience in this field, and we are fortunate to have access to his knowledge. Beautifully written, this book is an essential addition to our astrological understanding.
        Clare Martin, author of *Mapping the Psyche, Volumes 1, 2 & 3*

Copyright © Brian Clark 2016

All rights reserved. No part of this publication may be reproduced, stored in a retrieval system, or transmitted in any form or by any means, electronic, mechanical, photocopying, recording or otherwise, without prior permission of the copyright owner.

Brian Clark has asserted his right to be identified as the author of this Work.

ISBN: 978-0-9944880-0-8

First edition published 2016 by Astro*Synthesis
PO Box 111
Stanley, Tasmania 7331
Australia
www.astrosynthesis.com.au

The author can be reached at: brian@astrosynthesis.com.au

Charts calculated using Solar Fire software
Cover Designer: Cat Keane
Proof-reader: Jane Struthers
Project Manager and layout: Frank C. Clifford

All photographs from Brian Clark's personal family albums

Front Cover: This image is from a panel on the east facade of the Ara Pacis in Rome, the peace monument erected in honour of Augustus. While the central figure is uncertain, as are the two children she nurtures, the panel is named Tellus, after the Roman Earth Mother. The Romans embraced the traditions of family and ancestry calling upon their household gods to protect and honour ancestral customs and rituals.

THE FAMILY LEGACY

Astrological Imprints on Life, Love & Relationships

BRIAN CLARK

Astro*Synthesis

Acknowledgements

First I express my deep appreciation and gratitude to the many clients and students who have so openly shared their family stories with me in an astrological context. I have been enormously privileged to have been a witness to family threads that have been woven into the tapestry of their lives. My thanks to those who gave me permission to use their family portraits or fragments of their family stories.

I have been helped by many friends and colleagues who have read, proofread and assisted me to present the manuscript. My thanks to all those who have lent a helping hand; in particular Chris Bright, Michelle Proctor, Mary Symes and Barb Thorp for their much appreciated proofreading, edits and suggestions. Thanks to Carole Taylor who supported the presentation of the material through the Faculty of Astrological Studies in England. My gratitude to Rod Chang of the Academy of Astrology and Lilian Liou of Cite Publishing in Taiwan who were instrumental in the book being first published in Mandarin.

And I could not have written on family without the encouragement, love and support of my own family. But the one who has taught me most about family is my cherished wife and partner Glennys, who deeply knows the soul of family and who, by her integrity and honesty, consistently shows me how to be part of a family. Together we developed the family component of our four-year teaching programme, Astro*Synthesis.

My astrological circle is a close-knit collective worldwide which has always been supportive and encouraging and I am deeply thankful for their assistance. Many thanks to Frank Clifford who generously offered to steer the course towards publication. I am heartened by my close bonds with so many wonderful associates and friends in the astrological community; my colleagues here in Australia have been so embracing that we dub the FAA or Federation of Australian Astrologers as the Family of Australian Astrologers.

TABLE OF CONTENTS

Preface	7
Introduction *Soul and Family*	11
1. Soul and the Family System	13
2. Fate, the Soul's Imprint; Myth, the Language of the Soul	21
Part I *Behind the Front Door: A Look Inside the Houses of Family*	35
3. Water and Air, Together Apart: The Elements of Bonding	37
4. The Water Houses: Emotional Seas in the Harbour of Home	49
5. Planets in the 4th House: Delineating the Fundamental House of Family	65
6. The Air Houses: Individuality and Relationship	81
7. Planets in the 3rd House: Delineating the Formative House of Connection	97
8. Angles and Cusps: Doorways, Borders and Keys	109
Part II *Solar and Family Systems: Exploring the Planets*	123
9. Family Systems and Relationships: Parental and Sibling Dynamics	125
10. Planetary Archetypes: Personalities of the Family System	147
11. Planets, Aspects and Houses: Delineating the Family	163
12. The Moon: Love, Attachment and the Lunar Landscape	193
13. Moon Signs and Lunar Aspects: Attachment Impulses and Influences	203
Part III *Intrinsic Blueprints and Rites of Passage: Family Time*	223
14. Family Templates: Order and Chaos in the System	225
15. Patterns Through Time: Psychic Spells in Families	245
16. The Passing of Time: The Family Life Cycle	255
17. Full Circle: Family Passages from Conception to Death	271
18. Adult Children: Transits, Progressions and the Evolution of Family Relationships	317
19. Plotting the Ancestors: Genes, Genealogy and the Genogram	337
20. A Family Portrait: Freud's Legacy	357
In Conclusion	375
Birth Data	377
Bibliography and Endnotes	381

– PREFACE –

Even though it might be curiosity that opens the family closet, when the door is ajar a highly evocative and emotional encounter with our past emerges. Memories, stories, feelings, images, responses and reactions await us as we encounter our family history. Being the sons and daughters of our familial legacy, we are the genes and DNA, the blood and earth as well as the spirit and soul of our ancestors. We belong to a tribe and this is the group we develop in. Individuality is not forged outside family, but begins with our first steps taken within the intimacy of household.

Seminal psychoanalytic theory understood the family as the foundation stone for adulthood; buried in the family experience were the origins of adult complaints and the source of troubling patterns. Yet millennia before these ideas developed, myth had told stories of family curses and ancestral relationships that vividly illustrated the intensity of family patterning. Astrology too had mapped out family themes and connections nearly two millennia before psychoanalysis. Awareness of the powerful imprint that the family etches on personal development has always been a fundamental feature of mythological and astrological intelligence.

This book has organically grown out of the classes that my partner Glennys Lawton and I developed for our four-year teaching programme Astro*Synthesis. A component on family called 'Life Partners: Family Dynamics and Relationship Patterns' is the fifth unit in the foundation course; the module called 'Family Development: The Family System through Time' is taught in the advanced programme. These two programmes have also been developed as a module for the Faculty of Astrological Studies in the UK. Three student booklets prepared for these modules, called *The Astrology of the Family: The Family System*; *The Astrology of Brothers and Sisters: The Sibling System* and *The Astrology of Family Development: The Family System Through Time* are the basis for this book.

Family therapy principles fit naturally with astrological practice and its models and main beliefs are very helpful in amplifying astrological signatures. Glennys is both a registered family therapist and astrologer and has brought her ideas and understanding to the astrological programmes on family that we developed; therefore, she is a strong influence, mentor and collaborator on this book. My earlier book *The Sibling Constellation* (Penguin, London: 1999) precedes this edition and some of the ideas on the sibling relationship were first explored in that book.

I am Canadian by birth but an Australian resident, and my family background is Anglo-Celtic. My father was born in London, England of Anglo heritage; my mother was born in Saskatchewan, Canada of Irish lineage. Both were only children and I grew up with my parents and one brother with no extended family. Therefore, my early outlook on family had a narrow focus. But it broadened in my adult life when I became a stepfather to three adolescent children and later had the gift of five beautiful granddaughters.

Through travel, I've experienced how Mediterranean family life extends to include aunts, uncles, cousins and their partners, grandparents and closer family friends. In Bali the ancestral spirits are honoured as part of the family matrix while other Asian cultures are inclined to include ancestors and all descendants in the make-up of their family.

The concept of family varies greatly depending on culture, race, generation and social circumstances. The 'nuclear' family was generally classified as two heterosexual adults in a committed relationship with one or more biological or adopted children. In the 21st century the notion of family is fluid and changing. Today families can be a couple with no children or a same-sex couple with children. No matter what our cultural perspective and understanding is, we all belong to a family and the bonds created through family ties are often the strongest and most enduring of all human relationships. Ultimately we are all part of the human family and share similar needs, drives, instincts and desires beyond our cultural and familial differences.

Approaching the family as a human archetypal experience assists in transcending cultural divergence. The archetypal nature of astrological language supports this approach. Its vernacular is not words but images and symbols; its dialect is not pronounced but felt and imagined. It differentiates aspects of the character in order to assemble a holistic understanding of the Self.

A very great part of understanding ourselves is our family and familial history. We cannot know our soul until we have understood the souls of those who have been before us. This is the treasured gift that opening the door to the family closet brings about. For the compassion and understanding we demonstrate to our ancestors is the compassion and understanding we will display to ourselves and the families we in turn create.

INTRODUCTION
SOUL AND FAMILY

The author at five months old in Mother's arms
with older brother, Ted, standing by

*What if we thought of the family less as the determining
influence by which we are formed and more the raw material
from which we can make a life?*[1]
Thomas Moore

– CHAPTER 1 –
SOUL AND THE FAMILY SYSTEM

Though we might blame our parents or even the planets for our predicaments, we are participants in shaping our destinies from the raw materials inherited from family. Astrology allows us to reflect on these raw materials and offers ways we can be authentic in response to our ancestral inheritance.

While developmental psychology emphasizes the influence of the parents and family in human growth, astrological doctrine suggests their imprint is already etched upon the soul at birth. Each soul has an essential template for its familial experience which is revealed through the planetary arrangements of the horoscope. An astrological perspective challenges most psychotherapeutic ways of thinking about family, suggesting that the images of the parents, familial legacies and complexes are embedded in our horoscope. And if the family is inherent in the birth horoscope, then its images are innate in us. Family is our fate.

The family is a system moving through time. It is the container that holds one's genesis and beginnings. It is where we are deeply rooted, hopefully secure enough in our origins to grow and adapt to life. In a way, a family unit is a microcosm of society, providing continuity throughout life and a place in which to belong.

The Dictionary of Family Psychology and Family Therapy defines 'family' as:

> A basic unit of society characterized as one whose members are economically and emotionally dependant on one another and are responsible for each other's development, stability, and protection. The family serves as the basic unit of socialization to teach cultural values and adaptation to society.[2]

Importantly, a family unit consists of multiple generations. Members of each of these generations mature together within the same framework; therefore in the family grouping there are children, adolescents, adults and elders, all at various stages of the life cycle in their roles as siblings, sons, daughters, parents, grandparents and perhaps even great-grandparents.

An individual's natal horoscope is systemic. Its multidimensional symbols reveal the family system and the network of the extended family members through time. The horoscope not only imagines the individual's responses to family members but also how others in the family may engage and participate in the system. This systemic approach is an important model for astrological counsellors, as the horoscope contains images of the ancestors which provide a greater understanding of an individual's legacy. The images of the soul of the family are encoded into the symbols of the horoscope.

Understanding the influence of the family can support our understanding and acceptance of the 'real' self. The astrologer can take into account the family atmosphere and heritage in order to better appreciate the individual's disposition to particular planetary conditions. Our astrological inquiry into the family can be a journey into a fuller understanding of our role and place in society, as well as our relationships with other family members. It can also serve as a way to consider responses and patterns that have been shaped by the family, which continue beyond into other relationships.

Some Astrological Keys to Family

Astrology has a long tradition of ascribing familial images to its symbols. For instance, the 3rd house was historically seen to represent sibling issues and dynamics, while the 4th house was considered the sphere of the parents. Two millennia ago, Ptolemy stated that 'the sun and Saturn are by nature associated with the person of the father and the Moon and Venus with that of the mother'.[3] Conditions concerning the mother and father, such as death, illness and life span, were then delineated according to certain configurations with these and other planets.[4]

There are many ways to articulate familial images from the horoscope. Contemporary astrology includes not only the 3rd house but also the 7th and 11th to show how kinship, relationship and comradeship experienced in the familial environs are then taken out into the social world. These are the 'Air trinity' or the 'houses of relationship' where relationship patterns are shaped.

The 4th house has always been connected with the parents; by extension the 8th and 12th are the spheres most immediately concerned with ancestry and the familial inheritance. This 'Water trinity' focuses specifically on the family atmosphere, legacy and unconscious complexes that influence and shape our character. These 'houses of endings' or 'houses of soul' are the territory of in-depth feeling, reservoirs of the past and also the places where familial and ancestral themes are located and interred.

The two main axes of the horoscope resonate with the 'Air trinity' and 'Water trinity'. The MC-IC axis is the parental axis, the axis of the family. It combines the poles of the inner and outer worlds; the private and the public self. As the spinal column of the horoscope, this axis supports and/or hinders our ability to stand erect in the world. The other main axis of the horoscope, the ASC-DSC, is more aligned with the limbs of the family tree and the faculty of reaching independently into the world of social relationships.

As indicated by Ptolemy, the Moon offers a profile of mother. In contemporary times the lunar archetype has broadened. Aspects to the Moon reveal the inherited archetypal make-up passed through the lineage of mother. Systemically this might describe aspects of mother's character as well as those in her familial line, including grandmother and great-grandmother. From a contemporary psychological point of view, the lunar constellation (sign and house of the Moon and its aspects to other planets) illustrates the individual's perception and experience of their mother.

The Moon these days symbolizes a container of family life in all its multi-dimensionality. It epitomizes the family home, the experience of attachment and security in early life which becomes the emotional safety net for adult relationships. Astrologically the Moon suggests our own personal style of attachment, as well as our early sense of safety and well-being, which inform our ability to feel separate in later life.

Similarly the Sun personifies father and father's lineage. As an essential part of the solar system, each planet plays its role in the family system. For instance, the inner planets (Mercury, Venus and Mars) may indicate other family members such as siblings, aunts, uncles, while the social planets (Jupiter and Saturn) describe cultural influences on family life. Chiron resonates with themes of adoption and blended families while the outer planets (Uranus, Neptune and Pluto) illustrate the complex and collective patterns which influence the family unconscious.

More Threads to the Family Tapestry

When the helping professions began to view the individual in the context of the family and as a member of a larger group, psychology became more aware of sibling patterns within the family system. Psychological literature on the sibling started to appear from the 1970s onwards. Sibling research and theory have been mainly initiated from the areas of sociology and family therapy. Yet, long ago, myth and astrology already expressed the complexities of the sibling bond. One poignant example is found in the story of the constellation Gemini: the two bright stars, Castor and Pollux, personify the siblings that underpin this zodiac sign.

In exploring the myths of Gemini and Mercury we recognize the powerful imprints that the sibling or lack of a sibling leaves on both the individual and family life. Family therapy no longer sees the sibling relationship confined to the 'nursery' as the early psychoanalytic fathers did, but as a developing relationship maturing throughout the course of individuals' lives. In many ways the sibling relationship is our first partnership, and we can acknowledge the important turning points that occur within it over the span of a lifetime.

Beyond the sibling relationship and Mercury, other planets show different key influences. Using astrological symbols imaginatively in the context of the family experience reveals deeper insights into the influential relationships with these formative characters in our lives. Venus can be representative of women, such as aunts; Mars can signify men, such as uncles. All these insights can be gleaned purely through the analysis of one horoscope which acts as a family portrait.

Planetary aspects within a person's horoscope illustrate the impact of certain family members and the roles they played in our lives. While a planet may be embodied or personified by someone in the family, it is the attitudes and characteristics of this family member that help us understand these qualities within ourselves better. Aspects between the inner planets and the social and outer planets inform us of patterns embedded in family life and how these have shaped our character.

We can also compare and analyse other family members' horoscopes, and when we do it is apparent that a web of astrological connections is woven throughout the family. Repetitive patterns of signs and sign polarities, degrees of the zodiac, planetary aspects and angular planets, as well as planetary themes, emerge across the horoscopes from one family member to another. Family patterns are already inborn and recognizable in the interactive contacts between the horoscopes of family members.

It is curious that the Sun, Moon and angles of the parents' horoscopes are so often closely aligned with similar placements in the child's birth chart. It is as if the soul matter of the family discloses itself through these astrological patterns. Liz Greene expressed it in this way:

> ... planetary aspects repeat among the charts of family members without any perceivable or understandable causal basis. Families as much as individuals are driven by mythic patterns.[5]

Often similar planetary aspects, signs and zodiacal degrees are repeated throughout various generations, confirming the familial connections through time. Astrological symbols contain the family past that has become mythologized over the generations. When considering family ancestry we are presented with stories and images that have developed through the ages. Time has become invested with family memories, emotions, traumas, opinions, sentiments; its nature is no longer linear. Within the family system some symbols may no longer be characteristic of their potential as over time the archetype has been inhibited. The interplay of family story and time inform the specificity of astrological archetypes within each family.

For instance, a young man with a Sun–Neptune conjunction who had a noticeable gift for music was never allowed to play a musical instrument within his family home because music was not deemed an appropriate pastime, let alone a viable career option for men. The astrological symbol (the Sun–Neptune conjunction) carried the archetypal potential of a gifted musical vocation, but the evolution of this archetype within the man's ancestry was undeveloped and unfulfilled. The archetypal potential of the Sun–Neptune became buried beneath layers of family rejection. In order to engage with the potential of the Sun–Neptune archetype, he had to confront the family's resistance to individual creativity.

The Family Matrix Through Time

Family therapy's developmental ideas can offer the astrological practitioner insights into the individual's experience of family through the passage of time. The family's conscious and unconscious experiences of transits and progressions through the early life cycle of an individual are formative imprints on the child's own experience, influencing the way they relate to different astrological symbols and archetypes.

When considered systemically, astrological timing will not only be relevant to one individual's chart but also to the charts of their relatives. Major transits and life stages for one individual directly impact on other family members in the same system. Since the web of astrological connections often stresses certain astrological signs or degrees, planetary transits are often synchronous in many family members' horoscopes.

While we are aware of our own individual life cycle from birth through childhood, adolescence, adulthood, midlife, old age and on to death, family therapy also addresses the significance of the family life cycle. Like any organism, the family has a natural life cycle and each member moves through various stages and rites of passage in the family as they mature.[6] This life cycle corresponds with the natural astrological cycles of transiting and progressed planets, nodes and other celestial bodies. Nodal points in the family congregate around the entrances and exits of family members at important stages of family life; for instance, the 12-year rounds of Jupiter feature strongly in developmental stages, as we will explore later.

The family carries its own life force and momentum which extends across generations both living and deceased. Theoretically we might begin the life cycle at any stage but consensus suggests we begin at the engagement or commitment of the adult couple. This is the time when each individual moves away from their family of origin into their family of choice and a new cycle begins.

Entrances and exits are highly stressful for all family members because they represent transitional times in both the personal and family life cycles; these are the times when individuals are most vulnerable. Transition is generally a critical passage and awareness of these turning points in family life helps members to make these changes more consciously and functionally.

For example, the first child leaving home is a key passage in the family life cycle and signals a shift for each member. The younger sibling moves forward, accommodating the void created by the sibling who has left. Their roles, responsibilities and privileges alter. The parents, who have launched their first child, are acutely aware of preparing for a readjustment phase in their lives when daily family life will return them to being alone as a couple.

Traumatic events alter the course of the family. Divorce, remarriage, illness, relocation, retrenchment, loss and death all affect the course of the family life cycle. These variables are part of life and are symbolized astrologically by transits to the horoscopes of family members, each in their own way.[7] While planetary cycles will frame the life cycle for an individual and the family, personal transits create the interruptions and variations.

The Rich Complexity of Family Astrology

Many different types of horoscope can be generated when compiling family charts. In addition to each family member's horoscope, there are transits and progressed charts, composite charts, wedding and death charts. With so much information it's easy to become inundated. Therefore a genogram is helpful in organizing the family system through generations and it can also act as a useful foundational tool for grounding astrological data.

As astrologers we constantly marvel at the truth of the astrological symbol, yet I often feel confined when trying to express the essence of the horoscope through words. The astrological symbols and images are not bound by the nature of words. They reside in the mysterious and profound spaces of the imagination.

Astrological craft teaches how to read an individual horoscope for character, events, patterns and themes. This in itself shows the capacity of the astrological symbol to be revelatory and meaningful. Yet when it is extended beyond the individual chart into the matrix of family astrology, we are called to listen and respond to the deeper cyclical and repetitive motifs over time. In doing so, we experience a deeper soul patterning; the astrological symbols become more multi-layered and rich in history, aged and ripened by membership within the powerful container of the family.

– CHAPTER 2 –
FATE, THE SOUL'S IMPRINT;
MYTH, THE LANGUAGE OF THE SOUL

Like many other cultures, the Greeks used the constellations as a means to record and convey their myths. By the Classical period,[8] the constellations that the Sun and all the planets passed through on their journey around the solar system became known as the zodiac. This celestial highway, the zodiac, refers to a circle of animals which in turn tell the story of a wheel of life indicative of a deeply divine layer of human experience.

'Zodiac' is borrowed from the Old French *zodiaque*, derived from Latin; however, the original source is Greek.[9] The Greek root of the word is *zoion*, which refers to a circle of sculptured animal figures suggesting a living being, an animal or life; a circle of life. Embedded in the zodiac is this archaic wisdom; hence it also came to be known as the 'seat of the soul' or the 'temple of the spirit'.[10]

Humanity's First 'Book' of Myths – the Zodiac
While the myths associated with the images of the zodiacal constellations seem unrelated and almost random in their selection, a cohesive schema of life energies emerge as we unravel their plots.[11] In effect, the zodiac is one of humanity's first picture books. Rich with images of animals and human figures, it symbolizes the instinctual, 'animalistic' human journey, an imaginative way to view the schema of life. The narratives, drives, impulses and pathos of the 'collective unconscious' were projected onto these constellations; hence the zodiacal constellations are not just smatterings of images but representations of collective psychic energy animating the sky.[12]

Not all the luminous bodies in the night sky are fixed. The ancients came to know the wandering stars as the planets, imagining them as embodiments of divine forces, their deities journeying through the heavens. The planets were named after these gods and the sagas of these deities were intermingled with the narratives that were told of the constellations. Before science chronicled the heavens, the archaeology of the ancient skies was set down through the mythology. James Hillman suggested that mythology was the 'psychology of antiquity';[13] further to this, we could suggest that *astrology* was *also* a psychology of antiquity. Astrology is another way of engaging with mythic narratives. In astrology the mythic narratives are expressed through patterns in the heavens, one of the earliest attempts to link the world outside us to the world within.

Myth, whether expressed through the star stories, cycles and patterns of astrology or through tales unrelated to astrological phenomena, is a potent way of comprehending the world around us. The stories of ancient gods, goddesses and their heroic deeds narrate the soul's archetypal journey. As stories of inner events, myth unfastens a psychic portal through the language of the imagination. Carl Jung called imagination 'the mother of human consciousness',[14] as it nurtures our earliest attempts to find meaning and worth before the development of literacy.

One way to think about myth is that it is a dialect of the soul, a storyline strung together with ancient and archaic memories of human experiences. Myth offers an original view of our natural world beyond the limits imposed by rational thought. When we engage with myth, we suspend our beliefs and certainties about who we are and where we come from and cross into a dimension where these realities are less personalized. They are everyone's realities, like a collective dream, only we perceive and participate with them from our personal perspective. Myths engage the imaginative self and inspire us to play a part in the creative process.

Every family has its own myths and sagas, its own stories and dynamics playing out in the present yet tied into the myths of the generations gone before. Astrology offers a unique perspective on the family system and can support uncovering myths that might still engage us. Often we can feel tied to the fate of a family story, as if we are still living its mythic storyline as one of its characters.

Family Myths

Family inheritances are often viewed as financial or physical. Yet family myths are not only transferred through trust accounts and chromosomes, but also through emotional and psychological DNA. In this the early Greek myth-makers were well versed; their myths set down sweeping sagas of the dynasties of Crete, Troy, Mycenae and Thebes, detailing the complex intergenerational patterns that were inherited by each successive generation. Not only did the Greeks recount the fated threads with which each individual continued to weave the family conspiracy, but they also told of the interplay between gods and family heroes.

The myths were the earliest account of the family soul and useful modern-day metaphors for archetypal and familial forces that affected the individual. The mythological cycle became a boon for 5th-century playwrights who then dramatized the family fate through spectacular theatrical productions. Some of these tragedies were like living genograms in which the present-day hero was undoubtedly the heir to his family fortunes and misfortunes. For instance, Orestes, under the direction of the god Apollo, murdered his own mother. Yet each member of the audience, familiar with the mythic tradition, would have known the dynastic history: that his father had sacrificed his sister and his grandfather had killed his brother's children. But the fated patterns could be traced back even further to his great-great-grandfather who had originally betrayed the gods. Herein was the heroic challenge in all families: to become conscious of the fate dealt out by the gods for transgressions committed long ago.

Myth depicts the spectrum of familial relationships, whether that be the poignant relationship between mother and daughter, such as between Demeter and Persephone; the complex mother-son bond as portrayed by Oedipus and Jocasta; an intense father-son relationship like that of Theseus and Hippolytus; or a father-daughter attachment, such as the bond between Zeus and Athena. Mythology consistently recognized the sibling relationship and its influence throughout the lifespan. Myths honour the sibling bond through a complexity of relationships, both mortal and divine, such as the sibling marriage of Zeus and Hera; the solidarity of brothers Agamemnon and Menelaus or the fraternal rivalry of Romulus and Remus; the devoted companionship of Apollo and Artemis; the fate of sisters Iphigenia and Electra; or the envy of Psyche's sisters. Since myth was animated by family plots which visibly revealed ancestral patterns and trans-generational fate, it was no wonder early psychoanalysts like Sigmund Freud, Otto Rank and especially Carl Jung drew on its wisdom to articulate psychic patterns inherited through the family.

Alongside myth, astrology also addresses the soul's purpose, its patterns and its journey through its symbols and images. Each horoscope contains the myths of the family and its heritage; in each chart the family story is alive. With an imaginative eye an astrologer can begin to read the familial past that passes through the present

Pholus and the Myth of Four Generations in the Family

Greek myth is a treasure trove of family stories, and the story of Pholus offers some insight into the interplay between family mythology and fate. Pholus was a Centaur who gave his name to the Pholoe region in Arcadia where Mount Pholoe is located. His father was Silenus, an oracular forest god, who was associated with Dionysus and is often identified as his foster father. Hence Pholus inherited the family traits of prophecy and wisdom along with the skills of wine-making and preserving. Therefore it was natural for Dionysus to bequeath a jar of wine to Pholus with specific instructions that the wine must be sealed until Heracles would eventually arrive at his cave on Mount Pholoe.

Mount Pholoe is just south of Mount Erymanthus where Heracles was chasing the boar, the Fourth Labour in his great round of 12 initiatory tasks. It was during this time that Heracles visited his wise Centaur friend Pholus, who hospitably offered him some wine from the preserved jar sunk down in the earth. Four generations had passed since Dionysus had entrusted the jar of wine to Pholus, so the fragrance was strong and sweet when he lifted the lid to pour the hero his drink. It was this heady scent that attracted all the other Centaurs to the cave, where a confrontation between the hero and the chaotic Centaurs occurred.

It was Diodorus, the 1st century BCE historian, in *Library of History* (4. 12. 3) who details the full account of the myth and first draws our attention to the jar bequeathed by Dionysus and which remained in Pholus's care for four generations. Melanie Reinhart, in her work with the Centaurs, describes the chaos that erupts with the phrase 'the lid comes off'.[15]

Greek myth illustrates a template for what is often revealed by the great-grandchild, four generations later, and the link between this present generation and the one four generations ago. This past generation is usually unknown to the present generation and lives on through myth and family story. The myth serves as a potent metaphor for sealed contents stored in the jar of the unconscious that might burst into consciousness at some later point in the family history, hence why the narratives of family life are so essential to our sense of well-being.

In astrological imagery it is also interesting to note that the four generations could be imagined starting with the 4th house. The next generation, using the derivative house system, would be the 4th from the 4th, or the 7th house; the next house in the process would be the 4th from the 7th, or the 10th house; the next would be the 4th from the 10th, or the 1st house. All four angular houses are brought into the cycle of the four generations and, as we shall see, all of these houses play an integral role in family astrology. Interestingly, in the myth of Heracles, this is the Fourth of his Twelve Labours, and the astrological house most associated with family is the 4th house.

From the Chaotic Night of Fate to Conscious Collaboration

Fate confronts the individual and, indeed, humanity. Pholus unwittingly opened up the 'Pandora's Box' of the family fate. He had no conscious knowledge of what opening the wine jar would unleash. Pholus's predicament evokes core philosophical questions about fate. Is life predetermined or flexible? Is it God's will or free will? Carl Jung suggested that those who submit to their fate call it 'the will of God' but those who dispute it are 'more apt to see the devil in it'.[16]

The question of fate often polarizes into two extreme views: one viewpoint identifies fate as something we can do nothing about; the other implies surrendering to its will. Of course there are other perspectives, and one consistent with astrology is how we might consciously cooperate in weaving the threads that have already been allotted for the tapestry of our lives. Our understanding of fate is central to how we approach astrology and how we derive meaning from its symbols.[17]

In the first Greek epic by Hesiod on the birth of the gods, the Fates were personified as the daughters of Themis and Zeus. Hesiod gave them the individual names of Clotho, Lachesis and Atropos. However, earlier in the same epic poem, Hesiod had already introduced the 'ruthless' Fates as daughters of Night. They were categorized along with Doom, Death, Blame and a host of other dark figures.[18] Interestingly, over the course of the epic, the Fates' genealogy is changed from being children of chaotic Night to becoming daughters of Themis and Zeus.

Now as children of Themis and Zeus, the three Fates are under the jurisdiction of the new pantheon of gods and goddesses, reflecting their place in the new world order where chaos and feeling are becoming more contained and considered. I see this as a metaphor of how we might alter our fate from its unconsciousness by becoming conscious of the patterns that have already been woven for us before our birth. When born of night, our fate is unconscious; but when reborn in a more conscious light, it is a matrix that we can collaborate with through reflection and consideration.

Lachesis apportions the fibre that Clotho has spun at our birth. She assigns to us the length of the threads. When Atropos cuts the threads we enter our lives with the apportioned strands of our family inheritance. Our familial inheritance already exists as an essential aspect of who we are. It is our legacy, and astrology is a dynamic tool to help us understand this fate and how the family might collude to keep it in the dark, as if daughters of Night. Family values, beliefs, traditions and ways of life have woven patterns that exist before we are born and are the inherited cloth from which we forge our character. To be mindful of our familial patterns and legacies contributes to a deeper understanding of our own fate.

Signposts of Fate's Presence Across Family Horoscopes
With family astrology, there are many charts to contemplate and stories to consider. When looking at an individual's horoscope, the symbols are already powerful enough for us to perceive the family portrait. And when we look at a child's chart in comparison with their parents' or siblings' charts, we are able to see similarities and patterns which are carried through the family.

When looking at the family members' charts there are many ways that these patterns are visible. Like genes, sometimes these patterns skip generations or certain members of a generation. Often it is only some members of the family who carry the similar astrological statements while other members might carry another image. Sometimes the astrological statements flow through the mother's line while others flow through the father's. Analysing the horoscopes of the members of a family will reveal fascinating astrological patterns and legacies.

Repetition of Zodiac Sign or Sign Polarity

Often a particular zodiac sign is prominent in the family constellation. For instance, in the Kennedy family, patriarch Joseph Kennedy Snr had four personal planets – the Sun, Moon, Mercury and Venus – in the sign of *Virgo*. His wife Rose shared Venus in Virgo as well as having Saturn in Virgo.

Parents – Joseph and Rose Kennedy

Family Member	Zodiacal Degree of Virgo
Joseph Snr Father and Patriarch	Sun 14♍16 Moon 18♍12 Mercury 25♍59 Venus 29♍48
Rose Mother and Matriarch	Saturn 2♍33 Venus 8♍12

Both birth times are unverified; Joseph Snr is cast for 7.06 a.m. However, Joseph Snr's Moon was in Virgo all day on the day he was born (6 September 1888) as were the other planets, except Venus which entered Libra in the afternoon. Rose's chart is cast for 7.00 p.m. and both planets were in Virgo all that day.

They had nine children: four boys and five girls. The eldest, Joseph Jr, died at the age of 29 when his plane exploded over the English Channel during the Second World War. Of the remaining three sons, two had the Moon in Virgo. John's only planet in Virgo was the Moon; Edward had a Neptune-Moon conjunction in Virgo as well as the South Node in the sign. Robert had no planets in Virgo.

Rosemary, the third-born child and the first daughter, was institutionalized for most of her life after a failed lobotomy. She had three planets in Virgo – the Sun, Mercury and Venus – while her next sister Kathleen, the fourth child, had Saturn in Virgo. Like her elder brother, Joseph, Kathleen died in a plane crash at the age of 28. Eunice, the fifth child, had the Moon, Jupiter and Saturn in Virgo. Of the nine children, three had the Moon in Virgo.

The Kennedy Children

Family Member	Planet	Zodiacal Degree of Virgo
John	Moon	17♍12
Eunice	Moon	27♍58
Edward	Moon	6♍25

John Kennedy's son, John Kennedy Jr, was 38 when he died in a plane crash like his aunt and uncle. He was from the Pluto in Virgo generation but also had the North Node on his Ascendant in Virgo. His sister Caroline was also born with Pluto in Virgo. Another sibling, Patrick, who died when only two days old was born during the period of the Uranus-Pluto conjunction in Virgo, but also had Venus in Virgo like his grandmother and grandfather and his aunt Rosemary. Their mother Jackie was from the Neptune in Virgo generation and had Mars in Virgo.

Edward's first wife Joan was also from the Neptune in Virgo generation, with the Sun and Venus in Virgo and Virgo rising. They had three children all born in the Pluto in Virgo generation. Their two sons also had Venus in early degrees of Virgo.

Edward's other brother Robert had no planets in Virgo. His wife Ethel only had the Vertex in Virgo. Of their eleven children, four were female and seven were male. The fourth-born died from a drug overdose at 29 and the sixth-born died in a skiing accident at 39. Their first-born child had both Saturn and the South Node in Virgo. Two of the other children had the Sun in Virgo while two others had the Moon in Virgo. Half the siblings were born in the Pluto in Virgo generation and three were born during the period of Uranus-Pluto in Virgo. Four of the eleven children had three or more planets in Virgo.

While this is only a selection of the family, it is apparent that Virgo is prominent in many of the family's horoscopes, bringing the Virgoan themes into the family atmosphere. This also suggests that when there is a major transit of an outer planet through the sign of Virgo or the other mutable signs, many of the members of the family are affected by the transit. The first-generation parents, Rose and Joseph, shared the placement of Venus in Virgo which frequently appeared in the second and third generations of the family.

The erotic theme weaved its way through the men of the family; Joseph Snr was known for his Hollywood affairs, the most notorious being with the actress Gloria Swanson. His son John (later known as JFK) also had a similar reputation: his liaison with actress Marilyn Monroe was well publicized. It was also rumoured that Joseph's son Edward was having an affair with his campaign aide who drowned in the car he was driving after it careered off a bridge. The theme also plagued the next generation. William Kennedy Smith, the son of

Jean, the last-born daughter, was acquitted of rape charges in 1991. He has the Sun, Mercury, Pluto and the North Node in Virgo. Also from the Pluto in Virgo generation was Michael Kennedy, the son of Robert and Ethel, who was accused in 1997 of having an affair with his family's teenage babysitter.

The Virgoan theme of health, well-being and order also wove its way through the family's mental health, addictions and depression. Sign placements are commonly repeated in families through the angles, the Sun, Moon and lunar nodes of family members. The Kennedy family serves as a modern illustration of the classical idea of the family curse that was so well brought to light in ancient Greek myth and tragedy.[19]

Repetition of Stand-out Degrees of the Zodiac
Certain degrees of the zodiac are often emphasized in families. For instance, there may be one degree of a sign that is significant for family members; if this is the case then degree symbolism as represented by fixed stars, the Sabian Symbols or other astrological degree techniques enhances the meaning and imagery of this degree for the family. For example, if 8° Sagittarius continually stands out across different family members' charts, looking up any fixed stars at that degree or the Sabian Symbol for that degree can open doorways to reflective contemplation of family stories.

Sometimes one degree of the zodiac may be stressed in a family, astrologically uniting the members of the family through close aspects. Let's imagine 12° Capricorn is in one family member's chart and 12° Cancer in another's. Or there may be a range of degrees in a sign, element or mode – for example, 21° to 24° of Water signs.

When degrees of the zodiac repeat in the family, transits to these placements will be simultaneous, which not only enmeshes some family members through natal aspects but also through transits. Hence not only individual members are affected by transits but the whole family system. It is wise to be aware that transits to an individual's chart often affect the system of the family due to the close astrological links in the horoscopes of family members.

It is interesting to note which family members' horoscopes do not repeat the degree patterns that appear in the charts of other relatives. While we cannot make any general assumptions because of this, it does support the theory of sub-systems within the family due to alignments and collusions amongst certain members, or perhaps personality and character differences.

The British Royal Family serves as an example. There are some interesting repetitive degrees in the family system of George VI, The Queen Mother and their daughters Elizabeth and Margaret. Just looking at the Sun and Moon in the charts of the four family members, the Leo-Scorpio mix is strong, highlighting the tension between being thrust upon the stage and the urge for privacy.

The British Royal Family – Sun and Moon links

Family Member	Sun and Moon	Chart Contacts
King George VI	Sun 21♐54 Moon 24♏51	George's Saturn was 14♏45; in the same sign as his wife's and perhaps conjunct. He also shares the Scorpio Moon. George's grandson Andrew shares the Moon at 25♏29; interestingly, his Ascendant at 11♌33 is conjunct his grandmother's Sun.
The Queen Mother	Sun 11♌55 Moon 14–26♏	The Queen Mother's birth details are unverified so I have set her horoscope for 12 p.m. Even so, her Sun is still within 1° of her eldest daughter Elizabeth's Moon.
Queen Elizabeth II	Sun 00♉12 Moon 12♌07	Elizabeth's Saturn at 24♏26 is exactly on her father's Moon, which falls on her MC at 25♏33.
Princess Margaret	Sun 28♌01 Moon 25♋14	Margaret's Moon is exactly trine her father's.

In the next generation the theme continues because Prince Charles, Elizabeth's eldest child, has the Sun at 22♏25 and the Moon at 00♉25, exactly conjunct his mother's Sun. Charles's elder son, William, has Jupiter at 0♏ opposite his father's Moon, but was born with both the Sun and Moon in early Cancer, picking up the Cancerian thread of his great-grandmother's Venus in Cancer, his great-aunt's Moon in Cancer and his mother Diana's Sun and Mercury in Cancer.

There are many ways to explore the out-of-the-ordinary repetitive degrees in this family. Notably in these charts there is a strong emphasis on the fixed signs, but the areas of the zodiac between 22-25° of these signs are highly apparent.[20] What is more, those who marry into the family seem to carry these placements as well. Diana's T-square at these degrees might be seen as a trigger for this familial energy.

Repeated Degrees in the Fixed Signs in the Royal Family

Family Member	22° of a fixed sign	23° of a fixed sign	24° of a fixed sign	25° of a fixed sign
King George VI	♅♏		☽♏	
Queen Elizabeth II	♃♒ ♆♌		♄♏	MC♏
Prince Charles	☉♏			
Princess Diana		♅♌	♀♉	☽♒
Prince William				♀♉ ☿♉
Princess Anne	☉♌			
Prince Andrew				☽♏
Sarah Ferguson	⚷♒			

This suggests that the whole family will be sensitive to transits of the major planets through this sector of the zodiac. It implies that at those times there will be influences that affect the whole family system, not just the individuals concerned. For instance ♇ transited 22-25 ♏ from 1991-4; ♅ transited 22-25 ♒ from 2001-2; and ♆ transited 22-25 ♒ from 2007-10 along with ⚷ in 2009-10. As the slower-moving planets pass through this sector of the zodiac, individuals within the Royal Family system are affected and this in turn provides opportunities for the entire system of the Royal Family to be reinvigorated and transformed.

From Family Curse to Family Blessing

Powerful high-profile families are scrutinized and studied so intensively by the public that they almost take on an archetypal role, as if they were modern-day gods and goddesses, heroes and heroines. Therefore the astrological patterns are often more vivid. Yet the lives of ordinary people are just as open to the intense workings of archetypal mythic patterns.

As previously discussed, this truth is constantly exposed by the great playwrights of the 5th century BCE in their dramas about the dynasties of ancient Greece.[21] The plot of being caught up in parental and ancestral fate is a common theme and described in many of the plays. When Antigone is entombed alive by Creon at the end of a long and tragic family saga, the chorus of Sophocles' play asks: *I wonder ... do you pay for your father's terrible ordeal?*[22]

However it was not only Antigone who had been caught in the complex of her father's 'terrible ordeal'. Oedipus, her father, had been abandoned by his own father Laius and left to die on the mountainside. Liz Greene expresses the Greek dynastic dramas in this way: 'The image of the family curse, so beloved in Greek myth, is a vivid portrayal of what passes unseen down the family line, and embodies the experience of family fate.'[23] What the Greeks so intensely revealed in their mythic narratives of the family curse is the psychic reality of unprocessed trauma and transgression that continues to haunt successive generations.

Carl Jung expressed the fate of the ancestral lineage:

> I feel very strongly that I am under the influence of things or questions which were left incomplete and unanswered by my parents and grandparents and more distant ancestors. It often seems as if there is an impersonal karma within a family, which is passed on from parents to children. It has always seemed to me that I had to answer questions which fate had posed to my forefathers, and which had not yet been answered, or as if I had to complete, or perhaps continue, things which previous ages had left unfinished.[24]

Astrologically, the fate carried through the parental and ancestral legacies is often revealed in the houses of endings, strong aspects to the Sun and Moon or dynamic aspects between the outer and inner planets. Another way family fate may be carried through is within the sibling system. The inheritance of the ancestors might be shared among the siblings. Or sometimes, for siblings near the end of the familial line, fate seems to decree that their lives are in part to atone for those of their ancestors. We might astrologically consider the houses of relationship, strong aspects between the outer planets and Mercury, Venus or Mars, and interchanges between the houses of endings and the 3rd house or the zodiac sign Gemini to bring this theme to light. These astrological motifs are explored in depth in the succeeding chapters.

As astrologers we observe the world we inhabit and its hues in the horoscope so that we might better understand our birthright and work more intentionally with it. No matter what fate has decreed, we now live in times when the family curse might be transformed into the family blessing. When we bring consciousness to bear on our mythic stories, the family wheel turns in new directions.

PART I
BEHIND THE FRONT DOOR
A Look Inside the Houses of Family

The family. We were a strange little band of characters trudging through life sharing diseases and toothpaste, coveting one another's desserts, hiding shampoo, borrowing money, locking each other out of our rooms, inflicting pain and kissing to heal it in the same instant, loving, laughing, defending, and trying to figure out the common thread that bound us all together.[25]
Erma Bombeck

– CHAPTER 3 –
WATER AND AIR, TOGETHER APART
The Elements of Bonding

Salvador Minuchin, one of family therapy's seminal voices, describes the family as a laboratory in which the two fibres of humanness, the sense of belonging and separateness, are woven together:

> In all cultures, the family imprints its members with selfhood. Human experience of identity has two elements: a sense of belonging and a sense of being separate. The laboratory in which these ingredients are mixed and dispensed is the family, the matrix of identity.[26]

These facets of the human experience are symbolized by the astrological elements of Water and Air, which are the foundation for the houses with which these elements are associated. Houses in the horoscope demarcate life's environments and are divided into elemental trinities in the same way as the twelve zodiac signs. The Water houses are where the familial legacy is located, while the patterns of relationship are located in the Air houses.

Traditionally the 4th house, the first of the Water trinity, has since ancient times been referred to as the house of the parents, while the 3rd house, the first of the Air trinity, has been the place of brothers and sisters. Of the twelve houses, it is these six that most articulate and evoke the astrology of family.

The linear order of the elements places Air before Water. Air represents the principle of both separation and relationship. For Air, separateness is essential for relationship. The intention of Air is to separate from the object to become conscious of it. Awareness develops through standing apart. After Air has gained distance to observe, it is more inclined to move towards the object and forge a connection. In this way, Air develops and supports consciousness, allowing a relationship to develop with the 'object', the 'other'.

Air is known as the element of relationship because it cultivates the ability to relate consciously to another individual. However, the polar or unconscious tendency of Air is to remain disconnected or disengaged. Elements, because they are archetypal energies, have both bright and dark faces, which can be underdeveloped or overcompensated for in our lives.

Water, the element of merging and union, follows Air's otherness. Its function is to dissolve separateness to permit union. Vulnerability with another facilitates bonding and allows attachment to take place. Water is the element connected to emotional security, care and bonding. When union and merger develop, Water evokes love, momentarily obliterating incompatible differences.

Air and Water are positioned side-by-side in the elemental sequence – Fire, Earth, Air, Water – perhaps suggesting a constant shifting between feelings of separateness and belonging in our human experience. Water is the last element before the cycle begins again in Fire. A spark of imagination or vision – Fire – emerges out of Water and the cycle of life and energy recommences.

Water is a fundamental principle often bound up with the Divine as the source and renewal of life. It confers immortality or rebirth; rites of passage such as birth, death, marriage and other transitions are often symbolized by the crossing of water. Thales of Miletus, often named 'the first philosopher', commented that the world is made of one element and that element is Water.

In a sense, Water is able to permeate everything and to flood, flow and change its direction when needed. As such, it has become connected with feelings, emotions and deeply moving soulful experiences. The Water element encompasses this feeling life, not only in a single individual, but also in others who share a familial bond. Ancestral patterns are carried by the element of Water which meanders like a river through family channels. With this in mind, the discussion of the depths of family through the astrological elements and houses begins with Water.

The Element of Water: The Intensity of Belonging
The Water element expresses itself through the signs Cancer, Scorpio and Pisces and each contains a depth of feeling and emotion. Cancer is akin to the 4th house, bringing its instinct for care and concern, protection and mothering to this environ. Its natural ruler is the Moon, which governs the oceans' tides as well as the moods of family life. Scorpio is associated with the 8th house and brings its intensity and intimacy into the family circle, while Pisces is linked

to the 12th house where its boundless, intuitive and sensitive nature is in contact with the spirits of the ancestors. The modern rulers of the latter two signs are Pluto and Neptune respectively, which bring generational influences, attitudes and intentions to bear upon the family ambience.

Crustaceans are the emblems of the Water signs. Hard shells, crusts and scales – symbolizing the protective persona of the Watery element – cover the crab, the scorpion and the fishes. Not only acting as armour, these crystallized coverings also represent the age of these signs: primitive in nature and closest to the substance of the self. Hence feelings are often perceived as archaic, primitive and bothersome, yet ironically they connect us to the riches of the past and the wisdom of human experience. Associated with the feeling life, in a manner of thinking the Water element is closest to the depths of the soul.

Water is a storehouse of feeling, memory and images which reach deep into collective memories filled with familial, ancestral, social and collective patterns. Therefore the element of Water is easily influenced, possessed or entranced by the mnemonic power of these images. Mythic Water is associated with knowledge, wisdom and prophecy.

In human relationships this urge to dive into the mysterious waters of the unconscious can feel hypnotic and all-embracing, yet can also lead to symbiosis and enmeshment. When Water is entangled in familial issues it may be difficult to separate or forge alliances outside the family's control.

Water's ability to feel the other's feelings (or at least what we *feel* is the other's feelings), to serve the other's needs and to care for others' insecurities is admirable. However, in relationship this may be experienced by others as smothering or invasive and the Air element might rise to the fore to create distance. For the Watery person, this might be perceived as abandonment or emotional inequality. Although enormously painful, this is ultimately necessary in learning the difficult task of separateness.

Water often confuses the boundaries between self and other, and when it is important to separate the person may be unable to leave; when it is important to be there, the person may be unavailable. The family experience is the training ground in learning discrimination and boundary-setting in relationship. In the family circle we learn how to bond and separate.

Water is attracted by the sensitivity and creativity in others, drawn to their compassionate and caring qualities. Emotional manipulation, chaos, secrecy and moodiness are the shadows that lurk in Water that has been dammed up. But when Water flows freely, then warmth, emotional generosity and support are returned. When the flow of Water has been blocked in the family background, emotional floods are likely to pour through the descendants.

Graciously, Water is also connected with catharsis since it purifies, cleanses and washes away impurities. Fluidity, formlessness, beauty, power and even terror are all aspects of archetypal Water.

Mythic Waters

Thales of Miletus, often described as the first philosopher, commented that the world is made of one element and that element is water. Water is a fundamental principle and a core requirement for human life; put simply, we need it to survive. It represents mother's life-giving nourishment and the familial environs that keep the child safe; it is the element of attachment and emotional bonding.

Wherever water appears in myth it represents a multi-faceted symbol tending to be bound up with the Divine. Water is synonymous with the Divine, as both the source of life and the renewal of life. It is the realm of nature spirits and the gods and goddesses who represent the oceans, seas, lakes, rivers and ponds. Water plays a consistently important role in cosmogony; Pontus, Oceanus, the Nereids, the Oceanids and later Poseidon were all part of the vast watery dominion. Water is present in birth and death and mythic images of crossing over water often accompany the journey into life or death. Broken waters herald the child's emergence and entrance into family life after a long and arduous migration.

Water evokes images of power and beauty as well as powerlessness and dread, pandemonium and formlessness. Its fluidity and elusiveness suggest the absence of form, and the unsustainability and chaos from which the world will emerge. Various myths demonstrate the life-giving energies of the primordial waters, fecundity and the fertile birth.

Fecundity, procreative and oracular powers, fertility and birth characterize this element. It is also connected with catharsis because it purifies, cleanses, dissolves and washes away the impurities. Some waters have special powers that may restore virginity or youth, purify or cleanse the soul. Water is a common symbol of transformation. The 'night-sea journey' is a mythic aspect of the heroic struggle to consciousness. And it was on the river Styx that the gods would swear their oaths. This was the same river in which Thetis, the mother of Achilles, baptized him in order for her heroic son to become immortal.[27] Water confers immortality or rebirth, an image the Christians have borrowed for baptism. The crossing of a river or body of water was associated with rites of passage: birth, death, marriage and other important transitions in the life cycle where there are potent psychological and physical changes.

Water contains the mysterious and is often associated with the dark and dangerous. However, water is also associated with wisdom, knowledge and prophecy. The wisdom of water is gut wisdom, instinctual knowing. Akin to the element in nature, water meanders and changes course, ebbs as well as flows underneath the visible surface. Water flows towards the mysterious and mystical side of life, towards what is unknown, invisible and hidden. It is the water element where we reconnect to the depth and sacredness of life. Innate in the Water signs is the reverence for life, death and transitions in between, all aspects of family life and development.

The Element of Air: The Breath of Relationship

On first reflection, Air may not seem the element we would ascribe to relationship as it is can be non-committal, non-attached and distant. Air is the spectator, not always the participant, the messenger but not necessarily the message. However, Air encourages equality, individuality and consciousness, which are necessary in terms of relationship to permit union without the loss of self.

Astrologically, this is represented by Air preceding Water in the zodiac, and the houses of relationship preceding the houses of endings. Air ensures we can lose ourselves in relationship and then find our way back to the self, the part of our identity that remains separate. If there is a healthy sense of separateness, then this safeguards against regressing to a union of total merger or surrender where the self is lost.

Air encourages enough separateness to relate to someone different from ourselves. The houses of relationship provide a venue for this task, so that the merger into relationship can be conscious. Separateness and symbiosis, two polar instincts that underlie life, are continuously balanced by the element of Air.

The defensive side of Air uses detachment and separateness as a barrier against relationship, mobilizing the intellect to criticize the irrationality of emotional encounters. The analysis of relationship defends the uncertainty and lack of control that the actual experience of relating brings. The defence mechanisms most easily employed by Air would be projection and projective identification; that is, identifying in the 'other' the qualities we continue to repress in ourselves for fear of involvement.

The Air signs are Gemini, Libra and Aquarius. In the natural wheel, Gemini corresponds to the 3rd house; Libra, the 7th; and Aquarius, the 11th. The glyphs that represent these signs are dual, two lines detached from each other. Gemini and Aquarius are represented in human form while Libra is the only sign represented by an inanimate object – the scales. Duality, judging and weighing are all part of the Airy process of relating. The modern rulers of the Air signs – Mercury, Venus and Uranus, respectively – as well as Saturn, the classical ruler of Aquarius, preside over the territory of equal relationship. They are the deities we encounter in the archetypal process of individuation and relationship.

Duality is an important aspect of Air and its ruling planets. Mercury in the role of psychopomp travels between the two antithetical worlds of Hades and Olympus; Venus in her role as *Venus Urania* rules Libra and displays the heavenly and spiritualized side of Venus, while *Venus Pandemonia* is her common, earthly side associated with Taurus. Similarly, Uranus expresses duality through sharing the rulership of Aquarius with Saturn. Aquarius is split between the new order, ruled by Uranus of the heavens, and the old order, ruled by Saturn.

Different forms of rulership also connect these signs. Saturn, as the traditional ruler of Aquarius, is exalted in the sign of Libra. Venus rules Libra in traditional astrology and Gemini in esoteric astrology. Threads of amity run through these signs.

Throughout the Air signs and houses there are consistent symbols reminding us of the process of linking, connecting and bridging, as well as experiences of separation, duality and polarity. The dance between Air and Water is a perennial one that shifts and flows, or sometimes gets frozen or trapped, within each of us in our ongoing bonding and relating dynamics throughout life.

The Air signs and houses particularly introduce the theme of sibling bonding and show the powerful impact that formative relationships with siblings, or not having any siblings, have on future connections. The ability to leave unhealthy relationships or group situations later in life could be anchored in our first experiences of separating from siblings. With siblings we experience a series of separations that range from starting school to leaving home, which normalize the process of separation and return.

The only child might have a difficult time separating from destructive relationships, as the only child's sense of separateness is aligned with the parents, which maximizes insecurity and loss, whereas in our sibling relationships we have learnt to be equally independent and part of a group. Throughout childhood we experience a series of separations with our siblings which do not damage or destroy the relationship. The only child, lacking a sibling relationship, may not have adequately internalized a sense of separateness.

If You Leave Me, Can I Come Too? The Pathos of Gemini

The archetypal story of the Air sign Gemini profoundly illustrates the push-pull between the desire to stay bonded and the necessity of separation. Castor and Pollux are the celestial twins portrayed by Gemini. They are eternal reminders of the sibling bond, a relationship so important to the ancients that their story was written into the heavens. The Romans knew the twins as Castor and Pollux, but to the Greeks they were 'the Dioscuri', the sons of Zeus.

There are various versions of the myth of the Gemini twins. The following account of the myth became the popular version, originating from the epic poem the *Kypria*.[28] The twins' parents were the royal couple, Leda and Tyndareus, who were the queen and king of Sparta. Zeus passionately desired Leda and in order to seduce her he devised a plan which would render him vulnerable to the queen. Shape-shifting into a swan, Zeus was pursued by Hermes, who took the shape of an eagle. Trickster Hermes had colluded to drive Zeus, in the guise of the swan, into the safety of the queen's embrace. While in Leda's protective arms, Zeus ravaged her.

Yet Leda had already been impregnated by her husband the night before. Eventually Leda bore two giant eggs as a consequence of having been impregnated by both Zeus and her husband. From one egg emerged the divine progeny of Zeus: Helen and Pollux; from the other, the human offspring of Tyndareus: Castor and Clytemnestra. The duplicity of twinship offers diverse possibilities: one set of twins was divine, the other was mortal; one set was male, the other was female; and yet another combination arranged each set of twins as divine male/mortal female and divine female/mortal male. Their duplicated and symmetrical fourfold sibling constellation is an integral part of the Gemini myth. This complex constellation of 'others' at birth, and the ultimate loss of this connection, is often the fate that underlies the experience of Gemini.

In this version of the story the twins Castor and Pollux were in conflict with their cousins Idas and Lynceus, also twins, over the division of a large herd of cattle. All four had successfully raided a neighbouring territory and returned with the cattle. Conflict arose over its possession, which precipitated Pollux's separation from Castor, a powerful Geminian theme. Both sets of twins battled with each other and during the conflict Castor, the mortal twin, was killed by a spear. The opposites were no longer fused but torn apart. Their destinies were now revealed: Castor must die as a mortal whereas Pollux, who had the gift of immortality, lived.

Pollux was now alone. Seeing his brother killed in battle and separated from him evoked an unbearable grief. Ultimately, Pollux became aware that Castor completed something in him that was now missing and, with his loss, Pollux felt empty and incomplete. His grief at the loss of his brother-other was so intense that he could not bear to be separated from him. In his despair, he petitioned Zeus to allow him to relinquish his immortality and join his brother in death. In a rare bequest, Zeus granted Pollux, his divine son, this wish.

Geminian behaviour is typified as scattered, nervous and non-committal. Often what underlies this behaviour is a frantic search for something from which we feel separated. In essence, all Gemini placements contain a psychic image of a birth twin that feels as though it is missing. What is missing is often unconscious, but nonetheless it drives the individual forward to quest and question for the lost other. All of the Air signs and houses contain this theme to some degree.

In this myth, it is the severed connection to the twin/sibling that allows the other to cross the threshold to the underworld. Through his death Castor, the mortal, became a psychopomp leading his brother across the threshold of death.[29] In Gemini, the experiences of separation awaken the Mercurial functions of perception and awareness of what lies beneath the surface. Gemini in the horoscope may carry the first experiences of consciousness, therefore the earliest images of separateness. Separation begets consciousness, and the consciousness of being separate is painful. In the pain, the emotions of the Water element are evoked.

Gemini is an early experience in the zodiac – it is the first sign in the trinity of Air, and the first mutable and dual sign. It is the first representation in the zodiac of the consciousness of duality, separation and opposition. Gemini, occurring early in the zodiac, is a metaphor for a primal stage in psychological development. In the context of zodiacal development, the ability to understand, reflect or analyse has not yet been developed and a secure sense of emotional attachment has not yet been internalized.

As a symbol of the developmental process of Gemini, Castor, now in the underworld, was too young to consciously hold the impact of Pollux's profound loss. He was in the underworld and not in a dimension to even become aware of the grief that Pollux was experiencing. Hence the impact and feeling of the loss is repressed, banished to the underworld realm. Feelings that are deeply buried in the underworld are thematic of Water. Grief, abandonment and separation when interred are rendered unconscious in the individual.

These feelings surface as restlessness and emptiness, an anxiety that something is missing or lost, and an incompleteness that beckons us to continue searching, which is an Air element function. Quite commonly this 'missing' feeling is projected on to the world, especially the compatible world of equal others. This feeling of connection to the missing half is often idealized as the soulmate (Libra) or the bonds of fraternal or sororal love (Aquarius). Underlying many Geminian placements is a feeling of profound loss which cannot be explained rationally; it becomes embodied in the nervous system, stimulating anxiety and lack of focus. The unconscious memory of a primal separation is awoken in the closeness of an adult partnership or intimate friendship.

There are many differing versions as to how the twins were reunited. While most references suggest the twins alternated between the two worlds of heaven and the underworld, how this occurred is depicted differently in various sources.[30] The Spartans saw Pollux, the immortal half, as the morning star while Castor, the mortal twin, was the evening star. While one rose out of the dark and ascended towards heaven, the other descended into the twilight of the netherworld, forever separated by the horizon. In a similar version, Castor spends one day in heaven while his brother passes the same time in the underworld. They follow each other between Olympus and Erebos but never meet.

This theme of rising while the other is setting has led authors to refer to them as 'the alternate twins'.[31] Another version has them together, one day in the underworld and the next day in heaven. Even though together, they can only be in either the underworld or in heaven. These similar motifs have the twins swinging in a manic-depressive cycle between the highs of heaven and the lows of the underworld, a common motif underlying Gemini.

The twins' afterlife has numerous possible interpretations. One suggests the theme of the constant search for the missing other which seems to be part of Gemini's fate. The twins, once fused and bonded together, are now eternally separated. However, we can also read into the myth another suggestion. With the consciousness of their differences now apparent, it is more possible for the twins to experience both opposites within themselves. An awareness of the elements of Air and Water and their functions within the self can facilitate the process of finding balance. In Libra, the next Air sign, the sign of the scales, the function of balancing opposites with the self is supported.

Castor and Pollux remind us of the eternal quest for the missing other and the life journey of bonding, separation, conflict and reconciliation in relationship, first with family, then with others. Castor's interment in the underworld is a poignant symbol of emotional waters that are blocked or stagnant until an experience of consciousness – Pollux's awareness of loss – breaks open the dam. It is in the laboratory of the family where the balancing act of closeness and separation is first practised so that the emotions of Water and the consciousness of Air are integrated within our self and within our relationships.

Astrological Architecture: Designing the Houses

Before we open the doors to the houses of family, let's reflect on how they are constructed, as there are many house designs. In astrological tradition different houses systems have been used over time. This can be very perplexing for the student, especially when planets change houses using a different method. Which one is right? Each house system has its own logic, its own history and its own rationale and a case can be presented for which approach is better. Yet, in actuality we cannot debate which house system is best or most precise as the meaningfulness of the house is revealed through a symbolic approach, not a logical one. Perhaps underpinning the need for the 'right' house system is an urge for clarity, as astrological delineation is often open-ended and indistinct. The dilemma about the right house system subsides when we craft our own astrological approach and appreciate that subjectivity and ambiguity are essential in shaping a symbolic attitude to chart interpretation. Therefore the value and validity of a house system is in the hands of the astrologer, even if they cannot concisely articulate why.

Astrologers all agree on the position of the angles. How the boundaries of the houses are defined is where there are differing methods. The charts in this book are calculated using the Placidus house system which is a quadrant-based system; therefore the four angles are also the cusps to the four angular houses, similar to other systems in this category. However, in equal-based house systems such as Equal House or Whole Sign, angles do not always define the cusps of the angular houses. In the Equal Houses system the Ascendant-Descendant axis demarcates the $1^{st} - 7^{th}$ house cusps, but the IC-MC exists independently of the $4^{th} - 10^{th}$ house cusps. No matter what the house system is, the four angles are primary and powerful orientating symbols.

House meaning can be accessed in various ways. The sign on the cusp symbolizes the qualities, ambience and mood that infiltrate this sphere. It is also symbolic of the environment and conditions of this house; therefore it is an important symbol in accessing and opening its door. The planet ruling this sign might be likened to a doorkeeper or more grandly the ruler of the house, suggesting that its condition in the horoscope symbolizes our attitudes and approaches to this area of experience. We can summon this energy when we need support or amplification of its house matters. But it is the planet or planets in the house that bring its archetypal nature, patterns and characteristics into the environment. When we are in this location, we are in the presence of this archetype and its universal patterning. It is sensible to pay homage to its presence. When no planets are in a house, the environment is defined by the sign on the cusp and its ruler; but when a planet is in a house the atmosphere is permeated by its presence.

While the delineations in the book are descriptive they are not meant to be read as literal interpretations, although at times this may be so. They invite you to reflect and consider the profound nature of the astrological archetype, its endless expressions and how its pattern functions personally in your life experience.

– CHAPTER 4–
THE WATER HOUSES
Emotional Seas in the Harbour of Home

Every child, whether biological, adopted, fostered or step, is baptized in the ancestral waters of the family atmosphere. Immersion into the family atmosphere often provides a wellspring of nourishment but, sadly, too often the ancestral waters remain polluted with toxic feelings which have never been adequately flushed through the system. The pollutants find their way into the contemporary mood, undermining the emotional security systems of the family.

Each member's perception of the family atmosphere will be different, due to many factors. For instance, each child will arrive at a different stage in their parents' relationship, into a distinct family arrangement, a new family home or during a phase which is quite separate from other times in the family. We are born into the family system at a unique moment in the family's development; therefore we will have our own questions to answer. Numerous issues affect each one's experience of the family ambiance. Each child will have a unique participation in the parental marriage and with each parent, forming their own distinctive psychic bond with the unconscious of each parent.

The family atmosphere is an amalgam of many influences, many of which remain unconscious. The parents' behaviour, beliefs and values, their unconscious complexes and defences, unlived dreams and unresolved conflicts all impact the mood of the family. These influences in turn are shaped by the ancestral inheritance; hence we come into contact with family fate through the recurring inherited patterns that are passed down the family line and beyond our control to change. Unresolved conflicts and trauma, as well as unexpressed grief and loss, affect the family atmosphere, its security and well-being.

This family fate shapes our unique inheritance and inspires our character. However, consciousness needs to bring this inheritance to light. When viewed from this angle, the horoscope becomes a remarkable tool in helping to reveal some of the unique familial fate embedded in the family atmosphere.

Water Houses Overview – the Family Atmosphere

Through the 4th, 8th and 12th houses flow the currents of family life first experienced in the family home through the parental union and extended family as well as in the ancestral gene pool. In the Water houses we can begin to reflect upon the soul of the family. Each of these houses, in its own way, symbolizes our genesis and the familial atmosphere that shapes character and contributes to our inner experience of safety and belonging. These houses are the storage containers for our feeling heritage and where we locate our emotional security systems which nurture the growth of our fragile self.

Astrologically the 4th house is the house of family and has come to be more commonly associated with the parental and familial legacy. However, the 8th and 12th houses are also integral to the developmental themes of the family. The 4th house locates our participation in the family of origin where our earliest impressions and experiences provide the basic template for our emotional stability. This sphere signifies the living atmosphere of the family. In the 4th house we find the felt experiences of childhood that psychodynamic theory so clearly articulates.

Erik Erikson advocated the premise of basic trust, while John Bowlby's lifework explored the experiences of attachment throughout the life cycle that were underpinned by a secure family base. Ultimately the psychological drive of the 4th house is for the individual in adult life to find emotional security within the self; however, the attainment of this is heavily influenced by the childhood experience of attachment.

Psychotherapist DW Winnicott published a collection of reflective essays on family life called *Home is Where We Start From*,[32] inspired by TS Eliot's phrase in 'East Cocker V', from *Four Quartets*. The poet begins this quartet with the phrase 'In my end is my beginning', an image of the 4th house as the house of endings and beginnings. In traditional times, the 4th house was known as 'the end of the matter'.

The Houses of Endings: Excavating the Family Psyche

Indeed, all three Water houses bear the label 'houses of endings', as they mark the ending of developmental processes in the personal, interpersonal and transpersonal spheres of life. The 4th house is the ending of the deeply personal developmental process that begins in the 1st house of birth and beginnings. As we move across the threshold to the 5th house, we leave the familial sphere to create a more self-governing existence.

In the 8th house we are plunged into unconscious participation in the intimacy, or lack of it, within the parental relationship. This area symbolizes the emotional legacy of the patterns of personal relating of our parents, and their parents before them, which in turn models our intimate relationships in adult life. In the 8th house, we sort through experiences of intimacy to discover our own personal needs. Being immersed in parental intimacy dynamics can either stimulate or inhibit the emergence of a greater sense of self-mastery. As we internalize our own patterns of intimate relating, we enter the transpersonal spheres of life that begin within the 9th house.

Finally, in the 12th house, we receive the remaining soul threads of the generations gone before us and we are engaged with their shadows and shades. In recognizing the legacy of our ancestors, we become aware of the power and possibilities of our lineage. This house has often been referred to as the 'house of undoing'; in one way our task is to undo the knotted complexes of our ancestors so we may be freer to more fully participate in our own dreams and creativity. Our first independent breath marks the end of our 12th house connection with the Divine and participation in the ancestral waters as we cross the threshold of the 1st house into an incarnate life.

In the 4th, 8th and 12th houses we experience our sense of belonging on a personal, tribal and collective level respectively. Throughout our life experience, these sectors are the storehouses of our familial patterns and ancestral threads, representing our family inheritance as well as the secrets and fate that linger in the family's collective history. Transits and progressions passing through these areas of an individual's horoscope excavate the familial legacy and facilitate the cultivation of ancestral connections. These are the houses of ancestry, which contain our familial legacy, whether known or not, and assist in identifying the familial factors which influence individual development.

The lifeblood of the familial members past and present flows through these Water houses. Embedded in them is the past, not just our own past but also that of our relatives and ancestors. Therefore, the Water houses are the reservoirs of family patterns and fate. This gene pool of our ancestors is both the wellspring for our emotional security and also where we locate an underworld of ghosts and shades that have come before us. The Water houses are where we search for our emotional security yet also encounter the unlived lives and unresolved issues of the past; while striving to achieve emotional security, we will repeatedly return to address the lack of comfort, intimacy or sense of belonging from our past.

As symbolic storage containers for the contents of the unconscious, the Water houses psychologically represent what has been buried, contained, forgotten and repressed. Feelings experienced before conscious awareness or the development of language, even feelings from being *in utero,* are registered here. Since the unconscious is not only personal, the felt sense from others may also be recorded here along with familial or collective material. These are the houses of depth, where what is reflected on the surface is not always what exists below.

The 4th House: Creating a Secure Foundation
The primary function of the 4th house is to create and sustain a secure foundation. In the 4th house the groundwork for personal security, safety and shelter is prepared. This footing for life is shaped by the family atmosphere and environs. The tools with which to forge close relationships throughout life and cope with the complexity of human interaction are learnt here.

A basic issue of this house is the extent to which emotional security and nurturing help to secure the life base. From an astrological perspective this development of emotional safety and security begins at the IC and is brought to light in the 4th house. As the natural home of Cancer, the 4th house is also associated with the Moon; therefore embedded in this house are themes of how we are nurtured and how we learn to nurture. The experience of nurturing and care contribute to the infant's confidence in life, which in turn is the bedrock of trust in later relationships, one of the links between the 4th and the 8th houses.

Astrological houses represent both inner and outer locations. The 4th house is where we locate the physical structures, the psychological patterns, memories and attitudes that we inherit from our family and it shows how we have internalized them. The 4th house symbolizes the family atmosphere as well as its psychic foundations. As a signification of the past, the 4th house is our link to the psychological patterns that we share with the immediate ancestors that are genetically inbuilt or formed in our earliest life. These templates are acquired pre-verbally and are so bound up with who we are that it is often impossible to see them directly or objectively.

On a much more unseen level the 4th house may relate to the infant's felt experiences of mother's moods, perhaps prenatal senses and feelings, including moods from the family of origin and the family environment, even impressions from the atmosphere. These unconscious feeling reactions are part of the internal make-up of this house and an aspect of creating a secure base.

At the innermost level, the 4th house symbolizes the psychic functions that connect us to the rest of life. It governs feelings of belonging, being at home and being connected. This is the setting of the family home both literally and metaphorically. The astrological images of the 4th house will describe the physical climate of the family home as well as the attitudes and influences of the family of origin that shaped the individual's sense of safety and provided the foothold for life.

At the level of our conscious relation to others, the 4th house symbolizes intimate ties with our family and those who support and nurture us. These are the personal and inward aspects of our life and usually are unseen and unknown by others outside the family circle. Childhood patterns and roles, as well as our sense of safekeeping, are interred in this astrological landscape. These experiences shape our trust, our habits and the level of how safe we feel. We could say that, like our past, the 4th house conditions always catch up with us.

The 4th House/10th House Controversy: Father or Mother?
The 10th house belongs to the trinity of houses known as the houses of substance (the other two are the 2nd and 6th houses) and also represents the vocational pathway in the world, a course of life that is first conceived in the family and forged with their help and resources. Conversely, the path in life may also have been shaped in response to the lack of familial support. This trinity of houses is anchored and secured in the tangible world. The 10th house is the last in this trinity and also has strong connections to the family. Being opposite the 4th

house, this sphere is where the familial voices of what we might be, 'should' be or could be echo in the day world.

The shadowy attitudes inherited from the family about professional status, career and being someone in the world are exposed in the culminating light of the 10th. Here is the legacy of our family's social standing and how it contributes to who we become. Family businesses, family money and family attitudes about the world can be great assets or liabilities on the balance sheet of our professional life. This atmosphere of the 10th house has its early images embedded in the familial worldview.

Another family context of the 10th house is that it strongly represents the parents. The most controversial aspect of this house is whether it represents father or mother. While modern astrology mostly chooses the 10th as the father's house, traditional astrology specified that this was the house of the mother.

The controversy arose during the transition to modern astrological interpretation. With the advent of a psychologically-based astrology, the 4th house, with its association with Cancer and the Moon, became linked with the nurturing, inner-directed or emotional-based parent, most commonly the mother.

Howard Sasportas argues in his book *The Twelve Houses* that the 10th house is mother as 'she is the whole world to us'. This is consistent with astrological traditions that existed before modern astrology. This is the classical view stated in ancient texts; for instance, Bonatti in quoting Abu 'Ali suggests that 'in the day and in the night you ought to look for the father from the 4th'.[33] Later he uses the derivative house system to explain 'the matter of the mother' is the 10th since the father's wife would be the 4th house (father) from the wife (the 7th).[34]

The allocation of the house representing each parent has not been consistent, especially from traditional to contemporary authors. Llewellyn George reports:[35]

> Reference to twelve of the leading astrological text books, published during the last three hundred years, shows the tenth house ruling the mother; fourth house, the father. Only one of the early writers reverses this indication, while another who leans towards Eastern methods quotes the tenth house as ruling father in the horoscope of females, mother in male charts; the fourth house ruling mother in

female horoscopes; the father in male charts. My own experience confirms the teachings of the twelve older writers. It is an invariable rule in Horary Astrology to use the tenth house for mother and the fourth house for father in all cases.

Many authors steer clear of assigning a specific parent to these houses while some astrological dictionaries and texts mention both parents.[36]

The early bonding patterns with mother will be reflected in later life in the external world; therefore, how we might try to connect to society or the world at large will replicate this first experience with mother. As Sasportas says, 'we carry an expectation that the world will treat us similarly'.[37] Liz Greene also correlates the sphere of the 10th house with mother: 'planets in the 10th, the sign on the Midheaven, seem to describe many of the essential components in the image of mother and therefore of the World Mother'.[38]

In astrological tradition the 4th house is ruled by the Moon and the 10th is ruled by Saturn. Saturn and the 10th by nature are connected to power and influence; no doubt mother's authority could rest here. However, in a more patriarchal culture where authority and worldly figures are largely males, father would also occupy this sphere, as expressed by Jungian Vera von der Heydt:

> Father embodies consciousness; his realm is reason and knowledge, light and sun. In a patriarchal society it is the elders, the fathers, who govern, who pass laws and keep tradition alive. For the child it is the father who is the mediator between the exciting world outside and the home.[39]

From this view father inhabits the worldly sphere of the 10th, especially later when rules and structures become important for the child. But at the beginning of life the mother is the world as well. The 10th house shows the parent who has the most effect on the child's attitudes in the world, their social and professional persona or the one often referred to as the 'shaping parent'.[40] With this in mind, perhaps it is not an issue about *one parent*, but about the *parental system* and how that has shaped our view of the world.

It is wise to remember that the chart suggests the archetypal landscape and this is not always as functional, pragmatic or detailed as we might like. And it is also wise to remember that the houses have many layers. Like an archaeological site, each house has levels of influence and meaning and in the 10th each parent in the parental system is more visible at different times. As personifications of each parent, the Sun and Moon are more appropriate astrological representatives of the father and mother.

The 4th-10th House Polarity: Self or Social Norm?

When reflecting on the inner life from a Jungian point of view we could postulate that the axis of the 4th and 10th houses might not just sketch the relationship between the parents and the power exchange between the two, but the relationship between the anima, the inner feminine, and the animus, the internal masculine. Therefore, if the 4th is father, his inner feminine images reflected in the world by mother are also part of the territory. Father's anima was first shaped by his mother and other women in his family, and these images are embedded in the multidimensional layers of the 4th house. On the other hand, mother's animus might be a component of the 10th house. Hence the 10th could serve as the reservoir of fatherly imprints which shape mother's masculine side. In addressing the 4th and 10th houses psychologically, each parent's gender and their inner contra-sexual partner inhabit the terrain.

The 10th house plays its role in the family as the polarity of the 4th house, the familial root system. The 10th house illuminates the familial goals and principles and suggests what the family wants to attain. Carl Jung suggested children often 're-enact under unconscious compulsion the unlived lives of [their] parents'[41] and from a psychological perspective this house represents the tension and stress that the unlived life of the parent place upon the child.

This anxiety often compels the child to live out what is inauthentic in their nature to please the parent. The unfulfilled goals, the failed outcomes and the lack of success of the parents are lived through the child. Therefore, 10th house planets are invested with parental pressure on the child to succeed. The overt messages of what is expected permeate the terrain of the 10th house; hence the child often takes in two layers of experience. One is the layer of disappointment that contains the unfulfilled desires of the parent; the other consists of the obvious rules and goalposts set down by the parental system.

Since this sphere is where the family's worldly values and experiences are impressed upon the child, the 10th house could be described as the unconcealed familial expectations. We would differentiate this from the 12th house where the family's desires and passions have been concealed. The 10th house often describes the parental wish to succeed, which may be borne out of social norms rather than personal authenticity. Therefore, the parents' unlived lives and unmet goals that are projected onto the newborn may continue the inauthentic pattern of being true to the social norm rather than the self.

Is the Foundation Stone Strong Enough?
The 4th house foundation is reinforced by having a safe enough base to stand on and an adequate amount of care. The 4th house is the house of the parents. While there are differing opinions as to which parent this house contains, hopefully in a fairly functional family both parents played a 4th house role at some time. This fortifies the roots of our being and provides the nutrients and nourishment to develop a secure foundation throughout life.

The development of self-confidence and self-assurance involves standing on our parents' shoulders, and previously our parents stood on the shoulders of their parents, and so on. The IC symbolizes our primary roots and it is important to honour any planet on the IC because it is protecting and ensuring our safety. It personifies a potent legacy from the parental and familial line – the 'shoulders' we stand on.

The 4th is deeply personal, inward and private, as opposed to the outward and public nature of the 10th house found opposite. It is home, both physical and emotional; it is our piece of earth, our foundation stone where we settle and put down roots. It is our sanctuary and private space where we retire after a day of being in the outer, social world; it is our first experience of intimate space.

Our family members are the people who not only share the similar root system but also provide emotional support for us, as we do for them. Therefore, schisms in the system can destabilize the foundation stones. The innermost depth of feeling described by the 4th house, whether light or dark, is also a doorway to the soul; hence it is through reflection on and contemplation of our familial patterns and legacy that a deeper narrative of our soul's journey can be appreciated.

The following phrases summarize the 4th house experience in terms of family. Contemplate these phrases, not as keywords but as images and metaphors of the childhood experiences connected with the astrological imagery of the 4th house.

The Family Home
- Home is where we start from; home is where we belong
- The family of origin and the root system of the extended family
- The atmosphere of the family home and the climatic conditions of childhood
- Emotional foundation stones
- A secure base
- The family web and the familial alembic
- Familial patterns and roles
- Spirit of the ancestors as they affect contemporary life
- The 'homeland', the place we consider home
- Childhood patterns and the internalization of security

The 8th House: The Familial Inheritance and the Intimacy of the Parental Marriage

The 8th house is the house of inheritance and it is in this territory where we claim our familial legacy. Whether that legacy is psychological, emotional or financial, the 8th house is the depository where 'we find the inheritance we have been left by our ancestors'.[42] The ancestry of the 8th house is more personal and private than the ancestral shades of the 12th house.

To claim our inheritance we must journey into the underworld, down into the nether regions of the self that have been shaped and genetically structured through familial lines that stretch back through both sides of the family. This journey into the depth of self awakens the dead spirits of our familial past who are the executors of our legacy. The 8th house has been traditionally associated with the underworld where the treasures of the self are interred. In an ancestral sense the shades of our underworld are the skeletons in the family closet. In the 8th house we encounter this underworld of the familial past, these shades and shadows of what has not been allowed to live. Part of the 8th house journey is to confront the secrets, shame and shades of the past in order to reclaim our legacy.

The 8th house is the place where the two sides of the family merge into one; it reveals the search for intimacy and closeness in the family. Planets in the 8th house will describe the family inheritance, secret alliances and taboos in the family, as well as indicate the level of intimacy in the family system as a whole.

The 8th house is where we re-experience primal trust in adult life. It is the area where we once again become vulnerable with another, re-experience emotional safety and take the risk of losing their love. In the familial burial ground of the 8th house will be the legacy of loss and betrayal from the past and the repercussions of how this was dealt with by the family. The strength of our emotional foundation is tested.

Buried in the 8th house are the familial gains and losses which are passed down through the generations. These gains and losses might be financial, as in monetary bequests and inheritances, or a familial story of debt and economic disasters. In many cases the gains and losses are emotionally based. The sign on the cusp of the 8th house is the gateway to this intimate area and as such is important in considering how we access this part of ourselves. Often the sign on the cusp can also be employed defensively. By using the sign qualities of the 8th house cusp, the personality can defend against intimacy rather than use this vulnerability as an ally to closeness. Ironically, behaviours that are highly valued, such as caring, generosity and sacrifice, are effective defences against intimacy.

On a personal level the 8th house could also reveal participation in our parents' relationship or the lack of it. As a barometer of closeness, the 8th house refers to the degree of parental intimacy that was experienced when we were growing up. Complex 8th house arrangements might reveal a separation, infidelity, a form of abuse, all contributing to a lack of intimacy and influencing the adult sense of trust in relationship. Unearthed in the 8th house journey may be secrets and betrayals from the familial past which weaken the confidence of the present relationship. Secrets are poisons in the family as they undermine the integrity, honesty and intimacy of the system, leaving a deeply felt inner wound. This wound, often experienced as shame, divides each individual from the other and damages the cohesion of the family system.

The 8th house is the second in the trinity of Water houses; therefore the attachment, emotional security and parental issues of childhood experienced in the 4th, yet not resolved, are prone to being re-experienced through adult intimacy. Emotional and psychological issues brought into family life by the intimate partner are also aspects of the 8th house territory. In other words, we also 'marry' into and participate in our partner's familial line, which includes their family's psychological, emotional and financial composition. In the 8th house the collusion between both partners' unconscious patterns is highlighted. The will and testament of those gone before exert their influence on the emotional well-being of those in the present. Issues concerning legacies, wills, inheritances, shared resources and family trusts are all part of this terrain.

Contemplate the following phrases as images and metaphors to help deepen your understanding of the 8th house and your familial inheritance.

The Family Plot
- The burial ground of familial complexes
- Familial taboos and secrets
- Trust and betrayal in the family
- What has been abandoned and left incomplete in the family
- Legacy and wills of the family
- The familial inheritance
- Familial attitudes to intimacy and trust
- The atmosphere of the parental marriage
- The intimate other
- Inheritance through marriage and union

The 12th House: The Legacy of the Ancestors
The final water house is a mysterious and enigmatic place; perhaps why there are many astrological variants when delineating the 12th house. Paradoxically it is the house where planets have just risen above the horizon, yet in traditional astrology it refers to matters that are secret or hidden. It is a place of seclusion or isolation. In a familial context it is the place where secrets or shame may be stored, invisible to public view. In another way it might suggest a place of refuge and shelter for familial ghosts; therefore having planets in the 12th house may suggest that an ancestral spirit may seek sanctuary through you.

The 12th house could be likened to an ancestral resting place where the tombstones of our ancestors are not clear or able to be read. The granite is old but we cannot decode these tombstones of our ancestors. We need to be in touch with them in an imaginative way, connecting with them through our creativity and fantasy.

Modern astrologers compare the imagery of the 12th house to Carl Jung's notion of the collective unconscious. Since all humans are biologically similar, the contents of this pooled unconscious are common to all humanity; myths, images and symbols are shared by all human beings. This oceanic depth of collective and familial feeling underpins each being's life and is a key to understanding the vast and somewhat impersonal nature of the 12th house. For instance, while compassion and love might be deeply felt they may be focused more collectively than personally. Here in the 12th house, personal feelings are often flooded by collective ones or the past overflows into the present. From the family's perspective, the 12th house represents where communal and familial mythologies intersect and where the collective and the personal become enmeshed.

Embedded in the 12th house are experiences beyond the personal, sometimes arising through inherited and familial lines or surfacing due to our sensitivity to the collective. The 12th house is where our personal and emotional plumbline reaches the collective level and where we experience the commonality of being human. Usually this is experienced as an emotional or deeply felt response, carried not by thoughts or ideas but by images and feelings.

In traditional astrology the 12th house has been known as the house of secret enemies, institutions and asylums. In contemporary astrology this has come to represent the house of ancestral shades and the psychological resting place of familial ghosts. In the family system 12th house planets can often be depersonalized, used as a spokesman for the ghosts of the past. Often the planet can symbolize the grip of a familial shade that still tries to express itself through the individual.

Planets in the 12th house describe the legacy of the ancestors and what has not been adequately expressed in the family. Planets in this house may feel as if there is a compulsion to express what has been left unexpressed or unacknowledged in the past. The qualities represented by the sign on the cusp are important to consider as being the mechanisms that either open up this area for exploration or defensively close it down. Planets in the 12th house are potent, as they have just risen above the horizon. They personify archetypal energies that do not belong exclusively to the individual experience but are also part of the collective experience. This is a territory that does not respond to the literal or rational world but is more inclined towards feelings and images. The contents of the 12th house are known through the faculty of the imagination using metaphors, symbols and images. Dreams, reveries, fantasies, active imagination and myth are the language of the 12th house.

Scapegoat or Shaman – the 'Identified Patient' in the Family
Family therapists often refer to the identified patient or the one in the family who reveals the illness, expresses the denials and carries the shadows that the family turn their back on. In ancient cultures this person was often recognized as a shaman who could speak the truth for the departed souls; in other cultures this individual was the scapegoat, cast out for expressing the sins of the tribe. Twelfth house planets experience the spectrum from scapegoat to shaman and are therefore often very difficult for the individual to articulate or understand. Without conscious awareness, the feeling of being misunderstood, not known or invisible is often internalized as a sense of being unacceptable or marginal. Hence, there is often a history of mental frailty or chaos forged from this despair of not being understood. From a psychological point of view the 12th house planet unconsciously identifies with the repression of the familial past and can be the archetypal vehicle for the family's healing. Twelfth house planets can be experienced both regressively and therapeutically.

The 12th house is also a sphere of creativity and spirituality. Familial beliefs, ideologies and principles do not always support the individual's needs. The 12th house need is to find the soul's authentic spiritual expression which may have been cut off and sacrificed for social acceptance; therefore the 12th house is also a place where we locate the spiritual and creative longings which may be at odds with the family institution. The 12th can often reveal myths and stories in the family past, especially those that are inauthentic, falsely forged to fit in and which feel acceptable to the social paradigm of the time.

From a familial perspective the 12th house can also characterize family health, the inheritance of disease that is passed down through the ancestral gene pool. Therefore, qualities of the sign on the cusp of the 12th become important images for mental well-being and health. Planets in the 12th become keys to identifying any possible hereditary factors. Astrological images of the 12th house are passed down through the generations and therefore the denials of these over time may also somatize as symptoms.

The 12th house can be metaphorically seen as the last trimester of pregnancy.[43] Here in this house is where the feeling experience of being in the womb is registered. The ancestral history and legacy are impressed upon the child during gestation; however, these impressions are pre-verbal, stored as sensations and dream-like images. In the 12th house we are unintentionally involved in the tribal past and the collective unconscious of our clan, phenomena that anthropologists referred to as the *participation mystique*.[44] Subtly, 12th house planets are impressed by what has come before, the feeling life that has not been expressed, creativity not lived out and feelings not shared.

The following phrases apply to the 12th house experience. Contemplate these phrases, not as keywords but as images and metaphors of the experiences connected with the 12th house.

The Fate of our Ancestors
- *In utero* and pre-birth experiences
- *Participation mystique* with mother during gestation
- The vestiges of ancestral fate and embedded family patterns; family fate
- The identified patient
- Disenfranchised feelings and experiences from the past
- Contact with the Divine
- Participation with collective images, symbols, icons and feelings
- The familial institution; what has been imprisoned and incarcerated
- Ancestors and ancestral shadows and shades; the ghosts of the past
- Deep familial complexes

– CHAPTER 5 –
PLANETS IN THE 4TH HOUSE
Delineating the Fundamental House of Family

The planets represent the cast of characters possible within the family system as well as our own archetypal images of 'inner family'. For interpretations of the planets in the 8th and 12th houses, refer to Chapter 11: *Planets, Aspects and Houses:* Delineating the Family. To honour its prominence as the fundamental house of family, in this chapter we extend our journey into the 4th house, through an in-depth contemplation of each planet within the house.

The Moon in the 4th House

With the Moon in the 4th house, emotional security and a sense of belonging are shaped early in the family of origin. A dependence on family develops because of the need for support, protection, guidance, nurturing and safety. Of course these are typical human needs, but with the Moon here the process of attachment and bonding becomes highlighted. Mother is a significant image in the psyche, therefore she has a powerful influence upon the child. When a positive attachment to family is created, it is easier to leave the nest and return on your own terms because a sense of safety and trust has been created. However, if your family experience was fractured and unsettled, then it may be more difficult to separate and become independent. Sensitivity to others' needs and the moods in the family atmosphere might inhibit independence.

A sixth sense about what others need is developed in the family. This sympathy towards others in the family circle may not be conscious, but nonetheless the individual responds to what is in the atmosphere, sensitive to emotional undertones, jarring vibrations or darkened moods. This is not an intellectual knowing; rather, it is a gut knowing, as the emotional climate in the family is absorbed, often settling in the stomach or solar plexus. Without conscious knowledge of this pattern, the child may respond to everyone else's needs rather than their own, unaware of what it is they require because of the unfulfilled needs of those around them. If this occurs the child feels out of sorts, alone, unsupported, as if no one really understands. Creating an emotional boundary is difficult, but it is necessary. With an emotionally mature mother and family to help the child feel supported and separate enough, they learn to know what they need as opposed to what others might need. But if there is a volatile or dysfunctional environment, the child internalizes some of the stress, which results in feelings of insecurity and being unloved. In this environment the child may feel that to be loved they need to take care of others rather than put their own needs first. Love becomes dependent rather than unconditional. In adult life, it is always helpful to reflect to what extent you care for others at the expense of your own needs. The tendency to bond, merge and be symbiotic might be great for nurturing a child, but is not necessarily supportive in developing friendships and relationships.

Home and country are important, both literally and metaphorically, as images of belonging. The Moon needs a sense that it belongs; however, there is also a great need for privacy. In an adult context the task is to provide enough emotional containment and boundaries to protect your sensitivity; to be selective about whom you invite into that private and sacred space you call home. Ultimately, home is the reflection of your inner life and security. Being unsettled in your self is entwined with feeling unsettled in the home. Many of life's major transitions will probably be synchronous with an important move.

Being habitual suggests that change may not come easily. Leaving home may be complicated; however, on an inner level the image of returning home time and time again helps to recreate an adult home. Carrying transitional objects that are invested with memories and feelings from the family home to the adult home can help to make the transition easier. The memories of home linger into adult life and need a place to be housed. With the Moon here it is important to acknowledge the powerful imprints that the family marks upon the internal sense of safety, security and feelings of comfort and love.

The Sun in the 4th House

With the Sun in your 4th house, you were born nearing midnight when the Sun reaches its nadir. When we think of the Sun we imagine it shining brightly above us; however, here it is at its lowest point. As a symbol this suggests that identity is deeply ingrained and shaped in the family. Herein lies a paradox because identity is often singular and individualistic while family is plural and collective. The questions might be 'How do we define our self without cutting off family ties?' and 'How do we participate in the family traditions without losing our identity?' A deep sense of identity is already there; hopefully, the family encourages this.

When family supports the child's sense of being, they grow into their natural courage and self-expression. With the Sun in the 4th house, the child may have become the centre of family attention. When constructive, this means the child felt acknowledged, appreciated and had a lot of applause. When unconstructive, the child may have become the centre of attention through acting out, trying to feel noticed and acknowledged. This may have been compounded because of parental difficulties which took the focus away from the child. With the Sun in the 4th the child may have identified familial complexes and acted them out. Or parental narcissism may have drawn the child into identifying with the parent's need for approval and identity. It is helpful to reflect on the pattern of the Sun in the 4th house, as identity may have been forged through an ability to mirror others, rather than to express the true self. Later in life the individual may seek out others who mirror and approve of them. Without a healthy sense of separateness or individuality, differences become threatening. The family inheritance influences how the child expresses their identity, creativity and self-expression.

The Sun in the parental zone reveals that father is central in the child's psychology. It also suggests that favouritism may be an issue in the family. How much does the individual identify with the father? Paternity becomes important because the child's instinct will be to identify with the father. A Greek myth speaks to this dilemma: when Phaëthon found out that Apollo, the Sun god, was his father he begged him to let him drive his chariot of the Sun across the sky. Phaëthon was obsessed with the notion that he could master his father's solar chariot. However, the horses were too strong and wild for the boy to rein in and, when the horses bucked, Phaëthon fell from the chariot. With Sun in the 4th the individual may look for their identity through the mirror of a parent by seeking their approval or recreating their identity. Yet the task is to find one's unique creative expression through the contributions and talents experienced in the family of origin.

Mercury in the 4th House

With Mercury in the 4th house, communication patterns and ways of thinking are strongly influenced by the family. Early developmental stages, such as learning to crawl, walk, talk, starting school and changing schools, are important family markers influenced by Mercury. This could suggest that the familial background was academic or scholastic; if not that, at least intellect is highly valued in the family. When intellect is prized over feeling in family life, the expression of sensitivity and affection can be compromised. Rationality might replace emotion and the family unit may suffer from the lack of expressing closeness and intimacy. Mercury in the 4th suggests how the family communication system impacted the individual's sense of security.

Learning, whether that's learning to ride a bicycle or study the times tables, and schooling are parental concerns. What is important is whether the child felt supported and nurtured in their learning capabilities. School may have been challenging, not because the child did not want to learn but because learning was an issue for their parents. They may not have been able to see what the child needed because of their own educational experiences and ideas. Mental development, communication and learning are prominent in the family.

Mercury is the god of travellers and the marketplace. Early life may include a lot of movement and activity in the home, possibly even literally changing houses or moving neighbourhoods. Some of these changes may have been due to the emotional shifts in family life; for instance, moving between your parents' homes after they separated or becoming accustomed to a step-family after one of your parents remarried. A sibling may have become the transitional 'object' that provided continuity when changes occurred.

Mercury often signals a sibling relationship and in the 4th house this may suggest that a sibling story influences the stability of the early home life. Whether that is the child's own sibling, the parent's sibling or the loss of a sibling in the extended family, the pattern suggested is that the role in the family often requires you to be a sibling or friend. The roles of sibling and parent might be interchanged. To feel emotionally secure, the individual needs to express their ideas, talk through their feelings and feel comfortable when changing their ideas and opinions. Nothing is fixed and the individual learns to find their security in a world of flux.

Venus in the 4th House

With Venus in the 4th house, self-esteem and personal values are shaped early by family attitudes. Family preferences influenced the child's tastes, likes and dislikes, and from an early age they were taught the value of things. Parental attitudes towards money, fair exchange, possessions and valuables also exerted a strong influence. Therefore, if there were any emotional undertones associated with money, financial setbacks or hardships, the child's sense of values was affected.

Desiring a harmonious home life, the child may become the peacemaker, go-between or mediator in the family. They may have always become caught up in the centre of a family feud, feeling that it was their role to arbitrate. The child seeks fairness and balance, but is that possible in family life? Attitudes towards relationship are forged in the family; therefore in adult years the individual may still be conciliatory or find themselves in the middle of disagreements between friends or family members. Venus is prone to triangulation in relationships and this may have stemmed from earlier undercurrents in the family home. Whether the individual is aware of it or not, their parents' relationship patterns have a strong bearing on their own. The familial attitude towards the feminine and roles of women is stressed and this has left its impact on the way the individual orients themselves to women's issues. Femininity and sexuality may have been a theme that surfaced in the mother's life. Venus desires to be equal; therefore, the individual may champion the roles of women in society.

Relationship and interaction are aspects of security, so from an early age the child reached out to relate and partner others in the family. The template for relationship was strongly forged in these early years. Therefore it may be helpful if you have Venus in the 4th house to reflect on your relationships with family members and how this impacted your relationship patterns. Who were you paired with? Your mother? Father? A sibling? Or did you feel alone?

With Venus in the 4th, home and relationship are valued. Home needs to be both harmonious and attractive and to reflect the individual's values and tastes. Adult values, likes and dislikes and the ability to make choices have been strongly shaped through the familial experience.

Mars in the 4th House

When Mars is in the 4th house, the earliest examples of going after what you want, expressing desire, anger and being assertive, are modelled by the family of origin. In the family laboratory the lessons about fighting for what you want or getting your own way are learnt. A core issue is how to forge your own individuality and self-expression within a group. There is a fine line between compromising and giving in, co-operating and not having your needs met. The individual seeks their independence; but is this forged in a reactive or defensive way? Innately the child is independent, but they may only know this by acting out against others' desires, rather than by doing something on their own. It is important to identify the family attitudes towards anger. In a family where love and anger are split, it is difficult to feel safe with personal feelings or desires.

To the ancients, Mars was the planet of war, and in the 4th house it suggests that the landscape of the family may have been a battlefield at times. Living in a war zone is not conducive to feeling safe and secure. It might have been easier if the father was in the military or police force. The question arises about how anger was managed in the home and which patterns have been repeated from the family of origin. Instinctually the child identifies anger in the environment and if it is suppressed or denied then they may be the one to carry and express it. When anger builds, it develops into rage. This placement identifies issues of anger, assertiveness, sexual expression and competition within the family. When these issues cannot find healthy expressions there could be overt aggression, acting out or injury. However, these feelings may also be internalized as depression and lethargy. When Mars turns to self-harm, lack of vitality, passiveness or hopelessness, the individual's sense of safety and security is threatened.

The family's attitudes towards the masculine and male roles shape the attitudes of the individual with Mars in the 4th. This mainly influences how we go about asserting what we want but it impacts all our relationships with men. Attitudes towards sexuality are shaped in the family. Sexual acting out or other ways of behaving may be more influenced by repression in the family than the individual is aware of. Therefore with Mars in the 4th it is important to reflect on the legacy of the family in terms of anger and sexuality, confrontation and competition.

Jupiter in the 4th House

With Jupiter in the 4th house, religious beliefs, morals, ethics and philosophical outlooks have been strongly influenced by the family of origin. The deep-seated urge to find meaning beyond the familial is an essential characteristic. The family is where the child first reaches out to find their spiritual and mystical self, or where it first finds them. While there is a profound need to find meaning in life and to seek the truth, the individual might need to search further afield for the wisdom they seek. Even though the child first encounters the spiritual values and resources that the family provides, they might feel the urge to seek outside these beliefs in order to find their own philosophical foundation stone.

Sometimes with this placement the ghostly presence of an educator, wanderer, preacher or religious convert is part of the familial history. Jupiter suggests a familial legacy of the search for wisdom. Whether overt or hidden, a set of beliefs and a code of moral conduct underpin the family. Therefore it is important to reflect on philosophical and religious doctrines and how much they may have been shaped by the familial experience. These principles play a role in attitudes towards faith and security in the world. Even though a parent may not have sermonized or been overly dogmatic, moral principles were highlighted, either subliminally or through indoctrination. This affects the way the child viewed the world, their concepts, beliefs, opinions, educational choices and their urge to travel. Spiritual values, tolerance and judgements are coloured by the teachings of the family culture and any feelings of shame, even guilt, may have their origins in the family's belief systems. The individual's journey in the family is to find the truth for themselves and at times be the one to enlighten the family and change their rigid beliefs.

Underlying the family may be a motif of multiculturalism, whether that is accepted or not. Themes of migration, cultural exploration, education and faith are an aspect of family life. One of the parents may have come from a different social, racial, economic or cultural background and this shapes the child's cultural and social experiences.

There is a myriad of ways that cross-cultural themes in the family might manifest: an aristocratic family, an ethnic background in the family, a spiritual home, strong religious convictions, cross-cultural marriages or a family that travelled widely. However fate may have arranged this, the child's socialization process was affected by their family's social and educational standing. Cultural and religious standards may have challenged the long-standing beliefs of the family. Through a multicultural exploration the individual may end up living overseas, in a religious or educational commune, in a caravan, on the road as a gypsy or they may educationally go further than any member of the family has ever been. Destiny, thanks to the familial experience, is to reach beyond the borders of the family.

Astrologically, Jupiter is the planet associated mostly with expansion, inflation and luck. Taken literally, this might suggest a large or extended family when it is in the 4th house. Psychologically, it could suggest inheriting an attitude of entitlement or an air of extravagance, the darker face of this placement. This could suggest that the father might have been a larger-than-life figure whose social background has influenced the child's direction. The image of Jupiter in the 4th is to feel free to explore without the limits and responsibilities imposed by family structures, as freedom and discovery are vital to feeling secure. As an adult the individual may discover their family or place of belonging to be foreign and culturally distinct from their family of origin. Jupiter's cycle is 12 years long and therefore every 12 years there is a return to the question of belonging and settling on a deep level.

Saturn in the 4th House

Our attention is drawn to the impact that family rules, systems and traditions make upon the child when Saturn is in the 4th house. To feel safe and secure it is important for the child to know the rules. Having a predictable and organized environment is significant in developing emotional security. With Saturn here, the question is whether the family's standards and boundaries were too controlling or rigid. Regulations and controls are vital allies in feeling secure; however, if the family's policies engender fear, then the rigid systems leave the child feeling anxious. In this environment, self-esteem and personal accomplishments are compromised. Hierarchy and authority are essential in development, because the child needs to follow these guidelines and structures. It is important to forge a respect for and trust of power and administration; however, this may be jeopardized by weak or unavailable authority figures. In this case, the child rebels against authority rather than finding their own place in the system.

Therefore, the first authority figures, the parents, are highlighted with this placement. Have the Fates woven a pattern of an unavailable father figure, leaving the child in charge of their own destiny? Or has the child been conditioned to follow in the traditional footsteps laid down before them? Either way, the task is to develop authority and autonomy. The child needs to know that they have a strong safety net and that any lapses in judgement, mistakes or errors will be OK. Without this internal sense of security the individual may feel compelled to follow rules that do not suit them.

Being responsible and dependable, the child may have been accountable for other members of their family from an early age. If they were the eldest, they were entrusted with the care of their siblings; if they were a later child, they may have become a surrogate partner. Childhood may have felt constraining or lonely; hence in adult life there is often a strong sense of self-reliance, resilience and autonomy. It is in the family atmosphere where a heightened awareness of the law and a strong conscience develops. Over time the individual learns how to respect their inner law.

Saturn is a social planet; it is about the socialization process, the rules of the world and how to manage in the context of the society. In the 4th it suggests the lifelong task of finding the authentic self. How does one become the author of one's life when there are so many parental and governmental codes of conduct, standards, regulations and policies that are not supportive? If the parents abandoned their authenticity in favour of an external authority, then the child might feel abandoned deep inside their self. If traditions, rules and authority become more important than individuals in the system, then the child feels unsafe and insecure, because they recognize that no form or structure is present to contain their developing individuality. If the family's traditions are too rigid and stifling, the young adult separates from the family to find their place which is often geographically far away and certainly emotionally distant.

Whether overtly or not, the child seeks approval, yet often feels that no matter how well they do, it is not good enough. And when they do get approval for a task well done, it does not have the impact they thought it would. Ultimately, Saturn is about the internalization of authority. Soul-making in family life helps to develop the inner authority, often ironically through feelings of rejection and disapproval. Life is not as objective as the individual might like it to be; underlying the familial history might be melancholy, depression, anxiety or fears that leaked into the family atmosphere. Therefore a personal sense of angst and isolation may be overloaded by family denials. This subjectivity may pull the individual down into the melancholia of isolation. Alchemically, Saturn is lead and when it is at the bottom of the chart it suggests that there is heaviness, perhaps ruminations. But this gravity is also *gravitas*, the deep wisdom about the reality of life.

Saturn in the 4th can suggest the inner critic, perhaps shaped in the family atmosphere and characterized by a parental figure. However, this is also the personal pattern which is relieved through an innate capability and capacity to succeed. Through tenacity and commitment, long-term supportive attachments are forged both in the personal life and in the career. Saturn does not guarantee that it's easy, but is a warranty for forging secure attachments on your own terms. And due to the Saturn cycle, every seven years the individual re-examines and restructures their security systems and deep sense of self.

Chiron in the 4th House

Chiron is a maverick in the planetary pantheon of gods and goddesses. Similarly, with Chiron in the 4th house the first felt experience of being a maverick was in the family of origin. Perhaps the family was marginal to the mainstream culture or foreign to the system in some way. Themes of abandonment, estrangement or displacement may have permeated the family atmosphere. These may have been lingering feelings left over from an emigration, displacement, loss of home or schism that left the family feeling bereft and outside the social system. An important question is to what extent feelings of marginality contributed to the child feeling unsafe and insignificant. Chiron suggests being different from the herd, yet in the 4th these feelings permeate the family; to what extent was the family comfortable with these feelings of marginality?

If the family is the outsider in the society, then the child might feel that safety can only be sustained within the family, leaving them at risk of not venturing into the wider world. The family myth may imply that the pain of living is great, wounding the spirit that promotes adventure and exploration outside the family and culture. If a familial wound left the individual with a handicap, then it is important to reflect on how this essential aspect of character may be used to their advantage.

This placement might literally reveal that one parent was wounded in some way; generally, this is a loss of spirit due to feelings of excommunication that took place in their family. And with Chiron here the child is sensitive to the parental pain. Perhaps a trauma, injury or affliction may have distressed a family member and, because of this, the familial attention was directed towards pain rather than comfort. This contributed to making the wound the centrepiece in the family; however, this might also have been the inspiration for the individual to find their spiritual self. Deep in the inner self is a healing and compassionate side, born not from inspiration but often from desperation.

Freud wrote about the phenomena of Family Romance: the child's feeling of being alien to their family of origin and therefore romanticizing their parents and siblings. While the person may not have romanticized their origins they might have felt alien and adopted when growing up. This deep feeling encourages them to find where they truly belong.

In mythological tradition, heroes were often cast out and abandoned, left to fend for themselves. In Greek mythology the orphaned were brought to Chiron so he could raise them, and in his home cave he taught them the heroic skills needed to become a warrior, a healer and a poet. This mythic motif underlies the familial experience. It is the disenfranchised aspects of self that teach the child to be heroic. Ironically, they become heroic when they are helping others to accept their own personal limitations. Why the individual stands out is not because they do not fit in, but because they are one of a kind. Being one of a kind, they are drawn to others who are mavericks. With Chiron in the 4th there may be a deep feeling of homelessness which permeated the family, encouraging the individual not only to find their ancestral roots but the foundation stones which support their sense of security in their life journey.

Uranus in the 4th House

Like the other outer planets, Uranus describes experiences beyond the personal, and when placed in the 4th house it suggests that underlying the family were larger patterns of separation or disconnection that might have influenced safety and security. Uranus in the 4th is an image of a schism in the family, and it is worth reflecting upon how this may have manifested in the family. Perhaps the family was highly individualized, with everyone doing their own thing, or maybe a sudden separation, relocation or unexpected change created a sense of insecurity that reverberated through childhood. What this placement suggests is that the individual may feel uprooted or dislocated in some way. Whether or not this was an actual experience from childhood, the person may feel that they belong somewhere else.

A cornerstone of this astrological placement is being unique. Being a one-off might sound exciting, but not to a child trying to fit into the family. Therefore the challenge is how to accept being peerless in a group and comfortable being the different one in the family. Hopefully, the family atmosphere supported this. If not, the child might have felt disconnected and cold. An irony of this placement is that it may be the parents or familial setting that was alternative or eccentric, and the child the 'normal' one.

When this archetype permeates familial life then it might suggest a family atmosphere that is disengaged, an emphasis on individuality and separateness rather than closeness. If so, the individual might also swing between needing freedom in relationship and needing to be close. Usually what happens is that wherever they find themselves, they want the opposite. In a relationship they want freedom and when independent they want closeness, a pattern born out of the unpredictable climatic conditions in the family atmosphere.

Being a renegade and rebelling against the status quo may be natural, but it is important not to sever personal needs for an ideal of individuality. Family life may have been quite alternative, with many changes of scene. Often with such a changing landscape the child never quite knew what to expect when they came home. Hence they may have developed a hypersensitivity to help them cope with the various options that have arisen. This might present as anxiety; however, it also develops the faculty of intuition and the ability to read future possibilities. In adult life, it is important to know that this skill is a deeper part of the inner life and not just a defence born from trying to feel safe in the face of an unpredictable future.

The task of balancing the need to be nurtured and safe with the urge to be independent and free is a major challenge of adult life. The individual comes to recognize the impulse to take flight when there is an emotional stagnation but also comes to know that when they are free as a bird they also long for a nest. These were the paradoxes experienced in the family. But it is the family that provides the fodder for the individual to understand their independent spirit. The two extremes of freedom and closeness are polarities experienced early in life; as an adult the task is in finding space and distance in a relationship so that they can feel safe enough to attach.

Outer planets located in the depth of the 4th house suggest that some of the imprints of ancestral or familial experiences may be addressed in the adult years as relationships and partnerships are being forged. In the life cycle of Uranus, the defining moments present between the ages 20 and 22, 38 and 42, and in the early sixties. At these life stages the road less travelled becomes more apparent.

Neptune in the 4th House

Neptune describes experiences beyond the personal, and when placed in the 4th house it suggests that underlying the family were larger patterns, feelings and impressions that might have influenced early feelings of safety and security. When Neptune is in the 4th house, enmeshment with the family or a lack of boundaries is an issue; therefore, individuality and personal expression are often absorbed by the familial need for sameness and unity. Instinctively, the emotional undertones and unexpressed feeling of the family are absorbed.

If childhood was idyllic then the individual may yearn to return, to regress back to the garden of infancy where everything was perfect, in contrast to the confusion of adult life. The ideal of family is important; however, this might be at odds with the reality of family life. The tendency to idealize a parent or a familial situation may be the antidote to the pain of reality. Often behind idealization is loss, and with Neptune in the 4th house a child may re-imagine their family situation so as to manage the pain of not having the closeness they long for. The loss of a parent is not necessarily literal, although this is a possibility because this placement often corresponds with the loss of emotional bonding or a missing attachment to a parent. Often there are genuine reasons for this, such as illness, work, disability or separation. At other times the individual perceives the parents to be more involved in caring for the world rather than for them.

The motif of sacrifice smoulders beneath the family atmosphere. Therefore the child may feel as if they must relinquish what is important to them for the greater good of the family. Making concessions might be part of the family legacy; holding on to individuality may be difficult. Instinctually, the child feels the expectations of others and responds by trying to fulfil their family's unexpressed desires. Personal identity and individuality are surrendered to the group. Therefore it is important to recognize that in later relationships the individual might be prone to giving up something of value in order to keep the peace in the family they have created. Deep inside they feel that this is not right, but are almost helpless to change it. But changing this dynamic of sacrifice is the challenge.

Strong spiritual ideals may have underpinned the family. The way that the family expressed its religious attitudes, compassion and spiritual ideals has a formative impact on the child's beliefs and search for security. The yearning for something more, expectations of a better life and the search for higher ideals might the basis of the family ethos, shaping how the person feels about spirituality. A deeply felt sense of religious principles may permeate the family home. It is important to recognize the susceptibility to the images and impressions that are valued by the family.

Alternatively, parental addiction, whether that is to a substance, an ideal or a belief, might have left the child feeling unsupported. Neptune located in the depth of the 4th house brings its creative and spiritual imprint into consciousness through the ancestral and familial lineage. As Neptune's first square in its cycle occurs at around the age 41, the early forties are often coloured with these issues. The childhood patterns that reappear at this time contribute to the individual feeling that they are able to disentangle themselves from some of the family mythology.

Pluto in the 4th House

Like Uranus and Neptune, Pluto describes experiences beyond the personal. When placed in the 4th house, it suggests that underlying the family were powerful emotional patterns that might have influenced the child's feelings of safety and security. Whether or not they knew where these feelings emanated from, they were aware that the atmosphere of the family home was intense and at times tinged with darkness. The ability to feel secure within the family circle was dependent on the way the darker feelings of loss, depression and futility were managed in the family. This early template of feeling secure with a darker or negative feeling life affects intimacy in later relationships. Trust, honesty and integrity are important issues that underline the ability to bond and feel safe.

Metaphorically speaking, the underworld is an aspect of the 4th house, as Pluto was the deity assigned to this place. And since this is the area of family experiences and the innermost private life, we might expect that hidden below the surface are strong influences from the past. On one hand this might suggest that mystery, something unknown, secrets and denials might infiltrate the family atmosphere. On the other hand this could reflect a very private or isolated upbringing or a home where honesty and integrity were championed. Whatever extreme, it is probable that the atmosphere of the family home was concentrated and intense. Whether this was due to parental grief, a loss not mourned, an unacknowledged depression, an unspoken betrayal, a parent's shame or the denial of a secret life may never be known. But what is known is that the child taps into deeper and unseen feelings that flow beneath the surface.

Emotional control, especially concerning the issues of sexuality, resources, money and freedom, may have dominated the familial atmosphere. Power could be wielded as a means of emotional control; therefore, the child may not have felt safe enough to express their true feelings or desires. Located in the depth of the 4th house, Pluto uncovers ancestral or familial secrets, denials and lies. While not consciously known, they may surface in adult life as the individual creates his or her family. Trust and control issues arise like ghosts from the past. In adult relationships the individual can make peace with these ghosts and gain confidence in the depth of their feelings.

Privacy is important as well as the psychological resources of honesty, integrity and intensity of feeling. Deep inside there is a drive to get to the bottom of things, and in this case it might be to seek out the truth not spoken in the family. Research into the family tree helps to understand the passionate emotional inheritance.

What is unfinished, incomplete and not acknowledged emotionally from the past is brought into present awareness through the soulful participation in family life.

– CHAPTER 6 –
THE AIR HOUSES
Individuality and Relationship

Whereas the 4th, 8th and 12th houses are familial regions that symbolize how we experience and integrate a sense of belonging, the 3rd, 7th and 11th houses show how we forge our individuality and a sense of being separate. Egalitarian relationship is conceived and constructed in the three Air houses, which are known as the houses of relationship. This type of relationship begins in the 3rd house, which since antiquity has been the domain of brothers and sisters. The template for our relationship patterns, including how we experience equality in relationship, is founded originally in our sibling experiences and then transferred to relationships outside the family of origin. The sibling system is the first social laboratory where experimentation with peer relationships can take place.[45]

The houses of relationship form a trinity which reveals the patterns of peer relationship in a familial and social context. In these spheres the theme of creating and sustaining equal relationships, as well as our urge for social intercourse, develops. The Air houses are where we locate the witnesses, partners, companions, rivals and soulmates of our lives. This is where we discover the spirit of the family and build our identity through relationship, companionship and kinship. These territories do not model the parent-child relationship, which inclines towards unequal and dependent relationship, but instead model equality and individuality, the level of relationship first encountered with the sibling.

The psychological landscape in each Air house is interconnected; therefore our sibling relationships will be recreated in our partnerships and friendships. Equally, the experiences with partners and friends facilitate change and healing with our siblings. Ultimately, the sibling relationship extends to all our equal interactions, from our playmates to our co-workers.

The Oedipus and Electra Complexes

Early psychoanalytic theory suggested that we unconsciously model our adult relationships on those of our parents, unwittingly marrying our fathers or mothers as mythical Oedipus did. Sigmund Freud, identifying with Sophocles' drama *Oedipus Rex,* developed the Oedipus complex, which suggests that a son trapped in a triangular relationship has an unconscious urge to remove his rival father in order to capture his mother for himself.[46]

Freud's cornerstone theory echoed throughout psychology for the next 100 years. High drama was part of the Greek mythological cycle and therefore a boon to playwrights of the 5th century BCE as well as the fathers of psychology. It seems that a young girl also wants to remove her rival, and the Electra complex was named for the heroine who, complicit with her brother, helped to plan her mother's murder in order to avenge the death of her beloved father. Carl Jung describes the Electra complex as a daughter who 'develops a special liking for the father, with a correspondingly jealous attitude towards the mother'.[47]

The triangle formed at the birth of the first child is a unique arrangement in the family, not again repeated, but part of the elder child's fate. The second child born may be more likely to forge a triangle with the older sibling in pursuit of the affection of one of the parents. In the early psychodynamic theories of Sigmund Freud and Carl Jung, the parental impressions upon the older child were analysed but the impact of the sibling, as the earliest template for peer relationship, was left unexplored.

Working exclusively with the parental effect, the psychoanalytic fathers were unconscious of the impact of the sibling archetype, themselves becoming caught in the undertow of sibling politics. After their initial and rewarding encounters, Freud and Jung were unable to resolve their sibling rivalry with each other in their adult lives, which made social cooperation and professional contact with each other impossible. Both had Mars in their 11th house of friendship; both were aware of the feelings of being displaced by a rival and were acutely sensitive to competition from equals. Rivalry and conflict marred, and eventually destroyed, their working relationship.

Not all the early psychoanalysts accepted the Freudian edict of the Oedipus complex. Alfred Adler thought that the Oedipus complex was born out of the environmental climate of an only or first child, such as Freud and Jung. Adler, the second son, was born under the umbra of an older brother and did not relate to the parental triangle that first-born Freud described.[48] Instead, Adler was acutely aware of his older brother from the beginning and conscious of the role his sibling played in shaping his psychology.

From these observations and experiences, Adler proposed the 'inferiority complex'. Unlike the elder's Oedipal urge to triumph, the younger was in the inferior role, being born second in the system. From this vantage point Adler could understand the ordinal position within the sibling system and developed his theory of birth order and character. But Freudian theory triumphed in the first half of the 20th century. For the milieu of that time it was psychologically sensible to be mindful of the perils and patterns of replicating the parental figures in adult relationships, leaving the sibling layer of relationship uncharted.

However, by the end of the 20th century, patterns in the social fabric had changed. It was more apparent that the quest for equal relationships (as opposed to more traditional and hierarchical relationships) was primary. The impact of sibling dynamics on our adult relationships became more acknowledged than ever before.

The Quest for the Soulmate
Once the helping professions began to view the individual in the context of the family and as a member of a larger group, psychology became more cognizant of the sibling. Psychological literature on the sibling started to appear from the 1970s. Brian Sutton-Smith and BG Rosenberg wrote *The Sibling* (1970), and Stephen Bank and Michael Kahn published a thorough examination of siblings in *The Sibling Bond* (1982). While there is a growing awareness amongst psychological circles, sibling research and examination has been mainly initiated from the areas of sociology or family therapy.

Family therapy's 'systemic' approach views the sibling as belonging to a sub-system within the greater organization of the family. Family therapy realized that the lost sibling of the early psychoanalytic movement was important in shaping and influencing the personality. In systemic or group work, each member of the organism becomes a vital part of the system's life force. This systemic approach is an important model for astrological counsellors as the horoscope contains images of the family, their members and ancestors. These images are encoded into the horoscope's symbols. An astrologer examining the horoscope has ample imagery to enhance the understanding of the ancestral legacy, the family of origin, the parental dynamics and the sibling system.

Astrological intelligence has always revealed the link between the sibling system and the socialization process through the houses of relationship, which are the spheres of the horoscope that describe the developmental quest for the soulmate. In essence this trinity of houses describes a composite image of the soulmate shaped from fragments of the inner images of the sibling, the partner and the friend. While these images exist in our horoscope before our experience of them in the outer world, they also shape the way we experience these relationships in our lives. These houses also reflect developmental experiences in relating and the instinctual patterns we bring to the sphere of relationship. This quest for a soul companion begins with the sibling in the 3rd house, which is the first house in the trinity. Therefore our experiences of the actual sibling relationship play a large role in shaping the dynamics of our social interactions, including our adult relationships.

Perhaps these houses describe a sense of individuality forged independently of our heredity and ancestral expectations. The 3rd house symbolizes our inherent disposition to becoming an individual within a larger system, the sibling system. Within this system we develop our individuality in relationship to the sibling, learning to be independent yet part of a community. The other relationship houses have a similar task. In the 7th we strive to sustain our individuality within marriage, while in the 11th we experience our independence within our social circles.

Airy qualities of detachment, non-attachment and witnessing are all important in the participation of equal relationship. In these houses we meet the witnesses of our life. The 3rd house sibling witnesses our childhood years, shares the same history, the same culture and is the touchstone of our early life experiences. The 7th house partner witnesses in us the process of maturation and discovery in the world beyond the family. The 11th house colleagues and friends witness our personal and professional, individual and collective experiences as we mature in the wider world. In these houses, the record of our personal developmental history is shared and witnessed by the significant others in our lives. Without a healthy development of separateness and equality, we may adopt the compensatory behaviour of detachment, aloofness and indifference.

The 3rd House: The Sibling and Early Peer Relationships
The 3rd house symbolizes our primary encounters with others who shared our environment, mainly the sibling/s, but also neighbourhood friends and primary schoolmates. While the 3rd house suggests that siblings are equal, a hierarchy is created by the ordinal positions of the siblings. The beginning of the quest for equality is born out of the paradox of this situation.

As siblings we each have our own unique orientation to the family which is defined by birth position and personal experience of the family atmosphere. In this system each sibling is an individual striving for equality. Age difference, physical size, intellectual capability, social adaptability and parental influence may create inequality amongst the siblings; however, 'in the majority of cases there is usually equivalence in siblings' feelings of acceptance for one another which allows them to relate as equals'.[49] For this reason the 3rd house is critical, as it suggests how we may first experience peer relationship and the impact it will have upon subsequent relationships. We first test the response from the world through the reaction of our siblings, using them as a mirror to how we are received. As Salvador Minuchin says:

> In the sibling world, children learn to negotiate, cooperate and compete. They learn how to make friends and allies, how to save face while submitting, and how to achieve recognition of their skills.[50]

The 3rd house is the experimental ground for relating; habitual behaviour in relating may find its origins here. While the parental system is located in the 4th house, the sibling system is well described by the 3rd house and is the 'first social laboratory' of our horoscope, indicating our primary encounters with those who shared our early environment. Sibling/s, plus the extended family of cousins, neighbourhood friends and primary schoolmates, populate our 3rd house.

The 3rd house is the first social circle we encounter in life. Expectations we have of relationships, patterns we repeat with partners or even our choice of mate may be more influenced by the sibling/s, and the 3rd house, than we realize. Our seminal experiences and predisposition to being in a unit are located in the 3rd house and influence our choice of partner and friends. The astrological 3rd house configurations may clearly describe the sibling or 'at least those qualities we project onto him or her'.[51]

Before our birth, any planets in the 3rd house had reached the IC, the lowest and darkest point on the ecliptic, and were beginning to rise. At the 3rd house, the planets had ceased their descent, turned and started their ascent when they became fixed into a birth horoscope. The ascent towards the horizon symbolizes the 3rd house planets' urge for consciousness and individuality. This rising momentum is imprinted upon 3rd house planets.

Planets in the 3rd carry this experience of rising consciousness. When planets progress or transit, they do this from the 3rd house into the 4th house sphere of family and then continue beyond into the 'interpersonal houses'. Included in this category are the 5th to 8th houses, the second quaternary of houses where self-development through interaction and relationship beyond the family of origin occurs.[52]

From an astrological perspective, social development, communication and community begin in the 3rd house. What follows are images of 3rd house planets. These are important archetypal allies in forging relationships, equality and interdependence.

Our First Partners
- Primal patterns of equality which inform our relationships with partners, friends and colleagues
- The sibling; companion, friend, witness, rival and enemy
- Kinship and our experience of feeling part of a group or equal in the system
- The social laboratory where we test out our relationship skills
- Projections onto the sibling; how have we idealized or demonized the sibling? What qualities in ourselves might we displace onto our siblings?
- Earliest patterns of sharing, learning and communicating

- Birth order and our experience of where we place ourselves in a system
- Early patterns of communicating with others

The 7th House: Patterns of Relationship and the Early Imprint of the Parental Marriage

The next house in the trinity of houses of relationship is the 7th. Unlike the 3rd, it is above the horizon of the horoscope and therefore suggests more visibility or objectivity. Perhaps it symbolizes what we already know: that the arena of sibling relationships below the horizon offered no conscious choice of the 'other', it is a non-consenting realm. But on the horizon of the 7th, our partners are consenting, at least consciously. Siblings are contained by the larger system of the family, whereas 7th house partners come from beyond the familial system. Into the 7th we carry the *a priori* pattern of the sibling along with our experiences of relating in the sibling system.

The 7th house is the sphere of equality on an adult level where we encounter others who feel familiar and who complement what we sense is missing in ourselves. Inspired by Libra, this territory is the arena where we encounter the equal other and the soulmate from beyond the family system. Embedded in Libra are images of this other, who reflects the parts of ourselves that often feel incomplete or missing. The 7th house process embraces the experience of being with an equal other in a committed and intimate way. There is mutuality and reciprocity. Whether 7th house partners are marriage or life partners, business partners or close friends, they engage with us on an equal level of exchange. The word 'partner' contains *part*, the sense of being separate – apart, yet also able to join.

Traditionally, this was known as the house of open enemies; the opponent represented by the 7th house was an adversary and rival. Sibling rivalries may be re-enacted again with our adult partners. In a psychological context, the 7th house 'open enemy' may be our own shadow material rather than a literal individual. However, the unconscious is marvellously astute at choosing individuals who embody our own shadowy qualities. Therefore, unresolved sibling issues and repressed feelings from the family of origin may be transferred onto our adult partners.

The 7th house experience is directly influenced by the earlier effect and residue of our sibling relationships and can illuminate earlier relational patterns shaped through our experiences in the sibling system. In adult relationships, sibling dynamics are ever present and experienced through rivalry, competition, companionship, sharing, etc. The 'open enemy' may be our unresolved rivalries, differing values, leftover anger or unfinished challenges with our siblings that rearrange themselves with our partners. Unconsciously, we may have entered a new relationship in reaction to this unresolved material with a sibling. Our 7th house may be more influenced by our sibling relationship than we ever imagined, and we often marry a 'sibling' substitute or a close approximation.

Psychological astrology stresses the propensity to project the 7th house planetary qualities onto partners. All the while we remain unconscious of the 7th house energies, we continue to proclaim them as belonging to someone else, generally the partner. Seventh house planets are usually first recognized through a partner; hence the opus of the 7th house is the attempt to be more conscious of our inherent nature that is projected onto our partners. Projection is an unconscious defence mechanism; therefore the task of becoming aware of our projections demands self-reflection. Becoming conscious of these projections provides a greater facility to be authentic in relationship.

Projection is the psychological mechanism that helps illuminate unconscious aspects of the self through relating. The 7th house planets are the archetypal patterns that are catalysed as we enter into relationship. In essence they are part of the other side of ourselves; this is why they are so easily mobilized through the agency of the other. Once again, as with the 3rd house, we are in territory that stirs the images of the missing other and the shadow. This time, however, we are outside the familial alembic and the family taboos no longer apply. Emotional involvement with the partner also begins to shift the loyalties away from the family of origin into another system.

The 7th house is an area of mutuality which suggests we become the carriers of our partner's projections, being drawn into a mutual collusion. The 5th house, the first in the developmental process of relating, is where unrequited love or one-way projections are more likely to be found. However, in the 7th house the core of the projective material is generally a two-way street.

Projection: From Idealization to Denigration to Integration
Generally, there are three stages in the process of 7th house projection. First is the numinous stage: the bright side of the archetype is embodied in the individual to whom we are attracted. The qualities shine and we are in awe. Generally, the planetary energy is exaggerated or idealized, being drawn to the Divine aspects of its nature. For instance, we may first meet the 7th house Mercury as the brilliant and witty genius; Saturn as the success story; or Pluto as the magnetic and engaging powerhouse.

Next follows the waning stage: the very qualities that mesmerized us are now annoying and uncomfortable. The partner now is 'a know-all'. The shadow of the archetype begins to manifest. Mercury has become superficial and non-committal; Saturn is patronizing and cold; while Pluto is now obsessive and controlling. The 7th house planets reveal both sides of the archetype through the same partner. At this stage, consciousness of the presenting shadow material is possible. However, the possibility of regression is also available by choosing another partner with whom we can re-experience the magical first stage.

The last stage holds the tension between the opposite sides of the archetype which we come to recognize as aspects of ourselves. The integrative process begins when we become aware that these qualities which the partner is living out for us are also our own. The 7th house, like the 3rd, is a territory where consciousness occurs because of another; therefore, it is quite common for the 7th house partner to rekindle the relationship to the first partner, the sibling. Planets in these sectors can be blatant and transparent, as consciousness is not revealed as subtly as the unconscious.

The sign on the cusp of the 7th house is an important quality to us and is very often prominent in our partner's horoscope. The planets in the 7th house are representative of archetypal patterns constellated in the exchange between partners. As we have seen, they are generally first embodied in the partner before they can be successfully integrated consciously into our lives. There is an analogy between the arrival of the partner and the birth of a sibling. The 7th house experience is directly influenced by the earlier effect and aftermath of our sibling relationships. Powerfully conflicted feelings of love and rivalry, fascination and anger, are constellated with the 7th house other. The partner awakens an earlier stratum of psyche where unresolved or incomplete issues with the sibling may be transferred into our current relationship.

The 7th house is where the Sun is preparing to set. It is twilight, when the light elongates the shadows and we prepare to meet the dark. Partners can become the targets for unresolved hostilities that siblings cannot confront or resolve with each other. The partner is then 'triangulated' in the sibling relationship. Equally, it may be a partner's sibling who enters the triangle. We may be able to express the intimacy with a sibling-in-law that we find difficult with our own sibling. A family therapist confirms this when writing of the importance of sibling issues in new marriages:

> Siblings may also displace their problems in dealing with each other on the intrusion of a new spouse. Predictable triangles are especially likely between a husband and his wife's brothers or between the wife and the husband's sisters.[53]

Hera and Zeus – the 'Sibling Marriage'

Walter Toman's premise in his book *Family Constellation* was that adult partnerships replicating the sibling infrastructure were more complementary and therefore more successful.[54] For instance, a younger sister with an older brother might be more compatible with a partner who was the older brother of a sister. The younger sister replicates her position in her adult relationship by relating to a partner who has a younger sister. The hypothesis of Toman's theories confirmed that the sibling experience directly affected adult relationships.

In dealing with issues between couples, I find it enormously valuable and revealing to ask about their sibling constellations: their position in the sibling system, sibship size and gender, age spacing, etc.[55] These details can often open up the imagery of both the 3rd and 7th houses and reveal issues from the sibling system that are infiltrating the current relationship. Third house planetary energies that are still projected onto the sibling or unexpressed in us will find a new venue in the present relationship.

The brother-sister marriage is a mythic pattern, perhaps best seen in the relationship of Hera and her brother, Zeus. In fact their parents, Chronus and Rhea, were also a brother-sister pair. While the later myths of Zeus and Hera focused on their power struggles and dysfunctional marriage, the earlier stories told us of their secret wedding and sacred union. This sacred union was their sibling marriage, the level which contains the equality and companionship in all relationships. The 7th house experience rests on the 3rd house, and the relationships of the 7th house include the archetypal layer of the 'sibling marriage'. Opposite sex siblings may have been temporary carriers of sexuality. Transferring this powerful connection to another partner will undoubtedly awaken intense feelings between the sibling and the partner.

We enter a mystery in the 7th house where we are drawn to what appears as opposite and different, yet is only a partial reflection of what is still not conscious in us. What we sense is kin, congeniality and familiarity. Since the individual is not from the system we have known, they present as being different. The partner of the 7th house stimulates us to reunite with the missing parts of ourselves.

Our Adult Partners
- Marriage and the relationships that us bring into our family system
- The other, the partner
- Shadow qualities, the open enemy, the rival and competitor
- Mirror image of the projected self
- Projected qualities onto another
- The companion, the soulmate, the other half
- One-to-one, equality

The 11th House: The Social Sphere of the Family
The 11th house is our encounter with equals in the community outside the familial setting. These include the 'social others' – colleagues, associates, acquaintances, friends and professional equals. This is the house of groups, communes, sects, cults, fraternities and organizations, reminiscent of our first experience of a collective, the family. While the 11th house depicts the group, not bound by blood or kinship ties, nevertheless our experiences of family will still be stirred. As a member of the group our relationship to the other group members will magnetize unconscious memories of our earliest peers, our brothers and sisters, our childhood partners. In the

11th house we are still prone to recreating the unresolved familial issues in our chosen groups and associations.

Like the 7th house, the 11th is above the horizon, but now in the eastern hemisphere where the focus is on the individual. As individuals we are contained by the larger system of society, subject to its laws, influenced by its ethos and bound by its taboos. Our 11th house symbolizes the larger community, the groups, social structures and the circle of friends and associates that populate society, where we once again become part of a system. Our sibling system is the microcosm of this larger social sphere; therefore our experiences in the sibling system directly impact our ability to feel comfortable in other social systems.

Equality and Individuality in the Social System
Underpinning the 11th house domain is the sign of Aquarius, the humanitarian. In the 11th we are in contact with the wider human family through our participation in society. Teamwork, group effort, social improvement and human concern are all part of the vision of Aquarius and all located in the 11th house environment. No longer are we only part of the family system but now we enter a wider system created by our involvement in society. This social system recreates the politics, issues and concerns of the earlier sibling experience.

The 11th house can also be the territory where we redeem our conflicted sibling relationships. A loving friend, an encouraging colleague or supportive groups are healing agents for earlier wounds inflicted in the sibling system. We may also be able to accomplish in the larger world what we could never do in the sibling world. While we are influenced by our sibling system we are not bound to it, and the 11th house is the arena where we can amend this. Now we are able to choose our brothers and sisters. They come from the same spiritual tribe and generally look forward in the same direction as we do, carrying the same hopes and wishes for the future. They are partners, equals and kin in our worldly family. This is brotherhood and sisterhood and it is the 11th house where we find our social siblings.

Roles and positions have already been forged in the sibling system, and we instinctively take these into our relationships in the broader community. Our impact on society and society's impact upon us is related to our primary experiences in the sibling world. The last house of relationship is where we meet our extra-familial peers. Minuchin says:

> When children contact the world of extra-familial peers, they try to operate along the lines of the sibling world. When they learn alternative ways of relating, they bring back the new experiential knowledge into the sibling world.[56]

Our 11th house relationships feel familiar because they too are kin: allies who are kindred spirits. The spirit that is the bonding agent is the shared dreams, ideals and visions of our friends and colleagues. In a way, the 11th house is a return home to the missing other through a sense of congeniality and enjoyment of the shared spirit of life. Congeniality literally means 'with the generations', an apt description of the 11th house process of shared community. In the 11th we can find the sense of belonging to a larger family, being individuals in a larger collective. This is an important aspect of the 11th house as we learn here to be separate from the collective, which inherently prepares us for rescuing the collective soul of the 12th house.

However, the group of friends, the group of colleagues and the organizations we join reawaken the incomplete sibling experiences. Rivalry is experienced once again. Our group experiences are often regressive, reminding us of the infantile behaviour with our siblings, fighting for the attention of the parent who is now embodied as the leader of the group. If we have not yet learned to feel an equal, then we will react to perceived acts of favouritism bestowed on the rival colleague or group member. In this respect, therapy groups are hotbeds for sibling transference. Adults are vulnerable to playing out incomplete sibling hostilities and rivalries in their professional associations and organizations, as well as their therapy groups. Festering sibling rivalries may pollute the equilibrium of the organization. Sibling behaviour, such as acting out within the group, bullying, gossiping or conspiring with the other group members, all stem from the feeling of inequality. Quite often members of groups can polarize into their sibling positions of first, middle, last or only. Birth position may be replicated quite literally in our professional world. This certainly is apparent in the political world and organizations in general.

The 11th house social development is where we play out the quest for equality on the world stage. Alfred Adler suggested that equality started in the earliest social system with the siblings:

> Unless children feel equal, mankind will never be well grounded in social feeling. Unless girls and boys feel equal to one another, relationships between the two sexes will continue to pose the greatest problems.[57]

No longer is equality just having what others have but being valued as an equal individual within the group. In an adult context, an equal share is held by each group member even if one or more members receive more attention and time. Hopefully, as adults, we have introjected enough autonomy to be able to feel concern and equality in our adult relationships.

Our Social Partners
- Relationships in the wider community
- Participation in the community
- Friends and colleagues, acquaintances and compatriots
- The social sphere; attitudes towards socialization and belonging in a group
- Group experiences
- Kindred spirits, special friends, exemplary peers
- Mending the sibling bond; healing the sibling relationship through our adult friendships
- The spiritual family

The Family Houses – Air and Water in Summary
Each of the three Air houses precedes a Water house, as if the Water houses have been assigned the task of supporting or holding the relationship patterns that have been developed in the Air houses. In essence, each of the Water houses becomes a container for the relationships that are encountered in the houses of relationship: the family system of the 4th house contains the sibling relationship; the tribal system of the 8th encloses the partners; the communal and ancestral systems of the 12th house envelop our friends and colleagues.

- The 3rd house – *the sibling system*
- The 4th house – *the family system; the family of origin*
- The 7th house – *the parental marriage*
- The 8th house – *the familial legacy and intimacy in the parental system*
- The 11th house – *the social system; friends of the family*
- The 12th house – *the ancestral system*

– CHAPTER 7 –
PLANETS IN THE 3RD HOUSE
Delineating the Formative House of Connection

The planets represent the cast of characters possible within the family system as well as our own archetypal images of 'inner family'. For examinations of the planets in the 7th and 11th houses, refer to Chapter 11, Planets, Aspects and Houses: Delineating the Family. To honour its prominence as the fundamental house of relationship, we extend our journey into the 3rd house through an in-depth contemplation of each planet within the house.

The Moon in the 3rd House

The Moon in the 3rd house locates the nurturing and mothering instinct in the sphere of the sibling, suggesting that a sibling may have been in a care-taking role or that we ourselves were placed in this role. The early sibling relationships would have a direct impact on our sense of safety and security, and be important in forging a sense of emotional stability. Because of this emotional impact, there could be a strong attachment to the sibling if the sibling was the good mother or, conversely, a sense of alienation if the sibling constellated the dark mother. Given the Moon's propensity for symbiosis, separation from the sibling could have been difficult. Early separations such as going to school, being taken care of by another, etc., may have been traumatic if we were not adequately prepared.

The Moon in the 3rd carries an image of an older sister, one who may have shared in our upbringing, and one to whom we may still have a strong attachment. Whether there was a literal elder sister or not, we may have sought this sister-mother figure in our environment or, alternatively, made our mother our sister. Perhaps mother preferred the role of a sister rather than the responsibility of being mother. An early pattern of confusion between sister or equality and mother or dependence may continue into our adult relationships. A young boy with the Moon in the 3rd *and* a sister may feel the need for, or continue to expect, 'women' to take care of him. While he is very comfortable with sisters and the world of women, he may be habitually drawn to women who will nurture and take care of him. An important aspect which needs to be learned in the sibling system is not only how to communicate one's needs but how to fulfil them independently. Without this initiation in the sibling system, we will still try to make our adult relationships symbiotic and regressive.

The Moon in the 3rd could point to the sibling who was closest to mother, mother-identified, and given the role of taking care of mother. Therefore this could be the sibling most at risk during the leaving home stage, finding great difficulty in separating. The sibling story is woven around the image of mother and sister and includes the inheritance from mother and her siblings.

The Sun in the 3rd House

The Sun in the 3rd house suggests identification with the sibling/s, highlighting the role of the first or favoured one. This places the archetype of the personal father in the domain of the sibling, suggesting a composite father-brother figure. If the father was weakened, unavailable or missing, a brother or solar daughter may have replaced him as the authority or fostering figure. Father may be seen as a close confidant or ally, combining his role as a mentor/parent with that of a friend/equal.

Favouritism may have been an issue in the sibling system and father's favourite may have been seen to be acknowledged and encouraged more than the others. The Sun may have cast its shadow over the sibling system, splitting the system into those who were favoured by father and those who were not. A girl who was father's favourite may feel in a precarious position, caught between her brother and father. In adult life this may rearrange itself as feeling caught between her partner and son. This position suggests the individual may be the sibling who was most father-identified or the one most easily triangulated with father against the others, including mother. We may have a very different view of father from the rest of our sibs and are the one most sensitive to colluding with him. This suggests we may also be the one who 'looks just like father', but on a more subtle level may be the one who has inherited more paternal ancestral complexes or treasures.

If the solar energy is being projected, a sibling may appear to be more creative, dynamic, confident and popular than we are. Initially, the tendency may be to adore the sibling; however, as this projection wanes these qualities in ourselves start to become evident. The sibling acts as a hook for our emerging identity. With the Sun here, it may be the sibling we identified as either a rival or a hero. Ultimately, we strongly identify with others, but may pass through stages of feeling unacknowledged or unappreciated before we are able to claim an equal and authoritative position in our relationships.

Mercury in the 3rd House

Mercury is the natural ruler of the 3rd house and has an affinity with this territory and the sibling relationship. It is an image of the younger or middle sibling who feels the need to catch up with older sibs as well as being the interpreter for the familial dynamics. Mercury is less attached to either parent than the Sun or Moon in the 3rd. Its role is the messenger, the go-between, and in the 3rd it takes the role as mediator and guide in the sibling system. Mercury was not the only messenger god; he often shared this capacity with the goddess Iris, but she delivered the message intact whereas Mercury often rearranged it to suit his purposes. The sibling may have played the role of messenger and psychopomp, being disconnected enough from the family dynamics to be able to reveal what was going on. In the myth of Mercury and Apollo, Mercury's envy of his elder brother prompted him to steal resources from him. These actions helped to win recognition from their father, Jupiter, the prevailing authority. In the 3rd house, Mercury's task is to translate the envy or jealousy of sibling rivalry into a productive and satisfying solution.

With Mercury here, communication and interchange of ideas with the sibling was an important foundation for the ability to share ideas and converse as equals. A difficult placement of Mercury could point to a feeling of intellectual inferiority with the sib which still affects adult confidence. Issues of learning, education, communication and conversation are derivative of the sibling experience. Mercury has an affinity with the sibling system which promotes the ability to be able to translate and decode both overt and covert messages between siblings, a skill taken into the adult world.

Venus in the 3rd House

Venus in the 3rd house suggests an encounter with the sister archetype. For a man, the image of sister becomes a potent feminine or anima symbol for him. If he has a literal sister, she will have played an important transitional role in carrying this internal soul image for him. The sister may have helped to shape his image of a partner more than he might like to admit, and he may unconsciously find her image again in his adult relationships. Without a sister, the man would still seek this image of sister in his adult relationships.

A woman with Venus in the 3rd may be unwittingly drawn into competition with her sisters. In Homeric tradition, Aphrodite (Venus) was half-sister and rival to Persephone, Athena and Artemis. Zeus decreed that Aphrodite had to share her lover, Adonis, with Persephone. Aphrodite charmed Paris so that he would choose her rather than Athena in the competition for the fairest goddess. And Aphrodite clashed with Artemis over the young boy, Hippolytus. The mythic themes of sisterhood may be drawn up to consciousness through a clash of values or a shared love object. It is also through this relationship that social skills are developed. The sister could be an influence on our values, what we find attractive and how comfortable we feel in social circles.

With Venus in the 3rd we look towards our sibs of either sex for experimentation with the process of relating and sexuality. The sibling system may be where we first recognized that the feelings of loving and valuing another could be different from the way we felt towards our parents or other adults. We could project our own sense of worth or value onto our sibs, seeing them as more attractive or social, a sibling providing a mirror for our developing sense of creativity and sexuality. It is through our earlier relationships with siblings or friends that we developed our tastes, what we find attractive and the social skills that influence us today. In later years, those with Venus in the 3rd may yearn for a warm and supportive relationship with their siblings.

Mars in the 3rd House

Mars has an affinity with the image of the elder brother, the warrior, the competitor, and in the 3rd these images may be brought into consciousness through the sibling.

Clients and students with Mars in the 3rd have often told me stories of their experiences of aggression and even brutality from the sibling – being pushed downstairs, tied up and abandoned, and even of being rushed to hospital after an older brother stabbed his younger sister with a kitchen knife. Because these situations occur when both sibs are young, and are not adequately supervised, the family often makes a farce of the situation, thereby deflecting the rivalry. Students, describing their experiences in class, often laugh along with their classmates when regaling them with a sibling story that is volatile and violent. With sibs we learn to defend and stand our ground, and with Mars in the 3rd our aggressive and survival instincts are brought to consciousness, generally by a sib's taunting and goading. In many cases, sibling violence is not even reported to the parent and the secret brutality leads to alienation from the sibling. With Mars here we may first experience the aggressive instincts with a sibling. Some sibling fighting may be over territorial rights to the parent.

Mars also constellates the sexual instincts, and these too may be tested out with the sibling in various ways, ranging from sexual play to a consummation of the relationship. Siblings may want to test their sexual or physical virility with each other. The sibling system may be where we first experienced aggression, competitive feelings and anger. How these feelings were consciously managed will impact on our adult relationships, for unresolved sexual or hostile feelings towards the sib will certainly be constellated in our adult relationships. For a woman, this placement of Mars suggests that a brother image is part of her internal masculine realm and a literal brother would be an appropriate hook for the externalization of this animus. Mars often seeks role models and strives to emulate them, and in the 3rd we may have chosen a sibling as one of our role models.

With Mars here, the sibling system is an important training ground for taming the aggressive and sexual instincts. Mars is the first planet outside the orbit of the Earth, a planet that is outside the Earth's system. When Mars is in the 3rd house, we learn in the laboratory of childhood how to become independent and retain our individuality within a system. In adult life someone with Mars in the 3rd finds equality in relationships by authentically asserting their individuality and independence.

Jupiter in the 3rd House

Jupiter searches for a wider view of the horizon by questing beyond the familial experiences with siblings to prepare us for different beliefs, ways of life and cross-cultural awareness. Learning from our siblings and being open to their guidance and life experiences may be a valuable part of our education and socialization. In adult years, siblings and their families may continue to expose us to new ideas and adventures. Quite literally, I have often seen this placement representing many siblings; however, I suggest the statement of Jupiter in the 3rd talks more of the wide panoramic exposure that the sibling may provide. The sibling system could be cross-cultural in that it may have included step- or half-siblings, or we may have met regularly with cousins or others who introduced us to different ideas and beliefs. We may have had the opportunity to travel and explore new places with our sibs, giving us an early appreciation of other ways of daily life, beliefs and ideologies.

Jupiter is a planet of socialization, and therefore our siblings' social progress, their choice of studies, extra-curricular activities, and so on, were important to us. They may have become a benchmark against which we judged our own progress. A sibling may also have been our guide to a wider social world, introducing us to new horizons of belief and culture. However, siblings could also be experienced as rigid and unwavering from their beliefs and with whom we are at odds. One of the sibs may play the role of Zeus in the sibling system, claiming dominion over the others and constellating a larger-than-life figure. The early experience with our sibling-peers gives awareness of the need to feel spiritually compatible with our adult partners and friends. In later years we may find that although we may be physically, spiritually or morally distant from our siblings, the urge to reconnect is a catalyst for the examination of our own beliefs.

Saturn in the 3rd House

When Saturn is in the 3rd house, the themes of authority, duty and responsibility may have been constellated for the first time with the sibling/s. I have witnessed Saturn in the 3rd consistently with only and eldest children who feel they have been placed in positions of control and responsibility too early. There were many reasons for this; a common theme, however, was the sibling who filled a void left by an irresponsible parent. Often this placement also suggests wide age gaps between the sibs, so that they grow up virtually as only children, or for some other reason are not part of the sibling system. For an only child, this placement suggests that the world of equals may be overshadowed by the world of adults. For eldest children, it suggests they were responsible for their younger siblings, setting the example of upholding parental law, often while their younger sibs broke the rules. There could be difficulty in sharing or delegating as a result of sibling experiences. Issues around the division of labour may have caused resentment, as the individual may have felt they had a greater share of the chores than the others. Whatever the birth order, Saturn confers a sense of the law-maker upon the individual who may feel obliged to discipline or direct his siblings. There could also be a tussle for the top position in the sibling system, with the sense that the parent's approval was gained at the expense of feeling connected to the other siblings.

Another manifestation of this position could be the feeling of rejection by our sibs, or feeling completely alone and separate from them. We may feel the need to become self-reliant and not have to depend upon our siblings for support, encouragement or comradeship. It may become imperative to detach, withdraw or take care of ourselves on our own, contributing to an isolationist tendency. This pattern could be the foundation of feeling self-reliant in our adult relationships, not easily able to depend upon others.

In adult years, Saturn in the 3rd house could also be demanding, as we again feel it is our responsibility to bring the siblings together. Issues around family gatherings, rituals or special occasions polarize the siblings again into their childhood roles. One of the greatest tests concerns taking responsibility and making decisions about an elderly parent. With Saturn here, we learn to be responsible, but not at the expense of our own individuality. It is in the sibling system that we first learn how to delegate, discern and let go of control in appropriate ways. Learning to differentiate who is responsible and set the appropriate boundaries becomes an important lesson for Saturn in the 3rd.

Chiron in the 3rd House

Although Chiron is not classified as a planet, its archetypal imagery is too important to leave out of our planetary pantheon. Chiron, like the three older Olympian brothers Hades, Poseidon and Zeus, was a son of Chronus and therefore was their half-brother and part of the Olympian family. Chiron was not awarded the same status as his half-siblings, which is an interesting image for Chiron in the 3rd house. Here is the sibling who is exiled from the system or not granted the same status. As a sibling image, Chiron represents the adopted sibling, the step-sibling and the sibling who is not wholly part of the system.

When Chiron is in the 3rd house, it points to a potential wounding that has occurred through our siblings, or the image that the sibling himself is wounded, handicapped or exiled. Chiron is the wound that is inflicted unintentionally; with Chiron in the 3rd, this wound may have been inflicted by our sibling/s. This generally is not physical, although it may be; it is usually experienced through name-calling or other forms of verbal abuse or wounding. The teleological level of the 3rd house, I feel, has to do with the power of the *word*. With Chiron in the 3rd, the poisonous arrows that are the wounding agent could be the sibling's verbal abuse. A child being branded stupid, ugly or illegitimate by his siblings receives a lifelong wound. Chiron in the 3rd is also highly sensitive to the feeling effect that flows beneath what is said; so the wound can also be inflicted by the dishonesty and trickery of the sibling.

The wound could also be that we feel exiled from our siblings, completely separate and not a part of the same system to which they belong. I have often witnessed that someone with this placement experiences the death of a sibling in the family, and the individual with Chiron in the 3rd is the one most at risk of carrying the unresolved grief of this loss. Chiron in the 3rd seems to be a dominant placement for those who have a handicapped sib. Ambivalence accompanies this aspect: there is a love of the sibling, but also a feeling that they themselves missed out owing to the enormous attention focused on the handicapped sibling. The wound is opened through the relationship with the handicapped sibling.

Early patterns from the sibling system may be re-enacted later in adult relationships by drawing the wounded other into our orbit, constellating the primal polarity of wounding and healing again in relationships. Unexpectedly, our partners and friends may once again draw the sibling wound to the surface.

Uranus, Neptune and Pluto
The outer planets describe experiences beyond the personal, and when placed in the 3rd house suggest that the sibling may have magnetized images, feelings and experiences beyond our capacity to understand or integrate them. These outer planets in the personal house of the

sibling may stir deeper, mythic and archetypal experiences which we can only begin to address in our adult years. With any of these planets in the 3rd we are drawn into a larger and more collective story with our siblings. Since these energies seem to be larger than we are, we may tend more to project them onto the sibling. Here we must acknowledge that the sibling-other has been the personal spokesperson for an impersonal archetype.

Uranus in the 3rd House

Uranus in the 3rd house may suggest a sense of abandonment, separation or distance from the sibling. This archetype often suggests separation and splitting and in the 3rd this may have applied to the sibling system. Uranus is disengaged and this may have characterized the nature of the sibling system. The sibs may have been highly differentiated, so much so that they may have nothing in common. They may have been separated for a variety of familial reasons including divorce, relocation, education or even the unexpected death of another sibling. Uranus's nature is sudden and unexpected, so this could characterize our relationship with a sibling, never knowing what to expect in the relationship. One day we may be welcomed into their circle of friends and the next firmly rejected. This image suggests that the sibling is highly individualized and, in the best-case scenario, we feel like an individual within a system and that our sibling is also our friend. More often there may be a feeling of disconnection or alienation from the other. Uranus's sense of separation can be so severe that once the bond is severed it cannot be reclaimed. Therefore, with Uranus in the 3rd we could have experienced a sense of irreconcilable differences which led to an irrevocable separation from the sibling; or our feelings towards the relationship are frozen, remaining in contact yet being virtually unreachable. It may be with a sibling that we first experience Uranus's ability to sever, detach, stand apart and split off from feelings.

Within the sibling system we may have been the one to rebel or take a stance contrary to that of the others. We may have found our individuality by rebelling against the others. This early pattern of independence and individuality in relationship to our sibs will influence our attitudes towards other relationships, continuing to seek out the different, the unusual and the unique in our partners and friends.

Neptune in the 3rd House

When placed in the 3rd house, Neptune's urge to sacrifice may be a pattern lived out with our brothers or sisters. We may be the one to take the blame for actions perpetrated by our siblings or allow them to set us up, even to use us. Neptune's urge to merge is so strong that we may discard our sense of self in order to experience this sublime union. We may feel that we are not giving up that much to the sibling when the self is fragile anyway. However, a pattern may be created that continues into our adult relationships. Ultimately, this sacrifice comes at a high price as it weakens our sense of independence. Quite literally, we may have had to sacrifice our education or our dreams for another sibling.

There may be a lack of boundaries between ourselves and our sibs, so we may be highly sensitive to their psychic life. One of the most difficult Neptunian patterns in family life is to know intuitively what is going on but for this to be continually denied by the other members. We then begin to mistrust our intuition and often feel that we are going mad. In this scenario, Neptune in the 3rd becomes the classic 'identified patient' in the sibling system, manifesting the anxieties and the disease that is repressed by the other members of the system. In the 3rd, the sibling could play the role of the liar, the deceptive one, even the mad one. Enmeshment with siblings is high and we are often unable to distinguish what the truth is. We may get caught up in the web of the sibling's deceit or addictions. Neptune in the 3rd is a potent image of a primitive yearning to surrender oneself to the other, disappearing as a result of fusing oneself with that person.

Neptune in the 3rd often describes a missing sibling, one who has disappeared or become estranged, leaving a void in our lives that we try to replace with friends. Equally, the missing sibling may be idealized so that the feelings of loss are numbed and defended by the idealization. Since the 3rd house is the first of the houses of relationship, it is quite likely that the image of the missing sibling surfaces in our later relationships where we once again address the issues of sacrifice and invisibility in relation to our partners and friends. We are vulnerable to recreating a fused relationship and losing ourselves in it.

Pluto in the 3rd House

When Pluto is in the 3rd house the underworld domain may be brought into consciousness through an experience in the sibling system. Often this may be through the experience of grief over the death of a sibling, a profound sense of loss that may continue to permeate life. The loss of the sibling may not be a conscious memory or literal event, yet this image may still be part of our psychic terrain. While there may be no awareness of a death in the family, we sense the shadow of loss in our sibling system. This may happen when a child is a replacement child, or when the family atmosphere is clouded by the unresolved grief of the parents.

The underworld could also be constellated through the experience of feeling dominated and controlled by the sibling. The sibling may have been manipulative, wielding power, confronting us with feelings of powerlessness and loss of control. Pluto's placement in the horoscope could locate one of the entrances to our own underworld. Here in the 3rd house, it is through our early relationship with our siblings that we are exposed to the underside of life, confronted with dark and dangerous feelings.

Within the sibling system we may have been coerced into keeping a secret or may be privy to a secret we still feel obliged to keep. If the secret has gathered intense feelings of shame and guilt, it becomes a complex that keeps the participants in the secret bound together in an unholy alliance. Over time the sense of feeling powerful is diminished as the secret is a constant reminder of being in the grip of something more powerful than oneself.

Pluto represents an innate aloneness, which we come to understand later in life as part of the human condition. As children this is difficult, since it feels threatening to our survival and our sense of well-being. With Pluto in the 3rd, we may have felt alone in the sibling system, which also felt painful and terrifying. Pluto constellates both extremes of the feeling spectrum and in the 3rd we may have experienced either a deep sense of betrayal with a sibling or a deep sense of union and trust. It is in the sibling system where we may need to look first to understand our feelings of mistrust, suspicion and control, and we may need to return here to heal a primal sense of betrayal before we feel able to trust in an adult context.

– CHAPTER 8 –
ANGLES AND CUSPS
Doorways, Borders and Keys

Astrological practice gives strong focus to the four angles of the horoscope: the Ascendant, Descendant, Imum Coeli and the Midheaven. These 'four corners' are astrology's customary compass points of the horoscope and pointers in life.

Each angle indicates a particular direction. The Ascendant (ASC) is the eastern point that rises over the horizon, symbolizing an entrée, an emergence, a dawning. When the Sun is at this point dawn is breaking, which is a consistent image throughout world mythologies for being born, youthful awakening and the bringing of the light. Hellenistic astrologers likened this to the ship's helm[58] – a steerage metaphor for the Ascendant's role in manoeuvering the ship of life. Opposite the rising Ascendant is the angle of the Descendant (DSC), the setting point characterizing the approaching darkness, the end of the light. In Greek myth this was the land of the Hesperides, the nymphs of the evening located at the edge of the world. These western maidens tended the orchard where golden apples grew in the grove of immortality, a gift from Gaia to Hera on her marriage to Zeus. The Descendant reveals to us the darker life-giving aspects of soul not always visible in the daylight of consciousness; in a psychological way the angle proposes how we might deal with what is in shadow, especially when that is encountered in others.

The Medium Coeli or the Midheaven, commonly known as the MC, is the apex of the ecliptic representing goalposts and brightly-lit summits. It is our own Master of Ceremonies. As the highest point on the ecliptic at that moment, the MC is something we look up to, like the top of a cathedral spire or the ship's mast. It is the peak above, an uppermost limit and a symbol of something worth reaching for. Opposite the apex of the MC is the rock bottom angle known as the Imum Coeli or lower sky, commonly abbreviated as the IC, or as some students say, the 'I see'! As the low point on the ecliptic, it is like a portal where the root finds its entry into the dark, cold earth. It represents the ballast on our ship of life, the dim depths from where we draw our sustenance.

The MC-IC axis forms the vertical axis of the horoscope and symbolizes the upstanding orientation to life while the ASC-DSC axis is horizontal, representing reaching out to life. The early family environment and dynamics impact on the strength of the individual's limbs (ASC-DSC) and spine (MC-IC). Early experiences of both the parental and the sibling relationships inform the adult blueprint for relationship. Each of the four corners of the horoscope describes significant bonding patterns that affect the development of relationships later in life.

As the root system of the family, 4th house images are the deepest layer of emotional safety that supports the extent to which secure relationship can be formed later in life. The IC is the border into the 4th house – a powerful cusp that influences deep-down security needs in relationship. As a polarity, the 4th and 10th houses reveal the hierarchical axis of parental influence. Through this hierarchy we can glean images of how the parental pair and their relationship informed an individual's relationship development.

The 4th house is below the horizon, the 10th culminates above it. The 4th is located underneath what is visible; the 10th is on top of the seen world. Therefore the 10th is more representative of the seen or overt expectations of the family, as well as the attitudes towards the world at large. Dane Rudhyar described this vertical axis as the 'axis of power', while the horizontal axis of the Ascendant-Descendant was the 'axis of consciousness'. The influence of the 4th house is private, whereas the authority of the 10th house exists in the public domain. Along this axis we experience the familial effect on our attitudes towards privacy and publicity and the encounter with our private and public selves. Each influences and informs the other.

Rudhyar expressively imagined the 4th house as a 'taproot able to reach the centre of the earth'. He described the cusp of the 4th house as 'the point of deepest sustainment and most secure foundation for the building of anything that is to rise above the ground'. Thus the IC refers to the ancestral tradition and 'the great images and symbols on which a culture is built'. Rudhyar suggests that in the 4th we find out where we belong in the 'narrow field' of our families, but in the 10th house the individual 'meets experiences which result from the fact he has succeeded, or failed, in gaining a social position'.[59]

The 10th house is where the familial programming comes to a head. Therefore, always underpinning the 10th house solidity of our social power and position are the foundation stones laid down by our family of origin as well as the familial expectations and attitudes towards success and achievement in the world. The 10th house becomes the outer sphere where the values, traditions, experiences and memories from the family of origin are lived out in a developmental context.

The 7th and 8th houses are the sectors of the horoscope most akin to adult relationships, and the Descendant plays a key role. When considering the 7th and 8th houses and the patterns interred in the layers of these houses, reflecting on the parental relationship offers insight into an earlier and often unconscious influence on our adult relational patterns. For the child, the parental relationship becomes an early model of all adult relationships. Equality and intimacy are key factors in the parents' marriage that shape the adult experience of the 7th and 8th houses. These houses and the DSC also contain critical aspects of our sibling relationships.

When there are no interceptions, the signs on the cusps of the houses of relationship are either sextile or opposite the Ascendant, conjunct or trine the Descendant; naturally these houses are sympathetic to the personal horizon of our life. This trinity of houses supports our personal view of the world, our personality and our urge to strive forward. Conversely, these houses are at odds with the meridian, the vertical angle that is familial and inherited, forged by the parental legacy. These houses describe relationships that are compatible with our urge to be equal but naturally clash with parental and hierarchical expectations. Within this trinity of houses we uncover the primal patterns of relating which include the expectations and projections we will carry into our adult connections.

The roots of the parental legacy and the branches of our sibling experience are two core family tree systems carrying patterns that shape our character. The parental system, which is the hierarchical or vertical system, carries the ancestral fate. This is analogous with the MC-IC axis and the Water houses or houses of endings. The sibling or horizontal system reaches out into the social environment and is our social template shaped by our birth position and individuality. This is analogous with the Ascendant-Descendant axis and the houses of relationship.

Opening the Doors to the Houses – Working with Cusps

Each of the four angles and the eight intermediary house cusps of the horoscope is a borderline for a new, yet unfamiliar, terrain of life experience. Like gates, house cusps suggest a division of territory and are markers between these territories. Each house is governed differently from the preceding territory and therefore there are different procedures, customs and rules for each one. In antiquity, gates and doors were common symbols of threshold crossings and the entrance to new domains and rooms of life.

As a symbol of threshold, the house cusp alerts us to the entrance into a state of liminality as we cross from one realm into another. Liminality is the experience of being between two fixed points of reference and is a time of suspension and reorientation. Therefore, the sign on the cusp of a house is a potent symbol of initiation into a new sphere of life. The essence of the sign colours the experience of the house and may be the first image that we meet as we enter this territory.

When the natural wheel is mentioned, it is assumed there are no intercepted signs in the horoscope. If there is an intercepted polarity, the order of signs on house cusps is disturbed. There will be a doubling-up of zodiac signs on house cusps, and signs missing from other cusps – these signs will be 'hidden' within the house rather than appear on the cusp.

For each individual, the horoscope reveals their personal images of the dweller on each threshold, or the gatekeeper, symbolized as a starting point by the sign on the cusp of each house. The cusp sign is an archetype, an energy waiting to be honoured. Its ruler is a deity who is a guide to entering this domain. When beginning to excavate any house, contemplating the element of the sign on its cusp opens a doorway to a first glimpse within.

Elements on the Cusps: The 4th, 8th and 12th Houses

When there are no interceptions in the horoscope, the same element will be on all three of the cusps to the houses of endings. This element will then play a major role in the family of origin and in the familial and ancestral inheritance as well as the legacy of the familial past.

As the table below shows, the element that repeats on each of the houses of endings (assuming no interceptions) is in resonance with the elemental polarity of the MC-IC axis of the individual's horoscope. Yet the elements on the Ascendant-Descendant axis of the individual's horoscope are different and out of resonance. Let's imagine your chart has no interceptions and Fire is the common element on the cusps of your 4th, 8th and 12th houses. In this instance, you would find that your IC is also Fire (masculine element) and the MC is Air (also a masculine element). But your Ascendant would be the Earth element (feminine) and the Descendant would be Water (feminine).

This is consistent with the houses of endings being linked with themes of destiny and fate similar to those of the MC-IC axis, which is at odds with an individual's urge to express the self, as symbolized by the themes of the Ascendant-Descendant axis.

The element on the cusp of an individual's 4th, 8th and 12th houses ...	... results in these compatible elements on the MC-IC axis in the natural wheel of the horoscope	... and these incompatible elements on the Ascendant-Descendant axis in the natural wheel of the horoscope
Fire (Masculine)	Air (Masc)-**Fire** (Masc)	Earth (Fem)-**Water** (Fem)
Earth (Feminine)	Water (Fem)-**Earth** (Fem)	Air (Masc)-**Fire** (Masc)
Air (Masculine)	Fire (Masc)-**Air** (Masc)	Water (Fem)-**Earth** (Fem)
Water (Feminine)	Earth (Fem)-**Water** (Fem)	Fire (Masc)-**Air** (Masc)

When an interception interrupts the flow of the elements on this trinity of house cusps, one house cusp may contain a different element from the other two. In these cases, the individual experiences two elements influencing their family houses. Take note of the two houses with the same element, as these may be more similar in temperament than the house that is ruled by the dissimilar element. You might reflect on the house with the different element as being the one that might not be as easily integrated into the familial spectrum or one that offers a distinct building block to family life.

The following summary for each of the four elements represents some of the qualities and virtues that were or were not appreciated in the family. In considering a horoscope, first identify whether the 4th, 8th and 12th house cusps hold the same element, then reflect upon the element on the cusps to sketch an initial picture of the essential qualities and orientation to family life.

Fire as the Gatekeeper to the 4th, 8th or 12th Houses

When the signs ♈, ♌ and ♐ are on the cusps of these houses, Fire becomes a gatekeeper for the family story. This suggests that the planets that rule these signs, ♂, ☉ and ♃ respectively, will be important in the family mythology. With Fire as the dominant element of the houses of endings, the qualities sought through the family experience include:

- Independence, competitiveness and drive
- Inspiration and passion
- Optimism, idealism and positive thinking
- Strong beliefs, morals, philosophical constructs
- Self-motivation, encouragement
- Playfulness, sports, entrepreneurial spirit
- Risk-taking, movement, travel
- Spontaneity and change

Reflect on how the fiery spirit might have permeated the 4th house family atmosphere, or have influenced the 8th house familial inheritance or how it might have affected the 12th house legacy of the ancestors. Is Fire an element that feels compatible with a need for security and safety? How has this element been honoured and integrated in the familial experience? What were the myths, stories and experiences of this elemental quality in the family? How were the planets ♂ ☉ and ♃ expressed in the family and do they support an innermost sense of security?

Earth as the Gatekeeper to the 4th, 8th or 12th Houses

When the signs of ♉, ♍ and ♑ are on the cusps of these houses, the Earth element is focal to the ambience of the family story. This suggests that the planets that rule these signs, ♀ ☿ and ♄ respectively, are important in family values. When Earth is the dominant element of the houses of endings, the qualities that an individual needs the family to respect and maintain include:

- Reliability, predictability, honouring routines and rituals
- Stability, security and continuity
- Coherence, constancy, fidelity
- 'Family values', loyalty, affection
- Tradition, conservation, caution
- Career, success, objects of worth and value
- Preserving and taking care of possessions
- Work ethic, strength and determination
- Duty, responsibility and the completion of tasks

Imagine how an earthy perspective might have influenced the 4th house family atmosphere, or have changed the 8th house familial inheritance, or how it shaped the resources of the 12th house legacy of the ancestors. Is Earth an element that feels compatible with the need for security and safety? Are the qualities of Earth well supported by the family and ancestry? How do the archetypes of ♀ ☿ ♄ play out in the family? Are they accessible in ways that provide security in life?

Air as the Gatekeeper to the 4th, 8th or 12th houses

When the signs ♊, ♎ and ♒ are on the cusps of these houses, the element of Air becomes a gatekeeper for the family story. This suggests that the planets that rule these signs, ☿ ♀ ♄ respectively, will be important in the ethos of the family. ♅, the modern ruler of Aquarius, also needs consideration. Air being the dominant element of the houses of endings might suggest that the qualities important for family to emphasize and support are:

- Relationship, conversation and interaction
- Separateness, space and distance
- Objectivity and rationality
- Versatility, multi-faceted ideas and ideologies
- Diplomacy, fairness, harmony and idealism
- Multiplicity of interests
- Learning, reading, writing and the exchange of ideas
- Activity, movement
- Culture

Imagine how the energy of Air might have energized or depleted the 4th house family atmosphere, stirred up the 8th house familial inheritance or what its effect on the 12th house legacy of the ancestors might have been. Is Air an element that feels compatible with the need for security and safety? Contemplate the qualities of Air in family life: the ability to communicate, express ideas, connect and feel separate. Are these qualities well supported by the family? How do the Air sign qualities help to secure and support the innermost sense of self? How do the planets ☿ ♀ ♄ ♅ sustain a sense of self?

Water as the Gatekeeper to the 4th, 8th or 12th Houses
When the signs of ♋, ♏ and ♓ are on the cusps of these houses, the element of Water becomes essential in the well-being of the family. This also suggests that the ruling planets ☽, ♂ and ♃ respectively will influence the character of the family. ♇, the modern ruler of Scorpio, and ♆, the modern ruler of Pisces, are also important rulers as these planets bring their collective power into the experience of the sign. Their archetypal essence will underpin the family atmosphere. With Water as the dominant element of the houses of endings the qualities the individual needs the family to value and appreciate include:

- Closeness, compassion and warmth
- Emotions and feelings, emotional security
- Protection, shelter, nurturing
- Memories and family bonds
- Love and tenderness
- Spiritual ideas and beliefs
- Mystery, privacy
- Creativity and imagination, fantasy, dreams
- Romance
- Suffering, healing

Imagine how Water might have flowed in the 4th house family atmosphere, or have influenced the 8th house familial inheritance or how it shaped the nature of the 12th house legacy of the ancestors. Is Water an element that feels compatible with a need for security and safety? Were the watery qualities of feelings, expressing emotions, affection and care developed enough in the family to give a sense of belonging and security? Do the qualities of the Water signs add to a sense of being safe and private? Are the archetypes of ☽ ♂ ♀ ♃ and ♆ well supported by the family? Do these energies help to provide peace and privacy?

Elements on the Cusps: The 3rd, 7th and 11th Houses

When there are no interceptions in the horoscope, the same element will be on all three cusps of the houses of relationship and naturally this element plays a large role in the formation of equal relationships. Note the dominant element of this trinity of houses in an individual's horoscope and consider how this element plays a role in peer relationships.

With the Air houses, as the table below shows, the element that repeats on each of the cusps is now incompatible with the elemental polarity of the MC-IC axis of an individual's horoscope. Yet the elements on the Ascendant-Descendant axis are now in resonance.

This is consistent with the houses of relationship being linked with themes of personal self-expression (ASC) in relationship (DSC), showing that the cusp element facilitates this process in resonance with the Ascendant-Descendant axis. Yet the MC-IC polarity is not linked in this way.

The element on the cusp of an individual's 3rd, 7th and 11th houses ...	... results in these compatible elements on the Ascendant-Descendant axis in the natural wheel of the horoscope	... and in these incompatible elements on the MC-IC axis in the natural wheel of the horoscope
Fire (Masculine)	**Air** (Masc)-**Fire** (Masc)	**Water** (Fem)-**Earth** (Fem)
Earth (Feminine)	**Water** (Fem)-**Earth** (Fem)	**Fire** (Masc)-**Air** (Masc)
Air (Masculine)	**Fire** (Masc)-**Air** (Masc)	**Earth** (Fem)-**Water** (Fem)
Water (Feminine)	**Earth** (Fem)-**Water** (Fem)	**Air** (Masc)-**Fire** (Masc)

Fire on the Threshold of the 3rd, 7th or 11th Houses

With this element guarding the thresholds to the arena of equal relationships, we could suggest the individual may approach relationship in a courageous, competitive, challenging and inquisitive way, empowered with a sense of self-discovery and urge for excitement. The sphere of relationship is a vital area for investigation and experimentation of the self. Fire would desire that its partner share this sense of adventure, travel and wanderlust.

Fire demands its freedom and needs to explore new territory, which often leads us away from relationship. In the early experience of relationship with siblings, Fire needed to feel free enough to do its own thing, yet also wanted to compete and play with its sibs. In the sibling relationship we may have first experimented with competitive and assertive behaviour. Fire also needs to inspire and empower and this could be an important aspect of relating both in primary and adult years. The necessity to be in relationship with those who are able to meet our need to adventure, quest, philosophize and discover the truth is very important. We may have tried to share these ideas with our siblings. How disappointing if this was not reciprocated; perhaps we decided early on how relationship may or may not be able to embrace our powerful needs for exciting activity and the eternal quest for truth.

Earth on the Threshold of the 3rd, 7th or 11th Houses

The most incarnate of all elements, Earth needs stability and security; therefore it is important that relationships provide this ongoing structure. It is vital that partners are committed, reliable and stable, serving the needs of the relationship. Relationships are nurtured through attention and work. Earth individuals are serious about relationships, as they represent an investment of emotional and material resources as well as a commitment of time.

Earth on the cusp of the 3rd house values commitment, fidelity and devotion in sibling relations and also feels responsible and protective towards siblings. Equally this may manifest as duty and obligation towards the sibling, which could inhibit the formation of other relationships. Feeling a sense of duty for others might be scripted in early relationships. Earlier patterns of stability or lack of it are reawakened in adult relationships where loyalty and responsibility are keynotes of relating.

Air on the Threshold of the 3rd, 7th or 11th Houses

This element is constantly seeking its other half through the process of relating. However, Air seeks a multiplicity of experiences and may share its ideas and experiences in many differing relationships, sometimes being indiscriminate about privacy and containment. Relationships may be an arena of curiosity and often Air's inquiring and interactive manner is mistaken for a deeper emotional or more intimate interest.

With Air on the 3rd, the sibling becomes important as the first equal with whom to share ideas, learning and the experiences of life. The sib is the partner with whom it can relate, gossip, experiment emotionally and satisfy its curiosity. Communication on all levels within relationship is important, and in the sibling system interaction, consultation and the sharing of ideas influences the level of connection possible in later relationships.

Water on the Threshold of the 3rd, 7th or 11th Houses

With this element on the threshold of these houses, the inclination is to bring sympathy, empathy and concern to the sphere of relationship. When Water is on the cusp of these houses we enter relationship with a sense of deep connection, moved by our need to nurture, fuse or merge with the other.

With Water on the 3rd we may have experienced a deep bond with the sibling. Yet, on the other hand, enmeshment or a lack of boundaries may have permeated the sibling system. This could have manifested in many ways: being bound together in the sibling system because of a dysfunctional family atmosphere, through sharing inappropriate feelings with the siblings or through a powerful secret that binds siblings together.

This could also manifest as the individual being the emotional caretaker for the other siblings, or one of the siblings needing more attention and support than the others. Water here confuses boundaries, and when it is important to separate, the person may hold on; when it is important to be there, the person may be absent.

Cusp Rulers – Further Keys to Unlocking the Houses

In the previous sections, we have explored the technique of contemplating the element of the zodiac sign on the cusp of a house as a first step in delineating houses. Next it's important to engage with the archetypal imagery of the actual zodiac sign itself.

When delineating any house it's essential to interpret the ruler of the sign on the cusp. Once you have identified the ruler, you should note this planet's placement in the horoscope. Notice the house it's in, the zodiac sign it's in and the aspects it makes to other planets. The sign on the cusp is an indication of the qualities that lead us into the area of life represented by the house. Its ruler's condition in the horoscope helps us to ascertain the ease or difficulty in accepting and participating in this sphere of life.

Once we've entered a house, we discover its innate complexity. Each house has its own archetypes and energies to interpret. When excavated, houses reveal potent symbols and images of importance to the individual for quickening the understanding of patterns in their life. The environmental atmosphere described by a house is multi-dimensional. Firstly, the house can often describe the literal and manifest environment, e.g. the 4th house can describe the actual childhood environment and family home. Secondly, a house describes the psychic layer – the psychological landscape and atmosphere underpinning this terrain. Always there is a teleological level to any house: what is the meaning of this area of my life and how may this sphere be integrated into the whole of my life?

Most important to interpret are the planets that reside inside a house as these symbolize the archetypal energies encountered in that area of life. In previous chapters we have explored delineating a planet in a house by looking at interpretations of planets in the 4th house and in the 3rd house. In the future chapter Planetary Systems and the Family, the importance of planets in the houses is discussed in detail, including the essential technique of working with aspects.

House Keys

1. Let's briefly consider the MC-IC axis to explore ways to combine these delineation techniques. With the 10th house opposite the 4th, a polarity exists and the signs on the cusps of these houses and especially the planets within them will shape the parental system and its roles. The rulers of these houses can

be indicative of the parental relationship and a key in assessing the equilibrium and stability of the relationship. The placement of the rulers also might suggest the focus of the parental roles. For instance, I have often witnessed that when the ruler of the 4th is in the 10th, or vice versa, one parent plays both roles, such as in a single-parent family. The placement of the rulers in the houses is metaphoric of the roles that each parent might play. Also, the 4th-10th polarity reveals how the parental pair and family environment shapes the active interplay in the self between the inner and outer worlds.

2. In the sibling sub-system of the 3rd, 7th and 11th houses, we first learn about equality. Our estranged or disengaged siblings may present themselves through others we encounter in the world beyond family. The link between the three houses is natural; however, if these houses are astrologically linked in an individual horoscope, then this pattern becomes more evident and visible in the individual's life. Linking factors might include:

- The ruler of the 3rd house cusp in the 7th or 11th house
- Gemini on the cusp of the 7th or 11th house or planets in Gemini in these houses
- Mercury in the 7th or 11th house
- Planets in the 3rd house in aspect to planets in the 7th or 11th house
- Planets in the 3rd house that rule the cusp of either the 7th or 11th house
- The ruler of the 3rd house in aspect to the ruler of the 7th or 11th house

PART II
SOLAR AND FAMILY SYSTEMS
Exploring the Planets

The author's ancestors

*If you don't believe in ghosts,
you've never been to a family reunion.*

Ashleigh Brilliant

– CHAPTER 9 –
FAMILY SYSTEMS AND RELATIONSHIPS
Parental and Sibling Dynamics

The Parental System: Mother and Father

Carl Jung, like all other psychoanalysts who have investigated parental influences, wrote about the potent imprint that the parents' psychological state marks upon the character of the child:

> Fathers and mothers deeply impress their children's minds with the stamp of their personalities; the more sensitive the child the deeper the impression. Everything is unconsciously reflected, even those things that have never been mentioned at all. A child imitates gestures, and just as the parents' gestures are the expressions of their emotional states, so in turn the gestures gradually produce an emotional state in the child, as he makes the gesture of his own. His adaptation to the world is the same as his parents'.[60]

Each child's horoscope also demonstrates the parental influence in many ways, profiling the parents and their legacies, the parental system as well as the dynamic between the parents. The chart is an indispensable aid in illustrating and amplifying the child's encounters with his or her parents.

The Luminaries

Since the Sun and Moon are the dominant lights in the heavens they have perpetually been the cross-cultural representatives of the god and goddess, the king and queen, and father and mother: collective, cultural and personal images of the parental pair. In astrological tradition these two luminaries have always represented the father and mother; therefore we first look to their astrological condition to profile each parent. The sign and house position of the Sun and Moon, their dispositors and especially planetary aspects to each of the luminaries describe layers of the parental system in the family.

First and foremost, their astrological composition suggests the individual's personal perception and experience of their parent.

However, systemically the symbols of the Sun and Moon can also portray the parents' legacy and at times sketch an exceptional picture of the parent themselves. Listening to an individual's experience of their parents synchronous with examining the horoscope reveals a dimension to the luminaries which is valuable in understanding the dynamic interplay between the primal masculine and feminine principles.

From a psychological point of view the active experience of mother and father shapes the development of these inner feminine and masculine archetypes and their outer expression through relationships. Hence psychoanalysts first looked to the father for the development of the animus or masculine principle and to mother to signal the anima or feminine awareness. The horoscope provides the confirmation of the authenticity of these patterns. While we may have first experienced the impact of the solar and lunar archetypes through the parental relationship, ultimately these are contained within our own chart and hence our own soul. Father and mother are inner figures as well as embodied ones. When focusing on a client's solar constellation I will discuss their perception and relationship with father. Their description of their father is so metaphoric of the Sun in their chart that I often comment, 'But this is your horoscope; how do you feel about this pattern within your own self?' I use a similar approach with the lunar constellation and a client's perception of their mother. This helps to disempower the projection onto a parent and bring awareness back to the individual's innate patterning.

While the astrological placements of both luminaries will help delineate the parental system, I have found that it is the demanding aspects between the Sun or Moon and the slower-moving planets that reveal the parents' heritage. For instance a Sun-Chiron aspect may describe the father whose spirit has been damaged, who perhaps was adopted or relocated from his homeland. Perhaps he feels marginal in the world he lives in due to some racial, cultural, economic or educational dislocation. A Moon-Uranus aspect might point to a cerebral mother more equipped to intellectual pursuits than emotional ones; perhaps an out-of-the-ordinary or independent mother. The outer planets' aspects strongly colour the parental experience; hence they characterize their influence on our developmental 'gestures' and temperament.

The secondary progressed Sun and Moon represent the development of these archetypes throughout the life cycle. As they progress through the chart in aspect to the natal configurations they reveal the maturation and individuation of these archetypes. When dynamic aspects occur between the progressed luminaries and the natal configurations, the time period in which they occur suggests a separation from or an awareness of parental and family patterns. The opportunity to identify a more authentic and personal expression of the parents' legacy is heightened.

Transits to the Sun and Moon stimulate the deeply ingrained patterns inherited from the parents. Systemically these transits also reveal changes and developments in the parent. An outer planet transit to the Sun or Moon reverberates through the family system. When reading the transits to the luminaries I am often alert to any changes that are taking place in the parent, the parental marriage and the parent's familial relationships, as this parallels what might be shifting and transforming in the individual.

As we have already explored, the astrological Moon specifies mother and her legacy as well as our inclination to bond and feel safe. Aspects to the Sun, its sign and house placement contribute to profiling the personal father and his effect upon the family system, his legacy and ancestry. Other planets are also associated with the parents in specific ways. For instance Jupiter is often described as a father figure, especially the abundant parent, whereas Saturn is portrayed as the conditional one. Jupiter and Saturn characterize the social parent whereas it is the Sun and Moon that best encapsulate the personal parental system.

Saturn: Parental Laws and Regulations

From a traditional point of view Saturn is synonymous with the father. Mythologically this is certainly true, as Chronus in the Greek pantheon (Saturn in Roman myth) was the patriarch, father to the new order of the Olympians. Under the leadership of his youngest child Zeus, the Olympians eventually overthrew him. He was a rejecting and devouring father, swallowing the life force and creativity of his children. Hence Saturn is often an ambivalent astrological figure, representing the necessity for boundaries and control but also epitomizing domination using authority and restraint. In classical astrology Saturn was also representative of the father, and Saturn is still recognized as a father figure in many contemporary texts as well. However, one way we might think about differentiating the rulership of father is that the Sun is a personal planet and equates with the individual or private father, while Saturn as a social planet relates to the societal or public father. Saturn's laws, rules and regulations can be observed by the parents, but they are usually collectively shared and socially agreed upon; hence Saturn is a consensus or collective reality, not always personal.

Saturn in the family system suggests the traditional and structured aspects of the family, the boundaries, rules and expectations. Saturn is representative of the patriarchal or more conditional images that are projected upon the family. When the traditional and conservative values are unbending and the familiar rules are strict, one or both parents may be aligned with this archetype, colouring the parental experience as rigid or controlled. When Saturn is in a dynamic aspect to one of the luminaries the parental system is experienced as being contained and boundaried. With more conscious awareness on the part of the parent, this can be experienced as supportive guidelines that foster the sense of self; however, it is more often felt as limiting and oppressive when the parents themselves feel unacknowledged.

While Saturn is generally considered to be masculine, it is important to remember that by definition Saturn is feminine in its rulership of Capricorn and that the Saturnian domain of rules and regulations can be experienced as masculine or feminine, active or passive or in an external or internal manner, depending on one's conscious viewpoint. When Saturn is more focused on the self rather than the world, it tends to be more feminine in its approach. Therefore responsibility becomes the ability to respond to the self, not to external pressure or someone else's rules; authority becomes the authoring of one's authenticity, not an outer figure.

Assigning Saturn to the sole rulership of the father limits the expression of this archetype in the family. The Sun is the personal father and therefore Saturn is more the social and governing parent, whether that is mother or father. Mythologically, Saturn is time, the devouring and inadequate father who imprisons his own creativity and children in the dungeon of his belly. However, rather than interpreting this as the father, we might see it as the aspect of Saturn that keeps a tight rein on the freedom of others or whose autonomy is not self-determined but controlled by traditions, rules and laws which then 'swallow up' creative expression.

Saturn's natural house, the 10th house, as polar opposite of the 4th house is also important to consider in terms of the parental system.

The Parental Marriage
When exploring the family in terms of its life cycle, most family therapy technicians begin with the engagement and marriage of the couple, who in the next phase of the round become parents. From the newborn's perspective this coupling is multi-dimensional in that the physical parents are also identified as the mythic mother and father. In a sense we might suggest that the parental coupling is archetypal in that all human life is conceived by this pair; behind this human couple stands the Divine pair. In Greek mythology this primal relationship was expressed through many myths. In the beginning was the elemental union of heaven and earth in Uranus and Gaia; later it was brought to life by way of the stormy brother-sister marriage of Zeus and Hera. Aphrodite's union with the brothers Hephaestus and Ares illustrates the relational triangle while the heavenly marriage of Eros and Psyche reveals the tasks and trials faced on the way to the wedding. The horoscope brings our parental ancestry to light but it also reveals our participation in and experience of the parental marriage.

Liz Greene in *The Development of the Personality* introduces the archetype of the parental marriage.[61] Since the powerful imprint of the parents' marriage on the psyche of the child influences their adult relationships, it is important to consider this when examining the family portrait. As Greene points out, there are two sets of parents, as the shadows of the mythological world parents fall upon the mortal pair. Therefore the chart helps orientate us to both the archetypal parents and the mortal ones. The horoscope also uncovers our subjective expectations of our parents, their ancestral patterns and the atmosphere of their marriage that shapes our experience of adult relationships.

We are born into our parents' relationship at a specific time which becomes embedded in the parents' natal charts; the newborn's horoscope will always represent the transits to their parents' charts at the moment of their birth. The child's chart will also be the transits to their parents' composite chart. We could suggest that the child unconsciously experiences the images of the parental synastry and the forceful inter-aspects between the parents' charts. To some extent the child internalizes these patterns, especially when they resonate with the template of their own horoscope. I have often seen aspects between the parents reflected in the child's chart. For instance, Prince William has Chiron conjunct Venus in Taurus in his natal chart. His mother's Venus in Taurus is closely conjunct his. His father's Chiron in Scorpio opposes his mother's Venus; therefore in his parents' chart comparison there is a Venus-Chiron opposition. His conjunction of these two archetypes would be impressed with images from his parents' marriage.

Each child in the family will perceive the parental marriage quite differently and forge alliances and relationships with the parents in their own way. When thinking about the parental marriage these questions might be worth reflecting upon:

- Who has the power in the relationship and which parent do you identify with and feel safe with?
- What is the unconscious contract in the parental marriage? Why are they together? What unspoken rules and mores have been imprinted upon your psyche? How could the internalization of this behaviour have affected your values and attitudes towards relating?
- What were the unlived dreams and unanswered questions of your parents that may have unconsciously shaped you?
- How safe did you feel? Did you feel their relationship would last?
- Were your parents compatible? How did they resolve their differences?

To begin to consider the parental marriage, look through the lens of the aspects between the Sun and the Moon, because the Sun is the archetypal principle of father, while the Moon represents mother. Prince William has the Sun conjunct the Moon in Cancer. His mother shares the Sun in Cancer but her Moon is in Aquarius. His father's Sun in Scorpio squares his mother's Moon. Prince William's conjunction between the luminaries reveals the intensity of his experience of the parental marriage. Given the stressful square between the Sun and Moon in his parents' chart comparison we would wonder how his attitudes towards family relationships were shaped by his reactions and impressions of his parents' marriage.

The aspects between the Sun and the Moon reveal the orientation between these two archetypes and therefore give us a way of thinking about how the parental relationship between the parents might have been experienced. When there are no major aspects between the two luminaries you can reflect on the phase of the lunation cycle at your birth.

The Sun in Aspect to the Moon
Aspects between the Sun and the Moon form the lunation cycle and their aspects are actually visible in the sky, except for the New Moon when it is darkened at the beginning of its cycle. Although these two planets create a 29½-day cycle, they may not be allied psychologically. When the Sun and Moon form difficult aspects, stress and tension build in their relationship. This stress may also be indicative of your experience of your parents' relationship. This conflict may result in tension between what you need and what you want or what you want to do and what you feel. There may be an uncertainty about identifying what you need or discomfort at it being identified.

The parental marriage is emphasized when the Sun, personifying father, is aspecting the Moon as mother. In essence, the archetypal drama between activity and passivity, doing and being, masculine and feminine, is highlighted in this relationship. An aspect between the Sun and Moon often indicates that the individual may be subjectively identified with the needs of others. In this case the task is to become more reflective of responses and feelings in relationship. They may unconsciously identify so personally with others' moods and feelings that they are no longer aware of their own.

When challenging aspects occur between the Sun and Moon, it may be difficult to identify what is needed as the parental pair may be more focused on their own needs rather than the child's. A child learns to bond, feel safe and express their needs through being identified and mirrored by the parent. Without the parental support in establishing a separate self, the child remains vulnerable to identifying others' moods and anxieties as their own. Like a barometer, the individual may read the emotional atmosphere but unknowingly identify it as their own. If the parents have been more preoccupied with their own needs, the child may be at risk of lacking an identity in the system, unconfident unless they echo back what they perceive the parents need. With a major aspect between the Sun and Moon, we might consider the parental marriage in various ways. For instance:

> ☌ Since the conjunction is generally very subjective and at times difficult to express, the child may have internalized feelings about the parental marriage that are confusing and perplexing.

It may be difficult to separate each parent. The luminaries are together and therefore the marriage may seem fused, enmeshed, bound together, but not always in a healthy way. This might suggest that the parents are not able to be seen in their own right. They may express the same opinions and values; therefore the child may have felt that one parent could not make a decision without the other. The parents might always appear to be aligned, unable to be differentiated. When this is constant the child does not experience how differences can be spoken about. They may feel left out, not a part of their parents' relationship. Whether the parents' relationship was symbiotic or volatile, the feeling that the child was not a part of their unit may underpin a sense of not belonging or fitting in. In adult relationships this might manifest as singularity or difficulty in feeling part of a unit or team.

Being born near the New Moon could indicate that a beginning or a new cycle was unfolding in the parents' marriage when the individual was born. The dark of the Moon suggests that there is a subjective identification with others and that it may be necessary to be more reflective over responses and feelings in relationship. For instance, the individual may unconsciously identify so personally with others' moods and feelings that they are no longer aware of their own. If the Sun and Moon are in adjacent signs then the task of separating the Sun and Moon is moderated by the different element and quality of each sign.

> ☍ The opposition is more objectified and often projected onto an event or person, so that individuals might experience the difficulty as being outside themselves, not as an internal personal conflict or struggle.

When born at the Full Moon the disc of the Moon is fully illuminated by the brilliance of the Sun. On one hand this might suggest a strong working relationship between the parents with each working in tandem with the other; equally it could represent a split or antagonism between the two. Rather than allies they may be competitors. However, the key is how the parents coped with the polarity, as this informs the child's approach to resolving tension and disparity in relationship.

From the child's perspective there is the possibility of relationship as each parent may balance the other. However, if the relationship is unconscious, the parents may be in conflict, senselessly arguing or opposing one another without any resolution, commitment or perseverance. In this scenario one parent sees the conflict as being totally their partner's fault, setting up the pattern of projecting blame onto others. Or the couple may remain independent of one another when they are unable to agree or compromise on the outcome. Ultimately this will shape how differences with others are handled in adulthood.

☐ The Square combines psychologically opposed elements and becomes active through tension and friction.

The needs and urges at each corner of the square are difficult to bring together at the same time. Each planet is demanding a voice but since they cannot occupy the same space simultaneously, they appear to be in conflict; hence the experience is often abrasive or stressful. In terms of the parental marriage we might visualize one parent at odds with the other. When the parents are unconsciously driven by their needs and urges, the child might see irreconcilable differences in their parents. They might perceive each parent as being at variance in their needs, values and life direction.

How to be in relationship but also to do what we need to do is a core issue. How the parents managed to resolve their differences, achieve compromise, find the right timing and acknowledge the other's needs and desires shapes the child's ability to resolve conflicts in adulthood. Without consciousness in the parents' marriage, conflicts become irreconcilable and differences between the partners appear unmanageable.

This aspect reveals the tension in the parental marriage. How these differences were resolved becomes crucial. Are differences seen as diverse or discrepant? From a functional point of view this could suggest that the child internalizes a practical sense of conflict resolution. Ultimately the child views two different energies personified by the parents who are endeavouring to relate to one another.

> △ The trine unites the three signs of the same element. From an astrological perspective this suggests more affinity, more choice and fluidity between the planets; however this does not necessarily suggest consciousness. When using aspect orbs, planets near the cusp of a sign may trine a planet in an incompatible element. This suggests more discrimination and mindfulness might be applied to the planetary aspect.

Choice does not always add value to the relationship. Therefore how the parents utilized their resources and worked together to create their relationship informs how the child experiences the parental marriage. On one hand the relationship could be seen as flowing, yet on another it could also represent apathy, even indifference, in the relationship. If the parents are separated or divorced, this aspect suggests that the child might have more choices or a wider safety net to cope with the split.

> ✶ The sextile combines either feminine or masculine signs, so there is also more compatibility in this aspect.

The sextile between the Sun and Moon indicates opportunities. While the harmony between the signs increases the likelihood of parental accord, this depends on the nature and consciousness of the parental relationship. However it does suggest that the individual has greater scope to deal with parental discord and inequality and is able to weigh up both sides of the controversy. Since the archetypal bond between the two is compatible it eases the tension in the experience of relationship.

Separation and divorce are experienced more frequently by children these days. While this can be distressing, perhaps the factor that eases the suffering most is the conscious intent of the parents to separate as honestly and as consciously as possible. Aspects between the Sun and Moon are supported and shaped by the level of awareness that the parents bring to the task of interaction and relationship. When the parental relationship is handled as consciously as possible, the child's experience is not so affected by the unresolved feelings of the parents.

The Sibling System: Sister and Brother
Siblings are a vital part of family life, and the atmosphere and complexes of the family and ancestry greatly influence their development and relationship. As siblings are our earliest equals, companions, peers, partners, allies, comrades, associates, rivals and friends, their influence will permeate many other areas of the horoscope. One of the first experiences in our sibling system is sharing a common generation, one different from that of our parents.

Siblings share similar generational influences. They are born into the same collective atmosphere, symbolized by the placement of the outer planets, Neptune and Pluto, and often Uranus, in the same signs. Sibling systems are microcosms of their generation. Siblings have the opportunity to participate in the emerging collective spirit that will express itself throughout their lifetime. For much of the 1940s and 1950s, Pluto was in Leo and Neptune was in Libra. The elemental combination was also in the Fire-Air sextile at the turn of the millennium, when Pluto was in Sagittarius and Neptune in Aquarius. Now the elemental mix of Earth and Water has returned: the Pluto in Capricorn generation with Neptune in Pisces revisits the Pluto in Virgo with Neptune in Scorpio generation. The microcosm of the sibling system is influenced by the same outer planetary themes throughout the life cycle so that siblings participate in the same generational milestones and world events that define their early years.

Through the dynamic stories of brothers and sisters, myth continually demonstrates that the sibling is an archetypal reality, an inner reality as well as an outer individual. Therefore the sibling archetype is already inherent in the planetary pantheon. Traditional astrology grants Mercury the role of rulership over the sibling, and Mercury's domains of Gemini and the 3rd house are clearly sibling territory. Venus and Mars are archetypes that a sibling would most likely embody. Because Venus and Mars are equal archetypes that inspire relationship they are prone to being projected or transferred onto the sibling, especially as the awareness of gender differences develops. Olympian twins Apollo and Artemis were associated with the Sun and the Moon respectively, reminding us that another dimension of the Sun-Moon relationship might also apply to the sibling experience.

Confusion between the hierarchical role of parent and the equal role of a sibling is apparent in the horoscope when the parental and authoritative indicators are placed in the realms of equality or vice versa. When these systems are interchanged then inappropriate roles and uncertainty are likely. For instance, when the parental archetype of the Moon is placed in the 3rd house or Gemini, or in aspect to Mercury, there may be a lack of boundaries between the roles of sibling and parent. Or perhaps if a sibling image like Venus is in aspect to a hierarchical archetype like Saturn, tensions arise between the urge to control and the urge to share.

The following tables detail the differences between the two systems in the family: the family system of hierarchy and the sibling system of equality. The first table contrasts the difference between the two systems while the second lists how these are expressed in astrological terms.

As expressed in human experience

Parental system	Sibling system
Hierarchy	Equality
Vertical	Horizontal
Mentor	Friend
Boss	Colleague
Parent	Partner
Dependent	Independent
Power imbalance	Power shared
Therapist	Counsellor
Symbiosis	Separation
Regression	Progression
Matriarchy	Sisterhood
Patriarchy	Brotherhood

As expressed in astrological archetypes

Parental system	Sibling system
Meridian	Horizon
Houses of endings (4, 8, 12)	Houses of relationship (3, 7, 11)
MC-IC	ASC-DSC
Moon	Mercury
Saturn	Uranus
Neptune	Venus
Pluto	Mars

Commonly, clients with the Moon in the 3rd house have described how they were the mother to their siblings or that their mother wanted to be their sister and equal, not their mother. And in another case, a client with the Moon in the 3rd found out in adolescence that her older sister was really her mother. When the Moon is in the 11th house we may become the mother to our friends or when Uranus is in the 4th we may want to be an equal of the parent. When an authoritative archetype such as Saturn is in a house of equality (3, 7, 11) then the quest for an equal relationship may be complicated by an authoritarian approach. For instance, Saturn in the 11th might suggest the boss is your friend or that you feel parental towards your colleagues. Underpinning these astrological placements is often the familial experience of inappropriate roles, the parentalization of the child and the parent who is a child. These interchanges are one way of thinking about how the roles and boundaries in a family may become confused.

Since siblings share outer planetary combinations, inner planets and angles are the most important in chart comparisons between siblings. If one of the siblings has an outer planet aspecting an inner one, then the sibling born in the same generation sharing the same outer planets stresses that particular planetary combination. Because the relationship is on a more equal level, the possible outcomes of the planetary aspects between the charts have more scope and latitude.

The Astrology of Siblings

In our discussion on the houses of relationship, we looked at the 3rd house first for sibling themes. The sign on the cusp and its ruler help to delineate our instinctual approach as well as our experience in the sibling system. Planets in the 3rd are very indicative of the sibling themselves, our role in the sibling system as well as the impact that siblings have on the formation of our sense of learning, communicating and formation of equal relationships. Here in the 3rd house we find the seminal template for equal relationship; hence the sibling plays a major role in this patterning.

Gemini is the sign of the sibling and its patrons: the twins, the Dioscuri, represent this mythic archetype. Castor and Pollux, the two bright stars in the constellation of Gemini, are eternal reminders of the sibling bond, a relationship so important to the ancients that their story was written into the heavens. Whichever house Gemini rules is a sphere of our lives where the sibling story may be located. Inner planets in Gemini also are indicative of the sibling story. Interestingly, when the slower-moving planets transit this sign, there are often social movements arising that attempt to create a sibling society or a more egalitarian one. When outer planets transit Gemini the sibling story begins to surface in the collective.

The sibling experience is influenced by the planets that aspect Mercury. As a messenger, Mercury often allows full expression to the planet that it aspects. The aspecting planet's essence colours the sibling relationship, often quite literally.

The Sun and Moon are generally seen as the parental archetypes, but when a parent is not present in the family a sibling may become a parental substitute and therefore become solar or lunar. In Greek myth the Sun and Moon were the twins Apollo and Artemis, as we will explore. Sibling themes may also be constellated with the luminaries. To begin to reflect on the aspects to Venus and Mars from the sibling's perspective, consider the outer planets' aspects because these more readily evoke the archaic vestiges of fate in the family, hence shadowy residue from previous generations. A difficult aspect from an outer planet to Venus and/or Mars may bring ancestral patterns into the relationship with sisters (Venus) and brothers (Mars) or the feminine and masculine attitudes carried through the family line.

For instance, Sally has Venus in Scorpio in the 12th house squaring Pluto on the MC. We used this image in her consultation to explore the powerful dynamics that permeated Sally's relationship with her sister. She described her sister as dark, underhanded, dominating and obsessive, a powerful shadow image for Sally who could never forgive her sister for coming between her and her idealized father. Eventually the intrigue and secrets surrounding the sister's relationship haemorrhaged with the death of their father and the contents of his will.

Angela has a Chiron-Venus conjunction in the 3rd house and is the youngest of three sisters. During adolescence, her sisters taunted and teased her about her weight, the size of her breasts and how she dressed. Angela became convinced she was as her sisters described – ugly. The family atmosphere was permeated by this wounded image of the feminine. For instance, when Angela started menstruating, her mother's advice about sex and men was the proverbial message: 'men only want one thing.' The feminine experience of the celebration of womanhood and sexuality was severely damaged, not only by her mother, but confirmed by her own generation of sisters. As Angela told of these experiences, I was aware how striking and well presented she was, which seemed to be the opposite of how she felt. Like Psyche, Angela still heard the envious voices of her sisters in every relationship.[62]

Aspects to Venus and Mars are, of course, multi-dimensional; however, one of the potent layers of these aspects can be read in terms of the sibling relationship. Mythologically, Ares (Mars) and Aphrodite (Venus) were brother and sister as well as lovers. The brother-sister stratum is often forgotten in the examination of their archetypal dynamics, which is consistent with the overlooking of the powerful dynamic of the brother-sister relationship.

Brother Sun and Sister Moon
Artemis and her twin brother Apollo were loyal and devoted to each other from birth. Apollo was the brother she loved. The Second Homeric Hymn to Artemis[63] tells us that when Artemis had satisfied her urge for hunting in the wild, she went to her brother's temple in Delphi, hung up her tunic and arrows and changed into a beautiful dress. Here she joined her brother, the Muses and the Graces in song and dance.

Artemis and Apollo first bonded in the womb of their mother, Leto. During her pregnancy, Leto was refused refuge in every place to which she went. Finally, the rocky, abandoned island of Delos offered her sanctuary in exchange for the promise that the son to be born would build a temple on the island before he became too famous. The abandoned island of Delos was now guaranteed to become an honoured centre in antiquity. Myth suggests that Artemis was born nine days earlier on a neighbouring island, Ortygia, and then helped her mother to deliver her twin, Apollo. The twins had become bonded, even before they were born, through their shared gestation in the womb of their troubled mother. Artemis, the midwife for her twin brother, became his feminine guide and companion in the world. Apollo and Artemis were close allies, mates, and together they protected their mother, Leto, and her honour.

By the time of the later classical period, Apollo and Artemis had become associated with the two great luminaries, the Sun and the Moon, thereby fostering their relationship as a powerful couple. Artemis's association with the Moon may have come as late as the second century BCE, by which time she had become known as Diana. When astrology became of interest to the Greeks, Apollo and Artemis were firmly aligned with the Sun and Moon. Our primary astrological pair of luminaries has a sibling derivation which the alchemists knew and we have forgotten.

Ptolemy, writing in the second century CE, suggested that we first look to the opposite-gender luminaries when considering marriage in the horoscopes of men and women.

> With regard to men, it is to be observed in what manner the Moon may be disposed ... But, in the case of women, the Sun must be observed, instead of the Moon.[64]

In a modern context we translate this to mean using the woman's Sun and the man's Moon to delineate some of the characteristics of the inner partner. Contemporary astrology continues to look at the powerful union of the Sun and Moon as an image of the *conjunctio* or *hiero gamos*, forgetting the sibling story that underlies the luminaries. Apollo and Artemis are now part of the template of the Sun-Moon couple, and their relationship is an important reminder of the layer of the sibling bond that underlies adult relationship.

The traditional astrological statement that Sun-Moon inter-aspects are indicators of marriage inspired Carl Jung to conduct his synchronicity experiment that compared the aspects between the Sun and Moon in couples' horoscopes. Jung said: 'Ptolemy regards the conjunction of a masculine Moon with a feminine Sun as particularly favourable for marriage.'[65] With couples, my experience of the synastry aspect of the Sun-Moon is powerful in two ways: firstly it constellates their parental marriages and revisits their parents' issues and patterns. Secondly, it magnetizes their sibling experiences: their sense of equality, the ability to be an individual and be identified. Two layers of relationship exist and what often goes unnoticed in the 'marriage' is the sibling patterns that are affecting the partnership.

In their own way Apollo and Artemis were married. Artemis had already chosen to be a virgin and therefore remained true to her brother. Apollo's adult heterosexual relationships were also reflective of his powerful union with his sister. His most successful relationship was with Cyrene, a replica of his sister: a huntress, independent, strong, from the wild. The solar-lunar dyad as represented by Apollo and Artemis is companionship, friendship and sibling loyalty. Apollo was primarily bound to his sister, claiming substitutes for her as his partners. Unlike Zeus and Hera, who had a difficult time returning to their sibling marriage, Apollo and Artemis have a difficult time leaving it. This theme enters into adult relationships when separation between the siblings has not taken place. Perhaps, as in the case of Artemis and Apollo, the separation is difficult because of their mutual enmeshment in supporting and protecting their mother. The unbreakable attachment may be born out of a toxic family atmosphere, drawing the siblings into a union that permits no other relationship to exist.

In opposite sex siblings, the Sun and Moon may be of interest in assessing sibling dynamics, especially when the relationship has been symbiotic or fused. Either the Sun or Moon could also be cast onto a sibling when a parent is absent or disengaged. If father is missing there is a strong tendency for a son to take on the role of father, thereby attracting the other siblings' solar projections. Likewise, if mother is missing psychologically or physically, the daughter may be drawn into the vacuum of her absence, becoming the replacement Moon in the family. These situations will be clear through the examination of the family history and dynamics, and will resonate with themes in the chart that confuse the role of the sibling with that of the parent.

The Brother-Sister Marriage
We are often unconscious of the impact that the sibling has on our adult relationships. There is a tendency to believe that we leave the sibling experience behind us when we enter into intimate relationships. However, this is not the case, especially when the sibling has been a key to our relational patterns. The myth of Zeus and Hera is commonly depicted as a husband and wife who are endlessly in conflict over his love affairs. However, once they were brother and sister who were tenderly in love with one another and given special permission to marry.

Hera's Gamos
Hera was celebrated as the goddess of marriage and Hera's Gamos specifically refers to her union: *gamos* means marriage. In myth, the union of siblings was reserved for gods and 'was realized in Hera's Gamos, where the highest god of the Greeks joined her as brother-husband.'[66] While we know Hera as the wife of Zeus, the other layer of this marriage was as brother-sister. When Zeus finally defeated his father Chronus and ascended to power, Hera became his queen. Their marriage is often referred to as the most important marriage on Olympus. Yet the classical version of their relationship depicts a marriage that is 'at risk' due to Zeus's constant philandering and infidelity and Hera's jealousy and vengeful retributions. A power struggle arises from their tempestuous feelings.

However, there was an earlier time when the Olympian couple were not always locked in power struggles or scheming and lying to each other. This was when they first fell in love in the palace of their aunt and uncle, Tethys and Oceanus, where they were being hidden, protected by their mother Rhea from the familial wars that were raging with their father. Here, in the great palace beneath the sea, they consummated their relationship, a relationship that was to remain secret for 300 years.[67] But by the classical period their 'secret' relationship no longer existed and the infidelity and recriminations within their relationship had become public knowledge. As the supreme deities on Olympus, their marriage reflected the spectrum of experiences that adult partners undergo, both positive and negative.

But Hera and Zeus are also siblings. The sibling layer of every adult relationship is often the secret level that remains unconscious to the partners. Hera and Zeus's relationship reminds us of two important layers of adult relating: the sibling and the parental relationships. The sibling level of the marriage contains the feelings of equality, the facility to share both physical and emotional spaces, loyalty and -*philia* – the love of brother-sister. There is a symmetry and equality between siblings that is reflected on this level of the relationship. However, this level of relationship could also activate the incest taboo – the partners feel loving, supportive and caring of one another, but not sexual. On the other hand, the parental level of the relationship contains the tension of the opposites, the powerful feelings of love and desire, dependency and need. Here the unknown in the other is challenging, motivating as well as erotic.

Recognizing both levels within an adult relationship gives more scope to the union and allows the partners more flexibility when interacting with each other. Balancing both levels within an adult relationship/marriage is a task of mature relationships. Lynda Schmidt expresses these two spheres of adult relationship as the 'sibling archetype' and the 'marriage archetype':

> The sibling archetype offers the possibility of understanding, free of parental overtones. It allows for the natural expression of positive and negative feelings of peers whose relationship is for life. The marriage archetype offers the excitement and tension of non-understanding. It permits the instinctive, biological expression of extreme ends of the dimension of maleness and femaleness, thus keeping the charge of sexuality.[68]

Within the same article, the author highlights the need to balance these two archetypes that shape adult relationships. Traditional marriages could benefit from the equality and love offered by the sibling relationship while modern couples may feel more passionate and secure by being more consciously aligned to the marriage archetype. When we are engaged in a dominant struggle to be equal to our partner, the erotic tie may wane. Conversely if we are lost in the passion of the union we may be unaware of the inequality and power imbalance within the relationship.

In her union with Zeus, Hera as the goddess of marriage embodies both the sibling archetype, as sister, and marriage archetype, as wife. She has married her brother-husband and as the patroness of marriage has lived the secret of the sibling marriage. Cultural bias and religious ethic contributed to depicting Hera in a never-changing fixed role of the jealous wife, trapped by the marriage archetype. However, Hera, as the marriage deity, wed her brother-husband, Zeus, and was well aware of the other level of her relationship with her husband. By keeping her trapped in a one-dimensional role we fail to honour her history and her ancient tradition that brought her into union with her brother-animus, the aspect of her self and her marriage that represents equality and symmetry.

Antiquity was aware of the powerful sibling patterns that were an *a priori* aspect of psyche. The brother-sister relationship ranged from feelings of extreme closeness through to indifference and included images of sacrifice as well as the taboo feelings of sexual desire. In contemporary society, the taboo on brother-sister sexual attraction is rarely addressed. A silence has fallen over the relationship of opposite sex siblings and how feelings of love, desire, ambivalence and even loathing are an integral part of this dynamic. Psychologically, we are unaware that the way these feelings are handled will directly impact our adult relationships.

Astrologically, this theme arises naturally because the 7th house of adult relationship is a natural extension of the 3rd house of the sibling and early relating. However, when the links in the horoscope between the 3rd and the 7th, the 3rd and the 8th, or astrological archetypes connected to the sibling like Mercury are strongly aspected to relationship archetypes like Venus and Mars, then it is of interest to reflect on the pattern between the sibling and the partner.

The denial of the sibling impact on our present relationships is often greater when there are still unresolved issues or powerful feelings associated with our opposite sex siblings. This denial is supported collectively and therefore often slips past the trained ear of the therapist. However, the unconscious will often bring sibling material to the conscious forefront through dreams or uncanny coincidences between the sibling and the partner, such as them having the same name, the same birth date, the same birth position or similar personalities.

Astrologically, this transferential situation can be explored in the comparison of the horoscopes of the sibling and the partner. The similarities between the horoscopes reveal the patterns that are most likely to repeat in the current relationship. An exercise that is of interest is to generate two composite charts; the first is between you and your sibling and the second is between you and your partner. Compare these charts to see if any patterns are repeated in the matrix of the current relationship. This comparison helps to highlight where you may unconsciously be drawn into responding to your partner in the same way that you might have done to your sib. Recurring issues that are replayed in the contemporary relationship are revealed through this synastry.

Sibling Synastry
My only sibling, an elder brother, left home to get married when I was seventeen. My progressed Ascendant had reached my 1st house Uranus and I was surprised and delighted that my brother had found his soul mate. But when I calculated my sister-in-law's horoscope I had another shock. It was mine! We are both Librans, although she is two years older than me. However, we share the same angles: Venus is in the same degree in Scorpio squaring Mars in Leo which is conjunct Pluto, and so on. My brother, the eldest, is appropriately a Capricorn with Saturn opposite the Sun. His traditional values allowed me to rebel, and so it was many years later that I 'settled down'. My wife was born three weeks before my brother, thereby sharing his planetary placements from Mars outwards. Therefore in each case our adult partnerships replayed many of the astrological patterns we had experienced earlier in life.

Sibling dynamics are replayed in our relationships with our partners, friends and colleagues, who, as surrogate siblings, repeat similar patterns. This is one area of chart comparison that astounds students – a sibling's planetary placements, aspects and patterns are often replicated in the partner's chart. Sibling transference is more common than we care to admit, especially when we are estranged, angry or when there is unresolved grief or other incomplete issues.

Sibling synastry can be very revealing and informative as to the formation of early patterns of relating and attitudes towards the same or opposite sex. Generally, siblings have their choice of differing zodiacal signs for the Sun to Jupiter. If any of these planets is in the same sign as the sibling, or is strongly aspected to the sibling's inner planets, this will be an indicator of an important theme in relationship. These aspects may also be an inherited motif in the family history, and verifying the family's astrological ancestry often reveals the same planetary contacts between other family members. Synastry aspects between siblings may crystallize into a relationship pattern which exerts its influence on later relationships. Siblings belong to their own system, which is part of the family system and its ancestral legacy. The drama played out in the sibling synastry may also extend back through the family history. The individual and the family also move through time, and any aspects shared between siblings will receive the same transits during similar passages of time. The sibling relationship is continually developing and maturing.

For the most part the siblings will share the same outer planetary combinations; therefore the inner planets and angles are the most important in chart comparisons between siblings. As mentioned previously, if one of the siblings has an outer planet aspecting an inner one, then the sibling born in the same generation stresses that particular planetary combination. Because the relationship is on a more equal level, the possible outcomes of the planetary aspects between the charts have more scope and latitude.

I use the same rules for sibling chart comparisons as I do when working with other couples. Planets still have their traditional meanings and the inter-aspects symbolize how successfully we interacted with our siblings. When we have more than one sib we experience a multiplicity of relationships, therefore different parts of ourselves may be drawn out with each sibling depending on the synastry aspects. With a multiplicity of relationships we may not feel as intensely about relationship as people do if they come from a two-sibling system. The size of the sibling group defines whether our early access to relating was limited or varied. An only child may lack these early experiences in relating that help us to mould and define who we are in the context of another. We begin our life journey by encountering the powerful figures of our family who are evocative representatives, agents and diplomats for our astrological and genetic make-up.

– CHAPTER 10 –
PLANETARY ARCHETYPES
Personalities of the Family System

Looking at family as personified facets of our inner life opens up rich territory. Family and its members are not only 'real' people but could also be considered as metaphors of archetypal patterns and processes. As these familial fragments are aspects of our psychic make-up, their images are embedded into our horoscope. Reflecting astrologically on the family is profoundly revealing because the horoscope contains multi-dimensional symbols that uncover the family of origin. These include our ancestral lineage and our familial experiences, which shape the patterns of our psychological inheritance.

When considering the diversity of familial symbols, we can also utilize these as metaphors to understand our instinctual and psychic life. In a way the family functions as a metaphor through which certain reactions and patterns become clearer.[69] Innate patterns and characteristics that we can clearly ascribe to our parents and siblings are also images that help us reflect on our internal life. Father, mother, brother, sister, son, daughter are illustrated in the horoscope not only as literal figures but inner ones, personifying an instinctual orientation to this archetype. A helpful way of thinking about your mother or father is not only who they are, what they did and how they behaved, but their internal presence as a symbol of solar and lunar patterns in your life. The horoscope is a unique lens through which we can view our ancestral legacy and the inherited patterns embedded in our own soul.

Family Members Mirror Internal Archetypes
The planets and their aspects help to illustrate the family, its members and the inter-generational patterns that contribute to shaping our character. In essence the planets are all members of one system named the solar system in honour of its central focus, the Sun. In a way the planets belong to a family, which is just one system in a complex cosmos. Like our families, each member in the planetary

system is assigned roles and has its distinctive characteristics and soul. Similarly each planet in the horoscope marks out its own niche, outlining the way it is accustomed to instinctually experience and react to particular archetypes, which are the systemic energies of the family system. The horoscope reveals each planetary condition. When we look at the horoscope through the image of family we can reflect on our familial inheritance, as well as on each member within the family system.

Our inner world is animated by our close relationships; therefore emotions, behaviours, feelings and senses are often given a human face in order to better understand them. For instance when we are forgetful we may assign this behaviour to Auntie Pat; when we are careless, it could be our brother Frank who comes to mind. Hence it is natural for the objective attributes of particular family members to be resonant with inner patterns and qualities, no matter how much we deny our connection to them. Horoscope patterns that describe our literal mother and father also map the inner dynamics of the parental archetypes. These astrological patterns profile how this energy has been formed through family experiences over time.

This way of thinking could be used to describe how we might orientate ourselves in relationships, whether that is motherly, fatherly, sisterly or brotherly. At times we may be more one than the other; however, all four orientations are both personal in our experience and also archetypal in the human dimension. Astrology helps us to understand our inner world through the characters that inhabit our outer world. And the more we come to know the inner dimensions of these figures the more we are able to internalize their image, which aids in the withdrawal of expectations and projections we may have cast upon the outer individual.

Overview of the Planetary Characters and Archetypes

Metaphorically we can use the planets in a variety of ways. To begin, we can imagine the inner planets as personifications of family members. Since the experience of the outer family member often parallels the influence of a corresponding archetypal pattern, our response to the outer figure mirrors the internal archetypal complex.

For instance, Venus might be embodied as a sister or an aunt. Through our relationship with this family member we might become more aware of our own experience of the archetype of Venus through our responses to this individual. Venusian traits such as our self-esteem, values and attitudes towards the feminine might become more conscious through our interactions and relationship with her. Difficulties with the outer sister or aunt (as the embodiment of Venus) could be synchronous with our own struggle with this archetype.

Mars could signify a brother or an uncle; our outer experience of brother or uncle might help us to understand our unique relationship to the archetype of Mars, such as our ease or difficulty with aggression, desire, adventure, independence and going after what we want. The Sun and Moon consistently symbolize the father and mother and their astrological conditions clearly delineate both the inner and outer understanding of these archetypes. Even though Mercury may not be embodied by any particular family member it serves as a valuable image of the sibling and the sibling stories that are part of the ethos of the family.

Therefore the first way we might think about the planets, in particular the inner planets, is that they personify both the literal and the archetypal family member. Aspects to the inner planets identify the details of this archetypal influence. But inner planets can also be used as metaphors to characterize how this energy has been incorporated into the family through time. Each inner planet can convey an image of how this particular archetype has been expressed or repressed in the family atmosphere with the passing of time. When there is a complex aspect between an inner planet and an outer one then this might signify a difficult relationship with this archetype through the family history.

Embedded in the Moon are images of the family portrait; therefore the Moon and its aspects are very important in delineating familial patterns and trans-generational themes and complexes. The social planets, Jupiter and Saturn, in aspect to the Moon reveal social themes carried through family while the outer planets' major aspects reveal larger, even fated themes, patterns and complexes in the family archives. These themes are often beyond the control of the individual or their family of origin. More specifically, the Moon can reveal the mother's ancestry; therefore dynamic aspects to the Moon are part of the mother's story as well as of her own mother's and are symbolic of patterns carried through the maternal line. We can think of the Moon as the vessel carrying the mother's ancestral patterning.

On the other hand the Sun is the container for the father's heritage. The Sun, being characteristic of the father's lineage, indicates what has passed into the family and the individual's experience through his line. However, aspects to the Sun also suggest how the family has integrated the solar archetype over time. The more difficult aspects between the Sun and the outer planets may reveal family complexities over confidence, self-expression and creativity. We can consider Venus to be a barometer of how feminine issues and values were handed down through the family as well as the familial attitudes towards females. Similarly Mars is the indicator of how masculine concerns and values were handed down through the family as well as the familial attitudes towards males in the family history.

Finally, another way of thinking about the planets in terms of the family system is to reflect on the influence of the social and outer planets. These planets influence a communal and collective dimension of the family experience. They impact the family atmosphere and environment with broader social, cultural, racial and historical concerns and experiences. Jupiter and Saturn reveal the societal, educational, ethnic, legal and communal mores and attitudes in the family.

Jupiter speaks about the beliefs in the family, attitudes towards education and scholarship, cross-cultural experiences, religious faith and spiritual convictions. Saturn is family law, social status, the boundaries or lack of them in family life as well as the conventions and regulations that influenced our freedom. These are specifically highlighted when the planets are in one of the houses associated with the family or in a dramatic aspect to an inner planet. With difficult aspects to the outer planets, the inner planets are burdened with ancestral repression and control.

Chiron, Uranus, Neptune and Pluto symbolize the larger and more archaic patterns that affect family life over which there is little, if any, control. Each of these planets also talks about generations and sub-generations when they ingress into a new sign of the zodiac. As they make aspects to one another they describe the historical ambience. But the astrological arrangements of the outer planets to the inner ones identify the larger archetypal influences and pressures upon the family.

We might think of Chiron as the wounds in the family that have influenced our sense of well-being or the feelings of marginalization and disenfranchisement that permeated the family atmosphere and affected our sense of belonging. Often when Chiron enters the familial realm there is a story of emigration, loss of home, dislocation, relinquishment, excommunication: themes that point to feeling outside the system that encompasses the family. In the family atmosphere, Chiron reveals migration trauma or suffering because of the relinquishment of emotional attachments in the family

Uranus signals the schisms and separations of family life that have influenced our ability to feel calm and settled. It might point to a heightened anxiety in the family atmosphere, a severed family line or an unusual blending of familial members. It brings the theme of separation, even abandonment, into the familial realm, often accompanied by hyperactivity, hyper-vigilance, heightened tension or splitting in the family atmosphere. When schisms have occurred in the familial past that remain unresolved, they enter through the family atmosphere into the individual's unconscious, often leaving a sense of disconnection or an inability to feel connected. Another consideration might be that the urge for intellectual development has not been nurtured, engendering bright but undeveloped thinkers. Often Uranus's aspects to the Moon reveal a lineage of bright females in the family line who have not had the opportunity to develop their intellectual strength or who had to abandon this to fulfil the family expectations. Uranus suggests unconventional and atypical threads in the family fabric.

Neptune suggests what might be missing or unavailable; it symbolizes the dreams, expectations and ideals as well as the denials, disappearances and disappointments of family life. Neptune is also consistent with a familial illness, sensitivity or weakness. This fragility may affect each familial member's sense of self. Neptune also suggests the urge to merge, to become enmeshed in the family, leaving the individual entrapped in a system they cannot leave or feel separate from. Because of the lack of boundary and limitations, psychic complexes leak into the family atmosphere. The family might have at its core an addiction, a belief, a spiritual cause that keeps them bound to a system that suggests they are at risk if they consider leaving. When the addiction, illness or sensitivity remains unacknowledged, it permeates the family atmosphere, leaving its members unable to individuate out of the system and forge separate lives. Passivity and helplessness may be the long-term results of repressing negative feelings over the course of time. The family system may deal with negativity through forgiveness, forgetfulness, rigidity or even spiritual compensation. Often lying undeveloped in the Neptunian system is spirituality and creativity, which were shunned by ancestors in the familial past. Neptune is the archetype of imagination, artistic creativity, spirituality and compassion, all melodic tones in the family choir but which have been left unsung.

Pluto plunges us into the depths of family life by revealing family secrets, sensing the demonology of the past or confronting the ancestral taboos. Pluto symbolizes the family grave, the family trusts and the family secrets. When Pluto darkens the family atmosphere there is an unspoken rule about continuing in denial about the truth of what is being repressed. More often than not, a loss unmourned, a grief unfelt, a betrayal denied or a taboo that is broken keeps the family and its members bound to what is disowned.

The archetypal process connected to Pluto is descent, which often feels like abduction, yet it is a necessary course of action to find what has been buried and repressed in the family history. Untapped in the reservoirs of the family are torrents of power that when accessed can reinvigorate and rekindle the individual's life force and will to live. Pluto is power and in family life this may still be dammed up due to the misuse of authority, emotional, sexual or financial power in the past. Pluto represents the enduring, indelible, passionate and soulful strands that need to be woven into the family tapestry.

When any of these outer planets aspects inner ones there is a sense of something beyond the container of the family that affects the individual in its own unique, yet fated way. Since the outer planets represent archetypal blueprints, energies and influences beyond the visible boundary of our solar system, metaphorically we can suggest that they also represent unfamiliar, mysterious and complex patterns beyond the family system. These patterns may also have become calcified through their denial in the previous generations.

Considering the Planets and the Family Legacy

There are many ways of thinking about how we could use the planets as a lens to picture the family legacy. But based on what we have suggested about the planets so far, we will concentrate on four possible ways to contemplate each planet's effect on the family atmosphere. In considering this approach it is important to differentiate the inner planets as more personal, the social planets as more communal and the outer planets as more ancestral influences. To summarize, the four ways we might think of the family system from the point of view of the planets are:

1. The inner planets as archetypes of the family; these five planets are aligned with family members from both a personal and archetypal perspective. Each of the five planets also represents an aspect of the familial environment and atmosphere; for instance, Mercury represents communication within the family but may also suggest attitudes towards learning in the family atmosphere. Each planet will also contain certain circumstances, experiences and influences of the family, as well as the inner impact of familial and ancestral patterns and complexes.

   We will familiarize ourselves with the two luminaries as indicating the familial threads carried by the parents and the other three planets as indicating the strands carried by the siblings and other family members. Any aspect between inner planets highlights a unique personal energy originating in the family system and may also indicate the relationship between these two family members. Of prime importance is the Moon, as the vessel of the family's felt experiences.

2. The social and outer planets are representative of potent familial patterns that influence the development, well-being and self-confidence of the individual. We will amplify these planets and their effect from the perspective of family patterns and complexes.

3. The inner planets' aspects to the social and outer planets reveal the ways a particular archetypal motif has been carried through the family history. In context of family history, we can outline inherited social, cultural, moral, legal and responsible influences and patterns through the dynamic aspects made between Jupiter or Saturn and the inner planets. Potent aspects between Chiron, Uranus, Neptune and/or Pluto and the inner planets highlight trans-generational patterns and influences

that enter the individual's contemporary life experience. Each one of the inner planets also represents its own lineage; for instance, the Moon's aspects would be maternal, the Sun's paternal.

4. The planets in one of the houses associated with the family. When a planet, whether personal, social or outer, falls in one of the houses of endings (4th, 8th or 12th) then this planet has been immersed in the family cauldron and plays a role in the family circle. When a planet is in one of the houses of relationship (3rd, 7th or 11th) then this planet seeks its individuality in the family system and participates in the sub-system of the sibling. The template for relationships with partners, friends and companions is shaped by the family experience of equality and relating. Planets in the 4th house are specifically focused on the family of origin and its atmosphere while planets in the 3rd house are indicative of the atmosphere of the sibling system.

What follows is an introduction to considering the planets from the point of view of a family portrait. First we will examine the inner planets, then the social and outer planets from the familial perspective. Since the Moon is probably the most sensitive and most attuned to family life we will amplify her psychological influence separately in the chapter on Attachment.

The Inner Planets as Mother, Father, Sister, Brother
The five inner planets symbolize familial archetypes which may be embodied by a member of the family or may designate a sub-group within the family. Aspects to these planets will correspond to the individual's perception of this familial member or sub-group, their attitudes and responses as well as the bond forged with this individual. The planet may not always be personified as a contemporary family member but it does represent this branch of the family tree. For instance, Venus personifies a sister in the family portrait. However, you may not have a sister, in which case Venus represents the sisters in the extended family, such as your mother's or father's relationship with their sister.

It is helpful to characterize each family member because they serve as a metaphor for the individual's orientation to this energy, the inner experience of the archetype, as well as being an important influence on the individual's development, the outer experience of the archetype. Inner planets and their aspects will also partially profile family members since the inner images and outer experiences are so intimately entwined.

Aspects to the inner planets will suggest patterns carried by a particular member that exert their influence upon the family. These aspects are multi-dimensional by nature and not only describe the familial member but what role this individual personifies in our life and what archetypal motifs this person might constellate. For example, an aspect to Venus may help to delineate the relationship with a sister, the sister's influence on the individual and outer events and experiences in the sister's life, as well as characterizing the sister herself. However, an aspect to Venus might also describe an attitude towards the feminine that is carried through the family and which impacts the individual. The Venusian individual, most probably a sister or aunt, helps to bring this family pattern to light.

Here are some ways of thinking about familial archetypes as represented by the inner planets. A strong aspect from a social or outer planet to one of these inner planets may be a key to a familial pattern.

☽ *Mother and mother's lineage*
- The primary relationship with the mother and other maternal figures
- The impact of the mother's emotional and psychological atmosphere upon the individual
- Mother's ancestry and what she brings into the family unit
- Mother and those who mothered

☉ *Father and father's lineage*
- The primary relationship with the personal father; other father figures
- The impact of the father's ability to shine and instil confidence in the individual
- Father's ancestry and feeling experience that he brings into the family unit
- Father and those who fathered

☿ *Familial links, kin, siblings, cousins*
- The primary relationship with early peers and peer groups
- The impact of the sibling relationship on the individual
- The sibling images in the family of origin; sibling patterns carried through the ancestry
- The parents' sibling stories

♀ *Sister and the attitude to the feminine in the family (aunts, daughters, etc.)*
- The primary relationship with the sister/sisterly substitutes; the sister bond
- The impact of the sister's emotional and psychological atmosphere upon the individual
- The familial attitude towards the feminine
- The sister role in the extended family

♂ *Brother and the attitude to the masculine in the family (uncles, sons, etc.)*
- The primary relationship with the brother/brotherly substitutes; the brother bond
- The impact of the masculine on the family atmosphere
- The familial attitude towards the masculine
- The brother role in the extended family

The Social Planets as Moral Compass and Social Codes
Each family unit exists within a wider sphere of society which has its own mores and rules that impinge upon the family. Astrologically we see these influences as being Jupiter and Saturn, the social planets which symbolize larger lifestyle issues and life phase passages. Chiron and the three modern planets Uranus, Neptune and Pluto bring the patterns that are beyond personal control to bear upon the family. The slower-moving planets beyond the orbit of Mars make their astrological impact on family life through:

1. Aspects to the Moon
2. Aspects to the other inner planets – the Sun, Mercury, Venus and Mars
3. Their location in a house associated with the family, especially the 4th house of the family or the 3rd house of the

sibling. However, by extension the other Water houses (8th and 12th) and the other Air houses (7th and 11th) are also important in addressing family themes

The social planets symbolize the familial philosophy, beliefs, moral values, ethics and principles, its set of laws, rules, traditions and conventions as well as the attitudes forged in the family regarding socialization and the world at large. The following keywords will familiarize you with some of their familial themes:

♃ *Family philosophies*
- Open-mindedness within the family ethos
- Cultural, racial and social prejudices, biases carried through the family line, attitudes towards cross-cultural experiences
- The social codes and moral values of the family
- The level of optimism, certainty and affirmation within the culture of the family
- Ethics, morals, beliefs, principles
- Educational expectations and attitudes towards higher schooling and cultivation
- Religious dogma and doctrines, religious affiliations; the family's concept of God
- The attitudes towards foreigners and travel; cross-cultural themes in the family
- Emigration in the familial experience

♄ *Family Law*
- Family traditions, what must be adhered to in the family system
- Family attitudes towards authority and social rules
- Family etiquette and reputation
- Feelings of success through the family's position and standing in the local community and the world at large
- Family ambition and attitudes towards performance, achievement and success
- Success myths, performance expectations and status
- Attitudes towards work, authority and hierarchy; the 'should' and 'must' of family life
- Elders; elder children as well as the elders of the tribe

- Rules and conditionality, discipline, consequences and punishment for transgressing family law
- Family boundaries and regulations, whether these are experienced as strict and rigid, or too soft and ineffective

The Outer Planets as Archaic Vestiges of Family Fate

The outer planets symbolize larger influences placed upon the family that are beyond the control of the family system. Often these are the issues which feel fated, irreconcilable and beyond family management. Over time these patterns may have created schisms, complexities and difficulties in the family history. As with the social planets, the outer planets have an impact on the individual's family experience when they are in a dramatic aspect to the Moon or an inner planet or when they are in one of the houses associated with the family. The themes that are highlighted generally assume that the archetypal energy has been blocked or unexpressed by the family over time. When expressed by the family and integrated into the system, the archetypal force is liberated to express itself functionally. The following keywords are an introduction to the dynamic impact of the outer planets on family life:

⚷ *Family Wounding and Healing*
- Wounds carried through the family line, often due to displacement from the homeland, either through immigration or excommunication
- The archetype of refugee, orphan or outsider may influence the family atmosphere
- The feelings of being marginal or outside the system, even of feeling an outsider in your own family system
- Relinquishment, marginalization, adoptions and/or step-parenting
- Feelings that have been disenfranchised or relinquished in the family experience
- What seeks to be healed through the feelings of exclusion and dismemberment
- Loss of spirit in the family as well as the possibility of healing this loss
- Splits or disruptions in the continuity of family life

♅ Family Freedoms
- Bonding and engagement versus individuality and separateness in the family culture
- Freedom versus closeness
- An anxious and/or anticipatory feeling in the family
- Intellect valued over feeling
- Separateness and division, connections in the family past that may have been severed
- Unexpected shifts, changes or severances within the family
- Disengagement and disconnection in the family atmosphere
- Separations and schisms that invade family unity and security
- Familial themes constellate around individuality and independence at the expense of security and belonging
- An unconventional family system

♆ Family Sensitivities
- The sacrifice of the individual for the whole; the experience of giving up the self in order to belong to the system
- Enmeshment in the family system; entangling individual needs with collective ones
- Inability to separate personal and communal needs
- Idealization in the family, often of difficult feelings such as grief and loss, rage
- Spiritual ideals and compassionate helping may permeate the family atmosphere as a defence against negative feeling
- Something or someone missing and/or unknown in the family; a void in the family
- Disappearances in the family history
- Suffering, pain, undiagnosed complaints and patterns of illness may also be thematic and are important to note in the family history
- Feeling misunderstood or invisible to the family
- Creativity, artistic imagination, psychic sensitivity and spirituality in the family line

♇ Family's Underworld
- What has been denied by the family in the past as a means of concealing the truth

- Denials that haunt and disturb the atmosphere of the present and influence the individual's sense of safety
- Family secrets and shame
- Unacknowledged loss and/or abuse that pollutes the familial climate
- Unmourned losses in the family, grief, bereavement
- Unnatural or suspicious deaths in the family history
- Sexual intrigue, betrayals, the dynamic impact of emotional control and love
- Emotional or financial inheritances
- Emotional or financial manipulation
- Familial alliances that are based on power and control
- The strength of the family system to survive and deal with crisis
- Attitudes towards power and manipulation in the family

The Inner Planets as Symbols of Family Fragments and Complexes

We have highlighted the inner planets as archetypal images personified by actual members of the family. However the inner planets can also represent very personal experiences, family traits and motifs, as well as patterns that are part of our psychological constitution. In other words the inner planets also epitomize how this archetypal energy may have been expressed in the family of origin and how it seeks articulation through the individual. Was this archetype honoured or repressed in the annals of the familial history?

First, recognize the aspects between the inner planets only, as these will characterize a much more personal orientation to the archetype first felt in the family environs. Aspects between the inner planets and the social planets symbolize how the social codes, customs and traditions from the family of origin affect the individual. Aspects between the inner planets and the outer planets reveal how greater forces outside the family's control or jurisdiction have an effect on the individual. This impact on the family patterning is often transgenerational, initiated in the ancestral past. What is of importance here is to recognize that the social and outer planetary energies bring their pressure to bear upon the inner planet, having an effect on the way we experience this energy. These combinations reveal motifs carried through the family.

☽
- Patterns and complexes carried through mother's lineage
- Feelings of unconditional love and acceptance within the family circle
- The home, the atmosphere and moods within the family
- Acceptance and nurturing in the family system
- Shelter, safety, emotional security, bonding – the sense of belonging
- Attachment and our own unique attachment style
- Family changes of residence, home place or homeland
- The felt sense of being part of a system and community
- Transitions and important emotional phases in the family

☉
- Favouritism in the system
- Father's favourite or special treatment in the family unit
- Familial identity
- The family spirit; feelings of confidence and creativity portrayed in the family of origin
- The ability to be self-expressive and creative with the family; to be yourself
- Patterns of narcissism within the family; narcissistic parenting
- Patterns and complexes that are passed down through the father's side of the family
- Early experiences of being encouraged to express oneself, feeling applause and the permission to shine and perform

☿
- Communication within the family, learning patterns, how the family members were able to express themselves to each other
- Familial interactions
- Attitudes towards early learning and the sharing of ideas
- How peer relationships formed in the family
- The family language
- The family script about what should and should not be said
- Learning patterns carried through the family

♀
- Familial resources and values
- Affection and the expression of love within the family
- The family's attitudes and approaches towards sexuality and desire
- Familial feelings of self-worth and value; self-esteem issues within the family
- Family tastes; likes and dislikes
- Attitudes towards money and possessions, the familial mindset about what is worth owning
- Attitudes towards females and feminine equality
- Patterns and complexes involving sisters or females passed down through the family

♂
- Attitudes towards aggression and anger
- Familial attitudes towards competition, desire and sexuality
- Independence within the family system; the ability to do your own thing within the family
- Family attitudes and rules about freedom and autonomy
- Clarity and directness of expression; level of openness about expressing emotion and feeling
- How getting what you want was supported by the family
- Ways of thinking about males and the masculine
- Patterns and complexes involving brothers or males that are passed down the family

Having differentiated the planets as familial character types as well as social and archetypal patterns carried through the family line, we can develop a way of thinking about each planet in the horoscope from the perspective of our family system.

– CHAPTER 11 –
PLANETS, ASPECTS AND HOUSES
Delineating the Family

Let's differentiate each planet in the horoscope from a family point of view, such as the experiences with the family circle, family fate, inheritances and patterns. Each planet plays its part by bringing its particular archetypal influence and unique meaning into the family through its aspects or its position in one of the houses of family. Therefore we will also summarize each planet in the family houses. In earlier chapters, we have examined the planets in the 3rd and 4th houses in some depth. Now planets in the 7th, 8th, 11th and 12th houses will also be discussed.

We will also examine each planet in relationship to each of the inner planets to illustrate how family themes can be extracted from these aspects. The Moon will be explored separately in the next chapter since it plays such a major role in the astrology of the family, especially through her theme of early attachment.

I will be cataloguing some of the themes I have experienced in my consulting practice, although writing in this manner can appear limiting and deductive to the reader. This certainly is not my aim; rather I would hope that these short scenarios help to amplify and introduce you to ways of thinking about the family astrologically. Therefore these are not delineations so much as amplifications of possibilities.

The Sun in the Family System

The Sun is associated with the archetype of the father. In the horoscope the Sun represents the personal father, his lineage and inheritance within the family system. Therefore, aspects to the Sun amplify our own orientation to the archetype of the father, illustrating his felt experience and ambience within the family. Its position in our horoscope will reveal our perception and experience of our father as well as of father-substitutes or surrogate fathers. Archetypically the Sun suggests the inherited solar nature. The familial attitudes towards males and the masculine shape the promotion and fostering of the self; therefore the nature of our relationship to our father is often indicative of our sense of self-confidence, ego resilience, identity, self-expression and personal vitality.

☉☽ The Sun-Moon relationship is a template for the dynamic interplay between the masculine and feminine polarities, suggestive of the relationship between the mother and father. Aspects between the luminaries shape the phases of the lunation cycle. However, these aspects are also representative of the parental marriage. Consider the relationship between the mother and father as symbolic of the ease or difficulty experienced between masculine and feminine energies.

☉☿ Mercury is always within a 28° arc of the Sun; therefore its only possible aspect to the Sun is a conjunction. The combination of these two archetypes could be an image of father's intellect, his ideas or his ability to communicate; perhaps father as trickster. The pattern of communication with father is important to consider because his attitudes towards the intellect, learning and communicating may have been influential. This might also suggest a favoured sibling, the relationship between father and a sibling or it may perhaps point to the father's sibling and the relationship between them.

☉♀ Venus can only be 48° away from the Sun so aspects between them are limited. The possible aspects are the conjunction, semi-sextile and semi-square. Of these, the conjunction is the most potent. I would also differentiate between whether Venus is direct or retrograde, because Venus is emphasized in its retrograde position. Venus represents the sister archetype and if retrograde might suggest that its feminine expression through the family is unusual and non-traditional. Father's lineage might bring the legacy of the feminine into the family system and females on father's side, especially the sister or another close female, is highlighted. The Sun in family dynamics can often speak of a favoured one. Perhaps there is a favourite sister in the family system or the sibling system becomes split because of favouritism. Father's attitudes towards self-worth and his expression of affection and love are influential in the individual's development.

☉♂ When these two masculine archetypes combine, the roles of father and brother/s are highlighted in the family, as well as the relationship between father and his brothers or father and his sons. Through father's side of the family comes the legacy of the masculine spirit. How are the natural urges to be active, competitive, adventuresome and to take risks expressed in the family and is father an able role model for the expression of these masculine traits? Healthy attitudes towards rivalry, confrontation, anger and sexuality support the individual's vitality.

☉ **in 3rd** Father's birth order, role in the family and attitude towards his siblings are subtle influences on identity. This also highlights the role of the first child or the favoured one. The Sun may have cast its shadow over the sibling system, dividing the system into those who were favoured by father and those who were not. A boy in this system may feel obligated to identify with his father's values. Whether he rejects them or embraces them, they have contributed to what he identifies as being critical in his adult relationships. A girl who was father's favourite may feel in a precarious position, caught between her brother and father. In adult life this may rearrange itself as feeling caught between her partner and son.

☉ **in 4th** The Sun here suggests the impact of father and father's lineage upon the family of origin. His presence, or lack of it, influences the child's sense of security and safety because the child instinctually responds to the father principle. The image of the personal father is integral to emotional stability.

☉ **in 7th** With the Sun in the area of relationship, unresolved issues or complexes with father may influence adult partnerships because the partner may unwittingly constellate the relational pattern with father. Equally the individual may be drawn to qualities in their partner that are reminiscent of their father.

☉ **in 8th** Here we would consider the nature of the inheritance – emotionally, psychologically and financially – that is passed down through father's line. We might also consider any secrets or denials connected to father or his familial past. Therefore the relationship to father could have a bearing on our ease with and experience of intimacy in adult life.

☉ **in 11th** Innately this placement may suggest an inclination to father the group or be its leader, or at least be the spokesperson for what needs to be accomplished. Therefore, father's role in the community, his social circle and capacity to socialize model the ability to take a position and find an identity in society. In the social world the individual may find father-substitutes in coaches, teachers, bosses or mentors who help to reconcile the personal relationship to father and build confidence and identity.

☉ **in 12th** The Sun in the 12th house points to father's ancestral line. This might suggest a loss or unavailability of fathering and/or fostering in the family. Perhaps father or father figures were missing or weakened in the family line. The spirit of the missing masculine influences the present system, which might be experienced as a yearning to connect to the spiritual dimension.

Mercury in the Family System

As an archetype, Mercury is associated with the guide, traveller and trickster; the god who we meet in transitions and threshold crossings. His nature is multi-dimensional with many facets; therefore he has numerous human surrogates, mainly companions, fellow travellers, playmates and cohorts, but we often meet him first in the family through the sibling relationship or the sibling stories within the family. Since the sibling is often a witness, guide, escort, attendant rival, tease and lifelong companion, Mercury is present initially in our interactions and experiences with siblings. Therefore Mercury and its aspects reveal the sibling archetype and its expression in the family system. It also suggests patterns of communication and attitudes towards learning within the family.

☽☿ The aspects between Mercury and the Moon suggest how feelings might have been communicated in the family. A difficult aspect between the two might suggest that emotions and feelings were difficult to express in the family, creating misunderstanding, arguments and strong reactions. Mother's feelings may not have been taken into account or she may have been ambivalent in her expression of them. A Moon-Mercury aspect might also personify one of mother's siblings or the dynamics between the roles of a sibling and mother.

☿♀ Mercury and Venus are in a confined arc geocentrically; therefore the most potent aspect to consider here is the conjunction. When Mercury is conjunct Venus there might be a sibling story surrounding relationship, marriage or unrequited or unacceptable love in the annals of the family history. A sister story carried by the parents or grandparents may be in need of honouring.

☿♂ The role of a brother or the relationship with a brother is emphasized with this combination. The attitudes towards rivalry, envy and competition are rooted in the early interactions with siblings, and certainly with brothers. This might also suggest how the desires, goals and ambitions are passed on through the family story.

☿ **in 3rd** Mercury is at home in the 3rd house and strives to satisfy its urge for communication and learning with siblings and childhood friends. Drawing on early experiences the individual learns how to be heard, whether that is through clarity of expression, joking or persistence. Early patterns of communication are forged in the family with siblings; therefore language, expression of ideas, interaction, attitudes towards learning, mobility and travel are all strongly influenced by familial and sibling relationships.

☿ **in 4th** This suggests that a sibling story may be a feature of the family atmosphere. Whether this is a brother or sister of one of the parents or the sibling relationships within the family, these contacts are significant in childhood. These relationships contribute to securing the emotional foundation. This position also highlights the importance of communication between family members and its impact on the individual's sense of self.

☿ **in 7th** As Mercury is representative of sibling patterns and attachments, unresolved sibling issues may be drawn into adult relationships when it is in the 7th house. Our partners may constellate early patterns that were first established in the sibling system, reminding us of the issues and concerns that have not adequately been dealt with. Mercury here may also refer to a sibling of our partner as well as reactions to and consequences from them. In a way this image speaks to the fusion of the sibling relationship with the adult one.

☿ **in 8th** Trusting others, respecting privacy and showing consideration for personal feelings begins in the early relationships with family and builds the capacity for intimacy. Listening authentically and communicating honestly are first modelled in the parents' relationship; the level of sincerity and integrity in the parental patterns of interaction influence the individual's capacity for open and honest relationships.

☿ **in 11th** Mercury in the 11th recognizes the individual's impulse to express themselves in public and feel equal and accepted by the group. In adult years sibling politics or dynamics may surface when unfairness or favouritism emerge in the social order. When in a group the individual needs to feel equal to the other members; if the leader is displaying favouritism, then the trickster may emerge to disturb the equilibrium of the system. On the other hand, Mercury finds its brothers and sisters through friendships and in social activities, helping to readdress and heal the earlier wounds with siblings and schoolmates.

☿ **in 12th** This placement focuses on the pattern of communication, learning and the expression of ideas in the family ancestry. The family's mythology includes strong codes about what can be said and what is correct, which may have influenced learning and expression. The individual with Mercury in the 12th becomes the spokesperson and mouthpiece for the family, often expressing or exhibiting the shadow of what was previously denied and prohibited.

Venus in the Family System

Venus brings its themes of feminine values into the family system and helps to illustrate the familial orientation to the roles of women: the importance given to the feminine as well as the expression of affection and love. Complex aspects to Venus might reveal how familial attitudes towards sexuality impacted the individual and contributed to feelings of worth and self-esteem. Venus also constellates the spectrum of emotion that includes unrequited and unequal love, such as jealousy and revenge. Triangular by nature, Venus may reveal an involvement in family triangles, which in turn sets a pattern for three-way adult relationships. At a literal level Venus may talk of the familial attitudes towards money, possessions and acquisitions; complicated aspects may reveal unresolved issues of worth and value that affect the family members in the present. Generally I would suggest that Venus exerts her influence in the family through the attitudes towards the feminine and the way she is valued, and how this affects the individual's sense of self-esteem and importance. Venus also personifies the image of a sister and the sister archetype in general; from the familial point of view it brings the role of the equal and empowered feminine into the family.

☽♀ If Venus aspects the Moon the two potent archetypes of the feminine are in dialogue. The roles of the mother and the sister converge and either conflict or cooperate. When conflicting, mother may have preferred to be free, equal, a sister rather than a nurturer. On the other hand, a sister may have stepped into the mother role. This aspect also suggests that the roles of the feminine in the family history may have diverged and a family story concerning the feminine or females from mother's lineage still remains unresolved. This aspect could be personified by mother's sister or a close female relative in mother's family.

♀♂ When the two mythological lovers, Venus and Mars, are in aspect, there is a potent drive to express the inner life force, often through sexuality, creativity or personality. From the familial point of view this aspect brings together the archetypes of the brother and sister. While there may not be an opposite sex sibling in the family experience, an inner image of another urges the individual into relationship. Supportive familial attitudes towards desire, sex, intimacy and self-expression are paramount in helping the individual to feel free enough to express the self in an intimate relationship. Complex aspects might speak of the denial of these impulses in the family history.

♀ **in 3rd** In the 3rd house Venus is aligned with the sister archetype, and if personified by an actual sister then this sister brings to awareness Venusian attributes such as sexuality, attractiveness and beauty. The template for adult relationships, values and worth finds its taproot in the relationship with sisters and early female friends.

♀ **in 4th** With Venus in the 4th house the family attitudes towards money, wealth, esteem, worth and personal value are embedded in the foundation of the individual's sense of security. The family is where the earliest feelings of being valued and loved have either anchored or unfastened the individual's sense of security. Underneath the family facade lie deeper issues concerning gender, the role of women and the equality and acceptance of the feminine; the sister archetype needs excavation in order for the individual to feel safely anchored in their sense of self.

♀ **in 7th** From a family perspective Venus in the 7th draws on the images of the parental marriage, the relationship with siblings and earlier childhood friends to help navigate the adult world of relationships. Earlier patterns with sisters may be replicated in adult relationships or adult relationships may involve sisters.

♀ **in 8th** While Venus may be aligned with the 7th house in traditional astrology, she finds herself accidentally debilitated in the 8th; in psychological terms this might suggest that her nature now must turn its attention to what is not innately comfortable. And since Venus aligns herself with peace, in the 8th she may need to uncover the discord and darkness associated with her being. Being in this house suggests she may have inherited images of incomplete union, severed relationships, betrayals, affairs and triangles from the family records; therefore the avoidance of intimacy may be linked to a family complex. In the 8th Venus's journey takes the individual into the underworld of self in order to excavate the legacy left from past familial relationships and inheritances.

♀ **in 11th** Venus in the 11th might speak of the re-encounter with the family's attitudes towards the feminine and/or the sister through relationships in the social world. Far beyond the parameters and the perimeters of family life we once again encounter our sister and our familial attitudes in the world. And from this perspective, a conscious understanding and acceptance can begin to take place.

♀ **in 12th** In the 12th, Venus highlights the role of the ancestral feminine. Often conflicted, the archetype seeks understanding and acceptance. On an inner level, a trail of devaluation of the feminine may wind through the ancestry seeking acknowledgement and understanding. Inherent is the gift of creativity and life force when the feminine begins to be redeemed. Reflect on the ancestral attitudes towards women, the feminine gifts of self-worth, artistry, affection and love, and how these were upheld in the family.

Mars in the Family System

To the ancient mythmakers, Venus and Mars were consistently paired together as companions, either as lovers or close sibling allies. In the family, the archetype of Mars is held by a brother figure. Mars characterizes the attitudes towards the masculine spirit in the family; it represents the familial orientation to the roles of men, the importance given to the masculine as well as the expression of independence and self-assertion. From a literal point of view, Mars may represent the family's standpoint on the expression of anger, its approach to desire and getting what one wants, as well as virtues such as courage and being identified. By nature Mars is competitive and driven, and its aspects may allude to how this was first experienced in the culture of the family. As the archetype of the lover, Mars might also indicate how passion and sexuality were expressed in the family.

☽♂ The active and passive principles are aligned in an uneasy combination. Mars is desire while the Moon is need, and often these are focused in different ways. How the clash between these was modelled in the family becomes an important factor in whether the individual is able to clearly state what they want or if they go about this passively. Anger and love may be entangled in the family ethos, complicating the expression of anger and passion.

♂ in 3rd The archetype of Mars is experienced in the sibling system through rivalry, competition, jealousy and confrontation. With Mars here, the sibling system and early peer groups are important training grounds for taming the aggressive and sexual instincts, which when identified and honoured can be directed into conscious striving and determination.

♂ in 4th Mars seeks expression through the family here; when consciously expressed, the ability to assert oneself without disrupting the system strengthens the sense of being supported in going after what is wanted. However, if independence, competition and anger are not functionally expressed, conflicts and quarrels disturb the security and stability of both the individual and the family. The deep sense of feeling comfortable with one's individualism and freedom is shaped by the family experience.

♂ in 7th Through our adult partners we may be reminded of earlier patterns of competition and rivalry in our family. Mars in the 7th brings the brother image into the adult relationship; therefore, for a woman who has a brother, her relationship with her brother was an important training ground for later relationships. How our brothers and other males in the family react to our adult relationships is also signalled by this aspect; therefore masculine attitudes in the family have a bearing on how comfortable we feel when expressing our individuality in relationship.

♂ in 8th The expression of desire and sexuality in the parental marriage may impact the level of comfort the individual feels in their adult relationships. Sexuality and intimacy are woven together in the 8th house and the parental relationship is the first one we respond to in terms of feeling familiar with these themes.

♂ in 11th Early patterns of competition and rivalry with siblings are aroused in our relationships with colleagues and associates. The family's philosophy about ambition and expression of anger is met in social situations. Incomplete sibling rivalries and resentments may seep into adult relationship; therefore it is the 'sibling society' of the 11th house where we can reconcile earlier issues in the family through conscious relationships with friends, colleagues and acquaintances.

♂ **in 12th** The 12th house often reveals what has been undisclosed or unexpressed in the family history; therefore Mars suggests that issues of anger, sexuality and ambition may be themes that were not adequately honoured in the ancestral experience. The individual with Mars in the 12th is weighed down with the burden of ancestral repression. The individual's task is to redeem some of the more appropriate ways to express their individuality and desires.

Jupiter in the Family System

Jupiter brings its impact into the family through social and cultural themes, such as education, especially motifs concerning scholarship and formal study, religious beliefs and traditions, family philosophy – such as morals, ethics, principles and human values – cross-cultural alignments and skirmishes, as well as the family attitudes towards advancement, spiritual ideals, pilgrimage and travel. While Jupiter was considered a benefic in traditional astrology, its urge for expansion and integration may not always have been upheld by the family. Its flare for broadmindedness may be dampened by fear; its urge for cross-cultural unity may be discoloured by prejudice; while its attempt at optimism and idealism may end in disappointment and giving up. Family attitudes and past experiences contribute to shaping the spirit of Jupiter in the individual; therefore a retrospective understanding of the family's embrace of this archetype helps to free its expression in the individual, not through rebellion but through conscious understanding.

☽♃ When the archetype of expansion dialogues with the archetype of safety, two possibilities emerge: either there is a security in freedom, adventure and travel or there is an air of uncertainty and trepidation about movement and reaching beyond one's comfort zone. The resolution lies in the family's attitude and experience of safety in exploration. Often in the family history there is an emigration story, a cross-cultural mix to the family or the experience of living outside one's culture of origin. The degree to which the family embraced the foreignness of its experience is the extent to which an individual can feel comfortable and safe when exploring beyond the boundaries of his home and homeland. Through mother's heritage the motifs of religion, race, education, emigration and travel are brought into the family atmosphere.

☉♃ Two forceful and heroic masculine archetypes combine here, suggesting a spirit of adventure and optimism. However, the outcome is dependent on how father's spirit influenced the family. The motifs of adventure, questing, going beyond the perceived limits, searching for higher knowledge and truth as well as the spiritual journey are passed through father's lineage; therefore it is important to consider how these themes were perceived and lived out. Reflecting on father's legacy helps us to reconstruct our own beliefs and life philosophy. In father's family background are images that both support and inhibit our quest for understanding.

☿♃ When Jupiter aligns with Mercury an image of the youngest sibling arises. In terms of birth order, Jupiter could be seen to represent a youngest child: in Greek mythology, as Zeus, he was the youngest child who eventually became leader of the Olympians, confirming an adage that the last shall become the first. Whether or not the sibling is younger, the family theme centres on the urge to quest beyond the cultural inheritance of the family, whether that be educational, racial or moral. In the context of the family, there is often an issue involving education, cross-cultural affiliations or travel that is brought to consciousness by a sibling or siblings.

♀♃ Venus-Jupiter aspects suggest that the arena of relationship intersects with the cultural realm; in terms of the family this might suggest a cross-cultural marriage, which might combine partners of differing race, culture, education, religion or social/economic standing. How this mixture was managed in the family atmosphere affects the levels of intimacy, affection and expression of love. Spiritual values are a motif in the family matrix; the ability to value the search for meaning and feel open to life begins in the childhood home.

♂♃ Again, two potent masculine archetypes combine. As fuel for each other, it is important to note how the family handled the volatile emotions of desire and aggression and the human urge to compete and succeed. Family myths are inherited around taking the 'right action' or 'doing the right thing' and it is important to deconstruct the conceptual and philosophical attitudes towards anger and power to find an innate authentic approach for the individual. Consider how the family philosophy either supports or inhibits the individual's natural instincts to act.

♃ in 3rd Astrologically we tend to see Jupiter expanding the area it occupies; hence we might consider how Jupiter expands the sibling system. How is it big? In size, in a social context, a cross-cultural mix, step-sibs or because of a larger-than-life sibling? With Jupiter here, the motifs of education and religion, travel and questing beyond the familiar are aspects of the sibling experience which have influenced us.

♃ in 4th Below the surface there are beliefs that form a template for the family's way of life. Whether this is religious, spiritual, philosophical or moral, there is often a sense of what is right and what is wrong. If the definition is rigid the individual may feel unable to forge their own beliefs in life; hence it is important to consider the inherited family values and whether they are authentic. Travel, reaching beyond cultural constraints, prejudice, emigration and social compliance may also be part of the family tapestry.

♃ in 7th Familial beliefs, morals and prejudices may be entangled with adult relationships. Cross-cultural themes may be present in our own or our parents' relationship to challenge and expand the family's attitudes towards outsiders. Enmeshed with the search for a relationship is the search for meaning, and the extent to which these can unite begins with the familial permission and support to be free and explorative. The encouragement from our siblings to explore beyond the boundaries of the system is brought into the arena of adult relationships.

♃ **in 8th** Here, in the 8th, Jupiter symbolizes the familial inheritance. Underpinning this placement, I have often heard of a familial story of loss of this inheritance through gambling, overindulging or inflated business decisions. However, there may also be an abundant inheritance when the individual searches beyond the scope of the family. In most cases it is the inheritance of not only resources but ways of thinking, philosophy, optimism and generosity that is tested; the individual must often reach beyond the limits of the family's attitudes and values to find their own.

♃ **in 11th** Jupiter in the 11th might suggest that in our social sphere we begin to have a diversity of relationships that expand our perceptions of companions that were internalized early in the sibling system. Here in a social context we have an opportunity to be freer of the attitudes and behaviours learnt in our early childhood relationships and therefore to be more open, explorative and inquiring.

♃ **in 12th** In the family history there may be some religious idealism or spiritual principles that were not able to be lived out at the time. Inherited from the ancestry are spiritual urges and/ or inclinations to explore intellectually or physically that cannot be reconciled with the current familial mindset. The individual is usually guided by an ancestral spirit that seeks to express itself in a spiritual, scholarly or courageous way through the individual.

Saturn in the Family System

Traditionally, Saturn is the patriarch of the family. In Greek mythology Saturn, as Chronos, was the father of six of the Olympians; one was Jupiter (Zeus), who would become the supreme ruler. As a father figure Saturn is not personal like the Sun, but more socially focused on the rules, standards and customs that need to be respected in the culture. In the family system Saturn is experienced more as the authoritarian or traditional parent. And its dynamic aspects to any of the personal planets often suggest that the regulations and decrees of Saturn may have first been encountered in family life. The archetype is complex in that its nature is feminine, yet it may be experienced harshly as a result of its consequences and penalties for breaking the rules. In family life it represents boundary-making and authority. Saturn is also the process of maturation and ageing, and addresses attitudes towards the aged and respect for the older generations in the family.

☽♄ Saturn is often regarded as conditional, whereas the Moon is often seen as unconditional; therefore this combination seems to suggest that there are rules and regulations bound up with care and nurturing. Often the bonding between mother and child may be interrupted due to complications or difficulties with feeding or caretaking. When this occurs, mother's anxiety may be absorbed by the child. When attachment is complex, love may be felt as being conditional and dependent upon the 'right' response and behaviour. Mother's set of laws has a strong impact on the child's sense of security, so they need approval and mirroring from mother to know that they are doing what is appropriate.

☉♄ Two influential archetypes combine to characterize father as a strong authoritarian and disciplinarian. Regardless of how this may have played out, the inner image of the personal father is entwined with the conditionality of rules and performance. Father's approval and acknowledgement are very important to secure inner confidence and build strength of identity; therefore the father becomes an important model for defining and structuring the child's career. Whether father is physically present or not, he strongly influences the child's developmental sense of his confidence, well-being and vitality.

☿♄ Saturn, as the image of an elder or authoritarian, does not sit comfortably with Mercury, who personifies a younger, more versatile figure; therefore there may be a conflict between rank and privilege in the sibling system. This combination might suggest feelings of aloneness or exclusion within the sibling system. Or this aspect might point to a sibling who was overly critical, patronizing, depressed or excluded from the system. Duty and responsibility may become associated with siblings either through being responsible or having too many rules. Later this pattern might repeat in adulthood because of an earlier role of accountability. This aspect also suggests the sibling may have had the role of teacher, authority or parent to the other sibs.

♀♄ The developmental sense of self-worth and esteem is strongly influenced by the prevailing conventions and attitudes towards the feminine. In the early family life a strong attitude about the roles of women or the value of the feminine is imprinted upon the child. Therefore the child is often highly sensitive and responsive to the accepted and traditional ways, feeling they will be unloved if they do not have the same mindset. The family folklore and rigid beliefs about the feminine and relationships challenge the individual's development of self-worth.

♂♄ The Martian impulse to act and go after what one wants is tempered by Saturn's reins. Rules in the family, the familial attitudes about responsibility and parental fear of consequences all influence the development of this aspect. When the individual is mentored and coached, the combination suggests the spirit is fighting fit; yet when overlaid with strict rules and potential penalties the individual's willpower is compromised. The familial attitude towards anger, desire and the masculine in general shapes the child's motivation and determination.

♄ **in 3rd** Saturn in the 3rd house is analogous of an only or elder child. While this may not be the literal birth order, the child often feels they have been placed in positions of control and responsibility too early. There is often an early sense of aloneness or separateness from others, which is often exacerbated by the feeling of rejection from the sibling. The child may feel the necessity to become self-reliant and not have to depend upon others for support, encouragement or comradeship.

♄ **in 4th** The atmosphere in the family of origin is affected by its rules and regulations. While directives, boundaries and authority are essential in development, the child's security is affected by how consciously the parents enforced and regulated these rules. Familial boundary stones are fundamental for an inner sense of security; however this depends on whether the child felt these were stepping stones or roadblocks. Parental control is highlighted.

♄ **in 7th** Saturn brings its air of authority to the sphere of relationships here. Power and control might be an issue in relationships if the family atmosphere of authority was rigid and controlling. Saturn tends towards a more hierarchical position; in the 7th this parental relationship may be projected onto the partner, confusing the roles of parent and partner. Commitment in relationship is important and the stability or lack of it was first witnessed and experienced in the parental relationship.

♄ **in 8th** Saturn in the house of inheritance might suggest that the family inheritance is an issue; perhaps unfairly divided, mismanaged or fraught with parental control. On an emotional level this might suggest a difficulty in the expression of intimacy or affection in the parental marriage; on the other hand, it might point to a limited financial inheritance. However this works out, the consequences of how the family has expressed emotional closeness and financial values over time is highlighted.

♄ **in 11th** Childhood experiences of feeling alone could resurface through group participation in adult life. Feelings of aloneness when in a group or being responsible for others in the group may awaken the earlier experiences of being an only or elder child, having a lack of playmates in early years, experiencing an isolated family atmosphere, having much older siblings or having to shoulder responsibility when a child. With Saturn in the 11th the challenge in adult years is to consciously find support and respect from peers who value the individual's wisdom and guidance in the community.

♄ **in 12th** Saturn in the 12th house looks back upon the legacy of achievement in the family. Ancestrally there may be a myth of success that papers over the failures and lack of accomplishment. Therefore the child often feels compelled to be triumphant and successful for the family, forging a path not of their own design but built on ancestral expectations. The individual is sensitive to the performance expectations in the family and challenged to find their authority to forge their own authentic path in life.

Chiron in the Family System

Chiron is not a planet in the astronomical sense, but as a celestial wanderer it fits the ancient tradition of a planet. Like most other counselling astrologers I have found its influence to be essential in revealing dimensions of character not necessarily embraced by the other planets. In many ways Chiron is marginal to the herd of planets. Similarly, in the family system Chiron feels on the margins. This might be experienced as the family feeling peripheral to society or a member feeling foreign in the family system. Chiron is the archetype of the refugee, the displaced and the orphan. It also brings the themes of wounding and healing in the family unit and its aspects may point to an ancestral wound or an individual's healing journey within the system of the ancestry.

> ☽⚷ Chiron aspecting the Moon unites basic emotional security needs with wounding and healing. The lunar wound points to the early relationship with mother and the family system where safety and a sense of belonging may have been impaired. Mother herself may be wounded, having inherited the ancestral pain of feeling marginal or not fitting in. Therefore the child experiences the mother's isolation or depressions as rejection. Postnatal depression or family difficulties may have meant mother was disconnected from bonding with the child. Mother's ambivalence towards her role as caretaker may have developed during her pregnancy, leaving the child feeling emotionally unsupported, even drawing the child into complicity with her feeling life. The themes of dislocation and feeling foreign within the system run through the family.

> ☉⚷ When the Sun and Chiron combine, we could imagine that the familial wound might lie in the developmental relationship to the father and other solar figures. This aspect also points to father's own wounding and sense of being marginalized. His spirit may have been crushed through the process of living and this atmosphere overshadows the ability to be connected to him. Hence the confidence to be ourselves, to feel comfortable with our identity and to express our self in a creative and magnanimous way, may be wounded. However, this aspect could also suggest that a fostering father or mentor figure helps us to heal the

relationship to our own heroic self. It is outside the family system where we might encounter fathering.

☿⚷ Chiron in aspect to Mercury unites the themes of marginality with the sibling story. This might suggest feeling alienated or out of place in the sibling or family system. Later this might manifest as feeling on the periphery of our community of peers. Chiron is also associated with wounding and healing, and this may have been experienced in the sibling system. Literally, this image could suggest a sibling who is physically or mentally handicapped, an adopted sibling or the separation from a sibling through death or a schism in the family.

♀⚷ The wounding of the feminine in the family is highlighted. This would influence the attitudes towards female values, sexuality and roles. In the familial past there may be a dishonouring of the feminine position in the family which shapes relationships as well as the relationships between sisters and other women in the family.

♂⚷ The impulse to act is impeded by the fear of being wounded. This fear might be in the family atmosphere so the child learns to not be spontaneous or adventuresome for fear of being hurt. The familial wound points to Mars, the expression of anger and ambition and the will to strive for what one wants. This urge and willpower may have been damaged in the past, leaving its mark on the child's natural curiosity and spontaneity.

⚷ **in 3rd** With Chiron in the 3rd house the family images include an adopted or relinquished sibling, a step- or half-sibling, one who is not wholly part of the sibling system. Or a schism may have occurred. Again this may not be literal but the feeling is one of displacement and not fitting into the system. This might also suggest that patterns of communication in the family between siblings might be difficult.

⚷ **in 4th** With the archetype of the outsider in the 4th house of the family, this might feel as if the individual is an alien in their family of origin or perhaps the family itself was foreign to the culture in which the individual grew up. The family atmosphere is influenced by its marginality, whether that is cultural, racial or economic, and this impacts upon the child. Chiron in the 4th also suggests that the themes of displacement, adoption, immigration or loss of home or homeland may have an effect on the development of a sense of safety and security.

⚷ **in 7th** When Chiron sets in the 7th house, the individual may be vulnerable to being drawn to individuals who are marginal, displaced or wounded. How this individual relates to the injuries and wounds of others, and deals with their urges to heal and help was first mirrored to them through their parents' relationship. This will also redress the feelings of marginality and wounding that may have occurred with a sibling.

⚷ **in 8th** The family legacy may have been affected in a variety of ways; however, the underlying similarity would be due to familial displacement and upheavals. Perhaps emigration, divorce, separation and loss may have contributed to the emotional and financial inheritance within the family.

⚷ **in 11th** Chiron in the 11th is prone to recreating early feelings of marginalization in later relationships with colleagues and associates. However, it is in these relationships and with close friends where the familial wounds can be mended. Friends and associates can heal the wounds of feeling disconnected from others and can help to reshape earlier feelings of not belonging.

⚷ **in 12th** In the collective unconscious is an image of Chiron who may take the shape of an outsider, a wounding agent, perhaps a mentor or a healer. Whichever way the image presents in the outer world, the pattern of wounding and healing is carried through the ancestry. In the background of the family may be the unhealed wounds from migration, repatriation, adoptions, relinquishments, undiagnosed mental disorders, etc. The individual is sensitive to what has been left unattended and unhealed in the family ancestry

Uranus in the Family System

Individuality and independence are important hallmarks in the Uranian family system. Aspects of Uranus to the inner planets reveal the urge to be adventurous, to take risks and be emotionally self-sufficient. Whether these have been lived out in the family history or not, these characteristics want to be valued and experienced. Surprises and unexpected change may be part of the familial landscape. Uranus often accompanies adjustments and separation. Its aspects to the inner planets often suggest that changes or schisms may have been experienced in the family atmosphere. This archetype is often experienced in opposition to family life as its urge is to disconnect and be independent rather than to connect and attach.

☽♅ Uranus's urge for freedom does not always mix well with the Moon's inclination for dependency; therefore, we might suspect that in mother and her family are struggles between traditionalism and unconventionality. Often with this aspect there are female ancestors who have lived alternative lives, been activists and sought equality and freedom. There is a feminine legacy of intelligence and originality. However, this may not have been lived out by women of previous generations who had to relinquish their urge for independence and education in favour of motherhood.

☉♅ Uranus brings its extraordinary and unusual characteristics to the archetype of father. Literally, the father may be unconventional or chose an out-of-the-ordinary career or path in life. The father's legacy may have been severed or schisms and divisions may have separated him from his family of origin. Therefore what might have been cut off is the will and spirit to shine and be successful. There may be a pattern of disconnection with the father in the family; however, this also suggests the inheritance of an independent and original identity.

☿♅ Individuality, unconventionality and freedom are inherent to Uranus and therefore it brings this influence to the sibling stories in the family. We may have first experienced a sense of independence and individuality in the sibling relationship, yet on the other hand a sibling may also have been distant, aloof or cold.

This combination brings the human experience of separateness and separation into the sibling system; in this relationship we learn about our sense of a unique and independent self. This might also suggest the experience of different systems such as half-siblings, step-siblings, blended families, etc.

♀⛢ A thread of unconventional women runs through the family fabric. The combination of these archetypes suggests that value and respect for the independent feminine is part the family atmosphere. Yet, on the other hand, it may be the lack of value placed on independence and risk-taking that stimulates the appreciation of freedom and alternative relationships. The legacy of femininity and sexuality in the family is original, at times non-traditional, at others avant-garde. Familial attitudes to money and worth are also unorthodox.

♂⛢ Both archetypes are masculine in orientation and therefore represent the attitudes towards masculinity and male roles in the family. Themes of adventure, pioneering, competitiveness and bravery may be passed down through the family. However, if this archetypal combination has been suppressed in the family it could point to unexpected accidents, hostility and aggression with males in the family. An unusual relationship with a brother or uncle, perhaps an atypical brother figure, may also be part of the family landscape.

⛢ **in 3rd** Uranus's sudden and unexpected temperament may have affected early peer relationships including those with siblings. Never knowing what to expect in the relationship with a sibling, perhaps a sudden separation, feeling abandoned or an unusual relationship underlie this sense of apprehension. An underlying anxiety about the nature of relating may be brought into adult encounters.

⛢ **in 4th** In family systems theory, this combination would point to a disengaged family atmosphere where there is an emphasis on individuality and separateness rather than closeness. Either parent may have experienced schisms, divorce or separations in their family system which influenced their security in the family structure. Underlying the security and continuity of family life is the urge for independence and individuality as well as splits and separations from the past.

♅ **in 7th** The images of how two independent and separate individuals can forge a trusting and secure relationship would be first witnessed through their parents' partnership. Does separateness lead to divorce or does it open up new possibilities in relationship? Independence in relationship was also experienced with the sibling and these experiences will be brought into the adult relationship when Uranus is in the 7th house.

♅ **in 8th** As an archetype of independence, Uranus is not comfortable in this sphere of intimacy. Therefore this might suggest an early experience of separation or tension in the parents' marriage. However, this house is also the sphere of the family legacy and one of the inherited patterns may be the avoidance of intimacy due to divisions or splits in the past. This may also suggest an unforeseen inheritance or unexpected discovery in the parental or familial past.

♅ **in 11th** Perhaps, with Uranus in the 11th house, the freedoms and liberties that may have been denied or unavailable in the family can now be found through associations with others in the community.

♅ **in 12th** Uranus is unpredictable and often startling, so this may suggest unanticipated revelations from the ancestral past. As a familial motif it suggests that issues of independence, liberation and equality are highlighted in the familial system and the individual may feel a compelling urge to express this passion of individualism for the family. The ancestral history may include separations, losses and rifts that have ruptured the continuity of the family line.

Neptune in the Family System

Neptune suggests that the ideal of the family is important, even though the actual experience may be far from perfect. Creativity, spirituality and a heightened sensitivity to others are aspects of a Neptunian family life. Emotional understanding, compassion for others in the family and the community at large, as well as the urge to serve others, are all part of the ancestral ethos in some way. However there may also be many unspoken rules, ideals and expectations in the family that exert a great impact on safety. Themes of enmeshment, sacrifice, relinquishment and illness may colour the family atmosphere when Neptune is involved.

☽♆ When the two most sympathetic archetypes combine, it suggests that strong imagination, fantasies and expectations may be conjured up. In terms of mother this might suggest mother's dreams and visions for herself and her role as mother. The child is sensitive to mother's expectations and vulnerable to making her dreams come true. In the family there may be patterns of passivity or undiagnosed illnesses that represent past disappointments and helplessness. On the other hand, a legacy of creativity and spirituality is also part of mother's dowry.

☉♆ Neptune's pattern of invisibility may be connected to father; for instance, a disappearing father, one who was not there emotionally or one whose spirit was somewhere else. Or perhaps he was able to be a saviour and hero for others but not his own family. Father may have also been idealized in order to defend the loss. This also suggests that imagination and spirituality may be connected to father's legacy; if so, the individual's identity is caught up with the longing to express their inspiration.

☿♆ Neptune's domain is the vastness of the ocean and this image permeates the sibling relationship. At one level it suggests the multi-dimensional layers and boundlessness of the relationships, yet on another it suggests the lack of boundaries in the relationship. We may have first learned to sacrifice our sense of identity in our relationships by copying or mimicking the sibling. We may have idealized the sibling, yet this could also suggest a sibling who was ill or troubled. Either way, this may have left us feeling invisible. In adult life this might lead to an estrangement with the sibling in order to untangle the enmeshment.

♀♆ These powerful feminine archetypes have some bearing on family myths concerning women and their position in the family. This may range from being idealized to maligned; either way, the roles of women in the family may feel limited by these perceptions. The feminine carries the creative and spiritual impulses for the family. When these are denied, the feminine values are weakened and not valued, leaving women vulnerable to feeling invisible and misunderstood. However, when the family system embraces these values we can expect to find inspirational, imaginative and resourceful women in the family system.

♂♆ The pattern of anger in the family may have conflicted with cultural or spiritual ideals; therefore, the child may have learned to not recognize the feeling, to sacrifice it or to forgive others in order to avoid confrontation. This learned behaviour weakens the family system and its members, resulting in the child not knowing what they want or feeling they are missing something. A weakened vitality or lethargy in the individual may also be caught up in the familial pattern of not being identified or outspoken.

♆ **in 3rd** Neptune's penchant for both idealization and confusion is brought into the early environment of the family through the sibling relationship, whether that is with their siblings or a parent's sibling. This might suggest that there are misunderstandings or sacrifices in the system. The misunderstanding might fester and create a sense of estrangement. A sacrifice by one sibling to selflessly protect another might lead to either enmeshment or drifting apart.

♆ **in 4th** With Neptune in the 4th, the family atmosphere may have been flooded with dreams, yearnings and ideals that became washed away in the everydayness of family life. What are the expectations of family life that the parents carry and how much has the child absorbed through the family atmosphere? The family legacy may be one of creative potential and spiritual realizations; however, it may also be corrupted by illusions, deceptions and unrealistic beliefs. It is important for the child to be safely guided through the transitions from fantasy and make-believe into imagination and creativity.

♆ **in 7th** The romantic ideal of relationship is strong; therefore, there may be family myths around the parents' relationship or relationships in general. These romantic and idealized stories of perfect relationships may disguise the pain and disappointment in relating to others.

♆ **in 8th** Neptune yearns for the ideal and in the 8th this is focused on the ideal other who may have been unattainable for various reasons. As with its position in the 7th, this might speak about family mythologies around the parents' relationship or tragedies which occurred in relationships in the family history. There may be mystery and intrigue in the family background or a feeling of something being lost or absent. The family inheritance includes this otherworldly sense that there is something missing or misplaced in the familial archives.

♆ **in 11th**   With Neptune in the 11th, the task of differentiating between fantasy and reality in relationships is affected by how well the family created appropriate boundaries and consistency. Our dreams and ideals are tested in the more impersonal world of the social order. With Neptune in the 11th, soulmates and spiritual companions are found through friendships; perhaps the creativity and spirituality which we might have sought in the family can now be shared in social pursuits.

♆ **in 12th** In the house it rules, Neptune feels boundless and never-ending. In a family context this might suggest that finding ancestral records, facts and information may be shrouded in uncertainty and misunderstandings. But deep in the family psyche lie the imagination and poetry of the past which the individual may naturally express through music, art or spirituality. When the past is allowed to remain mysterious, the ancestors become muses for the channelling of beauty and the sacred.

Pluto in the Family System

Pluto is connected to privacy and secrecy, and therefore could symbolize secrets in the family system when in one of these familial positions. It might also reveal buried grief in the family past, losses not acknowledged, sorrow not accepted or feelings not allowed. Pluto does not always manifest in this way in the family system, but generally brings its realm of taboos, grief and power struggles into the family atmosphere.

☽♇ If Pluto aspects the Moon we might consider that the mother or the maternal line could be the carrier of a family secret. This mystery may even be concealed from the mother, who was shaped herself by what had been repressed earlier in the family archives by her mother or grandmother. Our astrological assumption would be that the secret is being transmitted through the maternal line of the family. Another pattern might be that there are losses and grief carried by the mother that affect the level of security and attachment. It is this history that exerts its impact on our feeling bonded and emotionally safe.

☉♇ In aspect to the Sun, our astrological supposition would involve the father and his line. This could suggest a secret about the father or one that is connected to his lineage, either a powerful or powerless mysterious father or father figures. This family story will impact our levels of confidence and self-expression as well as our sense of identity.

☿♇ When Pluto aspects Mercury, loss and grief may be connected to the sibling story; for instance, a sibling unmourned, a loss unacknowledged. Or there may be a broken taboo or secret connected to the sibling system in some way; for instance, an unwanted pregnancy, a secret only known to some sibs but not others, a dead sibling. Whatever the fragment is, it has helped to shape our freedom to communicate and join in.

♀♇ Venus-Pluto aspects signal the potency of feelings aroused through the relationship with women in the family, perhaps with a sister figure. These strong feelings might be focused on jealousy, envy or betrayal. A secret love, passionate relationship or love denied may influence the parental or other relationship in the family. This could also suggest the feelings of betrayal of the feminine in the family as well as the familial attitudes towards values, money and possessions. The feminine narrative of sexuality and power, love and desire, beauty and value are important in the family history. The way that this has been honoured in the past influences our orientation to this archetype and to the females who embody this for us.

♂♀ This powerful combination alerts us to the relationship with brother figures, such as uncles, family friends, etc. This might suggest power struggles between brothers or masculine attitudes in the family that strongly influence the individual. The masculine sagas of competition and triumph, aggression and direction, fight or flight are important to consider in the context of family history. The way that these motifs have been honoured or dishonoured in the past influences our orientation to this archetype and the males who embody this for us.

♀ **in 3rd** When in the 3rd house Pluto suggests a secret about a sibling or a secret shared by siblings, even a secret known to everyone but a sibling, or suggests that the sibling system is forced into colluding over a secret. There is intensity in the relationship to siblings or early childhood friends, perhaps due to a crisis or loss that occurred early in the system.

♀ **in 4th** Pluto in the 4th may point to a family secret that affects feelings of security and honesty. This secret may not even be conscious, yet its mystery infiltrates the family atmosphere. This might suggest too that there is a pattern of loss or grief that affects the stability of the family, such as a death or sexual tension that pervades the home. Pluto's pattern is brought into the familial sphere through the 4th house where the foundation stones of security and safety are laid down.

♀ **in 7th** Pluto in the 7th could describe something that is undisclosed in the parental marriage or the loss of a significant other in the life of one of the parents that influences their partnership. The impact of the parental relationship on the child will be reflected in the way the couple dealt with crisis and how they handled honesty and integrity with one another.

♇ **in 8th** Here, in the 8th, Pluto might suggest a secret from the past about intimacy or inheritance affecting the family. There may be feelings of betrayal or loss that affect the levels of intimacy in the parents' marriage. Pluto in its own house suggests opening up the family closet which might contain some taboos and skeletons that are ready to be released. Excavating the deeper layers of the family may reveal hidden resources and wealth that can be brought to the surface.

♇ **in 11th** Pluto in the 11th could describe a social taboo, perhaps a secret alliance, that may have occurred outside the family circle but which affected the system's atmosphere. Loss and grief that are experienced through friends and colleagues may trigger earlier grief from the family of origin.

♇ **in 12th** Adrift in the 12th, Pluto suggests the shadows of secrets and shame buried in the familial history. It might refer to unexpressed grief, unacknowledged deaths or shameful taboos that have been violated in the annals of the family. Life and death are often entwined with Pluto, and these life and death issues may be an aspect of the ancestral environment. Researching the family history is a conscious way to acknowledge the ghosts of the past and lay them to rest.

One final note is to remember the multiple ways in which astrological symbols reveal themselves. Planets may show familial patterns in other subtle ways, such as:

- Ruling one of the houses of endings (the 4th, 8th or 12th house)
- Ruling one of the houses of relationship (the 3rd, 7th or 11th house)
- Ruling the 10th house
- The planet in a sign sympathetic to familial issues, such as ♊ (sibling issues and experiences) or ♋ (familial issues and experiences)

CHAPTER 12
THE MOON
Love, Attachment and the Lunar Landscape

However providence has arranged it, your family is where you forged your earliest relationships, took your first steps and first experienced an attachment to another. Attachment or the experience of secure bonding has a decisive influence on your capacity to feel safe enough to explore relationships beyond the boundary stones of your family. If you experienced a secure attachment, then being masterful over your environment was enhanced because of feeling safe and knowing you were loved. Attachment is developed day-to-day as a result of caregiving, through the participation in family rituals and belonging to the family circle. In the shelter of a safe nest, and with adequate protection, a greater sense of self is developed by mastering individuality alongside a sense of belonging.

The Moon, as the symbolic vessel of our earliest feelings and reactions, contains our felt experiences from our first bonding rituals and familial experiences as well as all the impressions inhaled in the family atmosphere. The effects of our lunar attachment may vary widely from an internalization of love and security to an interior sense of rejection or abandonment. The Moon suggests our own personal feeling life yet it will have been affected by ancestral and familial feelings that have permeated the family atmosphere.

Hence the Moon is of prime importance in childhood. For the rest of one's life it is always symbolic of the inner infant. The family atmosphere and the attachment to the caregiver influence our earliest experiences. As the memories of these times are preverbal, lunar contents are imaginative and feeling responses, not rational or cognitive. Changing emotional climates, which might be registered as a feeling of being unsafe or insecure, are harboured by the Moon. Issues of survival, dependency, feelings of safety and security, nurturing and feelings of helplessness are issues constellated around the lunar archetype; hence in adulthood these may be some of the issues triggered by transits to the natal Moon or as the progressed Moon moves through the horoscope.

First Love, Mother Love

Astrological tradition associates the Moon with mother. Psychological theory has well documented the psychodynamic imprint of the mother bond upon the emotional security and social adjustment of the infant, as well as the impact this brings to maintaining intimacy in adult relationships. Astrologer Howard Sasportas used the chapter title 'First Love' in his exploration of the Moon.[70] The inspiration for the title came from Maggie Scarf. When speaking of the mother-child bond, she suggested:

> But it is in this *first love* relationship of existence that the immature human will have developed a crude template, or pattern, for being in a loving relationship.[71]

Sasportas draws our attention to how our natal Moon reveals the mother-child bond. Set in this early bond is the blueprint for our adult attachments, the Moon being the container for our childhood memories of affection, connection, tenderness and warmth, plus all the emotions associated with these states, whether they are hope, fear, joy or disappointment. 'Mother love' is an important aspect of the lunar landscape and, when analysing the natal Moon, we are capable of glimpsing and better understanding the instinctual and unconscious reactions that we carry towards attachment and intimacy in our adult lives.

Of particular interest is attachment theory, which explores the early terrain of mother-infant bonding, pioneered by Mary Ainsworth and John Bowlby. *A Secure Base*, a lunar turn of phrase, was the title of one of John Bowlby's more popular books.[72] In it he outlines his attachment theory, which basically asserts that secure bonding develops the capacity to safely explore beyond familial borders and initiates us into the world of relationship beyond the family. Attachment theory rests on the premise that if the individual experiences a strong place of safety, then mastery over the environment is more easily achieved.

The Moon is the most personal and embedded of all the astrological symbols. Due to its fast speed, it completes its revolution of the zodiac in just 27.3 days. This means that during the first 27.3 days of our life, we experience the Moon in every astrological variant possible within our birth charts, initiating us into our lunar temperament, a deep symbol of what stays habitual and instinctual in us. The Moon is the recorder of our earliest feeling impressions. In the family system it is important as it suggests the atmosphere of early life and the home, the extent of nurturing and bonding, and the ability to feel held and contained in an atmosphere of safety.

The Lunar Legacy: The Vast Influences of the Moon
From the context of the family, our lunar legacy helps us to reflect on how we might attach authentically and what we need to feel secure. While this may not have been the familial experience, it becomes important to re-parent this part of the self in adult relationships. While the Moon might symbolize the external images of belonging, home and security, it ultimately reveals the authentic way to find solace and comfort in the depths of the self. Here are some lenses through which to view the lunar legacy.

Attachment Figures and Caretakers
Attachment is the early experience of emotional security and the inner development of safety. Mother is usually the first attachment figure. However, in complex situations another caretaker, such as an adoptive mother, father or mother-substitute, may emerge as the attachment figure. The Moon sign and aspects to the Moon evoke images of attachment and the way the child felt bonded to the family in childhood, which contributes to the fund of emotional security that can be accessed in later intimate relationships. The Moon holds the secure and nurturing feelings experienced through the process of attachment with our caretakers and later our intimate others. In a way we might think of the Moon as being first love, the footing upon which other attachments through life are built.

Secure Attachment; Bonding and the Ability to Separate
Separation is intimately linked to bonding. The ability to separate without destructive emotional undertones is a product of a secure attachment, so the more secure an individual feels, the more likely it is that they are able to separate without negative undertones or agendas. Aspects to the Moon reveal the propensity for secure attachment and therefore the ability to separate successfully. The Moon alerts us to the possibility of complications in attachment, bonding and separating, which influence the capability to feel safe

and secure in ourselves and, by extension, the world. The degree of secure attachment experienced early in life influences the way we bond and separate throughout our adulthood. Stressful lunar aspects may point to attachment difficulties and the ability to feel close and connected.

The Primary Planet of Love

The Moon as mother love suggests the experience of being loved and therefore the ability to feel loved. From an astrological point of view, this luminary represents the primal foundation stone for our sense of physical and emotional security. This is the basis for the formation of adolescent, then adult, love, represented by Venus. Hence the awareness of Venus, which begins near puberty and matures throughout adolescence and adulthood, is enriched and supported by the Moon. As the earliest template for relating, the Moon underpins the progress and maturity of the Venusian archetype.

The Systemic Moon

The Moon represents the ancestral feminine; the women within the family of origin and ancestry. It not only suggests the legacy of the feminine within the family context but the feeling experiences carried by these women. Aspects to the Moon will reveal familial attitudes towards the feminine, especially attitudes towards mothering, caring and other intimate feminine issues. The progressed Moon signals entrances and/or exits in family life, changes experienced by its female members as well as emotional experiences shared by family members. In this way the progressed Moon is akin to a barometer of family life, often synchronizing with emotional changes that occur in the generational system of the family through grandmothers, mothers and daughters.

The Family Atmosphere

Aspects to the Moon, its placement by house and sign, as well as planets in its natural 4th house, symbolize the familial atmosphere. We might think of the family atmosphere as the moods and emotions, the expression of feelings and the extent of affection and connection within the family circle, as well as the patterns and complexes that are caught up in the matrix of the family. Those patterns which are unconsciously absorbed by the child can be excavated through a thorough examination of the Moon. The family climate or its weather patterns include the ethos, laws, attitudes, values, morals and overt or covert expectations within the parental home. In anthropology, the experience of being involved in a tribal unconscious was called the *participation mystique*. It is this 'primitive unconscious identity of the child with its parents' or the *participation mystique* which 'causes the child to feel the conflicts of parents, as if they were its own troubles.'[73]

Primal and Preverbal Feelings; Feeling Memory

Aspects to the Moon help us to imagine preverbal and perinatal feelings and images, even feelings or impressions experienced *in utero*. These images are not necessarily literal; however, the responses and reflexes are carried through bodily senses and reactions, dreams, visions, responses, illnesses, etc. These lunar feelings are also enmeshed with the mother or emotions within the family atmosphere at the time. The Moon records everything we ever felt, wanted, tasted, touched, heard and smelt, storing these psychic memories in the body. The progressed Moon in its second cycle through the horoscope, between the ages of 27 and 55, often unearths these earlier denied or repressed feelings, which are frequently part of the familial landscape.

A Secure Base: How We Secure and Protect Ourselves

The Moon symbolizes our deepest emotional patterns and reflects how we nest and protect ourselves. As previously discussed, this template is laid down in early childhood and is relived and reworked in our relationships outside the family. Reflecting on lunar topics, such as our feelings about belonging, our comfort with our literal home, how we might create our nest and living space, our eating patterns and habitual routines, helps us to reveal the effectiveness of our lunar safety mechanism.

The Home, Homeland and Familial Surroundings

The Moon is home, the external symbol of settlement and the feelings of being settled or unsettled. As the archetype of belonging, its placement in the chart symbolizes our instinct for place. Aspects to the Moon help to describe what is necessary in the home to reflect our inner needs. In the quest to belong, aspects to the Moon indicate how we might support our own need to settle down or journey further afield. Symbolically, the Moon is the home place, whether that is the country or family of origin, the home itself, the symbolic hearth or the place where we feel most comfortable and secure. Changes of residence, moves away from the family environs or homeland, and feelings of belonging and feeling settled are lunar by nature and reflected in aspects to the Moon.

Authentic Attachment for Inner Security
The family is designed to be the sanctuary, where the emergent and fragile identity is kept safe, where we learn to feel protected enough to explore our boundaries and eventually secure enough of them to leave the nest. In astrological imagery this is lunar geography. The Moon symbolizes the inner strongbox where these feelings and memories are stored. By affinity the IC, which is the gateway to the 4th house (the natural sphere of the Moon), is the touchstone for the environmental atmosphere of the familial home.

In the shelter of a safe nest, the fledgling learns to tell the difference between protection and intrusion. With adequate protection the child develops enough strength for exploration, knowing that the shelter of the guardian is within reach. A supportive survival instinct is fashioned from the container of the family, in which the child learns to distinguish between the sounds of safety and the sounds of danger. Hazard signals are developed which alert a physiological response to flight, away from danger and back once again to the safe haven of familial protection. Theoretically, as this secure sense is internalized, the child begins to distinguish protector from predator and gains a sense of self, distinct from the family refuge. Should the protector become the predator, the family is no longer a refuge and the child aligns with the predator in order to survive. The 4th house is not the safe haven the child needs. Therefore, along with the Moon and its aspects, planets in the 4th house are also vital in understanding the levels of inner security and attachment.

Attachment behaviour endures throughout the life cycle. Internalizing the capacity to differentiate the sounds of safety and the sounds of danger develops the faculty to recognize when it is safe to leave, knowing we can always return to the secure base that we have internalized. But in order to develop this base we also need the approval to leave. The watchful eye of the parent must also be an encouraging glance. Under the shelter of parental protection the caretaker facilitates the tenuous amalgam of the encouragement to explore and the safety of homecoming.

When feeling safe enough to investigate and leave, the child's return is hopefully greeted with praise and applause. Psychologically, this capacity to explore outside the matrix of the family can only come from feeling secure within its precinct. Astrologically, this suggests that the capacity to leave home successfully into the exploration of our creative potentialities, the 5th house, is drawn from the resources embedded in the 4th house. Astrological wisdom suggests that in order to gain a sense of self, as distinct from the familial terrain, we first need to integrate our lunar legacy.

Successfully Leaving Home – The Influence of Attachment

From his clinical studies, John Bowlby developed an early model of attachment theory which has been expanded and developed. His theory asserts that the facility to be separate is based on the premise of how the mix of attachment was experienced in the early years of family life. In astrological terms we might also begin to consider how the Moon in an individual's horoscope addresses the ability to effectively separate from difficult and/or non-supportive relationships.

His research led him to formulate the following three attachment styles, which are a way of thinking about the lunar legacy in familial terms. In amplifying his theories it becomes evident that aspects to the Moon, perhaps planets in the 4th as well as other astrological indicators, will help us to articulate not only an attachment style but the individual's needs and reactions to a particular attachment approach.

The first attachment style is *Secure Attachment*, which suggests that care comes when the child calls; therefore the child feels sheltered and safe enough so that images of being cared for and loved are internalized. The second is *Anxious Resistant Attachment*, when protection is sometimes available, sometimes not, setting in motion an insecurity in the child who then attempts to anticipate what will happen in order to feel secure. Safety is compromised and the child resists connecting as a means of self-protection. The third is *Anxious Avoidant Attachment*, which occurs when adequate caregiving is not present and therefore the child avoids closeness to save themselves from harm. What follows is a précis of these attachment styles.

- **Secure Attachment**
Adequate care comes when the child calls
A secure base develops when an atmosphere of safety in early childhood promotes exploration past the boundaries of familiarity. Encouragement to explore further, coupled with congratulatory applause on our return, supports our ability to meet the challenges of the unknown. The sense of home is internalized and not projected onto a place, an individual, a community or a lifestyle.

- **Anxious Resistant or Anxious Ambivalent Attachment**
Protection is sometimes available, sometimes not
With this attachment style, bonding has been compromised by feelings of ambivalence, anxiety and disassociation. Bonding rituals have been unsafe, irregular or neglectful; therefore the ability to separate or leave is compromised by uncertainty. If separation occurs, there may be a fear that safety is not possible; consequently there may be a reluctance to leave home or explore outside its boundaries.

- **Anxious Avoidant Attachment**
Adequate caregiving is not present
Attachment and bonding are avoided as a means of protection against feeling ignored or rejected. The child becomes self-contained and self-reliant. Attachment is dangerous as it renders the individual vulnerable to disapproval and hurt. However, if we can't connect, we can't separate. Therefore this influences the ability to engage in life and relationships outside the familial circle, as there is a difficulty in separating and trusting in the continuity of relationship.

Immediately on reading about these attachment styles, we might recognize that our own attachment style has elements of all three: ultimately, an attachment style is unique. However, the theory is presented to deepen our appreciation of the far-reaching effect of the Moon across the lifespan and the life cycle of the family.

Continuing the premise that separation and attachment are interconnected, three groups of separation can be categorized: Bond – Separate; Bond – Can't Separate; and Won't Bond – Can't Separate. In amplifying this approach to separation it becomes evident that embedded in the experience of the Moon is the ability to separate effectively. Since healthy separation is fostered by secure attachment, the lunar constellation in the horoscope is important to consider in cases of complex separation. Without secure attachment, separation might be experienced as an ending, leave-taking or a departure without any guarantee of return.

- **Bond – Separate**
Secure attachment facilitates a sense of belonging and feelings of nourishment, which assist healthy separation. The ability to separate functionally can only occur if we have been encouraged to explore beyond what is familiar and to have been acknowledged and highly praised for our adventures. A secure base supports the exploration beyond what is familiar, helping to create mastery over the environment, which is an essential component of secure development.

- **Bond – Can't Separate**
When attachment promotes dependency and symbiosis, the inability to separate becomes complicated by rigidity and the pressure to conform. A chaotic atmosphere engenders fear and anxiety because no safety net or secure base has been developed. When astrological archetypes prone to rigidity, enmeshment and chaos (Saturn, Neptune and Pluto) are in challenging aspects to the Moon, the tendency towards this style of attachment is heightened.

Saturn in difficult aspect to the Moon may evoke guilt when we feel we are not acting in a responsible manner towards those we leave. It may trigger self-criticism about being able to go it alone or even fear at how we may manage.

The Neptunian attachment style may constellate fears of being unable to survive outside the family circle or the fear that those we leave will be weakened by our departure.

Pluto signals the dread of betraying those we leave or being betrayed by those we trust outside the familial environs. A complex Plutonic attachment may also indicate the grip of a family secret that stops its members from leaving.

- **Won't Bond – Can't Separate**
  An inability to bond promotes disconnection, which is not separateness but a sense of cutting off from the bond of relating. When attachment has not been successful, the individual instinctually feels isolated, removed and unconnected. Separation has been compromised by the inability to attach. With this lack of attachment, the urge for space and distance is often heightened as a defence against the possibility of being left. Astrologically, Uranus in difficult aspect to the Moon might reveal this attachment style. Even the simplistic astrological statement of the Moon in Air could identify this dynamic.

The Moon and its natural habitat of the 4th house are the harbours where the identity feels safe, connected and in the right place. The Sun and its playground of the 5th house are the stage where the experience of being separate promotes creative self-exploration. Identity is broadly shaped by the astrological archetypes of the Moon and the Sun as well as their derivatives. Similar to the Water and Air houses, we might think of these two strands respectively as the sense of belonging and the sense of being separate.

We will now look at the Moon in each zodiac sign and by aspect to sketch the possible attachment styles revealed by these astrological signatures.

– CHAPTER 13 –
MOON SIGNS AND LUNAR ASPECTS
Attachment Impulses and Influences

The sign of the Moon illustrates what is needed to be secure in order to attach. In some ways the Moon is always childlike; therefore, in an adult context it is important to recognize these lunar needs so they are not unconsciously transferred into later relationships by expecting friends and partners to fulfil regressive needs. Unmet lunar needs contribute to feeling dependent. The Moon's sign reflects the qualities needed to feel at home and the needs that may come to the surface through living with others. The idiosyncrasies, habits and routines that are brought into adult relationships are a function of the Moon. One of the first ways to begin to consider the lunar legacy through astrological delineation is through the Moon sign.

☽♈ The Moon in Aries

The Moon in Aries suggests that love and playfulness are entwined; in other words, attachment is natural when caring and loving are accompanied by adventure and play. A catchphrase might be 'If you love me play with me, have fun with me, but don't control me', suggesting that when the strings that bind are secure, but loosely tied, there is more leeway for relationship. The felt sense of being loved and cared for is absorbed by the child when they feel expressive, curious and inquisitive. While fiery emotions might simmer just below boiling point, these are only likely to erupt when the child's needs are blocked or threatened. Therefore the Moon in Aries population is probably familiar with temper, as it might have blown a few times as a kid when they didn't get their own way or were told 'No!' or had to wait for what they wanted. Familial relationships are the training ground where compromise, being patient and staying emotionally present begin. In the family environs we also first learn about competition, winning and losing.

☽♉ The Moon in Taurus

With the Moon is Taurus, feeling comfortable, secure and sensing that physical needs are going to be met are preludes to bonding. Classically, the Moon is exalted in Taurus, as the rich fields, fertile valleys and luscious orchards of this earthy sign satisfy lunar needs. The connection between the Moon and the earth is strong in Taurus, highlighting the need for creature comforts, to feel well taken care of, settled and pleasured. Taurus's icon of the powerful bull is an image of domesticating the lunar needs because the harnessing and taming of the powerful ox settled nomadic life. The child needs a settled and secure base. Taurus ruling the senses suggests that the child is comforted when they are indulged and satisfied, whether that is through taste, touch, smell, sight or hearing. Feeling comfortable with the bodily rituals of life is important in developing self-esteem and personal worth. When these are not well managed then shame may be internalized and the child may overcompensate with food or possessions so as to feel comfortable. Attachment is facilitated through the relationship with objects, both animate and inanimate, that are comforting and secure.

☽♊ The Moon in Gemini

With the Moon in Gemini, the child needs to feel they have room to breathe before they are responsive to bonding. Space, whether that is physical, emotional or psychological, is important; ironically, as an adult they feel they need to be separate to have a perspective on relationship. As a child they need to feel the openness of space before they can feel the closeness of attachment. The Moon in Gemini, as with the other airy moons, has a complex and difficult psychological task because the drive for emotional security is constantly filtered through the lens of disconnection. Some of the earliest feelings recorded by this Moon may include an innate sense of separateness, space and distance, or a strange sense of dislocation; a feeling of being disconnected from where one is or where one settles. As a child, the polarity of separateness and closeness is bridged by variety, movement, sounds, light and play; as an adult, the duality is linked by conversation and communication. Bonding may evoke a sense of anxiety when the child feels smothered or unable to move freely, so attachment is promoted with diversity and change. Secure attachment is promoted when the child feels comfortable moving between the inherent duality of being single and symbiotic.

☽♋ The Moon in Cancer

Cancer is the natural habitat of the Moon. The element of Water suggests that feeling emotionally secure is intimately bound up with closeness. Hence the Moon in Cancer instinctively seeks attachment with the mother or close caretakers. A strong need to be protected and feel part of a clan is fundamental to feeling secure. There is an innate sensitivity to the mother's feelings and moods and a heightened vulnerability to the emotional climate in the family. If the deep need for safety and shelter in the family was compromised, so too was the natural ability to feel safe when being vulnerable and open. When the child feels unprotected or overwhelmed, they retreat into the hard shell that is their protection. Cancer is a Cardinal sign, suggesting that the child needs to act on their instincts, hunches and feelings. However, being so sensitive to others, they probably first learn to react to others' moods. Therefore, part of the lesson of attachment is learning to feel safe enough with their own feelings, especially when these are different from those they love. Dependency is a necessary aspect of family life and with the Moon in Cancer there is always a fine balance between taking care of their own needs and of someone else's.

☽♌ The Moon in Leo

Being born with a fiery Moon in Leo suggests that the inclination to attach comes when there is sufficient safe space to be expressive, adventuresome and playful. The inner image of feeling loved and cared for is stimulated when the child feels that someone is responding joyously to their being. A little bit of appreciation goes a long way, and the more applause, the happier they are. Being seen in a supportive way frees the child to be expressive, curious and inquisitive. As a child, warmth, tenderness and consistency, along with play, are essential for feeling safe and attached. The fires of affection and approval fan the flames of emotional closeness. Without this demonstration of love the child seeks attention by acting out, being difficult or unresponsive, and being caught in a narcissistic reaction. Instinctually the child is able to script themselves as the central character in a high drama if they feel left out. Demonstrating that they are loved, mirroring their creativity and reflecting back their accomplishments supports the development of a healthy self-esteem. As a child it was important to feel special, singled out and supported in creative endeavours and worldly goals. The child may instinctually lean towards the father for reinforcement and nurturing of their creative and expressive needs.

☾♍ The Moon in Virgo

With the Moon in Virgo, feelings of safety exist when the routines of daily life provide coherence and constancy. The child with this Moon sign instinctively needs order and consistency so as to attach, as there may be feelings of anxiety or apprehension when the rituals of daily living are altered. An adult can learn to adjust but an infant feels insecure when systems are chaotic; therefore this image suggests that secure attachment begins in the stability of a scheduled life. If there is no consistency, or if daily routines are changed too often, the child feels disordered and mistrusting. With the Moon in Earth these feelings are easily somatized: perhaps an upset stomach, nervousness or bodily discomfort. Virgo is an ancient image of the harvest maiden who knows the ordered flux of the seasons, the divisions of the year, the intervals and the duration of each phase. This is a metaphor for the child's need to know the rhythms of their life. The instinct is to order and introduce natural cycles into their life, and this needs to be supported early in childhood. Being attuned to the natural world, the child may react badly to synthetic and artificial fabrics, foods and vibrations because they need the nurturance and peace of nature. Secure attachment is provided through the natural environment, which includes the sacred rituals of home life: quiet time together, the respect of privacy and unaffected intimacy.

☾♎ The Moon in Libra

Libra, being an Air sign, needs space to feel comfortable but is also instinctively drawn to relationship. This sometimes seems paradoxical in adult life when they are in relationship but actively create their own space and separateness. With the Moon in Libra, attachment is promoted by relationship; if the first love is mother and the child feels suffocated by her, then this may seed ambivalent feelings about relationship. Having an innate instinct for relating, the child is prone to being partnered, whether that was with a parent, a sibling or a friend. To feel safe and comforted the child also needs an atmosphere of stillness and harmony. Their emotions are strongly affected by their surroundings, with their beauty, symmetry and aesthetics. It is difficult for the child to feel receptive and comforted when chaos, mess or clutter surrounds them. Therefore, one of their greatest learning curves in relationship is in accepting and coping with negative feelings, especially their own. What happens when feelings of anger or jealousy conflict with their ideals about relationship? The child feels insecure when someone they love is angry or upset; however, with maturity they learn to feel safer with these feelings, which ultimately help them to forge a more intimate bond with their partner. Secure attachment comes when the paradox of being close and having space is finely balanced in childhood.

☽♏ The Moon in Scorpio

Of all the Water signs, Scorpio is the one that occupies the interpersonal sphere of the zodiac, bringing its depth and intensity of feeling to adult partnerships. Instinctively, the Moon in Scorpio seeks an intense and powerful attachment and the first recipient of this strong feeling is the mother and the mother figure. Attachment is possible when there is a passionate connection and merger. Having a deep sense of closeness means the child is more likely to develop the ability to trust others and feel safe with their potent feelings. If this deep sense of merger was compromised, so too was the ability to trust by feeling safe enough to be the powerhouse that the child feels they are. Having such intensity of feeling, it is beneficial to express these needs without fear of reprisal. Sometimes the feverish feelings are potent, extreme or dark. When others react to these feelings in a judgemental way, the child senses that their feelings are dangerous. Scorpio is a Fixed sign. When water is fixed it can stagnate; hence holding on to these feelings implies that they might become murky, polluting the sense of feeling at ease and safe. Having the Moon in Scorpio implies a depth of feeling and need for trust and intimacy, yet not everyone is able to endure this level of emotional timbre. As a result, the child learns to emotionally discriminate and be circumspect; some might even say secretive. Therefore a secure attachment gives the child confidence in their deeper feelings and powerful instincts, allowing them to be honest in honouring their deeply instinctual self.

☽♐ The Moon in Sagittarius

Sagittarius, the third Fire sign, is often characterized as the wide-eyed adventurer, traveller and good sport. Some might suggest it recoils at the sense of feeling bound or hemmed in, and those with the Sun or Moon in this sign were probably born humming the tune 'Don't Fence Me In'. Therefore, with the Moon in Sagittarius, attachment is promoted when there is a sense of freedom. The enjoyment of freedom, wide-open spaces and foreign soil does not mean that they do not recognize the value of attachments; in fact, it is the anchor of attachment that allows them to be flexible and movable. Therefore as a youngster they might have conjured up images of walking across the Ponte Vecchio, climbing Everest, travelling through space or swimming in the Indian Ocean. These images of freedom reveal their instinct to venture beyond the borders of their familial and cultural heritage. Secure attachment comes when curiosity, feeling mobile and the urge to explore are satisfied. With the Moon in Sagittarius the child has strong images and feelings about what is possible, therefore promoting spontaneity, adventure and independence to build their faith in life. Ironically, with the Moon here, changes in residence, family conditions or living arrangements may occur early in life. But it is the way that these are handled in the family that make all the difference to feelings of safety. The child instinctually wants it to be an adventure, not a hassle. Among the child's emotional supports are optimism, positive thinking and faith; therefore, a secure base is built when these qualities are fostered.

☽♑ The Moon in Capricorn

In classical astrology the Moon rules Cancer, therefore it is in its detriment in the opposite sign of Capricorn. Detriment does not imply that the Moon is disadvantaged or impaired in any way, but suggests a different way of thinking about how the Moon functions through this sign. The Moon is fluid and reflective; Capricorn is structured and masterful. The Moon is dependent; Capricorn is more autonomous. Therefore, the challenge is finding ways to embrace these paradoxes so as to nurture the child's needs. With the Moon in Capricorn, love and respect are intimately woven together. Adult attachment is more likely when there is maturity, accountability and reliability. For a child, attachment is encouraged when caretakers are dependable, consistent and in control; the lunar needs are structure, containment and organization. The child is more receptive to bonding when there are enough boundaries to protect them from potential harm. However, early feelings of love and acceptance may have also been tinged with feelings of disapproval. If so, the child learns self-reliance and to depend on themselves because others may not be competent enough to meet their needs. Being attuned to discipline, authority and regulations, the child needs rules, limits and boundaries. However, in a household where boundaries are rigid, rules and regulations are ineffective or parental figures are irresponsible, the child reacts against their innate need for structure, having experienced anarchy rather than order. When the child feels that the parental authorities have been supportive and that rules have helped them to achieve their goals, love is not tangled up with control or achievement. As the need for acknowledgement and recognition is high, a secure foundation is laid down with the support and endorsement of authority figures who are encouraging.

☽♒ The Moon in Aquarius

With the Moon in Aquarius, the child's need for physical space, emotional stillness, intellectual stimulation and movement is high. When qualities like freedom and lack of restrictions are compromised, the child may have difficulty in attaching. When there is a highly disturbing or volatile atmosphere, they probably react anxiously, feeling insecure in an emotionally unpredictable situation. As children they find ways to instinctually defend against feeling overwhelmed or smothered. This may somatize perhaps as an allergic response or allergy; more often, it is expressed by creating ways to feel independent. One of the prime patterns of this Moon is to create enough space in life to feel independent, separate and singular. Without this they are inclined to push relationship away rather than invite it towards them. Therefore, a secure attachment helps to provide a smooth transition between periods of closeness and comfort with periods on their own. When this is successful the child learns to know the difference between personal and impersonal feeling. Born with a strong inclination towards humanitarianism and equality, the individual can often confuse their ideals for tolerance and humanity with a personal love. Or the line between first love and friendship might be blurred. Therefore, in the atmosphere where secure attachment can occur, the child learns to know the difference between their personal feelings and their altruistic ideals.

☽♓ The Moon in Pisces

Pisces is the Water sign that occupies the transpersonal sphere of the zodiac. These are the waters of the collective where the streams of familial, cultural and racial feelings become one. Therefore, with the Moon in Pisces feelings of love are flooded by images, impressions and reactions from beyond the personal realm. Hence from their earliest memory the child may instinctively seek out the comfort of being enmeshed with others, needing to feel at one with their caretakers and the environment in order to feel secure. And with this deep sense of merger they are more likely to develop an ability to feel safe. With such a high degree of emotional sensitivity it is important for the child to feel supported and guided to develop their creativity and compassion in healthy ways. Their propensity to sacrifice their feelings for the well-being of others, or to be invisible in the wake of what others want, needs to be well parented. If not, then feeling loved and secure is often confused with taking care of others, helping and responding to others' needs. Pisces is Mutable, implying that the feeling life is fluid, tidal, always in motion. Boundaries become an issue as the child might instinctually forge an attachment to someone in need. Since co-dependency is a natural part of the landscape of relating, it is imperative for the individual to be aware of how to differentiate their feeling responses. This begins in the relationship with the mother. Forging a secure attachment suggests that the individual recognizes their emotional responses and how best to direct those towards their own creativity.

Attachment Patterns Through Aspects to the Moon

Aspects to the Moon are our lunar legacies that describe the conditions of the past in the family, the habits, patterns and fate carried through the family system. The Moon influences the bottom line security systems shaped in the family of origin and brought into adult life. The Moon will describe the individual needs, which if not met need to be re-parented by the individual. While other lunar images in the horoscope suggest family concerns, the Moon delineates the important factors: the familial climate, the ancestral inheritance and family patterns and habits.

The Moon is also the gauge of our attachment style, illustrating how we attach naturally and how we form bonds and close relationships, building trust and safety. Aspects to the Moon suggest how attachment may have shaped our emotional sense of well-being, and also show how complexes or trauma that might have altered the natural bonding rituals, as well as how we might re-parent and provide safety for ourselves in adulthood. The extent to which we are able to attach is also the measure to which we can separate. Our quest for individuality and independence is ultimately bound up with the degree of our ability to bond.

From a familial point of view, attachment helps us to consider our felt experience in the family and the way in which a sense of safety was internalized as a result. From an astrological perspective, aspects to the Moon reveal the psychodynamic structure of attachment. Therefore, the planet aspecting the Moon needs to be honoured and acknowledged, as it helps to shape each individual's style of attachment. Theoretically, the more forceful aspects like the conjunction, square, opposition and quincunx highlight the obstacles to secure attachment which may be re-experienced in adult intimacy.

What follows is a way of thinking about aspects to the Moon from the viewpoint of attachment theory, first considering only aspects to the Moon from Mars outwards, as this is the first planet outside the Earth's orbit, symbolically lying outside the matrix of the family. Superior planets exert an enormous impact on attachment and separation, as by nature they exist outside the familial container. When in aspect to the Moon, the familial approach to the given planetary archetype will shape the attachment style and affect the development of autonomy and separateness.

Aspects between the Moon and the Sun, Mercury and Venus are, of course, also vital to acknowledge, as they certainly reveal heritage and essential signs in the family of origin. However, unlike the other planets they are bound to the orbit of the Earth and are not separate from this familial matrix. Therefore we will consider separately these astrological attachment styles and the way that these may lead to adult separation and relationship issues.

Aspects to the Moon reveal an instinctual way of being in relationship. Astrologically, any planet that aspects the Moon imprints the way we attach and our ability to be intimate. The more forceful aspects, like the conjunction, opposition and square, may suggest an attachment style that was first experienced in bonding rituals with primary caretakers, then re-experienced in adult intimacy. These aspects also imply that certain patterns of bonding and attachment were established in the family ancestry and these may not always support or nurture our personal need for closeness. When in aspect to the Moon, planets contribute to informing the attachment style and the development of autonomy and separateness which in adult years supports an ability to be intimate. Hence aspects to the Moon are strongly indicative of attachment rituals and patterns that influence our capacity for closeness, comfort and trust in relationships.

Astrologically we are a mix of various attachment styles. Even though one may be more prominent, the other attachment styles will be present at varying levels of intensity. This attachment style also influences the way we attach as adults; hence the Moon is a vital key to understanding the deeper needs and unspoken expectations we have of being nurtured and cared for in later relationships. Adult relationship is informed by our childhood experiences, which can be identified through our lunar legacy. This is presented as a way of helping us reflect on our early childhood experiences within the family and how these might still affect the way we relate, as well as how they may also reveal our own unique style and instinctual way of relating.

Superior Planets in Aspect to the Moon

The planets outside the Earth's orbit are known as 'superior'. This is not a judgement, but a category, and is a useful division between the 'inferior' planets, those inside the Earth's orbit, and those outside. In terms of Family Systems we might also use this division to suggest that the planets internal to the Earth's orbit may be more familial to the Moon which orbits the Earth. Let's begin by considering the lunar relationship to planets outside the Earth-Moon system.

☽☌ Moon-Mars Aspects

In the milieu of the family, Mars promotes the ability to stand up for oneself and focus on individual goals with the courage and strength to move forward. Aspects between Mars and the Moon may describe:

- Relationship with brothers
- Family attitudes to the masculine
- Aggressive patterns and expression of anger in the family
- Family stories of adventure and desire

Mars highlights how family members are encouraged to compete for what they want, assert their rights and points of view, as well as to be open and clear about their feelings. When thwarted, Mars is red with anger, builds up frustration and contributes to the individual's loss of energy and dynamism. When in aspect to the Moon, the interchange between individuality and belonging is highlighted in the family. The individual's will and the family's needs compete, and when the Moon-Mars aspect is stressed this may result in a collision.

When there is a secure attachment between the archetypes of Mars and the Moon, the parents encourage the expression of appropriate desires, self-assertion and using the will to achieve positive outcomes. The child feels able to express their individuality and their anger while still feeling they are loved and part of the system. Mastery and assertion are supported in the family framework, which leads to a healthier expression of anger and competitiveness.

When the Moon-Mars aspect is not well supported in the family environment, an atmosphere of passive-aggression exists, clouding the ability to express anger in a healthy manner. Or there may be a lack of clarity and decision-making which leaves the child to go after what they want in a covert or underhanded way. The script that forms suggests that 'if I go after what I want, love will be withdrawn'. A common family response to a difficult Moon-Mars is to split love and anger: 'If you loved me, you would not be angry with me' or 'If you are angry with me, you don't love me.' This confuses the child, who learns not to express their desires for fear of not being loved or accepted. When caught in this atmosphere of lethargy or lack of direction, the child may indiscriminately respond to the atmospheric changes in the system with the fight-or-flight response. When an insecure bond develops due to the lack of appropriate attachment, frustration and anger develop, leaving the individual vigilant and reactionary in relationships. This may also be complicated by a history of unexpressed anger in the family.

☽♃ Moon-Jupiter Aspects

The combination of Jupiter and the Moon suggests that social customs and values, beliefs and morals permeated the family atmosphere. The ethics and beliefs of the family have had an impact on the safety and feelings of belonging. These have included the family attitudes towards:

- Civil law
- Morality
- Philosophy and religion
- Educational expectations
- Foreign travel and living abroad

In the family setting, Jupiter promotes a liberal and extensive world view and in its aspects to the Moon it suggests that the family's acceptance of religious and cultural beliefs, human values, hope and faith in the future play a large role in the child's security and bonding to the family group.

When a secure attachment develops, the child is encouraged to think outside the box, to be accepting of all cultures and religions and to explore ways to extend their experience beyond the family circle. A faith in life is instilled, allowing the child to be confident in their beliefs and to trust in the future. This attachment style suggests being liberal, far-reaching and expansive.

When the family is limited by dogma, rigid beliefs and cultural attitudes, the ability to venture outside the safety zone of the family is impaired. The child feels a lack of vision for themselves and fears the world and its future. If the family dynamic encouraged a limited religious and cultural way of thinking, hope for the future becomes compromised. When family values have been short-sighted, the sense of security is minimized. Attachment then may be mixed together with false hope and cultural mismatches.

☽♄ Moon-Saturn Aspects

When Saturn and the Moon combine, the child becomes vulnerable and sensitive to parental restrictions and rules. The rules and regulations of the family influence the feelings of attachment and safety, including themes of:

- Natural laws
- Boundaries and control
- Authority, prestige and status
- Success myths
- Traditions
- Performance expectations and roles

Rules and regulations are an important aspect of family life, with the ability to perform, set goals and be successful being integral to the family atmosphere. The family ethos encourages the child to be a contributing member of society. When the attachment is secure this is experienced as setting appropriate boundaries to ensure safety and protection; however, with an insubstantial attachment the child may feel they do not measure up to the parental standards, leaving them feeling inadequate and unloved.

Rules, regulations and the consequences when the rules are broken help the child to set appropriate limits and goals. Boundaries ensure safety; therefore the child can feel empowered through setting limits and self-regulation. The predictability of family life encourages the child to feel in control and helps them to manage the gaps of aloneness. A positive attachment also internalizes a sense of autonomy and authority over one's destiny, helping to contain negative and sabotaging impulses and feelings.

When the attachment is inadequate, the child feels the rigidity of family life: rules and boundaries now are obstructions rather than support mechanisms. The parent is experienced as emotionally cold, adding to the child's fear of rejection. The child feels controlled and imprisoned through the enforcement of strict rules. When lacking the appropriate boundaries the child is unable to be in control, feeling limited and stuck. A lack of adequate fostering or authoritative guidance adds to the child's isolation in the family. The pattern that is then set in motion in intimate relationships is to feel that love must be earned. There is a need to be taken seriously; this often results in a mistrust or misunderstanding with lightness and fun. The fear of rejection and lack of optimism encourage self-reliance to the point of being unable to ask for assistance in intimate relationships.

☽⚷ Moon-Chiron Aspects

When Chiron and the Moon are in aspect, being foreign or marginal to the larger community is often a facet of family life, akin to that uncomfortable feeling of being a stranger in a strange land. Feelings of being an outsider in the family system, and in systems in general, include the themes of:

- Familial wounds
- Fostering, relinquishments and adoptions
- Loss of spirit
- Disenfranchisement and marginalization

The spirit of the ancestors and the choices they made regarding emigration and change, or a parental wound of displacement or exclusion, still affect the family atmosphere. For many this aspect might have been experienced as their mother's postnatal depression, a family separation, an adoption or emigration. However this presents, it suggests the process of attachment has been bruised by feelings of exclusion that infect the family atmosphere and feelings of security. This archetypal union is complex as it combines feelings of marginality with the need to be accepted, often resulting in a feeling of exclusion.

When the attachment is strong, the child learns to be heroic in the face of being foreign and marginal in the system. The parents encourage a healthy sense of feeling different and demonstrate the freedom in being foreign. A positive attachment helps to locate the inherited wound as a source of humility and depth, giving potency to the sense of being an individual.

However, without a guiding hand or forceful attachment, the child feels orphaned and disenfranchised from their family unit. A parental wound may permeate the family atmosphere with a lack of spirit, leaving the child feeling helpless and unprepared to become part of a greater community. In this way a pattern of feeling marginal and outside sets in, compromising the integrity of future relationships.

☽⛢ Moon-Uranus Aspects

Disengagement and separation are themes that resonate when the archetypes of Uranus and the Moon combine. Individuality and freedoms in the family influence the ability to attach and feel safe, including the experience of:

- Breaking traditions
- Disengagement
- Family schisms
- Disconnection

The possibility of a fractured or dislocated family atmosphere, or the lack of an unconditional bond, is suggested, whether it is perceived or real. Due to the inconsistency of security in the family, the conflict is activated between freedom and closeness, when one part wants to be separate and removed while the other part desires closeness and connection. There is ambivalence about being in relationship: one part feels connected but the other feels like bolting out of the back door. Individuality and independence are important family hallmarks, whether actualized or not.

With supportive attachment, the urge to have adventures, take risks and be emotionally self-sufficient was valued in the family matrix. Surprises and unexpected changes may have also been part of the familial landscape; however, this added to, rather than detracted from, the security of the family. The child is encouraged to be a unique individual in the family system and is given enough space and freedom to pursue what is important. The child is prepared for the possibility of sudden change and develops other support systems outside the family unit, especially peer groups and others with common interests.

Without adequate attachment, the disengagement of family life may lead to feelings of anxiety and disconnection. The child feels disconnected and separate from the family. Unprepared for sudden changes, the child becomes anxious that something unexpected will disrupt the status quo. The parents are seen as emotionally unavailable, unstable or absent, leading to an erratic attachment style in which the child feels unable to settle down and needs to keep moving to feel safe. Part of the ancestral denial might have been in not actualizing independence, rejecting intellectual pursuits or an inability to live outside convention. Scratching the surface of the family ancestry might reveal that the disowning of individual freedoms has contributed to a disengaged family atmosphere. When this continues, relationships may become erratic, with intimacy issues focusing on the pattern of freedom versus closeness and the split between separateness and belonging.

☽♆ Moon-Neptune Aspects

The ideal of the family is important. Creativity, spirituality and a heightened sensitivity to others are aspects of family life that were registered as important. Idealization and sacrifice are themes that influence our sense of safety and intimacy, including:

- Illusions and idealized loss
- Sacrifice and enmeshment
- Spiritual values and creativity
- What is missing, lost and unknown in the family

Unspoken rules, ideals and expectations are part of the familial language that impacts the child's level of safety. Therefore, in order to fit into unspoken expectations or live up to unexpressed ideals the child may learn behaviours that please rather than those that are authentic. Themes of enmeshment, sacrifice, relinquishment and illness may dominate the familial atmosphere when these two archetypes combine.

If the parental bond was secure, creativity and imagination are encouraged, helping to develop a healthy relationship between the inner world of fantasy and the outer world of reality. A sense of security can develop within a fluid and flexible family atmosphere, even without visible structures and limits. Perhaps some questions we might ask with this combination are: Was your family able to instil confidence in your improvisations and creativity? Are you able to feel secure with your own inner creative resourcefulness? Feeling understood and accepted allows creative feelings to be expressed, rather than relegating them to a world of make-believe.

However, if family bonding was enmeshed and attachment was weakened, the child may have felt overlooked and invisible in the family unit. The need to sacrifice independence and will for the sake of the unity of the family became an unspoken rule. This may have been due to an illness or tragedy in the family that demanded surrendering individuality to attend to the family. However it leaves the child caught up in a complex that cannot be unravelled and puts them at risk of leaving the family. A lack of boundaries might have discouraged development of a private or inner self. With familial difficulties, the danger of becoming psychologically stranded is increased, leaving the individual sensitive to either rescuing or being rescued. In adult attachment the pattern of sacrifice in relationship is continued.

☽♇ Moon-Pluto Aspects

Pluto brings powerful issues of loss and grief as well as taboos and secrets into the family system. Familial secrets and shame might be part of the family landscape that has been an unconscious influence over our feelings of security and belonging. These secrets include:

- Denials
- Neglect and abuse
- The power of love or the love of power
- Manipulation
- Grief and loss and incomplete mourning

Power and influence may have been issues in the familial past that have affected the integrity of the family. The familial need for honesty, trust and cohesion are strong, due to the ancestral denials and unexpressed grief that infiltrate the current family climate. When supported, the child feels protected from harm and part of a tribe that is bound by trust. Emotional honesty in the family encourages the child to be intimate and truthful about what they feel. Negative feelings may be expressed without fear of reprisal and the truth of one's feelings is not allowed to pollute the atmosphere. Grief and loss are acknowledged as part of the life cycle and the child feels better equipped to be able to let go and move forward with life.

However, when there is a weak attachment, power and control may be mobilized to suppress a secret. The child may develop in an atmosphere of secrecy and dishonesty, instilling a sense of shame, unable to differentiate between what is private and what is secret. Power may also be abusive in that it keeps the child from expressing who they are. Powerlessness induces rage, and therefore the family atmosphere may be polluted with rage and brutal feelings. The child feels vulnerable to attack and unprotected, learning to mistrust the world at large, which sets the pattern of mistrust in intimacy into motion.

Solar and Inferior Planets in Aspect to the Moon
When reflecting on the aspects of the Sun, Mercury and Venus to the Moon in the context of attachment, we could begin to think along the following lines.

☉☽ Sun-Moon Aspects

With aspects between the Sun and Moon, the child learns to bond and feel safe by being identified with and mirrored by others in the family. Aspects between the Sun and Moon may describe:

- The *participation mystique* with father; how strongly the child identified their feelings of safety with him
- The emotional atmosphere of the parents and their level of interaction
- The parental marriage
- Inheritance from the father's family
- Attitudes towards the feminine carried by the father's lineage

When the attachment is strong, the parent supports the child's development and identity, instilling a sense of confidence and achievement through active encouragement. However, with an inadequate attachment, the parent uses the child to mirror their own needs and is unaware of those of the child. This results in the child lacking an identity in the system and feeling unconfident unless they are echoing another.

☽☿ Moon-Mercury Aspects

Mercury and the Moon bring the patterns of communication and expressing the feelings into the family domain. Aspects between Mercury and the Moon may describe:

- Kin and connecting with family members
- Family ties, links and extensions
- Learning and communication patterns

- The sibling story
- Family attitudes towards learning

The child learns to feel safe and bonded in the family system through communication of their feelings. The ability to be open to learning is grounded in the family's attitudes towards knowledge. With positive support, the parent encourages the individual expression of feelings and asking for what one needs. The child feels secure enough to be open to learning new things and expressing their thoughts and ideas. However, when there is a lack of attachment, the child expresses the needs of the system, being the translator, go-between and deliverer of messages. The child's curiosity and urge to learn are compromised by the lack of security.

☾♀ Moon-Venus Aspects

These two archetypes bring feminine values into the familial experience. Aspects between Venus and the Moon may describe:

- Relationship with sisters
- Family attitudes to the feminine
- Feelings of worth and value in the family
- Familial stories of money, possessions and relationships

The child learns to bond through relationship and is sensitive to the values expressed in the family system, with the likes and dislikes of the parents being impressed upon the child. When the parents support a healthy sense of self-esteem, they mirror the child's attractive qualities and instil a sense of worth and value. Then the child's ability to choose what he or she likes is encouraged and supported. When the family system is dysfunctional, a male child may bond through partnering the mother, while a girl may feel unsupported by feminine values that have been denied in the family. The child feels they have no choice in what they like and feel unsupported in the development of their personal tastes and values

PART III
INTRINSIC FAMILY BLUEPRINTS AND RITES OF PASSAGE

St Mark's Square, Venice, 1954:
Mom, Dad, Ted and me

Family fate seems to be a product both of deeply unconscious archetypal factors, and also individual consciousness and responsibility.[74]
Liz Greene

– CHAPTER 14 –
FAMILY TEMPLATES
Order and Chaos in the System

One way in which we experience family fate is through our position in the family system. Birth order denotes certain roles and contributes to the formation of personality and individual characteristics while also influencing the life choices that we make. For instance, an elder child may be more prone to upholding the traditions of the family while a younger one may be more compelled and encouraged to break free from long-held conventions and values. The younger sister of a brother is more exposed to the competitive, aggressive and protective sides of the masculine, unlike the younger sister of a sister, who experiences feminine influences around her growing up. An only child inherits the fate of never observing a sibling growing up and is never witnessed themselves by a brother or sister. The only child is destined to be integrated into the adult world sooner than their friends who have siblings. The eldest child experiences an exclusive relationship with the parents, only to be forced to share this parental relationship with the next sibling that arrives; the youngest must share the parents from the beginning, never having the experience of being displaced by another sibling. The youngest is the eternal 'baby' of the family. Birth order and gender imply certain roles and give a unique orientation to life's horizon. Fate is already inherent within the sibling order and the gender of our birth but it also lives in the parental and ancestral stories which are the roots and sustenance of the family tree.

Our birth order and personal experiences of the family atmosphere help to determine the attitudes we will bring to accepting this fate. Our families are a system we may physically leave; however, they are not a system we can psychically leave, for the imprints of the family have been impressed upon the psyche through our participation in the family atmosphere and our sibling constellation.

Birth Order

Birth order theory was known in antiquity and part of the stories we grew up with. Myths, fairy tales, fables and biblical stories tell us of birth ordinance. The first sibling constellation in the Bible is Cain and Abel who are in conflict over their ordinal position in the family. The struggle between the firstborn and the youngest or last-born becomes a clear feature of the Old Testament. In Exodus, God unleashes ten plagues on the Egyptians as a result of the Pharaoh denying the Hebrews' release from slavery and Egypt. The last plague 'smote all the firstborn in the land of Egypt' (12:29). Birth order is part of our fate and a strong influence on the way we orientate ourselves to life, whether researchers are able to prove it or not.

In 1961, Walter Toman first published his theory and research on birth order in his book *Family Constellation*.[75] Toman furthers Alfred Adler's theories by delineating the sibling constellation in terms not only of rank but also of sex and size. He attempts to explore the difference between the older brother of a brother and the older brother of a sister, trying to include the variants of sex and sibship size as much as possible. He also suggests that when our position in the sibling system is recreated in adult relationships (through partners and friends), there is potentially greater compatibility. The relationships that recreate our sibling position in rank and sex have the greatest chance of a successful outcome. He applied the same model to friendship. Toman's findings were criticized for having too much of a theoretical base and not enough research. However, his work picks up the ancient theme of the brother-sister marriage and echoes the truth that astrologers already know about the houses of relationship, which link the sibling, the partner and the friend in a trinity. The truth of Toman's premise is also borne out in astrological chart comparison and synastry. Some features of the sibling's horoscope are often chillingly duplicated in the partner's horoscope. Toman's model of sibship position and gender taken into the adult world of relationship is a potent tool for viewing the immediate link between our adult relationships, with partners and friends, and our earlier sibling relationships.

Frank Sulloway's book, *Born to Rebel*, is his creation after 26 years of research and involvement with birth order. Because of its long gestation it has much more interest than most of the research conducted into birth order influences. It is an articulate and scholarly excursion through birth order from the Darwinian world onwards. However, the bottom line seems to repeat the constant theme that firstborns carry the parental and traditional expectations of the prevailing authority and that those born later are born to rebel and bring forth revolutionary thought. Firstborns find their niche by sabotaging change, while later-borns consistently challenge the established order.

There are countless methods of approaching birth order and many more theories as to what our birth position may mean. Alfred Adler pointed out that it is not only the birth order that dominates the formation of character but the atmosphere into which the child arrives and how this is interpreted. The family atmosphere, the attitudes of the parents, along with the dynamic of the inheritance of the ancestors, all affect the sibling system.

One of the first variants in birth order research is how we count the sequence of the siblings if the order has been interrupted by a termination, a miscarriage, neonatal or perinatal sibling death, an adopted sibling or a step-sibling? How old do children have to be before they are included in the sequence? I suggest that the labelling of the position is more important for the researcher than for the counsellor or therapist. The death of a sibling, whether *in utero*, at birth or shortly after, has an impact on all siblings. The shade of the child finds its place in the sibling constellation. The family atmosphere is altered forever by the loss of the child, no matter at what age death occurred. When there has been a schism in the sibling order due to a sibling death, life arranges itself in the position of those who have survived, but the unconscious life records the missing sibling. For therapists and counsellors, it is the sibling loss that is important to acknowledge and work with.

Generally, birth order is defined in terms of the firstborn, the middle child, the youngest and the only child. Other systems have delineated the first, second and third positions in the family with later birth positions being undifferentiated. Some systems have delineated a fourth position.[76] Karl Konig suggests that only three birth positions exist. He postulates that these three positions are repeated with subsequent siblings so that the fourth child is similar to the first; the fifth to the second; the sixth to the third, and so on.[77]

Astrologically, we can also offer a theory of birth order by applying the technique of the derivative house system. In this system we can locate anyone in the horoscope by deriving them from the house of the primary relationship, which is counted as the 1st house. For example, children in general are the 5th house and therefore the eldest child is located in the 5th house. The second child is the sibling (3rd house) of the eldest, and therefore is three houses from the 5th house (the eldest child), which places it in the 7th house. The third child is the next sibling and so we would count three more houses from the 7th, which takes us to the 9th house. To sum up, this system aligns the first child with the 5th house, the second child with the 7th house, the third child with the 9th house, the fourth child with the 11th, and so on. While on the surface this may appear contrived, this model is worth exploring.

5th House	7th House	9th House	11th House
Eldest	Second Child	Third Child	Fourth Child

It implies that the eldest child constellates the myth of the hero and is at risk of becoming the narcissistic mirror of the parent (the 5th house). The second child, aligned with the 7th house, is at risk of triangulation with the opposite sex parent when there is a dysfunction in the parental marriage. Often it is the second child who is most at risk in parental conflict, separation and divorce, as this child unconsciously displays the undercurrents of the parental marriage. Second children are more prone to taking on the role of mediator, negotiator or go-between, but also to becoming the surrogate partner. The third child, in the 9th house, is the explorer, the one who steps beyond the beliefs and mores of the family in a cross-cultural exploration that exposes the family to wider horizons.

Astrological themes are synchronous with birth order. For instance, a firstborn may be more prone to favouring Saturn and will often have a strongly aspected Saturn in their horoscope. Equally, those with a strong Saturn often behave like a firstborn. Later-borns favour the archetypes of Jupiter and/or Uranus, seeking adventure and freedom beyond the ordinary and familial. Or middle children may be at risk of over-identifying with Venusian or Libran energies in their sibling role of mediator and go-between.

Familiarizing oneself with the roles assigned to birth order will complement the understanding of astrological statements. To introduce birth order I have used four categories: the eldest, the middle, the youngest and the only child. There are multitudes of other factors that contribute to defining the birth position: gender, sibship size, age spacing, sibling loss, the family atmosphere, etc., so this can only be a general introduction. The second of *two* siblings will experience being the youngest very differently from the youngest of seven siblings. From the second child's point of view, the gender of the older child exerts a great influence. If there is an age gap of more than seven years (a Saturn square), this second child may feel more like an only child. All these factors should be recognized. Sibship size is decreasing while the phenomenon of step-siblings is increasing, thereby altering the destiny that birth order bestows upon us. Nonetheless, reflecting upon our own birth position can be highly evocative and can also illuminate a portion of our family fate.

The Eldest Child
Parents' expectations of both themselves and their firstborn child are high. By the birth of the second child, the expectations, idealism and fantasy have waned with the reality of actual child-rearing. Many parental expectations of the first child are overt; however, the firstborn is also in a position to constellate the unlived lives of the parents, to be imprinted with their unrealized dreams. Upon the newborn's shoulders rest the parents' expectations to accomplish what they themselves did not achieve and to possess what they could not have. Performance anxiety of the eldest child is due to the pressure to succeed, be productive and become a high achiever.

The eldest child is the first member of a new generation and, until a sibling arrives, the only member of this generation. The eldest is the focus of parental attention and the centre of the family. The first child receives more of the parents' resources and energy but the price demanded is to follow their values, mores, customs and traditions. This is why the eldest is often described as father-identified, aligned with the figure of traditional authority (equally, they could align themselves in direct opposition to the authority's values). This tendency resonates with Saturn, which is often a feature of the eldest child's horoscope. Certainly the eldest position comes with more obvious responsibility and traditional 'masculine' traits.

The pressure for the first child to identify with maintaining the status quo and continuing the familial traditions encourages the firstborn to be more family-orientated. Being first also encourages the solar qualities, as the child is the centre and at risk of becoming the narcissistic child who is called upon to mirror the parents' attitudes. With the Sun and Saturn highlighted in this position, approval, feedback, identity, self-esteem and getting results become important for the first child.

This position encourages a sense of responsibility and relationship to authority; therefore, firstborns are highly susceptible to rules, to keeping 'the letter of the law', and to seeing what is obvious but not always what is underneath. They often feel pushed aside when the next sibling arrives. Since their position has been usurped, they may continue to feel vulnerable and fear being dethroned once again in adult relationships.

The Middle Child
During the class on siblings in our Family Development programme, I break up the group into the four categories we are now examining. The firstborns gather together quickly, follow the instructions and ask how long the exercise will take. They go off to find a place to meet – usually *my* consulting room. The youngest ones usually end up outside, laughing, swapping stories of who was the most brutalized and how they managed to rebel and annoy their sibs. Ironically, there is often one only child in the class, so they join the eldest group. But the middle children remain in the seminar room and keep wondering what is happening with the other groups. 'I bet the youngest ones are having lots of fun', someone inevitably says.

Middle children identify themselves through the eyes of the other; when growing up this was through their older and younger sibs. The eldest and youngest are more vocal and demanding when asserting their needs, which often leaves the middle children feeling withdrawn or solemn. Parents frequently mistake their quietness or self-absorption for their ability to take care of themselves, when in fact they may be feeling withdrawn or depressed. The middle child feels left out, suspicious of what they have been missing. They often describe the sense of not knowing where they stand, being invisible or caught in the middle.

The middle child is in the position of the peacemaker and mediator. They are younger than the eldest sib, who they want to emulate, yet older than their younger sibs, for whom they may feel responsible. They are able to see both sides of the argument and have a difficult time in choosing either side. Conflict and confrontation may seem difficult and they are compelled to try to avert confrontation, not only with themselves but also between others. They may appear to be getting on with the task or amusing themselves, but this may be more a sense of resignation. Often middles will describe a sense of confusion as to their role and direction in life, and envy of those who seem to be surer of themselves. This envy may be a remnant of their childhood feelings for the elder sibling, who appeared to have more resources and parental support and guidance.

The middle child can often identify with the feeling life that is flowing underneath the family. The second child is particularly vulnerable to undercurrents and family alignments. The second child of only two siblings is often in two positions: being the youngest, but also being the intermediary or third party! In this way they become the emotional caretakers of the family, highly sensitized to someone feeling left out or something amiss in the family atmosphere. They may tend to instinctively act out these feelings or spontaneously respond to someone's needs. The second and middle children are both at risk of fulfilling the unspoken needs of others at the expense of their own, and becoming enmeshed in the hidden agendas of their other sibs.

Here the lunar temperament may be emphasized, as well as a stronger identification to the mother. The second or middle child is also attuned to the energies of Venus, as ruler of Libra, in the capacity of mediator and relationship counsellor for the family. Mercurial energies are called forth in the second and the middle child. These energies are needed to outwit and trick the elder child. A sense of humour and a resignation as to the way life is often accompanies this position.

The Youngest Child
The youngest child in the family is in last position and is the only sibling in the system who will not experience having younger sibs. The arrival of a sibling is a jolt to consciousness, bringing recognition of differences and separateness. The youngest does not have this experience and is often typecast as the baby of the family, which has both its privileges and its burdens.

The youngest is pampered with a ready-made support system. By the time the youngest arrives, family members have begun to find their niches and there may be a more relaxed atmosphere to child-rearing, so the youngest is often less supervised or less bound by parental rules and expectations. This greater freedom is often a contentious issue for the other siblings. However, the youngest child can also be the one who is ridiculed, bullied and scapegoated by older siblings. Their size and low status through the earlier years may make them the brunt of the elders' jokes. The youngest may be the common shadow figure for their older undifferentiated siblings. This is a common theme in fairy tales: the youngest son is the simpleton who is able to do what his older brothers cannot; the youngest sister is tormented by her elder sisters, but then released from her suffering and transformed into a beauty. The elder shadow siblings are the agents of individuation for the younger child. Youngest children carry the archetypal role of being challenged by tasks and trials, and of struggling to individuate, which will encourage them to move further afield than the others.

Myths also portray the youngest child as the carrier of the new order, confirming the old adage 'the last shall be first'. Both Chronus and Zeus were the last children in their sibling system, and they led the coup against the old order by establishing the new. Youngest children strive to extend themselves beyond the familial horizon. Through education, experimentation and travel, they reach beyond the family beliefs, values and customs. Their quest beyond the familial limits often leaves them confused as to where they belong. They challenge the status quo and rebel, bringing something new into the family. This revolutionizes, or at least challenges, the family beliefs and traditions. Youngest children struggle against their siblings' and parents' resistance in order to achieve their independence.

Having had no followers, the youngest child may compensate for this with their friends and in social situations. They are sensitive to the underdog and the 'have not's, befriending the powerless, and encouraging and supporting the underprivileged. This overcompensation as leader or saviour contributes to their vulnerability and tendency to be taken advantage of. They know what it feels like to be last and smallest, often overcompensating by becoming extroverted. Within the family, the last child can also side with the sibling or parent they regard as being powerless or oppressed, supporting the one they identify as the victim or disadvantaged one. A youngest child will also be at risk of being triangulated in an unhappy marriage, easily enmeshed in the parental battles, championing the underdog, especially if cast as mother's son or daddy's daughter or one of the parent's favourites and allies. The last child left at home is in danger of feeling that they have to protect and rescue a parent if there is marital discord, or if they are in a single-parent family, or when a parent is ill or unable to cope. In a family where the power imbalance between the parents has created an unhealthy situation, the youngest may have been parented by older sibs, thereby making separation from them difficult.

In childhood the older sibs always appear bigger, more capable and better adjusted. This attitude is often internalized in the youngest child. They can see the elders' attributes yet not their own. They are often surprised in adult years to find out that their sibs admired their personality and achievements when they were younger. Youngest children are the last to arrive, the last to take or find their place, and this may be a recurring theme throughout their lives. Often they are confronted with having to fight for their space or claim their place. Youngest children have more access to the archetypes of Jupiter and Uranus. In a system where everyone is older, more established and has more resources than they do, the youngest child feels the need to venture into other worlds to explore how others live. The urge to move further afield brings them in contact with their spirit of revolution and rebellion and their fate of founding the new order.

The Only Child
Only children are similar to eldest children in that they experience parental attention and adoration exclusively without the interruption of another sibling. Unlike the eldest, they do not experience being replaced or dethroned or the potent confusing feelings that accompany the arrival of a younger sibling. Winnicott suggests that an only child misses the experience of their mother going through the stages of pregnancy and the mysteries and secrets of child-bearing. But even more importantly, an only child does not feel the powerful emotions evoked when a new sib enters the family: '… and the only child's relative lack of opportunity for expressing the aggressive side of his nature is a serious thing.'[78]

Siblings draw out powerful feelings of love and hate. The only child does not have the sibling system in which to experience the ambivalence and polarity of feelings – to be able to experience powerful negative feelings that do not destroy relationship. This could contribute to the fear of expressing negative feelings, being confronting or angry in later relationships. As Winnicott suggests, the competitive and aggressive instincts do not have the safe container of the family and may spill out into the schoolyard. Observers studying the ramifications of China's one-child policy suggest an increase in aggression and bullying and a difficulty in sharing. It seems that the only child must find avenues to express their aggressive instincts and power with peers. A younger schoolmate may have to become the surrogate sibling. Growing up without siblings also suggests that only children do not have to share toys, clothes, valuables and especially the parents. Therefore, the issue of sharing and ownership may become a pattern throughout their adult relationships. There is also no division of labour or the tasks that are often shared with a sibling in family life.

The sibling is an archetypal image and a part of each individual's psyche. We need a caretaker, but not necessarily a sibling, to survive physically. However, to develop psychically, we need the sibling image. This image in an only child helps to compensate for the loss of a sibling, with the friend acting as a replacement sib. Friends become ultimately very important for an only child and it is the friends from childhood who became the surrogate siblings. In many cases of only children, I have seen fate arrange it so there is a replacement sibling: a cousin, a lodger or a neighbour. The inner image of a sibling is activated towards breaking the isolation the only child feels. With the increase in the number of only children and the rise of day care for working parents, the children at the day care centre are the surrogate siblings. Friendship is the sphere in which the only child will most likely find a surrogate sib, and therefore the attachment to friends is strong. Near the end of the natural life cycle, the only child may be left with no original family members, which stresses the importance of friends as familial substitutes.

An only child may have difficulty in separation and leaving home. There has been no opportunity to separate from a sibling while still experiencing the continuity of life. Siblings help to mark important separations and transitions in the earlier years. Separating from a parent is much more difficult and threatening for the only child, and often means that the initiatory phases of late adolescence and leaving home are traumatic. In adult relationships I often find that only children have difficulty in leaving relationships that are unhealthy, since there are few images to help them trust that life goes on after separation. An only child has no sibling allies to fight with against the tyranny of parental power or the oppression of the parental ruling class. The family atmosphere may also be ripe for triangulation. With an unhealthy parental marriage, the only child feels trapped and often responsible for taking care of the 'abandoned' parent. The only child also feels the full responsibility for an ageing parent's care, having no siblings to share this responsibility with. Nor are there siblings with whom to share the grief of parental loss. The only child may also be prone to wanting their mother to be a sister, thereby creating role confusion. With this high tendency towards enmeshment, separating is risky. Adler also echoed this when he suggested the only child was prone to a 'mother complex', for the only child has the exclusive focus of the mother.

As parents themselves, only children may experience difficulty in understanding their own children's relationships and unconsciously collude in keeping siblings separate from each other. They may be devastated by conflict amongst their own children since they have not had this sibling experience themselves.

Some only children blossom under the spotlight of the parental focus, not having to share their attention, aware that they are the sole beneficiaries of the parental legacy. However, this rich legacy is a singular one and sharing a life with a partner is often when the difficulties arise.

Only children grow up in a familial environment populated by adults and are prone to becoming strongly identified with the parent. They are conscious of rules and social customs. From an early age they are sensitized to Saturn. While this archetype may represent an only child's ability to perform well in the world, Saturn often symbolizes both the self-preservation and the loneliness of an only child. Only children may have access to all of the parents' resources, but they may also wonder why there is no sibling with whom to share this. They may feel they have missed out. This missing seems to be part of the myth of being a sibling, but the only child has the literal experience of it.

Following Our Orders

Alfred Adler first drew our attention to the fated role that birth position plays in our lives. As parents we are prone to replicating our sibling experience with our own children, being particularly sensitive to the child who mirrors our own birth position. Our experience of our position in the sibling system is taken into our adult relationships, associations, friendships and marriage. Birth order is taken into the workplace. Elder children strive for recognition, status and leadership positions, often becoming depressed when they realize that what they have achieved does not feel authentic because it was motivated by an urge for parental approval rather than their own creative impulses. The middle child shapes the atmosphere of the organization, creating links between the employees and promoting intellectual and social stimulation. And the third or youngest may feel left out or marginalized, yet they inject revolutionary blood into the organization. Being conscious of our birth position and the arrangement of our sibling constellation may help us to become aware of the roles and expectations assigned to us and the personality forged from this. We then may be freer to shift our perspective.

Dysfunction

We have been exploring fate and the family. Perhaps we might rephrase it as 'family *is* fate'. This statement becomes acutely evident when we consider a child born into a dysfunctional system that unconsciously repeats inherited negative patterns. Relationship complexes and patterns repeat through families, but what goes a long way to relieving the pain and trauma embedded in these recurring patterns is consciousness, acceptance, understanding, communication and forgiveness. While we may feel handicapped by past familial and ancestral disturbances, consciousness helps to temper this inheritance.

When a family is caught in the grips of its fate it operates instinctually, automatically repeating its pattern of complexes. A family caught in its dysfunction is often identified through its high level of anxiety. Because there is no secure base the family atmosphere is highly charged with anxiety and hyper-vigilance as a way to try and control the uncertainty. The family mood is anticipatory, trying to anticipate what *will* happen, rather than participate in what *is* happening. Boundaries may be lacking or highly rigid; either way, rules and regulations are not supportive of the real self. In a dysfunctional atmosphere, control becomes an important defence against the powerlessness and shame which are often prevalent due to the child's feelings of not being good enough. There may be a great need to get it right; however, what is 'right' disregards the child's sense of freedom. The family becomes locked in a system that repeats the denial of feeling free and its children inherit a fate they must become conscious of in order to regenerate their authentic selves. Without this awareness they are prone to blaming others, which is another characteristic of dysfunction.

Dysfunction in families is generally accompanied by shame. When shame lies beneath the family ethos its members feel impoverished, not good enough, lacking. Individuals who are fostered in a shame-based or a shame-bound family often feel the need to be in control or to blame others for what is or is not happening – any strategy to deny the feelings of anxiety and fear.[79] A perfectionist streak keeps them trying to always do the right thing. Shame is a powerful influence that often has its roots entangled in the familial past and keeps its members feeling unacceptable.

There are many ways in which the family system remains dysfunctional and many ways in which we might think about how this continues down the generations. While it is not our task to analyse the possibility of family dysfunction, it is helpful to be aware of its themes in human experience in order to assist an individual in working with this fragment of their fate. Some of the dysfunctional themes in families that we have identified in our practice revolve around the following dynamics. Often it is the outer planets that are suspect in these patterns, especially when they form complex aspects to the inner planets or are in familial houses.

Boundaries

Boundaries help to protect those within their precinct. They also help us to discriminate between what is acceptable and what is not, what is supportive and what is invasive. Boundaries guard our physical, emotional and psychological vulnerabilities and help us distinguish between friends and predators. Psychological boundaries help to fend off psychic infections and emotional ones help to guard us against inappropriate feelings.

When there is a lack of boundaries in the family, the child is assigned inappropriate roles, taking on unsuitable responsibilities and duties. The ability to become emotionally independent is impaired, as there are no guideposts or markers to know what is right. Unknowingly the child becomes enmeshed in a system where they are at risk of leaving. There may be many contributing factors astrologically; however, a lack of boundaries psychologically, emotionally and physically is mostly representative of the archetype of Neptune. Strong aspects between personal planets and Neptune, inner planets in the 12th house, or Neptune in the 4th, 8th or 12th house, address the issue of enmeshment and lack of boundaries within a family.

On the other hand, when the boundaries are too rigid or inflexible, the child feels diminished and insecure. Too many stern rules and regulations inhibit the freedom to be, to think, to feel and to act independently and individually. When boundaries are too rigid, performance expectation induces anxiety and guilt; equally this might also incite rebellion against the authoritarian regime. Again there are various astrological combinations that can be equated with rigid boundaries, but commonly these are symbolized by Saturn. Strong aspects between the inner planets and Saturn, or Saturn in the 4th, 8th or 12th house, might bring this theme to light. When issues concerning physical, emotional or psychological boundaries are identified it is important to work with the images in the horoscope to help address constructive ways to maintain one's sense of separateness.

Narcissistic Parenting

An important developmental initiation for children is to experience a stage of healthy narcissism: that is, feeling loved and lauded enough not to seek continuous praise and approval from others. When a parent has been denied this sense of adoration themselves, their child will be the most readily available focus for satisfying this compulsion. If the parent uses their child to reflect their own unfulfilled needs and desires, the child learns to mirror their parents' needs. A pattern of losing themselves in the reflection of others begins. Parents who feel deprived need their children to fulfil their needs; hence a child can learn to be the reflection of their parent's desires at the expense of their own developing authenticity. Over generations this becomes a cycle of feeling devalued, damaging the ability to know the self enough to discern when he or she is truly loved and valued. A repetition compulsion to feel loved continues into adulthood and challenges the ability to be intimate in adult relationships.

Forfeiting one's sense of self in order to be what others need can make one popular and charismatic, yet it also leaves one feeling unfulfilled and empty. A fine line demarcates narcissism and the urge to be loved. The oracle revealed to Narcissus's mother that her son would have a long life unless he came to know himself. However, Narcissus's life was short-lived and tragic. He came to know himself through the reflection in the clear pond, yet could never see beyond his own reflection, which bound him to a likeness he could never leave. Nor could he relate to any other without having the same reflection returned. Without adequate applause, acceptance and love, children are unable to move through the initiatory stage of being mesmerized by their own image and develop the capacity of psychological self-reflection and the acceptance of separateness.

I equate the 5th house with the story of Narcissus. To me the 5th house is the place where we re-encounter the pond-mirror and see that reflection of the creative self. But have we been narcissistically parented, trained to be the pleasing reflection for our unfulfilled parent? If so, the pattern of seeking approval for one's creative being is sought in adult relationships, with group leaders, bosses and others. When this pattern intersects with adult relationships the ability to accept others' differences is impaired. In the derivative house system the 5th represents the resources of the parent, being the 2nd house from the 4th; hence the child and their creativity may become resources for the parent. When the child is undervalued the resources are, too; then it is the reflection back from others that is desired, rather than the act of being involved creatively. In traditional terminology the 5th house was also known as the house of affairs. Underlying the impulse for an affair may be the repetitive compulsion of needing to be mirrored and loved, which has its roots in the early developmental stage with a parent who also was a narcissist.

We have been witnesses to a plethora of media stories about mothers who push their young daughters into beauty contests or fathers who train their sons to become business tycoons at the expense of the children's individuation. Strong aspects to the Sun and planets in the 5th are flags for this theme. We might also suspect that planets clustered near the MC or in the 10th house also play a role, because the unfulfilled desire of the parent may force the child into a world chosen by the parent, not the child. Synastry between the parent and the child would help to amplify these themes.

Abandonment

Greek myths have many motifs of abandoned children: Paris, Oedipus, Asclepius, Chiron, even the Olympian god Hephaestus was relinquished by his mother Hera. The theme is prevalent enough for us to wonder whether the abandoned child is an archetypal image. However, when this archetypal image becomes a living reality, then anxiety and dread are part of the child's experience.

When a child feels abandoned, or a schism in family relationships occurs, a common defensive position is either to disconnect from feeling or become hyper-vigilant. By disconnecting, the child learns to numb the pain of rejection, yet this contributes to an inability to bond or feel safe. Hyper-vigilance develops intuition as a defence because having a feeling about what could happen prepares the individual for what might happen. Yet, as a defence against anxiety, the child is constantly trying to read the atmosphere and its trends, and often misreading the situations. A continuous cycle of anxiety occurs.

Strong aspects between the inner planets and Uranus, or Uranus highlighted in one of the Water houses, can correspond with this theme. When Uranus is in a complex aspect with the Moon, the theme of abandonment or disconnection may be part of the mother's heritage, while of course an aspect to the Sun points to the father's lineage. When abandonment issues are part of the family legacy it is more challenging for the parent to be engaged with their children. Strong aspects to Chiron also resonate with the themes of abandonment, marginalization and relinquishment, or Chiron in a Water house might point to these themes coming through the family experience.

Family Secrets

We can distinguish two types of secrets in the family. One is the type that revolves around a surprise, gift-giving or a special event in the family. Everyone but the recipient of the gift knows the special secret. These secrets are part of family life and often joyous, although not always. However, they are generally not noxious. The other category is the toxic secrets that are held by families, which are very powerful and often are accompanied by feelings of shame. Thematically, these secrets may be about losses and incomplete mourning, poverty or loss of wealth, physical or mental health, broken taboos and betrayed intimacies, sexuality, death, abuse or illegitimacy in the family's past. This type of secret compromises the family member's authenticity and their ability to feel independent and self-focused. There is a tendency to bond not because of a sense of closeness but because of the fear of exposure. Therefore, 'secrets between family members are likely to inhibit trusting relationships and are therefore destructive.'[80]

Secrets are by nature divisive and systemic as they affect everyone in the system. Often it is not the literal secret that is destructive, but the powerful sense of shame that underpins it. What may have been shameful in a previous generation may no longer be so; however, the feeling that something is wrong or unacceptable still is. Therefore it is important not to focus solely on the literal nature of the secret. It is important to recognize that, as a consultant astrologer and counselor, it may be of great benefit to talk to your client about the secret openly and without judgement, as this helps to disempower the feelings behind it.

When we talk about secrets in the family, we distinguish between those that are acknowledged as actual events by a family member who keeps them secret from the others, and those which have no such factual foundation but arise from fantasies.[81]

'Fantasy' here does not mean something unreal but perhaps a powerful feeling that arises from jealousy, rivalry, hate, envy, love or a reaction to a felt experience of injury or pain that remains unexpressed in the family, so this taboo feeling or sensation eventually becomes a secret in the family. The line between fact and fantasy blurs through time as we reconstruct and remythologize our experiences in the family. Even if there is a 'real' event kept secret it is often the fantasies attached to the event that influence the familial response.

We live in a culture that seems obsessed with privacy laws. Ironically, this concern for privacy can actually help to keep secrets concealed. When working with secrets, a central dilemma 'revolves around the definition of secrecy and privacy'.[82] Since this is such a contentious demarcation, I generally think about it this way: privacy supports and contains the self whereas secrets separate and defend the self. Secrets generate shame but privacy does not. Privacy is a basic right. If a child is afforded privacy in the family of origin, then there is far less need for secrecy and withholding. Finally, secrets hide the self and are the source of fear and anxiety, whereas privacy is a consciously constructed boundary to contain oneself. Over time, in families, the secrets that have helped to conceal the self set up an atmosphere of mistrust and withholding.

When secrets are part of the family matrix, loyalties may be shaped by those who know the secret and those who feel left out. Dyads and triangles are formed as sub-systems to keep the secret hidden. Ironically, secrets are often kept as an attempt to avoid the guilt or pain that comes with loss. However, guilt and pain are embedded in loss. Fundamentally, secrets are about concealment to avoid shame; they are often about the breaking of taboos, power and dependence, love and hate, and 'are inevitably bound up with sex, birth and death.'[83]

While we are familiar with the sign ♏ and its modern ruler Pluto being connected with secrets, it is apparent how family secrets continue to keep this archetype from conscious consideration in the family. Therefore, strong aspects from the inner planets to Pluto may carry this theme as well as planets in the sign of ♏. A planet in the 8th house might be a trigger for examining this energy as being secretive in the family. Like the other outer planets, when Pluto is in aspect to an inner planet it makes a deep impression upon the soul whose pattern is already inherent within the family milieu. With Pluto this will be often revealed as a secret that wants to be disclosed.

Unexpressed Anger

Anger that is repressed or expressed inappropriately in families impairs the individual's ability to be assertive, self-determined or entrepreneurial. If either a fear of, or an inappropriate use of, anger is encouraged then the individual is unable to feel safe with anger or able to feel loved when they are angry.

Anger is often judged as 'bad' or immoral. Yet anger is a natural human response and often is helpful in addressing our feelings or determining what we truly want. Since it is physiological it can be physically felt as heightened adrenalin, a faster heartbeat, shortness of breath, redness. Due to its physiological response the repression of anger has been linked to physical and mental disease which can also be hereditary. Learning about anger appropriately in the family environment contributes to our ability to tolerate anger in our relationships as well as control our impulses. Yet when anger has been inappropriately learnt in families there is often a legacy of emotional or physical injury, abuse or complex and confused feelings.

As in every type of society, families also have taboos. Often there may a taboo or conscious myth about anger in the family which might suggest that if the child openly expresses anger or hostility 'it would upset a parent, who would become sick, have a nervous breakdown, or die.'[84] When the attitudes towards anger are oppressive in the family system, the expressive energy of Mars may be compromised.

Mars is the archetype associated with anger and therefore its aspects to other planets to help illustrate patterns involving anger. When in aspect to the Sun or Moon we would look at the specific parent's attitude to anger to give us some indication of our legacy. When intertwined with the Moon there may be a pattern in the family of confusing anger and love. Statements like 'If you are angry with me, you cannot love me', or even 'I won't love you if you are angry' weaken Mars's productive functioning. Aspects to Jupiter and Saturn suggest there may be social conditions around the expression of anger; for instance, a Mars-Saturn aspect may repress or deny anger for fear of its consequences, while a Mars-Jupiter aspect may philosophize and conceptualize anger in order to deal with its destructive tendency. When Mars is dynamically aspected to an outer planet there is a family inheritance. For instance, we might think about a powerful Mars-Uranus combination as pointing to a family theme of disassociating from anger or trying to rationalize or talk through anger. A Mars-Neptune dynamic suggests spiritualizing, forgiving or forgetting anger or being unconscious and unaware of anger. The possible influence of a Mars-Pluto is to hold onto anger, repress it or seek revenge. When Mars is in one of the houses of the family then it would be sensible to consider the legacy of how anger has been managed in the family atmosphere. These are simplistic scenarios that speak to the powerful inheritance of our attitudes towards anger.

Neglect and Abuse
When a child is neglected, mistreated or harmed, the inner sense of security and safety is compromised, leaving the child at risk of being unable to bond. Often children are mothered by neglect due

to their caretaker being hospitalized or ill, depressed, irresponsible, unable to cope or simply because the mother is a child herself. The spectrum from neglect to abuse ranges from lack of attention through to humiliation and shame; from disinterest through to inappropriate punishment, such as yelling, name-calling and hitting. These behaviours raise the child's adrenalin to fight-or-flight, a template that is transferred into adult relationship, leaving them at risk of repeating the abusive cycle.

Difficult aspects to the Moon, especially from the outer planets, are important to consider in this case. Since the Moon is symbolic of our fragile sense of self, difficult aspects to the Moon suggest energies we might be vulnerable to. Again, it is the depth of the feeling of being neglected that is important to consider.

Voids in the Family

An individual may introject certain ways of being because of a lack in the family, not necessarily because it is part of their conscious will or an authentic way to be. For instance, if there is a lack of harmony or balance in the parental marriage, the child may become the emotional spouse. Or if dignity is lacking in the family the child may feel obliged to be the hero. If warmth is lacking, the child may play the role of caretaker.

Our first socialization is in the family. Therefore, family attitudes about what it is to be a man, a woman, a partner, a friend, a good person or a success are seeded in the childhood home. It is important to reflect on roles that may have developed because of a familial lack. Some may be authentic but others may not. This tendency to take on a role is especially pronounced when there are aspects between the Moon and outer planets or when the outer planets are in the houses of endings. However, it is also important to consider what you feel is authentic to the individual, given the astrological statement. Ironically, sometimes an individual is defensive about the very talent and skill at which they are adept, as they feel inauthentic. The talent is used as a defence and therefore I often try to discover why this defence has formed around the very trait that is authentic. The source is often the family's assigning of roles.

– CHAPTER 15 –
PATTERNS THROUGH TIME
Psychic Spells in Families

There are many ways of thinking about time;[85] for instance, the ancient Greeks knew *chronos* as the unyielding passage of time. Like the eponymous Titan who devoured his children, time was seen to consume all things. Images of the passing of time, such as the hourglass and crutches, became linked with Chronos but, being an early agricultural god, the sickle was also his symbol. While this symbol was associated with power and prosperity, it also represented the cutting down of time. Ironically, Chronos also presided over a Golden Age, an era when man lived in peace and prosperity like gods, and 'miserable age rested not on them'.[86]

Once upon a time the age of Chronos was benevolent and undying, but now his time is all-consuming; hence, this ambivalence towards Chronos is an underpinning aspect of the astrological archetype of Saturn. Chronos time enters our vocabulary though words that represent the passing and recording of time, such as *chronological* which means the arrangement of recorded time; *chronicle*, a detailed account of events arranged sequentially; *chronometer*, an instrument that measures time. But perhaps the word that most reminds us of the troubling relentlessness of time is *chronic,* a mnemonic of the inevitability of temporal corrosion. Chronos remains a powerful symbol of time in our language and his surrogate Saturn continues to be one of astrology's great chronocrators.

But the Greeks knew another time and that was *kairos*, which had a subjective, nonlinear, even supernatural quality. While *chronos* characterized linear and measurable time, *kairos* referred to a critical moment, an appointed time or the right moment in time. In early usage it was linked with opportunity or the moment when possibility penetrated the present. In ancient Greek terminology it referred to an opening, so *kairos* was the critical moment to enter into and take advantage of the moment. In Homeric Greek, *kairos* was the 'penetrable opening' which may have originated with the archer who aimed at the cracks in the armour to seize the right moment, an early symbolic association between arrows and time. The word was also associated with weaving, which was often imaginatively connected to fate and time; it conjures up the sisterly alliance of the Horai and the Moira. Metaphorically speaking, 'An opening in the web of fate can mean an opening in time, an eternal moment when the pattern is drawn together tighter or broken through'.[87] *Kairos* is that moment when the veil of time lifts and the opportune moment arises, akin to the idea that the moment has arrived or the time has come. In contemporary ways of thinking we might align *kairos* with soul timing or the mysterious process of the ripening of time. *Kairos* might be likened to the birth moment which opens us up to the vital opportunity of life.

These two concepts embody the quantitative and qualitative nature of time and its literal and fictional qualities. As astrologers we constantly work with both, investing the literal planetary cycles with meaning, using *chronos* timing to become conscious of the *kairos* moments of life. Astrological time is filled with images and symbols; for instance the Moon in Scorpio not only refers to the 2½ days it is in this sign but measures the quality of that time.

The ancient Roman god associated with the thresholds of gateways and doorways was Janus, the patron of beginnings. As the spirit of the doorways, his blessing was essential at the birth of each life, as well as the beginning of each day, month and year; hence, he gives his name to January, the first month of each year. Janus had two faces: one that looked east to the rising of the Sun and the other west, to its setting. As a two-faced god of time he also reminds us of the different attitudes towards time in eastern and western cultures, the objective and subjective nature of time, its measurable and mystical aspects as well as the ancient Greek ideas of *chronos* and *kairos*.

When considering family and ancestry we are faced with stories and images that have developed over generations. Time has become invested with memories, emotions, traumas, opinions, sentiments; its nature is no longer linear. Astrological symbols also contain the family past that has become mythologized over the generations. Therefore, while the symbol might indicate a certain potential, this may no longer be characteristic of its present expression due to the imprint of the family past. For instance, a woman with a stellium in the 10th house is a successful ballet dancer but she is unhappy with her career. Her professional success and status have been driven by her mother, who had to relinquish her own dance career when she became pregnant with her daughter. So, like her mother, the daughter remains unfulfilled with her role in the world. Both still suffer under the weight of the familial edict to do the right thing at the expense of their authenticity.

Our craft teaches us how to literally read the chart for character, events, patterns and themes; however, it is important that we are also able to listen and respond to the cyclical and repetitive motifs over time. By doing so, we remain true to the astrological statements but we also allow the personal and subjective understanding to arise. In this way we experience the astrological symbols of our chart as multi-layered and historied, shaped by our membership of the matrix of the family.

Time and timing in the family occur in many ways. In the following chapters we will explore timing through transits, progression and planetary cycles, but it is also important to recognize the phenomenon known as family time, as well as to honour the patterns that come down through the family over time.

Family Time
A dimension to time patterning by family members is a phenomenon we could describe as 'family time'. This refers to the unconscious memory of important times and ages within the family experience. Generally, family time is the mechanism that psychically records traumatic transitions and unexpressed grief, releasing the memory in response to a significant age or anniversary that repeats the original age of the trauma. When a shock has been experienced in the family, the surviving members of the family are imprinted not only with the potent feelings but also with the timing of the event.

Averil Earnshaw suggested that family time was the bridge that helped us to recognize how events were timed through the family history. Using many case histories and examples she shows the repetitive ages that repeat in the family life cycle, which questions assumptions about how aware we are of timing in our lives. She suggested family time was the unconscious remembering of a family trauma:

> Family experiences tagged to human ages are the bridges that link the generations. They persist inexorably in body memories, even

if not in conscious thoughts, and they erupt at predictable ages, as physical and emotional events.[88]

For example, the loss of a parent at age three may become a psychic watershed in the individual's life. At the three-year mark of any important venture the affect of the trauma may permeate the individual with fear and anxiety, the residue of the unresolved grief and loss. At this time in their lives they are at risk of sudden separations or other unexpected losses which repeat the pattern of severance.

The age at which a parent dies is significant as this becomes an age at which something stops. We are often unable to see beyond this age or have any experience of age beyond this traumatic loss. As we approach this age we may unconsciously begin to feel a sense of unease. These times are experienced unconsciously throughout the family life cycle and operate autonomously; an individual may feel anxious when they reach the age at which a parent died, yet not consciously make the connection that they may be identifying with the timing of their parent's death. Any family trauma may be carried in a psychic time capsule, waiting to be released at the appropriate time. The unconscious identification with the trauma of a parent's death might generate dread and anxiety or it may repeat the pattern in some way.

A client developed severe migraines at the age of 8, but these disappeared when she was 24 ($3 \times 8 = 24$). At the time she consulted me, her father had been dead for 8 years. However, this was when her migraines began to recur. Since she had referred to the loss of her father 8 years ago and the return of her migraines, being cognisant of family time I asked if anything had happened in the family when she was 8 years old. At the 8-year mark of family time, the time that had elapsed since her father had died, she began to feel and remember the early trauma at age 8 when the migraines first started. Her father had left her at a neighbour's house for the weekend and during this time, when she was left in another's care, she was sexually assaulted by a man who was boarding with the family. She felt rage at her father's abandonment of her. When considering the father's timeline, she recalled that her paternal grandfather had died when her father was 8, another abandonment theme at the 8-year mark. This is family time; considering the traumatic timeline is bringing the awareness of a fault line underneath the family to consciousness. This allows a framework to understand psyche's timing and to become conscious of the patterning, allowing choice and consciousness. At times, a release from the pattern is possible. In this case, the client had felt compassion for her father's abandonment at 8, which allowed her to feel compassion for her 8-year-old self. She also realized that she had been fixed in a bigger pattern which she respected much more.

I will draw a family portrait of Sigmund Freud later. However, as an example of family time we could note that he was born when his father was 40½ years old. When Sigmund was this age his father died, which ignited the spark for his own self-analysis and which led to his creative birthing of psychoanalysis. Similarly, yet in reverse, Wolfgang Mozart's father was 36 when his genius son was born. Mozart himself died just before his 36th birthday. As astrologers we will note the important life cycles in each of these cases. Near age 41, the progressed Moon is opposite its natal placement while Neptune is making its waxing square to itself. Just before the 36th birthday, Jupiter returns. Being aware of both astrological and family timing provides a powerful tool for identifying significant ages in our life experience.

Trauma experienced at certain ages in the sibling system may also repeat itself throughout the family life cycle. If we have lost a sibling at an early age the unexpressed grief and shock of this experience may affect the stability of our adult relationships. The age we were at the time of this loss may be the length of time into adult relationships when we begin to experience unexplained anxieties and fears over the relationship. Important ages, especially when trauma and loss are experienced, are etched on the psyche. This timing can be carried down through the familial line and recur in our own lives. Familial timing is quite common, clustered around family and sibling trauma, and is detected through the ability to listen and link important ages in an individual's life. Earnshaw encapsulates time in this way:

> We are all living in two sorts of time: Clock Time and Family Time. As children, we learn to tell the time by the clocks, but no one teaches us how to tell Family Time. We believe that we have time, but in a mysterious way, time has us![89]

Family time works independently of transits yet may also synchronize with potent transits and progressions in the planets' individual or generic cycles. Family time is revealed by reflecting on the family history and by active listening. It is encouraged through assembling a genogram and creating a family time line.

To encapsulate your experience of the important times in the family, which may repeat in family time, reflect on all the times that the family group changed or experienced trauma, transition and loss, especially each time there was an entrance or exit within the family group. These changes could include:

- Death of a parent
- The birth or death of a sibling
- Death of a grandparent
- Grandparents or other relatives moving in and out of the family home
- Divorce and remarriage
- Relinquishment or adoption
- Abandonment
- Leaving home, a sibling leaving home or a sibling leaving you
- Sibling relationships, marriages and divorces
- House moves, house purchases or sales, relocation, emigration, all important shifts that affected the security and functioning of the family dynamic
- Others moving in or out of the family unit
- Acquisition and/or relinquishment or death of a pet
- Other family traumas, including retrenchments, losses, tragedies, etc.

The phenomenon of family time is the autonomous repetition of trauma through the family life cycle, generally occurring near anniversaries and significant dates. This is a powerful influence of family fate, as unmourned grief, unfelt feelings and unprocessed trauma remain tied to the wheel of family karma and return around an anniversary, using the same timing or in some other variation. We are often unprotected from the fallout from ancestral trauma, which continues to impact on our emotional development. Family time helps to locate the source of the stress. While transits to our horoscope and the horoscopes of family members are a profound timing device, family time provides a self-governing model based on the family experience.

Patterns and the Passing of Time

In the introductory chapter we noted that fate in families is often visible astrologically through signs and degrees of the zodiac. However, patterns over time in the family are also recognizable through planetary themes, aspects and angularity. Patterns through time are very evident in families through repetitive planetary aspects.

Planetary Aspects

Particular planetary aspects are often visible in successive generations of the family. These might reveal themselves in many ways, such as a continuing aspect between two planets which repeats through successive generations or a combination of three or more planets which might align in various differing aspects or midpoint patterns. Sometimes the repeated aspects are visible only through the female line in the family while others might be carried by the males in the family.

Like genes, an aspect may skip a generation and show up in the next generation. Generally speaking, the repetitive aspect does not occur in all family members' charts but is visible in some – those that do not carry that particular aspect often carry another thread of the family pattern which is visible in another set of planetary relationships. The following example traces the female line through four generations of a family that has shared a Sun-Mars conjunction as well as a Moon-Pluto aspect.

Here is a clear example of planetary aspects being carried over four generations by women in each generation. Margaret did not have a Sun-Mars aspect but her daughter Kaye inherited the Mars-Uranus aspect. Kaye's Sun-Mars aspect was then inherited by her youngest daughter and two of her grandchildren. The Moon-Pluto aspects are carried by the same women in the family for four generations.

Family Member/ Generation	Birth Data	Sun-Mars	Moon-Pluto	Comments
Margaret 1st Gen. Great-Grandmother	30 January 1908, 12.00 p.m. Bairnsdale, Victoria, Australia	Margaret had Mars in ♈ square Uranus	The Moon is in ♐ exactly ☍ Pluto within 3' of arc	Margaret has no recorded time of birth but noon local time brings the Moon within 7½° of the Moon's placement at any time during the day
Kaye 2nd Gen. Grandmother	5 December 1944 00.55 a.m. Melbourne, Australia	Kaye has the Sun ☌ Mars in ♐ ☍ Uranus	The Moon is in ♌ ☌ Pluto within 2° of orb	Kaye inherits the Mars-Uranus aspect from her mother; she has a Sun-Mars conjunction
Yvonne 3rd Gen. Daughter of Kaye	19 August 1970 06.15 p.m. Melbourne, Australia	Yvonne also has the Sun ☌ Mars, but in ♌ within 5°	The Moon is at 27 ♓ ☍ Pluto at 26 ♍	Margaret's Moon sign is ♐, the same as her daughter's Sun sign. Kaye's Moon is ♌, the same as her daughter's Sun sign. Yvonne's Moon at 27 ♓ is ☌ her daughter's Sun
Lauren 4th Gen. Granddaughter of Kaye	17 March 1996 06.07 p.m. Baltimore, USA	Lauren has the Sun ☌ Mars in ♓ within 3°	The Moon in ♓ is □ to Pluto within 4°	Lauren has a stellium in ♓ including the Sun and Moon. Her Sun is exactly conjunct Saturn which is ☌ her Mother's Moon. Her Moon in ♓ is also ☌ her father's Sun in ♓

Elsie 4th Gen. Grand-daughter of Kaye	23 June 2000 04.45 p.m. Chelsea, Victoria, Australia	Elsie's Sun ☌ Mars is in ♋ within 2°	Elsie also has the Moon in ♓ square Pluto in ♐	Elsie and Lauren are cousins and share the Moon in ♓. Like her cousin, Elsie also has a stellium in Water in the sign of ♋

The positive qualities of the Moon-Pluto aspect, such as emotional strength, resilience and integrity, have been experienced by these women alongside grief, losses and betrayals. With the support of the Sun-Mars aspects there is a tendency for these women to instigate change and separation. The weaving of the Sun/Moon themes between the mothers and daughters suggest that the relationship of mother to daughter is closely knit.

Angular Planets
The family legacy may also be passed down through strong angular planets. Angular planets are a high priority in any natal chart so when they are repeated this planetary archetype becomes a focus in the family experience. By their very nature, angular planets stand out and therefore the carriers of these angular energies will be the family members more likely to overtly identify with and demonstrate this energy. For instance, angularity is very evident when examining the charts of the Kennedy family.

In some cases the planet on the angle may not be the same but the focus on the angle is. For instance, planetary energies focused on the Ascendant bring the theme of individuality and selfhood strongly into the open; planetary activity on the MC would suggest that traditions, goals, social achievement and professional accomplishments play a leading role in the ethos of the family; planets focused on the Descendant bring the themes of both relationship and rivalry, collusion and cooperation, into the atmosphere of the family; while planets on the IC bring family values, principles and standards to the forefront in those members who share the placement.

Family members who share angular planets are either drawn together in a collusion or alliance to express this energy for the family or are naturally reactive and defensive of the other's command of the power. When those who share an angular planet become polarized, one side of the family may deny the expression of the energy, leaving the other side to exaggerate it. Because of the highly active nature of angular planets the family has at some point influenced their expression.

Planetary Themes

In a more subtle way, a particular planet or a combination of planets may be highlighted in the horoscopes of successive generations. When a planet's nature becomes emphasized through being a focal planet in family members' horoscopes, this planet characterizes much of the family's fate. For instance, if Uranus is strong in family members' horoscopes, Uranian themes become highlighted in the family. One member may have Uranus as a handle to a Bucket chart, another may have Uranus on an angle, another may have Uranus conjunct a luminary or another may have Uranus highly aspected. In each of the charts, Uranus becomes highly focused and therefore brings its archetypal influence to bear not only on the individual but on the family as well.

Family themes can often be differentiated through the planetary archetypes. For instance, Saturn themes may speak about motifs of success, performance, authority and status in the family. A prominent Uranus in family charts would point to themes of independence and freedom as well as separations and splits. A family with Neptune highlighted in the members' horoscopes may face the themes of chaos, disappearance, spirituality, creativity and even illness throughout their history. When Pluto stands out in the horoscopes of family members, there may be themes of loss, shared finances, inheritances and emotional control that affect the atmosphere of the family.

As a final note I would like to reiterate that it is possible to work with the influence of family fate by examining only one horoscope. However, when the charts of other family members are studied, the astrological symbols reveal the continuity of family patterns and the repetition of planetary aspects through the generations. In this way the astrological model becomes a living map which reveals the familial fortunes and fatalities.

– CHAPTER 16 –
THE PASSING OF TIME
The Family Life Cycle

In this chapter we will explore some techniques and approaches to amplify ways of thinking about the family through time. In turn, hopefully this will deepen the meanings of the astrological symbols and give us a richer understanding of *kairos* time. We will begin by addressing the concept of the family life cycle. While we are aware of our own individual life cycle from birth through childhood, adolescence, adulthood, midlife, old age and to death, family therapy also addresses the notion of the family life cycle. Theoretically we might begin the life cycle at any stage but consensus suggests that we begin at the engagement or commitment of the adult couple. This is the time when each individual moves away from their family of origin into their family of choice and a new cycle begins. We will examine these stages in family life to appreciate how astrological cycles echo throughout all generations of the family. This will allow us to review the astrological transits in terms of the life cycle and we will observe this using the 12-year rounds of Jupiter, as this cycle corresponds to these developmental stages.

The Family Life Cycle
The family pattern is circular by nature, because a newborn will eventually move through the stages of life that their parents, grandparents and ancestors have experienced. The stages of life repeat themselves; while each generation will experience a different social ambience, the pattern remains and is replicated by each generation. The family moves through time together. When the first child is born, the couple become parents and their parents become grandparents. When the adolescent graduates from high school, his or her parents are navigating the trials of midlife while their own parents are moving towards old age. From an astrological point of view, the planetary cycles are unfolding for each generation.

Social researchers were aware of this repetitive patterning of family life and recognized the powerful imprint that the comings and goings of family members made on both the family unit and its individual members. In researching the pivotal stages of family life, social researchers agreed that certain developments such as engagement, marriage, birth of children, their adolescence, their leaving home, growing old and facing death were critical passages of the family life cycle. At each of these phases of transition, the family and its members were altered. These comings and goings or entrances and exits in family life were recognized as defining moments and turning points. Entrances into the family became recognized as a 'crisis of accession'; exits became known as 'crisis of dismemberment', acknowledging the psychological impact and stress that reverberate through the system when someone joins or leaves the group. Researchers suggested that when the natural cycle of accession or dismemberment was impeded or denied, dysfunctional or pathological familial patterns were likely to surface through one or more of the family's members.

Hence a family is not static: it exists through time and, while its influence might be felt most acutely in childhood, its impact lasts a lifetime. It is a multi-dimensional organism of which an individual is part, not only genetically, but emotionally, economically and psychologically. Contemplating the family from an astrological position suggests that the nature of the family is already inherent in each horoscope; from a systemic point of view, the natal charts, transits and progressions are interconnected with the family patterns and dynamics. Transits to individual charts reverberate through the family system. This is evident astrologically because family members often share similar zodiacal degrees of planets, angles or other points in the horoscope, which are then simultaneously transited in many family members' horoscopes.

We live in a world that is always in transition; perhaps at present this is more pronounced than at other times. Therefore the family, which is always accommodating these changes in society, is changing with it. When there are transitional difficulties in society, it is more important than ever that the family's psycho-social task of supporting its members is as robust as possible. The composition of the family has also altered since early researchers studied the unit: blended families, single-parent families, same-sex relationships and childless couples are now legitimate family units. Therefore, when contemplating the family and its changes over time, it is imperative to be as open-minded and flexible as possible.

Like any organism, the family has a natural life cycle. The members of the family move through various stages and rites of passage as they mature.[90] This life cycle can also be studied in tandem with the natural astrological cycles of the transiting and progressed planets, nodes and other celestial bodies. There are many differing versions of the family life cycle, which is understandably more complex than an individual's life cycle, but ultimately an individual's life phase is framed by the larger sequence of the family life cycle. The eight-stage model of sociologist EM Duvall, which spans the life of the family, is the one most widely used.[91]

1 The commitment of the primary couple
2 Their marriage
3 Child-rearing years
4 Their children's adolescence
5 The children leaving home
6 The readjustment of the primary couple
7 Old age
8 Death

Other models include as many as 24 stages in the family life cycle. Entrances and exits of family members most often correspond to stages of the life cycle that are the highest in stress for all the members. However, we might imagine that the family life cycle, which includes all the developmental phases, unexpected traumas, entrances and exits, develops from the time a couple begins their relationship as a single unit. This cycle of family life, which includes having children, their growing up and their leaving home, has gone full circle when the parents' own children form relationships and move towards their own family life.

Transitional periods in the family life cycle are the times when people are most vulnerable. Transition is critical, and awareness of these turning points in family life helps members to make the transition more consciously and functionally. For example, the first child leaving home is a critical passage for the family and signals a crisis and change for each member. The younger sibling moves forward, accommodating the void created by the sibling who has left. Their roles, responsibilities and privileges will shift. The parents, who have launched their first child, will be more acutely aware of preparing for the readjustment phase of their lives when daily family life returns to their being on their own. This also applies in an astrological context. A major transit for one individual will affect all family members. When we view astrology systemically, we see transits to one individual's horoscope being echoed by the other members of the same system. Undoubtedly major transits and life stages for one sibling will directly impact on the others. Sibs share their formative years so their experiences are impressed upon one another. Their transits and progressions through the early life cycle are formative imprints on our own experience, influencing the way we relate to different astrological symbols and archetypes.

The following table suggests the milestones in a classic nuclear family, centred on the couple. As suggested previously, this view of the family is in some ways outdated; however, it serves us well as a prototype which can be adapted to other family situations. The family life cycle can start at any point, but we are beginning our exploration at the engagement between two adults, as this is when the possibility of creating a new family exists. At this point two individuals leave their family systems to create another, shifting loyalties from their family of origin into the development of a new system. Throughout the family life cycle the possibilities of triangular relationships and collusions is always present.

With each milestone of family life, common issues and challenges arise in this transitional time for all members of the family. Of course, highly individualistic and personal issues are revealed at these potent stages. Therefore, when looking at the following stages of family development, reflect on your own experience of the family life cycle and your issues and concerns at these times. I have also speculated on some of the astrological archetypes that are apparent at this time, but it is also important to consider other astrological themes and arrangements that must be acknowledged during these transitions. Transitional stages in the life cycle often correspond to the major aspects – the square, opposition and conjunction (return) – in the cycles of the social and outer planets.

We might think of the first stage of family development as starting from the initial engagement when two partners form their own unit, separate from their familial one.

Milestone	Familial Issues
Engagement	With the engagement of two individuals from different family backgrounds, a transfer of loyalties from family to partner occurs. Patterns of intimacy in the family, as well as trust and security issues, may arise as the new couple becomes integrated into a new family unit. Building trust and security are seminal tasks for new life, as Erik Erikson affirmed in his stages of life. From an astrological perspective, synastry between the partners is important; however, from an individual perspective, the intimacy and relational issues from the family of origin that may be rekindled are worth noting. Therefore 7th and 8th house issues, as well as Venus and Mars, will be highlighted. Note the planetary cycles as well as the important transits, as these will be formative influences upon the relationship.
Setting Up Home/Living Together	The sharing of resources, power and money are now highlighted: how do we share our resources and space with someone else? Habitual patterns from the family of origin are brought into the new household. Both these issues stress the 8th house. Yet the 4th house and the Moon will be important to consider, as well as living patterns and routines from the families of origin. Again refer to the couple's synastry for clues on how living rituals, values, communication and emotional expression may be managed.
Pregnancy	During pregnancy there is an energetic shift from the woman being the partner and lover to her now becoming mother. This mother-lover split shifts the relationship matrix and evokes many astrological images connected to the Moon and Venus, their relationship and aspects, as well as their progressions. Once again the 7th and 8th houses are important, as well as the 5th house, in both the natal and composite charts.

	A new family unit is formed with the birth of the first child. The couple now become parents and their parents become grandparents. New responsibilities and roles emerge as well as new relationships. With the birth of the second child, a new system emerges in the family: the sibling system becomes a sub-system in the family organism. There are now two tiers in the immediate family.
Birth of First Child	With a third person in the new family, an overt triangle is formed between mother, father and child: what Freud coined the Oedipal conflict. How do the partners become parents and how does the child find a place in their relationship? The 5th house is emphasized as the house of children; the 7th and 8th as the houses of parental intimacy; and the trinity of Moon, Sun and Saturn as parental images. A learning curve and many changes occur during this phase. The child's horoscope is also the transits to his or her parents' horoscopes at the time of birth. This synastry remains intact throughout the life cycle.
Birth of Second Child	With another child, a sub-system in the family is formed. The sibling system is created and brings with it the issues of equality and hierarchy. New roles and expectations are formed in the family. The older child feels displaced while the younger has both a sibling and parental relationships to navigate. The sibling is represented by the 3rd house, ♊ and aspects to Mercury.
	As previously acknowledged, both attachment and separation are crucial aspects of family life. Separations occur across the family life cycle and some are powerfully evident during the Oedipal and adolescent phases of development. These separations are important to consider, because the emotional and felt experience during these periods is likely to be remembered and/or instinctually evoked once again during other separations in later life.

School	When the first child leaves to go to school there is a separation from both the parent and any other siblings. The parent revisits their initial separations and feelings of leaving the security of the family for school while the younger siblings may also experience a loss. While this may evoke issues of separation for the younger sibs, it also evokes the issues of education and schooling for the parents in their own experience. Again, Mercury and the 3rd house play a key role in the early experience of learning and schooling.
Adolescence	This is a very potent time in family life, as it stirs up rebellion and the urge to be free in the adolescent, while evoking memories of adolescence and youthful exuberance for the parents. The cycles of the social planets Jupiter and Saturn, as well as the progressed Moon, play an important role during this phase. Note any links in these cycles between the adolescent and their parents at this stage of the family life cycle. A teenager often triggers adolescent angst in the parent who is at midlife and may be faced with unlived and/or unexpressed feelings from this period.
Leaving Home	Another separation occurs when the first or perhaps another child leaves home. Power struggles emerge and roles in the family begin to change. Our reasons for leaving home and the way in which we leave home are often part of the family complex which, if unrecognized, are repeated in subsequent separations throughout the life cycle.
	Once the child is launched, their own journey begins outside the everyday interactions of the family. The family may no longer be part of the child's everyday experience but they are still immersed in the family ethos, both emotionally and psychologically. Changes in life expectancy, gender roles, economic uncertainty and social norms have all impacted this transition, altering the expectations about leaving home, securing the future, professional success and starting a family.

Children Marry	When adult children take partners and form primary relationships, the cycle begins to repeat itself. Patterns, habits, learned rituals and complexes from both families of origin influence the formation of the new unit. Once again, issues of loyalty and trust arise. These issues may be recycled from the parents and/or grandparents' engagement stage of the family life cycle.
Grand-children	When grandchildren are born, the issues of ageing are evident. Three generations are now moving through time together. A new triangle may emerge, consisting of the parent, the adult child and the grandchild.
	As the original couple ages, life matters and values are reworked and the questions of retirement, life focus and goals, physical health, occupation and facing death become priorities.
Retirement	Retirement continues the theme of ageing but also brings up issues of status, value and inheritance.
Death	When a parent dies the whole system is rejigged. Abandonment and loss, incomplete feelings, issues of inheritance and unresolved family issues arise.

While this examination has been from the perspective of a 'nuclear family', the stages will be the same for all families. For instance the stage of pregnancy will describe the creative changes in the relationship, while the other changes concerning children will be representative of maturation and developmental stages in their unique family unit.

Of course there are many variables that occur in families and which disturb the natural cycle. Parental illness and death, redundancy, divorce, dislocation, immigration, separation as well as role-reversals all disrupt the expected flow of the family. However, reflecting on the family through time is a powerful way to think of the family multi-dimensionally and our place in that cycle. These variables are part of life and are symbolized astrologically by the planetary cycles and the transits to the horoscopes of the individual members of the family. While planetary cycles will frame the life cycle for an individual and the family, personal transits create the interruptions and variations.

When working with cycles it is important to recognize that while you may be in a particular phase of a cycle, older family members have already gone through this stage and their experiences may subtly influence your understanding of this passage. The younger member may feel supported by the elder or might reject their experience as being unhelpful. If you have already experienced a planetary cycle that a younger family member is living through, it is helpful to reflect on your expectations and unconscious judgements about how this member is coping. Your subjective understanding and memories may distort your expectations.

A female client whose son was 29 was anxious about his lack of direction and difficulty in finding the 'right' job and 'settling down'. Like her son, she was experiencing her Saturn return and so I encouraged her to reflect on where she was when she turned 30: what were her memories, feelings and desires at that time? Interestingly, she remembered her uncertainty and lack of direction, which allowed her to separate from her son's confusion by remembering her own process at this time. Also sharing a Saturn return, albeit one cycle apart, allowed her to be more compassionate for her own internal 30-year-old by discriminating between her own process and that of her son's.

Consider the progression of the Moon in an adult horoscope. Even though we are alert to this as the symbol of an individual's emotional development during this stage of life, it can also parallel the development of other family members to whom they are bonded, such as their children and/or their parents, during this phase. From a familial context the adult's emotional development is sensitive and responsive to their child and parent. Therefore the progressed Moon in the adult's chart might also reflect emotional developments in another close family member. I would first consider mother and then a child. This is an example of the *participation mystique* which occurs in family development.

From a child's perspective, a transit of Saturn will be felt individually perhaps as learning about consequences of actions, new rules or boundaries being set. But it might also be synchronous with changes in the parents. Perhaps at this time in the family atmosphere there is more of a sense of restriction because of a shift in the parental system, which the child registers as their own experience. When viewed systemically the cycles of the planets can be regarded not only in terms of the individual but in the context of the other members of the family as well.

As an astrologer it is necessary to be aware of the repetitive aspects within the life cycle and reflect on whether these are also occurring for other members of the family or what they might mean for the family system as a whole. In acknowledging the family life cycle, astrologers can recognize the power of the planetary transits reverberating through the whole of the family and not only within the individual's experience.

The Astrological Life Cycle
There are many ways to view the life cycle astrologically. All planets have defined cycles; their cyclic returns symbolize homecoming and mark the maturation of a cycle. In terms of the life cycle, the planetary cycles that stand out are those that demarcate the phases of life. Saturn and the progressed Moon are valuable markers as they measure the distinct cycles of 27.3 and 29.5 years respectively.

Three of these cycles map out the current life span for many individuals living in developed countries. Three cycles of the progressed Moon measure 82 years, which is the life expectancy for individuals in countries such as Japan, Switzerland, Israel and Australia.[92] Three cycles of Saturn add up to 88 years. The lunar nodes also map out the life span with 4-5 phases of 18.6 years each. Four nodal cycles span 74-75 years, which is the average life expectancy in countries such as Serbia and Argentina. Therefore these astrological cycles also measure family life and are critical at turning points in the family. The table below *approximates* the opposition and return ages which we might consider in terms of our own and the family's development.

Cycle	1st Cycle		2nd Cycle		3rd Cycle		4th Cycle	
	Age at 1st ☍	Age at 1st Return	Age at 2nd ☍	Age at 2nd Return	Age at 3rd ☍	Age at 3rd Return	Age at 4th ☍	Age at 4th Return
Saturn	14-15	29-30	44-45	58-59	73-74	88-89		
Prog. Moon	13-14	27-28	41	54-55	68-69	81-82		
Lunar Nodes	9-10	18-19	27-28	37-38	46-47	55-56	65-66	74-75

Another cycle spanning the whole life is Uranus's of 84 years. The squares and oppositions in this cycle are important turning points in both our own development and that of the family.

Planetary Cycle	Age at the Waxing Square	Age at the 1st Opposition	Age at the Waning Square	Age at the 1st Return
Uranus	20-21	38-42	62-63	84

Within this cycle we could measure 7 cycles of Jupiter. Using Jupiter's 12-year cycle we can map out 7 distinct phases of the life cycle astrologically. These stages are also important in family life as they suggest socialization phases, chapters in development and when initiations into life as well as changes and growth will take place. In coming to understand the major cycles you will also begin to see the repetitive themes of these cycles in family life.

The following table separates the life cycle into 7 Jupiter cycles. Since the Jupiter cycle is actually 11.88 years, the returns may vary by 1-2 years in the latter cycles. The timing of planetary aspects will vary slightly for each individual because of Jupiter's direct and retrograde motion through the zodiac, so the ephemeris must be consulted for the precise dates. However, this serves as a prototype model of ages astrologically. Studying this map will also help us to be more familiar with the astrological life cycle; once we become fluent with this map we are more equipped to be able to move back and forth across the life span and the generations within the family.

The Astrological Life Cycle from the Perspective of Jupiter
I have sub-divided some of the cycles into phases in order to honour the astrological phenomena, such as the first returns of the inner planets and the powerful repetitive cycles of the social and outer planets. Once again, these ages are generalized. This is only one way of thinking about the life cycle but I have found it helpful and useful when moving back and forth through the different stages of development within the family and its different generations. Chiron's cycle of the waxing and waning squares and the opposition has not been included, as these ages are specific to each generation due to the ellipse of its orbit.[93]

Life cycle theory and research have been popular in psychology, sociology and in contemporary non-fiction writing.[94] Erik Erikson, an earlier psychological researcher, not only developed his theory of 8 stages of the life cycle but also suggested tasks that corresponded with these stages of life.[95] His first stage of life spanned the first 12-18 months when the infant's undertaking was dealing with trust versus mistrust and the task of bonding and connecting. This first stage was about attachment and trust as the infant's needs and view of the world was dependent upon the parental response. This task re-emerged in his fifth stage of life as a young adult from the ages of 19-40, which brought back the attachment task of intimacy versus isolation. However, most of his other stages were more individually orientated and outside the family circle. Family therapy brought to awareness the powerful sense of the family moving through time.[96] However, the astrological model using planetary cycles has always mapped out the phases of life.

The First Jupiter Cycle: Childhood (Ages 0-12)

Infancy	
Lunar Return	27.3 days
Mercury Return	11-13 months
Venus Return	10-14 months
Solar Return	1 year
Mars Return	22 months (17-23.5 months)
Early Childhood	
Jupiter Opposition	6 years
Waxing Progressed Moon Square	7 years
Waxing Saturn Square	7.5 years
Latency Period	
Nodal Opposition	9 years

Middle Childhood can be viewed as the period between 7.5 and 9, or the time between the waxing Saturn square and the nodal opposition. Late Childhood can be viewed as the period between 9 and 12, from the nodal opposition to the Jupiter return. Note the powerful impact of the 4 inner planets returning in the first year of life.

The Second Jupiter Cycle: Adolescence (Ages 12-24)

Early Adolescence

First Jupiter Return	12 years
Progressed Moon Opposition	14 years
Uranus Waxing Sextile	14 years

Middle Adolescence

First Saturn Opposition	15 years
Second Jupiter Opposition	18 years
First Nodal Return	19 years

Late Adolescence

Waning Progressed Moon Square	20.5 years
Neptune Semi-square	20.5 years
Uranus Square	21 years
Waning Saturn Square	22 years

While we are inclined to think of Adolescence as the 'teens' the World Health Organization defines adolescence as the years covered by the second Jupiter cycle, as do many other psychological researchers. During this period the brain is still developing and growing. Note the cluster of planetary cycles around the age of 21, a time in life that many cultures suggest is 'the coming of age'.

The Third Jupiter Cycle: Young Adulthood (Ages 24-36)

Young Adulthood: Pre-Saturn Return

Second Jupiter Return	24 years
Progressed Moon Return	27.3 years
Second Nodal Opposition	28 years
Neptune Waxing Sextile	28 years
Uranus Waxing Trine	28 years

Young Adulthood: Post-Saturn Return

First Saturn Return	29.5 years
Progressed Lunation Phase Return	29.5 years
Third Jupiter Opposition	30 years
Progressed Moon Square	34 years

Adulthood continues beyond this phase. However, I have used Young Adulthood to describe this powerful time of emergence into the responsibilities and experiences of becoming an adult.

The midpoint of this period is the Saturn Return, which is a living symbol and metaphor for this period of the life cycle which initiates the individual into autonomy and self-regulation, conscientiousness, dependability and accountability.

The Fourth Jupiter Cycle: Midlife (Ages 36-48)

Phase One: The Late Thirties

Third Jupiter Return	36 years
Second Saturn Square	37 years
Second Nodal Return	37 years
Waxing Pluto Square	36-40 years*

(*Note: only for the ♇ in ♍ and the ♇ in ♎ generation; other generations do not experience this aspect as early)

Phase Two: Shifting Perspectives entering the Forties

Uranus Opposition	39-42 years
Second Progressed Moon Opposition	41 years
Waxing Neptune Square	41 years
Fourth Jupiter Opposition	42 years

Phase Three: The Mid-forties

Second Saturn Opposition	45 years

Midlife embraces the fourth Jupiter cycle when all the outer planets are configured in difficult aspects in their generic cycle. Uranus is at its opposition point; Neptune at its waxing square. Each generation will experience the transition differently. For example, for Pluto in Virgo and Libra, the Pluto square is experienced during this midlife stage of the life cycle, whereas this was not the case for their grandparents. Some generations will have their Uranus square earlier than others; therefore the sequence of the Uranus opposition and Pluto square is altered.

The Fifth Jupiter Cycle: Middle Age (Ages 48-60)

Entering the Fifties: The Chiron Return

Fourth Jupiter Return	48 years (usually 47)
Chiron Return	50 years
Second Saturn Waning Square	51-52 years
Fifth Jupiter Opposition	53 years

The Mid-fifties: Reflection	
Second Progressed Moon Return	55 years
Uranus Waning Trine	55 years
Third Nodal Return	56 years
Neptune Waxing Trine	56 years

The Saturn Return	
Second Saturn Return	59 years

The fifth Jupiter cycle encompasses the decade of the fifties, which starts with the Chiron return and ends with the Jupiter and Saturn returns. Note the number of returns in this decade. For some generations, Pluto also was trining natal Pluto. However, this will occur earlier for the Pluto in Virgo generation.

The Sixth Jupiter Cycle: Seniority (Ages 60-72)

Fifth Jupiter Return	60 years (generally 59 years)
Waning Uranus Square	61-63 years
Third Waxing Saturn Square	66 years
Sixth Jupiter Opposition	66 years
Third Progressed Moon Opposition	69 years

Note that this cycle begins with the concurrent returns of Jupiter and Saturn, which harmonically coincide before the age of 60 (i.e. 29.5 years x 2 = 59; 11.88 years x 5 = 59). The Jupiter/Saturn synodic cycle is 20 years and at age 60 both planets return to their natal place. Twenty years is known as a 'score', a way to keep a tally on life. At 60 we have reached three score years and the achievements and experiences of life are being transformed into wisdom, which is the great task of this Jupiter cycle.

The Seventh Jupiter Cycle: Eldership (Ages 72-84)

Sixth Jupiter Return	72 years (generally 71 years)
Fourth Nodal Return	74 years
Third Waning Saturn Square	81 years
Third Progressed Moon return	82 years
Seventh Jupiter Return	83 years
Uranus Return	84 years

Retrospection and contemplation of one's life are the keys during this phase. This is the balsamic phase of life where the accomplishments and disappointments of life are internalized to forge a sense of integrity at having lived and fulfilled an authentic life.

Another way in which we might think of this sevenfold life cycle is that it has four phases with three transitory phases or times of transition between one way of being and another. The four phases of the life cycle could be viewed as Childhood, Young Adulthood, Middle Age and Eldership, with the transition phases being Adolescence, the transition between Childhood and Young Adulthood; Midlife, the transition between Young Adulthood and Middle Age; and Seniority, the transition between Middle Age and Eldership.

While it is impossible to define some stages of life as being more fixed or stable than others, the in-between stages do represent times of change. It is during these phases of transition that life may be more uncertain or turbulent and more vulnerable to the repetition of family patterns.

Life Cycle Phase	Phase of Transition	Life Cycle Phase
Childhood	Adolescence	Young Adulthood
Young Adulthood	Midlife	Middle Age
Middle Age	Seniority	Eldership

In context of the family we are interested in how we and other living members of each generation in the family may be experiencing and re-experiencing similar planetary cycles. It is also important to note which cycles are repeating themselves as well as which other family members are experiencing an important stage within the same planetary cycle as yourself.

– CHAPTER 17 –
FULL CIRCLE
Family Passages from Conception to Death

Sociologist EM Duvall's work concentrated on the nodal points in the developmental life of the family. Erik Erikson studied the stages of the individual life cycle. Each theorist used eight phases of the cycle to differentiate the changing experience of both family and the individual throughout the course of life. While we could argue that the use of eight phases is arbitrary, as astrologers we are already familiar with the eightfold developmental sequence of the lunation cycle. This 29½-day cycle of the Sun and Moon, from New Moon to New Moon, is a visible reality each month and has always served as the quintessential round.

The lunation cycle is the classic archetypal cycle that marks out every nuance from birth to death. Its eight phases suggest the inevitability of growth, change, maturity and death. As an archetypal cycle its essence underpins all cycles and knowing its sequence helps us to instinctually identify the conventional stages within other cycles. Within the family there are predictable phases of change as the couple embarks on their relationship, lives together and creates their family life, as their children and other family members mature, leave home, forge new relationships and start their own families. The carousel of time goes around and around.[97] Understanding the unfolding lunation cycle as a metaphor for the life cycle acknowledges the natural human experience of the stages and phases of time and helps us to appreciate the changeable process of family life. When we plot the lunation cycle against the family and individual life cycle then we might also question the task of each phase of the family life cycle and how its members might best participate in this process. The natural rhythms of the lunar cycle are metaphoric of personal and familial stages of life.

The following table demonstrates how other concepts and theories broaden and deepen our understanding of astrological principles. While we cannot impose one system of thought directly on another, other ideas can inform the astrological wisdom. Each phase of the lunation cycle is a stage of personal and familial development that can be amplified by psychological and sociological suggestions.

The Waxing Phases

The Lunation Cycle	Keywords for this Phase	Personal: Erikson's tasks and challenges for the eight stages of life	Familial: Duvall's eight nodal phases of the family
New Moon	Birth	Trust; Basic trust versus basic mistrust	The courtship of the primary couple
Crescent	Struggle	Autonomy; Autonomy versus shame and doubt	Their marriage
First Quarter	Action	Initiative; Initiative versus guilt	Child-rearing years
Gibbous	Preparation	Industry; Industry versus inferiority	Their children's adolescence

The Waning Phases

Full Moon	Culmination	Identity; Identity versus role confusion	Leaving home
Disseminating	Convey	Intimacy; Intimacy versus isolation	The readjustment of the primary couple
Last Quarter	Edit	Generativity; Generativity versus stagnation	Grandparenting; Older age
Balsamic	Withdraw	Ego integrity; Ego integrity versus despair	Death

Familiarity with the cycles of the planets and some planetary pairs, such as the Sun and Moon, allows us to appreciate the individual and family life cycle in the context of the planetary cycles. Cycles are already well known to astrological students, so it comes as no surprise that family passages congregate around critical planetary aspects and are synchronous with major transits. We will now turn to some of the major phases in the personal and family life cycle that warrant further amplification for our understanding of our own and others' processes and experiences. Each of these phases is critical in informing the other phases of our lives and family life in general.

Birth
While life exists long before birth, it is birth that commonly marks the beginning of life. Birth acknowledges our separateness, independence and individuality. In both the personal and family life cycle, birth is one of the most intense and evocative watersheds in human experience.

William Wordsworth's *Ode: Intimations of Immortality from Recollections of Early Childhood*[98] is acknowledged as one of the poet's masterworks which mused on the magical fragments of childhood's exceptional relationship to nature and the reflective experience of this loss as an adult. While we cannot return to childhood, the remembrance of this state lingers, even though the feelings may be unconscious. Wordsworth's journey into childhood reminded him of his immateriality and, as he later expressed, it was his imagination of this time that connected him to understanding his immortality. Birth marks the transition between the Divine and the secular worlds and the felt experiences of this time are beyond the scope of explanation. As Wordsworth expressed:

> Our birth is but a sleep and a forgetting:
> The Soul that rises with us, our life's Star,
> Hath had elsewhere its setting,
> And cometh from afar

It is this birth transition that often characterizes and summarizes the way an individual will face all future transitions in their lives. In Greek myth, souls crossed the River Lethe or the river of oblivion as they entered or departed the underworld, which was a metaphor for the forgetting that Wordsworth associates with birth. The world before birth and after death remains forgotten, a mystery to the conscious life; its contents are sealed in an unseen vessel, accessed at times through reverie, imagination and/or feeling states. Felt experiences, myths and stories are carried through time by the family in both conscious and unconscious ways through remembering and forgetting.

Birth is the beginning of the human journey and our introduction to our human family. As the culmination of an epic journey, birth is an arrival after a long and demanding migration. In common with all arduous migrations, an ambivalent mixture of possibilities is carried with us into the new world. The exhilaration over these possibilities lives alongside the sense of displacement. Life is at the side of death; the beginning, also an ending. Birth is both the conclusion of a symbiotic and suspended experience and the initiation into an independent and down-to-earth world. The womb of mother opens onto the womb of the world and our exclusive time with her is forever altered. The mythic realm begins to slowly fade into the world of visible shapes and concrete structures. Birth is when the horoscope is cast; this is the momentary initiation into our individual journey and when the resources we have to navigate the passage become impressed upon the soul.

Birth, and to some extent childhood experiences, must be amnesiac states to survive this transition and move forward. This first potent transition involves grief at the loss of what we are no longer able to know or see. Wordsworth's poem also describes this poignantly:

> There was a time when meadow, grove, and stream,
> The earth, and every common sight,
> To me did seem
> Apparell'd in celestial light,
> The glory and the freshness of a dream.
> It is not now as it hath been of yore; –
> Turn wheresoe'er I may,
> By night or day,
> The things which I have seen I now can see no more.[99]

We muster defences to help ourselves undergo this transition between life in the womb and life outside it. One of these defences is forgetting, but the soul remembers and instinctually knows an authentic way to cope with this transition and all others. In the horoscope, birth is generally equated with the Ascendant, as the eastern horizon is where planets actually rise into view; hence the symbol of dawning or beginning. As the planets rise, they emerge out of a vast and darkened region below the horizon. At birth the babe emerges out of unremembered space from beyond the visible world.

The Ascendant is sometimes associated with masks or the appearance we assume to face the world. Astrologically, the Ascendant can reveal many things about our birth and perinatal conditions, as well as how we instinctually confront the world. Planets that are on the horizon (on the Ascendant-Descendant axis), especially if they conjoin the Ascendant, symbolize not only conditions surrounding the birth but how this energy is called upon every time a transition or new beginning occurs. The planet also illustrates the threads of a theme that run through the familial experience, as any ascending planet is met first by the family and is often thematic in family charts. In my experience it is common for the sign on the Ascendant to be highlighted in siblings' and parents' charts, especially if it appears on the horizon, meridian or the nodal axis. For instance, the four children of Queen Elizabeth II all share the same signs on their angles:

	Ascendant	**MC**	**Descendant**	**IC**
Charles	5♌24	13♈18	5♒24	13♎18
Anne	25♎02	3♌18	25♈02	3♒18
Andrew	11♌33	22♈37	11♒33	22♎37
Edward	15♎34	20♋26	15♈34	20♑26

Edward's MC-IC axis does not repeat the pattern; however, it is exactly the same axis as his mother's Ascendant-Descendant and nodal axis. The Queen's Ascendant is 21♑22 and her South Node is 20♑06, exactly conjunct Edward's IC. The Queen's Moon at 12♌07 contacts the angles of her other three children.[100]

In 2013 the Queen became a great-grandmother again when Prince George was born. Her great-grandson was born just before a Full Moon and his Capricorn Moon, at 28♑17, is in the same sign as her Ascendant. But it is her great-grandson's Ascendant, at 27♏07, which is so closely linked to her horoscope. Queen Elizabeth's MC is at 25♏32 and her Saturn is at 24♏26. Four generations later, the angles of the family charts are still intertwined.

In Chapter 15 we met Kaye and two of her grandchildren, Lauren and Elsie, who share her Sun-Mars conjunction and a Moon-Pluto aspect. Kaye has five granddaughters and the interaction in their charts between the Ascendant and other angles is quite remarkable. I have included the Vertex angle as well. Note that Trinity's Ascendant-MC mix is very different from that of her half-sisters and cousins, but her Vertex is conjunct Kaye's and Lauren's MCs, conjunct Mae's IC, conjunct Elsie's Descendant and conjunct Grace's MC.

	ASC	MC	DSC	IC	Vertex
Kaye	16♏57	22♊39	16♓57	22♐39	24♓25
Lauren	26♏43	26♊16	26♓43	26♐16	20♓35
Mae	25♓26	24♐51	25♍26	24♊51	16♍19
Elsie	27♐38	5♍49	27♊38	5♓49	17♉09
Trinity	8♒33	28♎15	8♌33	28♈15	23♊16
Grace	10♍00	18♊41	10♓00	18♐41	21♓22

The life force that is channelled through the Ascendant and spills into the 1st house is also indicative of our early environment and the vital life force that can be channelled and focused to support the growing and forward-moving personality. Our immediate environment is also our physical body, as it is the vehicle which transports the self; however, the familial environs also shape our responses and experiences of the new world. One way of thinking about the Ascendant is to compare it to birth, in that it is a moving and luminous transitional zone. Stephen Arroyo describes it as 'transcendent':

> ... the Ascendant symbolizes a way that the entire self is expressed so immediately and spontaneously that no mere words are capable of capturing its essence. It thus has almost a transcendent significance from the viewpoint of its importance in one's total integration as a fully functioning, dynamic individual.[101]

The images of birth and early family experiences are often constellated when working with the Ascendant. Howard Sasportas describes the Ascendant as being how we might hatch;[102] in other words, the way we open the shell of the self onto the world. Any planet on the Ascendant might tell a birth tale or a family story. For instance, Pluto may be the life-and-death feeling surrounding labour or the perinatal loss that heralded the birth; Neptune might symbolize the uncertainty and complications surrounding the delivery, the bleary and bewildered sense of feeling lost; Uranus reveals the unexpected disconnection or severance that took place near birth, an abrupt sense of entry and feelings of disassociation. Saturn rising might suggest a long and difficult labour, while Chiron on the horizon signals foreign feelings, a birth scar or a variety of other scenarios sympathetic to the planetary symbol.

With no language to be understood or thoughts to convey, the memories of this time are stored in the body and in the brain. But they are also etched onto the parchment of the horoscope. The sign on the Ascendant, its ruler and the angular planets convey images of the atmosphere that surrounded the birth and this includes the family condition at the time. The Ascendant is symbolic of birth and beginning and in a way we can think about the houses that follow as representing the next stages of initiation and development in the soul's journey through life. The birth narrative is an important story, especially if there is perinatal trauma. Birth trauma impacts upon all the other transitions of our lives and underscores all attempts to inseminate constructive beginnings. With this consciousness we can begin to acknowledge the birth story in the horoscope and how its pattern may continue to play out. It also serves as an entrée into understanding how we respond to transitions.

The Moon and its aspects are also important to note, as they not only symbolize the perinatal atmosphere but can also help to develop prenatal imagery. The symbolism of the Moon is multi-dimensional and aspects to the Moon could be thought of as images during gestation, since the Moon refers to both mother and her womb. Prenatal images are also revealed through 12th house imagery; hence planets in the 12th, or connected to the 12th, symbolize situations during gestation, especially associated with the mother's feeling life and events within the family. One way of thinking about the Moon is that it records the gestation journey.

Birth is such a highly-charged transition in family life, yet we have few tools to help us understand the process or the uninvited feelings or sensations that arise in respect to this. However, astrology can help to illuminate this for us. In my consulting practice I have had ample examples of planets in the 12th synchronizing with prenatal experiences and often these are accompanied by strong aspects to the Moon or planets on the horizon. With these placements, prenatal or perinatal disturbances may be at the heart of later distress. I am also alert to the familial conditions and whether these experiences have ever been acknowledged, mourned or even identified, and am also attentive to family patterns and stories. The following example is one I described in my book *The Sibling Constellation* but it again serves as a reminder of the capacity that astrology has of helping to unlock personal and familial imagery:

Wendy has Gemini on the 12th house cusp with Saturn in this house. Saturn is involved in a Yod pattern with the Moon and Mercury and is the apex of a T-square with Venus and Chiron-Neptune. The Chiron-Neptune conjunction falls exactly on the IC with Chiron taking the 3rd house side and Neptune the 4th. Mercury rules both the 12th and 3rd houses and is opposite Pluto. The powerful aspects focusing on the 12th house Saturn draw our attention to the collective and familial realms of the 12th and also supply us with pre-birth images that illustrate how the feeling life of a mother can be absorbed by a baby while *in utero*.[103]

Wendy's mother suffered a horrible trauma when three months pregnant with Wendy. She was standing on the porch of her midwestern home waiting for her daughter, Patti, to cross the street. It was Patti's seventh birthday, and both mother and daughter were excited about the celebrations planned. A car swerving down the road, totally out of control, hit and knocked down Patti before smashing into the tree which brought it to a halt. Patti was killed instantly. The family later discovered that the woman driving the car had suffered an epileptic seizure. We can see the loss of the sibling reflected in the images of Pluto opposite Mercury, ruler of the 3rd; Chiron on the 3rd house side of the IC and the Moon opposite Uranus. The family atmosphere of the missing sister can be seen through Chiron-Neptune conjunct the IC opposite Venus, the ruler of the IC, both squaring Saturn in the 12th. But Patti's was not the only life lost that day.

When Wendy was ten she was rushed to hospital because the attending doctor thought her appendix had ruptured. However, the problem was later traced to a growth, the size of a grapefruit,

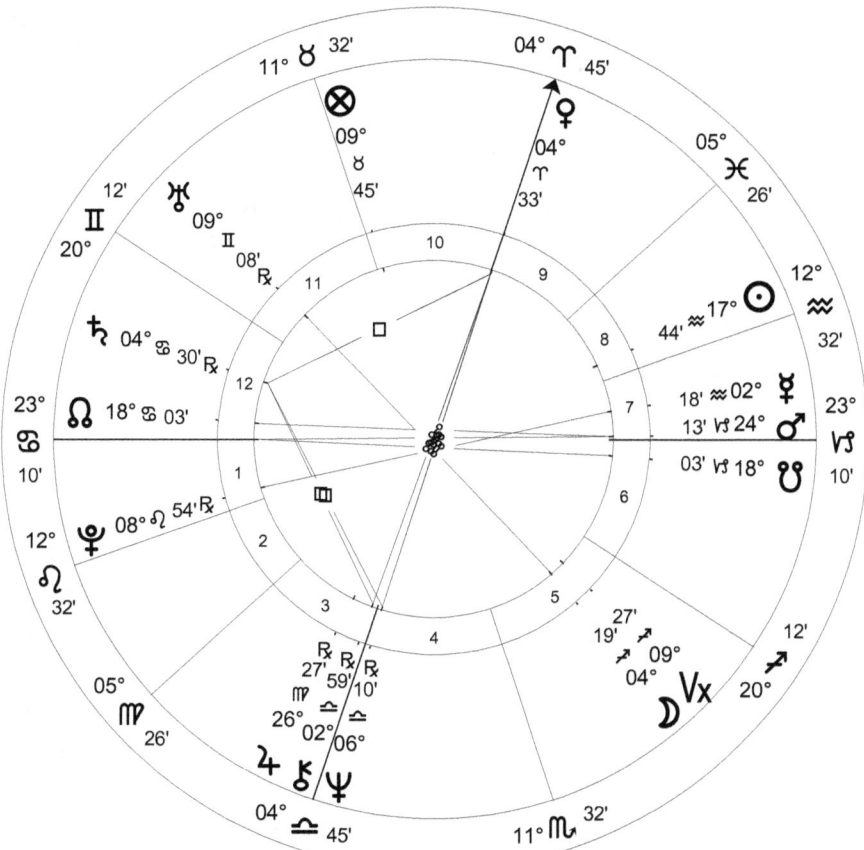

connected to her spine. Part of her bowel had to be removed in the operation and, because of the complications, the doctors thought Wendy had little chance of surviving. It was Easter, 1955.

At this time, progressed Mars was conjunct natal Mercury and progressed Mercury was just separating from the Sun. By transit, Uranus was exactly on Wendy's Ascendant with Jupiter close behind. These two planets would conjunct the following month just over 1° from her Ascendant. Wendy did survive. The emergency of the Uranian experience often allows us to be separate enough from the trauma – through shock, disbelief or numbness – to survive such tumultuous events. But eleven years later, complications arose and Wendy was back in hospital; an infection from the first operation was beginning to have an adverse effect. The doctors operated again.

The progressed Sun was now squaring Uranus. The progressed Sun, as her evolving ego strength, was ready to identify the part of herself from which she had been severed. The Moon was progressing through the 3rd house for the first time, contributing to the consciousness of Wendy's sibling story. Within days of the operation, Uranus and Pluto were making their second exact conjunction in her 3rd house. It was after this operation that the doctors told Wendy what had been removed eleven years before.

Wendy was a surviving twin: her twin was absorbed possibly due to the traumatic episode in her mother's womb. Part of her twin had become joined to her spine. Saturn rules the spine, and in myth he interred his progeny. Saturn, in Wendy's 12th house, is consistent with this pre-birth atmosphere.

Since ultrasound technology has been able to reveal earlier stages in the gestation process, it has shown that many twin pregnancies result in a single birth. One of the twins is either absorbed into the body of the other twin or expelled unnoticed by the mother. Wendy had participated in the womb phenomenon that is commonly known as the 'vanishing twin' syndrome. Hence *in utero* events and trauma are registered by the developing soul and we might be able to first recognize these through the lens of the Ascendant, the 12th house and aspects to the Moon.

Following the thread of her Uranus-Moon conjunction a student unravelled her own *in utero* imagery. Scorpio is on the cusp of the 12th and its traditional ruler Mars is also in Scorpio conjunct Saturn perching on the 12th house cusp. However, it was the symbolism of her dynamic Uranus-Moon conjunction that she correlated with the prenatal shocks that her mother experienced. The revelation helped to put some of her feelings into perspective. She writes:

> Astrological symbolism had helped me to explain or at the very least to ground a suspected connection between an absolute fear and loathing of blood and sharp objects and the knowledge that when my mother was 33 weeks pregnant with me she was subjected to a huge shock involving large amounts of blood after a shocking interaction my brother experienced with a sharp object.
>
> My mother was standing in the kitchen when a farmhand working for my father arrived at our front door carrying my brother in his arms. He had a deep cut in his leg which left the impression in her memory of the bottom part of his leg hanging off and dripping blood. A blade from a threshing machine at the back of a tractor had

sliced through his leg and there was lots of blood. My own repetitive dream when I was a small child (three to five years old), of being under the threat of attack from two workmen wielding a saw, bears an uncanny similarity to that experience and I have a sense that the trauma may have been transmitted to me *in utero*, reinforced by a serious haemorrhage when my mother gave birth to me.

It was much more recently that my mother told me that she also experienced a blow out of a tyre on the highway to Brisbane when she was heavily pregnant with me – with my brother (aged five) and my sister (aged two) in the car. While she managed to pull over without hitting any other cars or crashing her own, she reported having received quite a shock and having been extremely worried for the safety of her three dependants.[104]

Pregnancy and birth are tenuous times. While medical technology has lessened the incidents of perinatal trauma and death, nonetheless they are still prevalent and a source of much anxiety. The source of the concern may be unconscious, carried through time by unresolved family trauma or mystery. Nonetheless, the fear is still felt and real.

A birth in a family affects all rungs of the family system. The sibling system expands to accommodate another member; the parental system has additional stressors and the extended family widens to embrace the new arrival. Birth is usually surrounded by a charged and electric atmosphere; any new arrival into the family is destined to change its dynamic as the status quo is shaken up and the unit will never be the same again. This moment, immortalized in the birth horoscope of the child, is also the transits to each family member. This time, the child's horoscope, endures through the synastry between the child and the family members living at the time.

The birth horoscope also represents the dynamic of change that the child births into the family structure. Therefore it is worth reflecting on the passage of your birth, as it offers a deeper appreciation of your Ascendant through the atmosphere of this early entry into the family dynamic.

Childhood

Wordsworth wrote 'Heaven lies about us in our infancy',[105] words that are reminiscent of the magical and other-worldly aspects of the infant's atmosphere that contain both the wonder and the fragility of these early days. For this poet, childhood's end was abruptly marked at the age of eight by the death of his mother. He was sent away to school and separated from his 'dear, dear sister'[106] for nine years as she too was sent away to school, but to another part of England.

For some the memories from infancy may feel innocent, while for others 'sad' or 'unhappy' feelings still pervade this time. Or, like Wordsworth, there may be loss and grief interlaced with this period. Depending on the felt experiences of those first years of family life, childhood may have been an idyllic playground or a relentless battleground. Whatever our experiences or memories, the passage of childhood has been the architect of who we have become.

The term 'childhood' does not refer to any specific period of time but generally implies the phase between infancy and puberty. Perhaps we could think of early childhood as a prelude to the literal world, a time of play, an age of innocence or an interlude when magical thinking is the norm and imagination is real. During this phase the child's psychic life is still very influenced by the psychic life of the parent. Once we experience the dynamic impact of the first Jupiter opposition, the first progressed Moon square and the first Saturn square, this phase of childhood cedes to a period of social discovery beyond the perimeters of the family. School has begun and a new sense of being, as well as a new way of adapting to the world, heralds the next phase. This watershed in human development occurs around the age of seven, the first Saturn square, when imagination yields to reality.

Psychoanalytic theories about the passage of childhood are numerous, and while the roles and objectives of an astrologer are not the same as those of an analyst or psychologist, nonetheless the theoretical maps charted by these clinicians can amplify and ensoul our astrological images. Astrology naturally classifies the sub-stages of childhood based on the cycles of the inner planets Mars and Jupiter, but psychological and sociological hypotheses can amplify our understanding of the human processes that take place at this stage of the life cycle. We can see in the following table that the returns of the planets are clearly defined marking posts for early development.

The first initiation at 27 days old is evident by the Moon's return. In these first 27 days of life the Moon has travelled through each sign, transited every house and made every aspect possible to every planet and point in the horoscope.

Sub Stage of Childhood	Age-related Developmental Period	Astrological Developmental Cycle	Initiation of the Planetary Return
Newborn	Ages 0-4 weeks	From birth to the first lunar return at 27.3 days	**Moon**
Infant	Ages 4 weeks- approximately 1 year	From the first lunar return at 27.3 days to the first solar return which will also include the phases of the first Mercury and Venus returns	**Mercury Venus Sun**
Toddler	Ages 1-2 years	From the first solar return to the first Mars return	**Mars**
Pre-school	Ages 2-6 years	From the first Mars return to the first Jupiter opposition	
School	Ages 6-12 years	From the first Jupiter opposition to the first Jupiter return	**Jupiter**

As previously mentioned, psychodynamic theories can amplify the important stages of childhood development in different ways. For instance, Freud's psychosexual developmental theory categorizes stages of childhood based on the focal point of the child's libido. Freud noticed that the child became centred on the primary erogenous zones of the mouth, the anus and the genital region at certain stages of development. This stimulated certain age-specific behaviours in the child's maturation. When the progress and natural gratification of these stages were compromised, generally because of unmet needs, he claimed that the consequence could be a fixation that repeats throughout life. As a way of thinking about childhood development, the three phases Freud identified are:

1. **The oral phase** describes the passage when the child is focused on the mouth and receives pleasure from sucking and accepting things into the mouth. This phase is generally seen to last from birth to the second year. When the child feels deprived of nourishment, unsatisfied from sucking the breast or unfilled during this time, the adult response is to gratify the unmet urges physically through the mouth and psychologically through dependant behaviours. Oral fixation might include biting, chewing nails, smoking, and excessive drinking and eating habits. Psychologically, oral individuals recreate the child's dependency on others to nurture and take care of them. They may be gullible and undiscerning, swallowing inappropriate ideas and promises. Emotionally they may be unable to hold down any feelings of negativity or, as Hugh Crago suggests: 'They tend to express their emotions wholeheartedly and unguardedly, "throwing up" their feelings without much regard for the effect they have on others.'[107]

    This phase embraces the first returns of the Moon and the Sun as well as Mercury and Mars. Aspects to the Moon are brought to life during this phase because the primary object of contentment – the mother's breast – is lunar. A challenging Moon-Saturn aspect might be experienced during this phase as feeling hungry or cold; literally, there may be a shortage of breast milk or physical touch while emotionally there may a lack of feeling held. The continuation of these feelings into adulthood is experienced as lack of support or encouragement and emotional coldness. Our Moon sign is descriptive of our orientation to this phase.

2. **The anal phase** is generally placed between the ages of two and four and is focused on the anus, the bowel and bladder elimination. Control becomes an issue; physically, the control of the sphincter muscle becomes the focus. We might suggest this phase is ushered in by the Mars return between 17 and 22 months and the chapter commonly known as the 'terrible twos'. Hence will, mine or mother's, becomes an issue, as does the urge to express and separate. Toilet training becomes a focus for this will.

An adult anal personality is one who becomes fixed and unable to let go; they stockpile assets as well as withhold their feelings and ideas. Emotionally, they may be able to let loose with anger or resentment but they have an inability to express connective feelings such as love, or vulnerable ones such as grief and fear. They often cling to the past rather than feel confident about the future. Hanging on to the way things were can constrict maturity and development. Freud referred to the anal adult as the obsessive personality: over-organized, compulsively tidy and emotionally tight.

Astrologically, Mars is prominent during this phase as the will and urge to separate are awakened. However, the Sun is also roused during this time and therefore the role of the father becomes fundamental at this stage. Aspects to the Sun and Mars will focus on the development of the will, identity, creativity and ease of separation as well as the dynamic input of the father. During this stage the 2nd house is highlighted through the ability to master the body and feel a sense of worth and value. Therefore planets in the 2nd house are active in this process; the 3rd house is important as well, due to the mobility and movement associated with this time. Planets in the 3rd house that are activated at this time will provide an indication about how we might have navigated this phase and its implications for adult life.

3. **The phallic phase** begins near the age of four and is centred on the genitals. It is at this stage that the child becomes aware of desire, sexuality and parental dynamics. Aware that he is part of a triangle, he seeks to unite with his mother by 'killing off' his father. At least, this was Freud's idea, which was his cornerstone Oedipal theory; hence this segment is often known as the Oedipal phase. Thematically it is suggested that the subject matter arising during the Oedipal phase is re-encountered during adolescence and again at midlife.

Since sexuality and our identity are beginning to intertwine during this development phase, the aspects and placements of Venus and Mars are important to note. It is at this stage, and again at puberty and during adolescence, that these two archetypes are starting to awaken. The 4th house is also significant as the house of the parents and how we feel connected to them.

I would note that each of the first four houses could be linked to these developmental phases from birth to seven or eight years of age. In this way, the 1st house aligns with birth and the atmosphere of the following months. The 2nd house is akin to the anal phase of the development of control, autonomy and will. During this period we also take in the familial values and experiment with the pleasures of the senses. It is a time when we experience feeling valued, loved, appreciated. The 3rd house is the conscious awakening of separateness, the image of the sibling as other and the atmosphere of having mobility and freedom. The 4th house is the family and parental atmosphere. These first four houses could be imagined as childhood; therefore planets in these houses might have a strong affinity and influence from this time.

As astrologers, what we can reflect on here is not the literal nature of these phases, but the use of this theory as a way of thinking about how an individual's horoscope is aroused during childhood. For instance, we can begin to recognize that a strong Venus-Pluto aspect might have been vulnerable during the Oedipal sense of development when the child was picking up the emotional nuances of the parents' relationship, sensitive to the intensity of love or lack as well as sensing when the bond was broken or betrayed. These impressions shape the adult orientation to trust in relationship and inform the development of the aspect throughout life. Working with the astrological images and arrangements in tandem with the familial influences during these times helps to illustrate how the archetypal arrangement is animated in a client's life. A Taurean Moon opposite Saturn in Scorpio may be very akin to 'anal' behaviour such as holding on or being controlled. Your understanding of these phases helps a client to question their experience and family story at a particular time in their life so they can amplify the image and encourage links and feeling memories in order to feel the inner experience of this aspect. A Moon-Uranus conjunction in the 6th house may be synchronous with an allergy to dairy products; however, you can also draw on images and metaphors from the oral phase to elicit earlier responses to the feelings of comfort and nurturing, and to encourage the individual to have a felt experience of the aspect. Liz Greene has also explored these phases of childhood in terms of the defences of the personality.[108]

The progressed Moon's journey over the terrain of early life is highly significant. I imagine that preverbal encounters, precognitive impressions, feeling responses, inner imagery and emotions of early childhood are sensed by the progressed Moon and stored in the lunar vessel until ego development is ready to experience these senses. During the second round of the progressed Moon through the horoscope, between 27 and 55 years of age, memories of childhood can be more easily integrated. Hence the progressed Moon serves as the museum where our felt experiences throughout life are stored.

Erik Erikson's childhood life stages speak about the tasks and challenges during this phase. In considering the tasks we can reflect on the archetypal arrangement of our horoscope because astrologically it will be evident that certain phases will be more difficult to navigate, given certain aspects. For instance, the task of trusting others during the first year of life would be much more complex for a Moon-Pluto individual, especially if there were losses, taboos activated or unspoken mysteries.

Erik Erikson's Life Stage

Approximate Age	Task	Struggle	Outcome
Infants; birth to 18 months	Trust	Basic trust versus basic mistrust	Drive and hope
Toddlers; 18 months to 3 years	Autonomy	Autonomy versus shame and doubt	Self-control and willpower
Preschool; 3-6 years	Initiative	Initiative versus guilt	Direction and purpose
Childhood; 6-12 years	Industry	Industry versus inferiority	Method and competence

Therefore it is helpful to know the family story of the time so as to be in a better position to understand how this aspect might be felt. Perhaps Mars in Taurus squaring Uranus in Leo might be experienced as an absolute severance from resources once valued, the rationalization of intense anger or perhaps hanging onto something for dear life but then abruptly and cold-heartedly walking away from it. What happened during the early stage of development around the two-year mark?

Jean Piaget studied the mental growth of the child and articulated the child's development from prelogical and magical thought through to the development of logical and concrete thinking. He articulated the egocentricity of young thought in that everything that happens is connected to them. This natural development shows that at this stage no sense of separateness is conscious and the child is immersed in the world around them, losing interest in what they can no longer see yet also panicking when their security system, i.e. mother, ventures out of sight.

Yet by three years old mother can disappear from sight and the child knows she still exists. Individuation and separateness develop. Piaget and others help us to reflect on how the astrological images in the horoscope might make the transition between the preliterate and literal ways of knowing or the preverbal and the oral ways of communicating. Here we are immediately drawn to the development of the Moon and Mercury. For instance, an astrological image of a complicated Neptune aspect to the Moon and/or Mercury might lead us to suspect that the transition from the imaginal to the literal way of thinking would be difficult. Therefore it might be helpful to examine the early stages of childhood for signs of how the family's emphasis on cognitive development supported or neglected this development.

Transactional Analysis (TA) postulated that three ego states were shaped during childhood and that damaging early development may lead to fixating on one of these states. TA's founder Eric Berne's most popular book, *Games People Play* (1964), presented his theories while his colleague Thomas Harris followed these up in his book *I'm OK – You're OK* (1969). The three states of development were referred to as the Child ego state, the Parent ego state and the Adult ego state. As you will see, these states resonate with the astrological archetypes of the Moon, Saturn and the Sun, as well as the Freudian model of the Id, Ego and Superego.

According to TA, the Child ego state is the most primary state and begins at the moment of conception, which supports the concept that aspects to the Moon may reveal pre-birth images. Psychologically, this state is the feeling of the personality and is a complex of all the things that we ever felt, wanted, tasted, smelled and experienced as children. The Child ego state is always retained, no matter how mature we become. In astrological terms, the Moon can always be prone to regression to the Child ego state, responding at the preverbal or pre-social levels. I find this TA description is a helpful metaphor for the Moon and what it contains, as if it is the vessel of all sensory, emotional and familial feeling. The progressed Moon too becomes the dynamic movement of this through individual development.

The Parent ego state begins at birth and records all the verbal and non-verbal interaction with the parents. It consists of their spoken rules and regulations, the 'shoulds' and 'should-not's of family life impressed through nonverbal clues and body language. This state helps to socialize the child mainly through imperatives, such as 'No', 'Be careful' or 'Watch out', but also includes the authoritative 'Mark my words' and limiting remarks such as 'You can't do that'. This state contains the fears, concerns and defences that we grow up with. Astrologically, we can see this state as being represented by Saturn and it is worth reflecting on the early developmental experience of this planet. An elder child and/or a child with a dominant Saturn will be highly attuned to this stage of development. Without the appropriate support and approval through this stage the child internalizes Saturn as a punitive, harsh and negative inner critic.

The Adult ego state begins at about ten months old, just as Mercury, the Sun and Venus approach the completion of their first cycles. The Adult state suggests the beginning of integration from several sources of information – the feelings from the Child state, the rules and regulations of the Parent state and the understanding that is possible in the Adult state. It is more reflective and considered and allows new understanding of previous difficulties and dilemmas.

Transactional Analysis demonstrates the developmental states that correspond to the archetypes of the Moon, Sun and Saturn, which are the energies also strongly connected to the parents. Childhood is such an important stage in family life, because the child who is immersed in the family pool needs the parents' support and consciousness to navigate the passage in a healthy way. It is in childhood where we obtain the seminal pictures and impressions as to how the astrological images and aspects may have begun to take shape in the inner life of the individual. Childhood is the shaping influence for the development of the inner planets, which are the founding principles of how we will respond socially and responsibly. We look to our childhood for seminal images of our planetary development. But we also reflect on childhood because it informs us of early patterns that recur at other times of transition in our lives.

Moon	Mercury	Venus	Sun	Mars	Jupiter	Saturn
Id			Ego			Super-ego
The Child			Adult			Parent
	language	values		will	beliefs	

The inner adult learns to mediate between the child and the parent

In writing about the Family Constellation, Carl Jung suggested that one of the most important aims of education was 'to free the growing child from his unconscious attachment to the influence of his early environment, in such a way that he may keep what is valuable in it and reject whatever is not'.[109] In many ways, this is a lifelong task and one that is tested in adolescence.

Adolescence

In the family life cycle, adolescence is an extremely important and critical transition between childhood and adulthood, when a plethora of physical, emotional, psychological and spiritual changes occur. It is also a period when predictability is replaced by uncertainty and security is compromised by all the changes that are taking place. These changes are often rapid and physiologically awkward, resulting in adolescent angst – a temperamental condition well known to parents of teenagers. Teen angst and its resulting mood swings are common to this passage, but they adjust throughout the developmental transition of adolescence. The anxiety that accompanies hormonal and bodily changes subsides throughout the period while the emotional changes also begin to even out towards the latter phase of adolescence.

As adolescents begin to want more mastery, control and responsibility in their lives, there is a natural movement away from parental regulation towards peer influence. In this gap peers play a prominent role. However, there is also the danger of becoming psychologically stranded if the teenager abandons or is abandoned by their parents. Important relationships outside the family, on both equal and hierarchical levels, begin to develop. The life schema is broadening and the overt attachment to the secure base of the family is being reduced.

During this passage the changes in the adolescent's attachment to the parent are very observable as they experiment with new relationships, friendships and families outside their own. The first trimester of adolescence occurs approximately between the first Jupiter return and the first Saturn opposition. During this phase of adolescence 'being normal' is the main concern and for the most part parents and adults are not considered part of this category. From the perspective of an adolescent, friends are in the know about things, while parents are mainly ignorant and badly informed. When the worlds of friends and parents converge accidentally, young teens are often embarrassed to be seen with their parents. In an attempt to assert their independence, young teens often disregard and disobey rules and parental authority, while simultaneously grieving the loss of their earlier relationship with their parents. Sadness and grief for the loss of childhood and parental closeness become muddled with rebellion.

We could place middle adolescence as being from the first Saturn opposition to the first nodal return, when teenagers continue to sever the umbilical cord with their parents. Clashing with the parents, challenging authority and attempting to renegotiate rules becomes the norm. Physically, the adolescent grows in height, often surpassing their parents. Psychologically, the parents are 'shrinking' in stature and developmentally the adolescent is beginning to internalize the parental voice and authority. Peer group conformity is well established and the values, styles and goals of the adolescent's peers replace parental values and tastes. Peer pressure culminates during mid-adolescence.

By the last stage of adolescence the teenager is on the verge of adulthood. This coming of age is accompanied by some very powerful astrological transits, starting first with the nodal return but then followed by the waning progressed Moon square at approximately 20.5 years of age, the Neptune semi-square at 20.5 years, the first Uranus square and the waning Saturn square between the ages of 21 and 22. The nodal return between ages of 18 and 19 heralds the later adolescent phase. This time could be likened to a calling, an awakening to the soul's impulse to forge the life path. During this later adolescent phase, the intensity of peer relationships changes and it is more likely that the relationship with the parents is rekindled and conducted in a more adult manner. The adolescent's own intimate relationships may start to be introduced into the family and the parents' guidance and experience is more likely to be called upon to help launch them into the world. The waning of the adolescent phase is synchronous with the next Jupiter return just before the 24th birthday. Another Jupiter cycle introduces a new phase of the life cycle, with the experience of adolescence supporting the next phase of development.

The seminal and potent experience of the planetary cycles during adolescence will be repeated throughout the life cycle. For instance, Jupiter will return again, Saturn will oppose itself, Uranus will square itself. What is of significance here is that the cycle of the adolescent often converges with the planetary cycles experienced by their parents. How the parent experienced their own adolescence plays a role in how they deal with their adolescent child acting out in front of them.

Initiation follows separation, and through adolescence we first experience whether the familial container has supplied us with adequate emotional resources to feel safe enough through this passage. When young saplings are in the path of a hurricane, it is their root system that ensures their survival. Similarly, during the stormy period of adolescence it is the strong root system of the family which holds the adolescent. Family schisms and complexes weaken the secure base of the family.

In terms of family, the adolescence passage is re-experienced by the parents and grandparents of the adolescent. There is a chance of healing and accepting their wounds from the adolescent passage, but if they lack consciousness the parents are also susceptible to projecting their own limits onto their adolescent children. Life recycles the unprocessed psychic substances. There are many ways of thinking about when parental complexes may present themselves again; one is when the child's passage ignites the parent's unresolved transition. The parent is always challenged by their children's transitions if their own remain untreated. This is family time. However, astrologically we can also chart the repetitive cycles that reverberate through the family life cycle.

For instance, during early adolescence the first Jupiter return is experienced at 12 years of age. How did the parent experience this time when new beliefs, hopes, goals and desires are awakened? This could be complicated if the parent is undergoing a Jupiter return themselves at age 36 or 47. The progressed Moon opposes itself at approximately 14 years of age and indicates a swelling of complex feelings and the heightening of adolescent angst. At 41 and 68 we re-experience this aspect. How it was initially experienced in family life plays a strong role in how it is re-experienced at these ages.

The first Saturn opposition at approximately 15 years is re-experienced at ages 44 and 74. But what is of great importance is how the parent demonstrates the Saturnian principles of responsibility, power, control, self-regulation, authority and goal-setting without exhibiting an overbearing, inflexible and dictatorial attitude. The parent's personal experience of their own Saturn opposition will inform how they handle their child's transition. When the adolescent experiences this transition, the parent's recollection of their adolescent passage is brought to the surface. Hierarchy is essential in early childhood. However, this must loosen if adolescents are to develop a sense of personal autonomy. If it does not, structure and safety, predictability and controllability become rigid and imprisoning, threatening the creativity of the individual at this crucial period of transition.

The first nodal return at age 19 is a calling to the world; this is repeated at ages 37, 56 and 74. The first return at 19 will awaken the memories of the parents' hopes, dreams and wishes at this point in their lives. In this way transits and cycles are systemic as they reverberate throughout the family system. But what is significant with the first return of the nodes is how the family supports and encourages our pathway into the world. This is flavoured by their own experiences of how their dreams were realized.

In our early twenties the Uranus waxing square at 20-21 and the Saturn waning square at 22 are powerful initiations into adult life. Again, the attitudes and experiences of our parents and ancestors influence these initiations. During the forties these two planets have a combined effect as Uranus opposes itself somewhere between the ages of 38 and 42 and Saturn opposes itself between 44 and 45. The second Saturn return at 59-60 is closely followed by the waning Uranus square. From the ancestral perspective, how are we shaped to meet these transitions? From a familial perspective, we can see that the parent has an opportunity for redemption at each transition that the child experiences.

Each life stage presents us with important tasks. At adolescence there are many important tasks, but concentrating on the following three helps the transition to adulthood become more effective. From an adolescent perspective these tasks might feel superfluous, yet they are vitally important. This is where parental direction and support become essential.

- The direction and focus of your vocation as an adult
- Becoming autonomous and responsible
- Maintaining intimate relationships

Without the parental support for these factors throughout adolescence we face them again at midlife, when we are called upon to re-parent what was not fostered in us.

The final stage of adolescence and freeing ourselves from the family home is an important stage in itself. The task of leaving home is important to consider, as without conscious awareness of this transition we are often condemned to repeat it in all future separations. From an astrological perspective we might imagine how we step across the threshold between the 4th and the 5th houses.

Leaving Home
The lyrics to the mid-1960s Beatles' song 'She's Leaving Home' encapsulated the desperate way in which many adolescents from the Pluto in Leo generation left home. The daughter leaves home by leaving a note on the kitchen table. Turning her back on her parents, without any goodbyes, she sneaks away into the early morning darkness to rendezvous with her destiny. Her parents, who claimed to have given her 'everything money could buy', are in shock.[110]

Her parents are full of disbelief; they feel abandoned and betrayed. The heroine leaves the stifling atmosphere of her parents' home for the promise of more fun with a car salesman, who represents a new and exciting liberated life. Unprepared for the road ahead and unaware of the grief her separation from home will stir, she is at risk of having no security or safety net once her new relationship fails. The familial environment and her parents have failed to help her prepare for the initiation of 'leaving home'. Without the encouraging messages that will support her in crossing the threshold to the outer world, she is at risk of recreating the stifling home atmosphere she desperately wants to leave. Astrologically she is at risk of regressing to the 4th house, unable to separate from the powerful and archaic patterns that underpin her foundation stone, the IC. Her future security rests on the base constructed with the material supplied by the family of origin and their ancestors.

An earlier pop song sung by Sue Thompson, 'James (Hold the Ladder Steady)' in a more light-hearted way told of elopement, the only option left after both mother and father had rejected and ridiculed the daughter's pleas to be allowed to marry her sweetheart.[111] Leaving home for the Pluto in Leo generation was often a traumatic experience for everyone involved in this stage of separation.

One of the most common ways for this generation to leave their parent's home was to go into a marriage, romantically being carried over the threshold of their new home, yet poised to recreate the same familial scenario they had vowed to leave. Or they went into the arms of a lover who held the promise of a new life or onto an aeroplane or ship that transported them to a faraway adventure. Naively there was an assumption that the world would provide nourishment in the way the parental home should have done. Unfortunately, this important transition was often poorly executed with no rituals or process of conscious separation, so those left at home often felt abandoned or betrayed while those who left felt guilty and unworthy.

However, it was not only this generation who struggled to cross the straits between the familial home and the outside world. This stage of the life cycle is an archetypal experience, a passage that myth and religion often detailed, such as in Adam and Eve leaving the Garden of Eden or Medea leaving her father's house.[112] Mythic heroines left their parents' homes, leaving behind them a storm of feelings and a web of betrayal.

Ariadne fell in love with the shining face of the young hero Theseus who had been sent to her Minoan palace from Athens to face the Minotaur, her half-brother. Besotted, she arranged to help Theseus slay her monstrous sibling who had been hidden in the labyrinth below the palace. Having conspired in the murder, Ariadne fled the palace with Theseus and escaped into the dark Mediterranean night on her hero's Athenian ship. She abandoned her father's palace. Not only had she colluded in killing her half-brother but she left behind Phaedra, her younger sister. Phaedra, on the threshold of puberty, watched the course her older sister took to leave home, being impressed and influenced by her actions and choices. Having betrayed her family, Ariadne herself was betrayed, left stranded on the island of Naxos, the first port of call after their departure from Crete.

Similarly, Ariadne's cousin, Medea, betrayed her father, killed her brother and abandoned her homeland to help a foreign hero. Without Medea, Jason could have never succeeded in his quest to retrieve the Golden Fleece. And like Theseus, Jason also turned his back on his helpmate/lover. Betrayal was recreated in both relationships. The partner, who had been the impetus for leaving home, was now the one to leave.

The trauma of the severed relationship with family and homeland is a haunting and powerful force, which will reverberate throughout an individual's life and be replayed during other endings. The success of this transition from the homeland not only signifies the end of childhood and parental dependence but also is a pattern that re-emerges whenever old ways of being are no longer valid. During major life changes the unfinished business of 'leaving home' is revealed, emotionally catapulting the individual back into the earlier patterns of separation turmoil. To leave home emotionally requires not only the heroic impulse but the support and encouragement of those we leave behind.

Leaving home represents a transitional time in every family member's life. This pivotal time is crucial, as leaving home represents the movement away from the safety and security of the familial womb out into the world beyond the family. Astrologically, the crossing of the threshold between the 4th house of family and the 5th house of the heroic self represents this liminal phase. Developmentally, the 4th house marks the ending of the first four houses of personal initiation, ideally ending with the internalization of the 4th house sense of inner security. The 5th house marks the first of the four interpersonal houses and the beginning of the labours of forging identity outside the family, as well as the beginning of the transference of loyalties away from the familial matrix and onto the beloved. The 5th house cusp separating the homeland from the world beyond is the threshold that the hero and heroine cross, often a vivid clue to the process of leaving home.

Like the other cusps of the houses of life (the 1st and 9th), the 5th house cusp represents the emergence into new worlds of discovery. The Beatles' heroine turns the 'back door key' and steps across the threshold into the arms of her lover. Like Theseus and Jason, he is the embodiment of the hero who stimulates the urge to leave and venture into the world beyond family. Lamenting, the chorus realizes that 'fun is the one thing that money can't buy'. The 5th house represents a world of exploration that can no longer take place in the familial home. The heroine falls in love with the foreign hero, the representation of the world outside her familial container. The lunar world of the 4th house and the symbiosis with the family matrix are left behind in the transition towards the solar hero. The 5th house constellates the mythic hero who battles the dragons of the Great Mother and who ventures outside his comfort zone. When the 4th house environment is polluted by the toxicity of secrets, lies or repressed monsters (like the Minoan Minotaur and the dragon that Jason slays), the heroic impulse is to 'kill off' the monster which sets the circle of betrayal in motion.

Underpinning this change is an enormity of grief invisible in the excitement of separation. Childhood is finished; adolescence is waning. Unconditional acceptance is threatened. When the leaving home process is complicated, the individual indiscriminately places their trust in the outsider. The assumed reality is that the world outside will be supportive. Disillusionment often follows, shattering the assumptions that the external world will be more welcoming than the familial one. The misplaced loyalties and love rebound. Mourning is generally not ritualized at this stage and sits as a hollow feeling of emptiness under the upwardly mobile urges to discover the world outside. Without the proper mentoring the mourning can turn to despair, self-destruction, at worst self-loathing. The courage to leave what is familiar is often projected onto another who then must betray us in order for us to find the interior courage imbedded in the 5th house.

Separation is intimately linked to bonding. As already discussed, the ability to separate without destructive emotional undertones is a product of secure attachment. When the familial home has been violated by abuse or the atmosphere is clouded with violence, the world outside is also unsafe. Without secure attachment the individual is often at risk of making the wrong choices, trusting the wrong individual and therefore constellating betrayal. At the transitional point of leaving home, our sense of secure attachment becomes a primary indication of the transition's success.

The Moon is systemic in nature because it also describes the mother and her feeling life; quite literally, it may also describe the route that mother took to leave home, a roadway we may have instinctively travelled. Young people often repeat the leaving home pattern of their parents. The lunar statement in the horoscope suggests how we bond and how our urge to bond was met in the atmosphere of the home, directly shaping the way we separate and leave home. When the lunar constellation or 4th house is too difficult to deal with, we may split off from that aspect in favour of a more supportive one. Perhaps our Beatles' heroine left her Moon-Saturn constellation to pursue a more favourable aspect of her horoscope. However, without the necessary support to help her cross the threshold that leads to the outside world, she is destined to carry this Moon-Saturn image into her relationships.

Jay Haley, a pioneer in Family Therapy, suggests four important messages to help us leave home without guilt, shame or feeling encumbered by parental grief.[113] The roots of these messages are held in our early experiences of attachment and separation and are important in encouraging the development of ego strength. Mythically, this is similar to the commencement of the heroic trial or labours where the gods offer the hero important gifts for their forward journey. These four messages are:

You can go Released by the parents' love and encouraged to pursue their life away from home, the individual is free to explore themselves away from parental control. Their journey forward is buoyed by memories of approval, support and encouragement. However, often the unconscious message is 'You should not go', which hovers like a ghost over every successive adult relationship. With this negative message, the individual feels compelled to seek freedom from every relationship and to be constantly reassured that they will be free. This message begins early in each experience of separation and initiation. For instance, at the first Mars return is the child encouraged or held back? The message of being able to separate and leave home accumulates through the life cycle and is facilitated when the child has felt encouraged and assisted in becoming independent and autonomous.

We believe in you Armed with faith that was instilled by the parents, the hero is free to learn from his mistakes. But when the parents do not trust that their child can make their way in the world and be successful, their message becomes toxic and inhibiting. If the message is 'We don't believe in you' the individual constantly struggles to believe in themselves, driven to prove themselves to the world at large.

We will miss you Feeling valued frees us from the compulsive need to be loved by another. Knowing that we are loved allows us to love. When the message fails and 'We won't miss you' is internalized, then the feelings of not being valued seep into each successive relationship, creating the need for each partner to provide constant reassurance that we are desired and needed.

We will be fine The young adult is launched into the world, freed from feeling responsible for those they are leaving. They leave home with a sense of completion and an authentic knowing that this phase of their life has ended. Failing this, the individual may fear that the parental message will be 'If you abandon us we will be destroyed'. The individual then feels unable to cope with others relying on them or unable to leave difficult situations. Without the freedom to go, the individual may feel imprisoned in a situation they cannot leave.

Successful Leaving Home Message	Unsuccessful Leaving Home Message	Unsuccessful Leaving Home Message is Internalized by the Individual
You can go	You should not go	Prove to me I can be free in this relationship
We believe you can succeed	We do not believe in you	Show me you take me seriously
We will miss you	You are not valued here	Prove to me that you want and need me
We will be able to manage without you	If you abandon us, we will be destroyed	I cannot cope with you needing me too much

With security in their attachment to the family, the crossing to the world beyond family is accompanied by memories of encouragement and applause. These internalized memories form the foundation of ego strength, an anchor for future separations or times of fear and despair. This strong base enables the person to move through the dark nights of their lives, rather than become paralysed and impotent. The solidity of the IC and the 4th house provide the launching pad for the solar and heroic impulses explored in the 5th house.

The prominent factors in the familial environment that place the individual at risk of a rough crossing include rigidity, enmeshment, chaos and disengagement. The individual who finds themselves swinging between being tightly bound by the rigidity of the familial container and completely unbound and uncontained lacks a centre, a secure base. The foundation stone at the IC is weakened and the lunar container is vulnerable. Another continuum stretches from one pole, where the individual's personality may be engulfed and smothered by the family, to the other pole, where the individual could feel cut off from the heart of the family. Both extremes complicate the leaving home process. In a healthy familial environment we feel more centred and less dismembered by these extremes. Astrological themes that combine the lunar archetype with other planets sketch the landscape of the familial terrain.

When the Saturnian archetype is overemphasized, the family structure is probably rigid. Family members may be at risk of disavowing their authenticity in favour of an external authority. Important in the rigid family are accepted traditions, rules and authority, not individuals. When Saturn is weakened, a chaotic family atmosphere may be present and there is no form or structure to contain the developing individual. No safety net is available to help the individual feel secure in exploration and discovery outside the familial structure and rules. In a chaotic atmosphere, hierarchy is non-existent and the young child may feel responsible for their parents and/or siblings, and feel the need to take charge of the situation.

In a disengaged family, with a feeling of parental distance, the separation process is weighed down by anxiety. Here the archetype of Uranus is constellated. The individual instinctively pulls away at any sign of dependency or emotional bonding. The urge to bond unconsciously attracts others, but when they respond they are pushed away. This engagement-disengagement dynamic sabotages both the attachment and the separation processes.

High enmeshment between family members also inhibits the process of separation. When there are inappropriate or inadequate family boundaries then it is difficult to leave for fear of hurting or injuring those left behind. Astrologically, this can be described through the archetype of Neptune. Placements such as Neptune in the 4th house, the Moon in Pisces or Moon-Neptune aspects are signals for the individual's propensity to sacrifice themselves for the communal well-being of the family. If this is the case, the webbing of the family traps the individual and leaving home is difficult.

Plutonic enmeshment occurs through family secrets or the binding threat of familial betrayal.[114] It is difficult to leave when we feel emotionally obligated to others, and strong aspects to Pluto, Pluto in the 4th or the Moon in Scorpio all resonate with this image.

Midlife and Beyond
These lines from Dante's *The Divine Comedy* have been referred to as the most recited lines in western literature. Perhaps they are the most translated lines as well; the lines quoted here are by the poet Henry Longfellow.

> Midway upon the journey of our life
> I found myself within a forest dark,
> For the straightforward pathway had been lost.[115]

While oft used to illustrate bereavement, they have also been used as a poetic metaphor for midlife and the passing of youth, sentiments that other creative artists such as Anton Chekhov, Paul Gauguin, TS Eliot, Dylan Thomas and countless others have expressed in their work. In fact it is often during the midlife crisis that the great creative works of life are gestating and being brought to life.

Carl Jung's recognition of the individuation process emerged from his own midlife journey which ritualized the transition between focusing on being in the outer world and the adjustment to being with the inner world. He suggested that his journey into the self was akin to a mythic descent to Hades,[116] a journey he personally described in his autobiography and in *The Red Book*. At the age of 38, Jung experienced his own descent when 'the ground literally gave way beneath my feet and I plunged down into the dark depths.'[117] Like Dante, he was experiencing the 'forest dark'. While these dark depths at midlife are often experienced as despair, depression, lethargy and disappointment, these very feelings are the necessary downturn that quickens the descent to recover the aspects of self that have been lost while pursuing outer goals and ambitions. At midlife, soul beckons and seeks depth and meaning.

It was Elliott Jaques, a psychoanalyst and organizational consultant, who first coined the phrase 'midlife crisis' in 1965 in his article 'Death and the Midlife Crisis', published in the *International Journal of Psychoanalysis.* He concentrated on artists and their encounter with death; nonetheless, his characterization of the critical passage of midlife resonated with many. In popular culture today it is a well accepted notion, so much so that people from all ages of life claim to be having a 'midlife crisis'. Due to the dramatic changes in the life cycle, such as the increased lifespan and the later age for leaving home and having children, many of the early descriptions of the midlife crisis no longer apply to the contemporary generation navigating midlife. However, underlying issues such as transition and death, life review and the questioning of priorities, creative angst and spiritual barrenness, and an overall search for authenticity, still apply.

The midlife crisis is not solely the individual's mission for meaning. This passage also occurs within the context of the family, and the spouse, children and parents also participate in the crisis with the adult. At this stage of life, the death of a parent and/or grandparent confronts the midlife adult with the ageing process. Or the midlife adult and his family may become caretakers for their ageing parents which affects the dynamics of the family. It is always sobering to remember your parents at the time of life when they were your age, and then to see them as they are today. By midlife the individual looks back to their children and ahead to their parents.

In previous generations, midlife often paralleled children approaching or experiencing adolescence or becoming more independent. Today, midlife can be the time when the first child is born. For many it is a time of grieving for the unborn child and the awareness that time is running out to create a family. Family life is a mirror for what has not yet happened and what could happen; therefore the gap between the individual and the family widens. Extenuating circumstances, such as financial difficulties, the loss of job or illness, are often the external stressors that accompany the transition. The adult crisis spills into the family atmosphere. Each generation seems to have their own outer collection of disillusionments, yet the inner landscape remains the same.

Most writers seem to place the midlife decade between the ages of 35 and 45. Murray Stein suggests in *In Midlife* that 'the midlife transition lasts several years and occurs somewhere between the ages of thirty-five and fifty, usually falling around the age of forty'.[118] Stein instinctively picks up the important life phases, beginning with the third Jupiter return at 35 and ending with the Chiron return that ushers in the decade of the fifties. Astrologically we might suggest this phase lasts from the third Jupiter return at 35 to the fourth Jupiter return at 47, that it is especially potent between the ages of 37 and 42, and that it is consolidated during the mid-forties with the second Saturn opposition. This period revisits some important cycles experienced in adolescence. The midlife passage is systemic in that the individual's experience is replicated in the family by others who have been there before or are actually there now. Also this passage magnetizes the psyche's untreated experiences that were caught in the web of the last cycle. Let's review the astrology of midlife systemically.

The Jupiter return between the ages of 35 and 36 heralds a crisis of meaning which questions the dreams and analyses the priorities that have been dominant to date. The plumb line plunges down to the advent of adolescence at age 12 but also stretches ahead. Big dreams, the optimistic outlook and the core beliefs are reviewed and reprioritized at this time. Shortly afterwards, two other major cycles reverberate throughout the family life cycle: the second square of Saturn to its natal position and the second nodal return, both at approximately 37. The second square of Saturn recalls the period near the age of 7 but also revisits the decisions, changes and goals that were set 7 years previously at the Saturn return. The second nodal return cycles back to the age of 19. Here, at the onset of midlife, the soul is calling once again. The following table summarizes this. When the individual looks backwards or forwards through the lens of the astrological cycles, other family members may also be at these points in the cycle.

For the Pluto in Virgo and Libra generations, another potent aspect influences the individual's centre of attention at this time.

Pluto begins its square to itself and heralds the descent into the chasm that Jung described at this age.[119] For these generations, the early phase of the midlife passage is heightened by a darker passage of the soul. The Pluto square suggests the honest confrontation with one's values and integrity at this time.

Planetary Cycle	Midlife Age	Previous Ages of Note	Forward Ages
3rd Jupiter Return	35-36	Previous returns at 12 and 24; the opposition between 29 and 30. Reflect on your dreams and ideals at these times and also your present relationships with family members at this age.	Note the next returns between 47 and 48, and 59 and 60, to reflect on how you might imagine yourself at that age but also your memory of your parents and/or your grandparents at this age.
2nd Saturn Square	36-37	The first waxing square at age 7, the opposition at 14-15, the first waning square at 22 and the return at 29-30. Consider your ambitions and driving forces at these times and also your current relationships with family members at this age.	The Saturn opposition at age 44-45 and the next return at 58-59. How might your decisions and choices at this time influence the outcome at 59? What did your parents do at these times in their lives and how rewarded did they feel? How did your parents age?
2nd Nodal Return	37-38	The first nodal return at 19; contemplate the soul's yearning at this period of life.	The next nodal return at 55-56. How do you imagine you will be able to participate with the soul's desire in this next phase of life?

The quintessential midlife transit is the Uranus opposition that occurs between 38 and 42. Its close resonance with an average life expectancy of 84 years is now well and truly at its midpoint. And in Uranian style this symbolizes the internal urges to change, take a risk, disconnect from the past and, like the tarot's Fool, step off the cliff face into the future. The midlife urge to reinvent the self and remodel the future is heightened. The restlessness agitates the family system. Around the corner are the powerful accompanying cycles that characterize the deep shifts that take place in the psyche during midlife. What follows is a table that reviews these cycles. The early forties seem to conspire with the psychodynamic task of internal reparation with the past.

Planetary Cycle	Midlife Age	Previous Ages of Note	Forward Ages
2nd Progressed Moon Opposition	41	Previous opposition at 13-14 as well as the return at age 27-28. Look back on your sense of security in the family and your ability to nurture your needs.	The next return at age 54-55 ushers in the 3rd cycle. The work done at midlife to ensure the safety and emotional well-being of not only you but your dependants allows the phases of family life to organically renew themselves.
Waxing Neptune Square	41	The first semi-square at age 20-21. Consider your dreams and ideals at this time of life. Which dreams are still real and possible? Which are not? Reflect on the dreams of your parents at this age and what became of these.	The Neptune opposition at 82. As with the Uranus opposition, the Neptune square marks the halfway point in the human life cycle, offering a review of our creative and spiritual self. How does the familial legacy help us to engage with our spirituality?

4th Jupiter Opposition	41-42	The second opposition at age 18 is in focus – where were you heading and do you need to pick up any of these threads, such as lost educational opportunities or travel?	The next return at 47-48 will complete this phase. Which necessary changes are needed to ensure that the vision and goals for ourselves and our families are being supported?
2nd Saturn Opposition	44-45	A direct plumb line to the adolescent opposition at 14-15 awakens the fragility and the strengths in the self to succeed.	The return at 59-60 can reap the rewards of the work done now. How can we be as honest as possible with our authentic needs and goals?

In terms of the family life cycle, the midlife individual is now in the middle generation, looking back to the Oedipal and adolescent phases of life and forwards into the cycles through which his or her ageing parents are journeying. The dynamic cycles during this period prepare the individual for their next decade of the fifties, which contains a mix of potent planetary returns that both the individual and their family need to navigate. As the central parental couple move through the decade that prepares them for older age their children are launching themselves in the world while their own parents are retiring and leaving the world they knew behind.

The Fifties and Beyond
Five potent planetary returns take place during the decade of the fifties. All have occurred before except the first return of Chiron at age fifty. No other decade has five returns except the first decade of life with its returns of the inner planets for the first time.

Chiron's return at fifty is a powerful reminder of ageing and the loss and burial of youth. It is a stark cue that more of life lies behind us than ahead of us. In youth, the differences that were exciting, moving out into the world, our exploring and experimenting have receded. What is familiar and favourite becomes more satisfying as this corner of life is turned and a new task presents itself. Peter O'Connor's subtitle to his book *Facing the Fifties* is 'From denial to reflection', the task that he argues underpins this specific phase of our lives.[120]

While death still seems to be on a faraway horizon, nonetheless it is visible, more visible than ever before. Moving towards this inevitability paradoxically holds the key to a renewed release of spirit. Survivors of an encounter with death report one common experience: the will to continue to live in the moment has been forged through their rendezvous with death. In writing on this period Jung suggested that 'too many aspects of life which should also have been experienced lie in the lumber-room among dusty memories; but sometimes, too, they are glowing coals under grey ashes.'[121] At the Chiron return the 'glowing coals' of the imprisoned spirit are rediscovered and the subsequent period is spent reintroducing them into life. The initiation of the Chiron return at the age of 50 asks the question: 'What am I going to do with this last part of my life?'[122]

Fifty marks a new paradigm. While this new state has immense possibilities, the map needed for the waning period is different from the one used in the waxing period, the first half of life. Chiron returns in the period post-midlife. The midlife map, with its potent astrological cycles, looked back; it took a psychodynamic approach to understanding where we had come from. Childhood demons were exorcised, the inner child liberated, adolescence was revisited, and the road less travelled was explored. The decade of the fifties, however, looks ahead into an uncertain new world. As we turn towards the western horizon of our life, our quest for meaning is coloured with a different hue. What was a priority in the morning of one's life may not be as important in the evening. Erica Jong expressed it this way: 'All the things you suffer from when you're younger become far less important at the age of fifty.'[123] Priorities are shifting; a redirection has been seeded.

Age	Planetary Return	Previous Return/s	Next Return/s	Comments
50	1st Chiron Return			Chiron's cycle is unique depending on its sign and should be mapped individually for the critical points in its cycle
54-55	2nd Progressed Moon Return	27-28	82	The progressed Moon trisects the life cycle
55-56	3rd Nodal Return	18-19; 37-38	74-75	The nodal return occurs within a year of the progressed Moon return
58-59	2nd Saturn Return	29-30	88-89	
59-60	5th Jupiter Return	12; 23-24; 35-36; 47-48	71; 83	The 2nd Saturn return and the 5th Jupiter return occur very close together and mark the close of the decade that Chiron has initiated

The next major astrological return will occur just before the 55th birthday. The Chiron return is followed by the second Saturn waning square at age 52, then the fourth Jupiter opposition at 53, when the process of reinvention is starting to take hold. While a lot of reshaping and reinventing is occurring between 50 and 55, the individual may feel they are in a liminal state, suspended. Yet an orientation to a new life is occurring. During the fifties the demands of the outer world do not subside; however, the response to them originates from a deeper and more considered place. Chiron's symbolism consistently repeats the theme of contact with the 'other' world, and at the Chiron return the veil between the mundane and the spirit world is finer.[124]

Just before we reach 55 the progressed Moon returns for the second time in its cycle. The progressed Moon throughout the life cycle has three separate, yet interwoven, phases. Each cycle of the progressed Moon lasts approximately 27.3 years, charting important transitions in the individual and family life cycle. Circumnavigating the horoscope three times in an average life span,[125] the progressed Moon defines three distinct developmental stages: youth, adult and elder. Three stages of life are symbolized by her three phases; the youthful maiden at the waxing crescent Moon, the adult woman at the Full Moon and the elder crone during the dark of the Moon.[126] The alchemy of these three distinct phases of life helps distil the life experiences: the white goddess presides over the youthful phase, while the red goddess enlivens the adult. In the last phase the black goddess contains the wisdom of the cycle. The secondary progressed Moon symbolizes these three stages of the life cycle. A few months before the 55th birthday the progressed Moon commences its third cycle through the horoscope, returning first to its natal position. This is the third and last phase of the Moon, represented by the dark goddesses, especially Hecate. In Latin her epithet was *Trivia*, which translates literally into three roads or three ways.

At the triple crossroads Hecate is encountered. At 55 we stand at the intersection of these three life paths; we look back to reminisce about our youth, turn around to see the adult path that is just behind us, and look forward along the untrodden path of eldership. Three roads merge, and we prepare to take the road not yet travelled. At this life stage there may be synchronous developments in the family: a grandchild may be just beginning to walk that road of our childhood, while our child may be just starting on the adult journey we are leaving behind. Familial rituals and turning points include the birth of grandchildren, death of parents, and children's weddings. Symbolically the child, the adult and the beginning of this new elder phase meet at the crossroads. So often in my practice clients have presented at this time with significant dreams or active imaginations of a child, mother and grandmother or an external crisis or event which characterizes the enormous shifts taking place on all levels of family life. All three roads are converging. The child and adult are ready to be internalized through life's experiences and memories and the final path of eldership lies ahead.

While living in a culture where the crone, the image of the third phase, is outcast and marginalized we are susceptible to rejecting this elder phase and our role as mentors. We are encouraged to remain stuck in the images of our youth. Hence we may regress by returning to places in psyche that are inappropriate, continuing to recreate our youth by defying the natural processes of ageing, rather than embracing the mystery which lies ahead at the dark of the Moon. The mysteries of ageing are rejected and feared by our culture, like all other aspects of the waning cycle.

The return also marks another complete cycle of emotional and physiological development. The body has undergone many hormonal changes up to this return. For women the onset of menopause at the beginning of the decade is probably the most obvious shift, yet hormonal changes have also occurred for men. Men begin to voice these changes: the night sweats, the waning libido, bodily aches and pains, the flooding of feeling. Both sexes experience the natural reshaping of the body. The body moulded in youth shifts its shape for later life. In our fifties 'something changes and it's just not the body'.[127]

The second progressed lunar return is a time of both remembering and forgetting. Lunar memoirs are stored in the psyche as images, symbols, feelings, impressions, instincts or are imprinted upon the body through disease, allergies, aches or pains. Lunar memory is not linear, memorizing dates and statistics, but is revealed through dreams and senses. At the midpoint of the decade we are ready to gather together the threads of our life. Memories are awoken through the body, the feeling life, dreams, visions and other images, either internal or external. Here at the crossroads we are starting to weave the story of our life, recollecting and remembering. During the mid-fifties Uranus and Neptune are trining their natal positions and encouraging the gathering together of the threads of our life story.

The lunar nodes return just before we turn 56. Each nodal return also brings a repeat of the eclipses before and after our birth. At each nodal return the solar identity is challenged to become more soulful. Each nodal return is like a calling, a rendezvous with destiny, a purposeful awakening and a reminder of the soul's intention. This nodal return occurs at the intersection of middle and old age, a pivotal point defining a new branch on the path. Like a signpost, the nodal return points the way. The South Node return suggests a completion of the past cycle, an emptying out of the contents held from the past so that forward movement becomes possible. Possibilities of a new life are ascending. At this point a more authentic quest begins, when the heroic ego relinquishes the battle with the worldly dragons to seek the solace and security of a relationship with the internal world. Chiron's return at the beginning of the decade signalled the withdrawal of the hero. This nodal return marks the entry into the spiritual realm of one's life. Erin Sullivan describes this nodal period as 'insight into one's true purpose in life. Because the nodal cycle marks the return of inspiration and the re-evaluation of one's spiritual path, this is a time when religious and spiritual commitments are reviewed.'[128] We are ready at this return to live more fully in the spirit of our life.

Nodal transits often literalize as important encounters with others or special events, which reshape our beliefs, values or attitudes. Here the effort and work of the midlife passage, which began at the last nodal return, can be reaped. The search for authenticity and for a deeper sense of meaning, which began at midlife, culminates at this nodal return. The emergent spirituality is not an evangelical awakening but an assured sense of one's morals and values. A calling occurs which inspires us to relinquish what is no longer meaningful for the next cycle. The nodal return marks the beginning of a new cycle of soul progress, and thereby signals the ending of the liminal phase experienced through much of the fifties.

During her second Saturn return May Sarton wrote her *Journal of Solitude*. The struggle she articulated was to make space in her life to be, to forge a balance between reflection and relationship, to find solitude. The decade of the fifties helps to reorganize our priorities so we may create time for this solitude. Saturn's return offers the opportunity to build the structures to support this new way of being that has emerged. Outer life structures have reached their capacity; the soul yearns to fortify its inner life.

At sixty Tina Turner embarked on a stadium tour destined to be her last: 'I have no problems being sixty', she said 'but I want to hang up my dancing shoes. I know I have the energy to do it one more time, but I don't want to become a caricature, to diminish the memory of my great little dresses, my great legs. I don't want people saying "Oh, she was once a beauty, she used to be great". I have too much pride for that.'[129] At thirty our gaze is on the world ahead of us, outside of ourselves. At sixty this is internalized, focused on the creative self. May Sarton wrote that her second Saturn return was about being, not doing. The end of the fifties is marked by two potent returns, which characterize a return to wisdom, not information or knowledge. Both archetypes of Jupiter and Saturn have matured and been socialized; now they are more self-directed and reflective. The second Saturn return, coupled with the fifth Jupiter return, marks the commencement of living in the world of the intangible, the internal and the sacred.

At her second Saturn return Germaine Greer wrote *The Whole Woman*. Critics suggested this was a sequel to her groundbreaking *The Female Eunuch*, written at her first Saturn return. Greer has been a potent voice on women's issues throughout her adult life. In an interview at her second Saturn return she shared that the greatest sadness of her life was not giving birth to a child. At sixty her inner dream world still carried the expectancy of giving birth: 'Though I have no child of my own, I still have pregnancy dreams. I'm in a huge abdomen floating in the warm shallow sea of my childhood. I'm waiting with vast joy and confidence. But I'm waiting for something that will never happen'[130] Greer typifies the Pluto in Leo loss of the magical child: a loss which helped to initiate this generation into the wisdom of the third age which begins at the second Saturn return.

The landscape of old age has changed; retirement as it was once known is no longer the preferred option, or even the goal. The question is what do we retire from? Conscious preparation during the previous decade has helped to define a path beyond sixty. What has emerged during our fifties that is creative, rewarding and of value can be honoured and attended to. Saturn's quest for autonomy, hopefully, now can be realized. Saturn's urge for acknowledgement, hopefully, has now been internalized. At this stage of life we depend more on our investments and it is the investment into self which yields the highest return at this stage of the life cycle.

The end of the fifties marks the transition into elderhood for which the previous decade has prepared us. The angst of ageing has been spent and the inevitable has arrived. Saturn's gifts at this passage are the time and encouragement to pursue the true opus of one's life and the conviction and dedication to structure the brave new world. Jupiter supplies the optimism, vision and the sighting of the new horizon. At her Saturn return, Sarton wrote: 'I am proud of being 58 and still alive and kicking, in love, more creative, balanced and potent than I have ever been'.[131]

As we contemplate these changes from a family perspective, the elder role of grandparenting becomes invaluable during this phase. The grandparents' energies that were once focused on the outer world have been drawn in and there is more time just to be with the grandchild. And because of this, grandparents can be more present, more giving and more tolerant. The mentoring of the grandchild is life knowledge that is 'passed on' from life experience and allows the grandchild to cultivate values and opinions that are different from those of their parents but still within the family circle. Temperamentally, a grandparent is often able to accept and encourage aspects of the child that are unseen by their parents and teachers. But the gift the grandchild offers to their grandparent is the experience of the continuity of family life and the rising flame of youth and spirit.

Death
A common saying that I have often pondered is that we die as we have lived. I understand this as meaning that our character becomes us, etched on our face, in our movements and gestures, and in the way we approach and separate. If the ego is still strong and identified with the self, then death must feel intimidating. Yet knowing who we are and feeling loved surely must make the transition easier. The life cycle has come full circle. The soul who undertook its massive migration at birth prepares for its next transition into the unknown.

Another common idea is that we die alone. This is often the case; the person on the deathbed dies at the very moment that their loved ones are not in the room. Does the soul sense the moment? Does it know the time? But even if those we love are gathered around the deathbed, the transition is made alone. The landscape of the final years prepares us for this transition. Disease and decay are aspects of this, but so is the necessity for homecoming and the revisiting of the past to say goodbye. These are the rituals of emptying out the life but also taking in the soulful feelings that give comfort and solace. Remembering will help us to forget, just as the sense of place and attachment will help us to separate.

In terms of the family, death confronts the adult child with their own mortality. Everyone on the family ladder moves up a rung; the adult children of the parent become the elders while the grandchildren are initiated into the reality of death and the fact that their parents too will die one day. At this point in the family life the 'crisis of dismemberment' is profound; hence ritual becomes a focus for the grief, anger, sadness and often ambivalent feelings that the loss evokes. Funerary rites, memorial services and family gatherings support the process of bereavement and acknowledge the loss and grief that is often complex due to the mixture of feelings and previous unmourned losses. At these moments of loss the accumulation of the other losses throughout life are also brought to mind, complicating the grieving process. For many families, the unresolved schisms of life amputate the bereavement process; therefore the emotions remain muddled and unexpressed, leaving future generations to untangle the knotted feelings of love and loss or anger and sadness that permeate the incomplete relationship. Bereavement offers an invitation for closure.

The death of the parents will be a turning point in the sibling system. This is the crucial stage that will either bring the siblings closer together or keep them in isolation. Without the parents, hierarchy is altered. Childhood has truly gone and the siblings no longer have the parental buffer or the roles that were part of the family ethos. Quite often siblings rediscover one another as the only remaining witnesses to their childhood. When the parental inheritance is announced, sibling rivalry can reawaken, especially when the legacy is not distributed evenly. Favouritism in the parental legacy can be a blow that the sibling relationship may never be able to recover from. However, in other instances, I have witnessed that the fight for the parental legacy brings siblings together. Two sisters, estranged since their early twenties, joined forces to contest his will when their father died. Their father's will decreed that his de facto partner would receive everything, including their mother's estate, which was inherited by their father when she died. Their father had told each of them that they would inherit everything when he died. Therefore they were suspicious that his partner had forced him into signing a new will. During the trial, the sisters rediscovered their relationship. They were the only ones left from their family of origin and externalizing the fight for their father's inheritance provided a setting for coming to terms with their shared legacy.

Death brings the awareness that the 8th house of inheritance and intimacy is inseparably bound to its other half, the 2nd house of objects and values. Since family and parental objects are invested with the felt experience of the intimate relationship, the fight for the object becomes the quest to acknowledge the value and importance of the relationship. The object links the dead to the living and serves as a meaningful symbol for the connection. Possessions governed by the second house may be inherited at death but it is their intimate value, not necessarily their monetary worth, which is priceless.

Separation is intimately tied to attachment; hence in death our sense of attachment and belonging helps us to separate more easily. Again, aspects to the Moon might offer us an insight into how we might face the separation of death. While the aspects to the Moon do not reveal the type of death we experience, they may be indicative of how we approach death if the adage that we die as we live has substance. Classical astrologers had many ways to examine 'the length of life'. Interestingly, the houses connected to death, such as the 4th and 8th, are also connected to family. The individual might die but the family lives on. However, in contemporary practice, the prediction of death is not as popular or prevalent as it once was. Death is often seen as a metaphor for change and the traditional aspects of the chart associated with death are more often seen as a psychological rather than a physical death. Nonetheless, the death chart is quite revealing and the moment of death can astrologically summarize the legacy of the life.

Surviving members' horoscopes often reveal the loss through the transits and progressions. Since the members are part of the same system, many of the aspects are similar. Death of a family member reverberates through the system but their place in the system always remains. They are eternally part of the family matrix but it is the legacy of their lives that indicates whether their spirit haunts or supports the system. For all family members, death confronts each one with their own mortality, yet also allows each one to participate in the eternal wheel of life.

– CHAPTER 18 –
ADULT CHILDREN
Transits, Progressions and The Evolution of Family Relationships

Even death does not guarantee that we can leave the family system. Though we may not be in contact or consciously aware of family, our relationship to the system continues; for instance, our sisters and brothers are part of our sibling and family systems for life. For many siblings, leaving home marks the beginning of a gradual movement away from the familiarity of the sibling relationship and out into the world. Even though contact may continue, there is less daily involvement between siblings. Regular meetings between adult sibs generally occur for anniversaries, birthdays and ritual holiday gatherings. This contact, often in the family home, exerts a tremendous pull back to the past, and rather than meeting siblings as they are now, we engage with them as they were then. The tension of growing apart is abated by this regression to the past. Quite instinctively we slip back into the old patterns of relating, find our old niche and claim back our comfortable roles, share the memories rather than our current lives and sentimentalize rather than feel.

Sharing the way it used to be inhibits the forging of an adult relationship with our siblings. Instead, we continue to sacrifice a new relationship for the comfort of what we had. Adult relationships may also become complicated by our siblings' partners, their new families or lifestyles. Primary loyalties have shifted from the family unit, forcing us to readdress sibling relationships. To establish healthy adult relationships we also need to accept our siblings' significant others.

Marian Sandmaier, the author of the book *Original Kin*, explores 'the search for connection among adult sisters and brothers'. In fact this is the subtitle of her book, reminiscent of the Geminian theme of questing for the sibling-other. She writes of her own journey of reconnection and reconciliation with her estranged brother. In one poignant moment she describes the unique bond between siblings. They have just shared a funny story and she observes her brother's reaction. She says: 'I leaned back and watched my brother, who was shaking with glee like a ten-year-old. And I understood in that moment that my brother and I belonged to each other in a way that nobody else in the universe ever would or could and that it was going to be worth the continuing struggle to stay in each other's lives. And it seemed important at that point to communicate my feelings to him on this subject.'[132]

Removed from the family atmosphere, adults are challenged to find a mature relationship with their siblings. Restoration of the sibling bond 'that nobody else in the universe' could replicate is often an integral part of midlife and beyond. While this can take the form of a literal reconciliation with our sibling/s, it is most important as an internal journey of reconnection with the sibling archetype. Adult siblings may continue to place their brothers and sisters in the same roles they had in childhood, by still competing and persisting with rivalry, avoiding the formation of a new relationship. What we may in fact be avoiding is the consciousness that our early familial experiences have bound us into a common destiny. The sibling relationship survives throughout our lifetime, unlike our parents who leave us, or our kids who join us. In this way, the sibling relationship is unique, as it may be the only familial relationship that spans the course of our lifetime: the only possible lifelong companion is the sibling. They provide continuity from childhood through to adult life.

What makes this bond so unique is the shared past of the familial bond. Siblings are co-participants in the family drama, witnesses to our early years and the custodians of memories long forgotten. Sometimes we may wish to forget the memories that are reflected back. When the pain of living with our siblings has been too great, then adult estrangement protects against reopening and re-infecting the wounds. The memories of who we were in the past that are carried by our sibs are powerful. As Laura Markowitz puts it:

> Siblings are the living remnant of our past, a buffer against the loss of our own history, the deepest, oldest memories of us as we were almost from the beginning. But in these memories lies a terrible power: every time we see our siblings, they hold up a mirror before us, forcing us to look at an image of ourselves that may be either comforting or devastating, perhaps evoking self-acceptance and pride, perhaps shame and humiliation.[133]

The astrological movements in the horoscope cannot determine how the adult sibling relationship will develop – that is in the hands of the individual – but they do suggest when the archetypal image of the sibling may be highlighted. Throughout the passage of our lives, the effect of the sibling relationship will be constellated through other adult relationships, not only the primary sibling relationship. The sibling world is an archetypal world that not only seeks its expression in our future but also has its roots in our and our ancestors' past. Transits and progressions are powerful images that are reflective of the evolving relationship with both living and deceased family members. Transits are systemic since a major transit to one family member's horoscope affects the other members, including the siblings. We will now explore some of the progressions and transits that could synchronize with the evolution and understanding of familial relationships.[134]

The Progressed Moon: Our Emotional Archives
The secondary progressed Moon is the most appropriate astrological tool for tracking the emotional development and evolution of an individual. The progressed Moon's movement registers our emotional reactions, the impact of the familial atmosphere and the climatic changes that occur in the family system. The Moon has no personal container in the early years, being contained by mother and the family, and therefore participates freely in the feeling life. Through the *participation mystique* the child feels, senses and records the moods and feelings of the family members within the system. The Moon registers and remembers these feelings and the emotional reaction to them, becoming the record of our feeling life. Hence the progressed Moon represents the archives of all that we have tasted, touched, wanted, smelt and felt. Memories are mostly unconscious, stored in the psyche as images, symbols, feelings and instinct, or imprinted in the body. Lunar memory in the body may be stored in the adrenal or olfactory glands, the tension in the muscles, or our allergies and illnesses. These primal lunar responses may find their way into consciousness through our eating habits, our moods, our body shape and also the emotional patterns repeated throughout our adult relationships. The Moon is habitual and it is through its steady progression around the horoscope that we can become conscious of the feeling life that underlies our emotional responses.

The progressed Moon journeys around the horoscope three times in an average lifespan, symbolizing the three distinct developmental stages of the youth, the adult and the elder. The average time for the Moon to progress through a house is 2.3 years, a period when the emotional life is focused on a particular sphere. These three progressed cycles also correspond with the contemporary family life cycle of a child, parent and grandparent, which the ancients saw as the maiden or child, the mother or bride, and the crone or widow respectively. The three generations of the family are continually part of the progressed lunar cycle; therefore the movement of the progressed Moon can also describe atmospheric changes in the family – either the family of origin or the family of choice or both, specifically the mother and children. Systemically the progressed Moon often symbolizes the emotional atmosphere around the child or the mother.

The light of the Moon reflects the feeling life, instincts, habits, emotional patterns and motives, as well as the level of emotional safety and security in the house it is progressing through.

In terms of the sibling relationship, the progressed Moon is of most interest when it is progressing through the houses of relationship, especially the 3rd house. When the Moon progresses through the 3rd, the archetype of the sibling will be activated. In the first cycle, an important emotional statement in relation to the sibling may have been recorded – recognizing feelings of love or care towards a peer, sharing with others, familiarity with the duality of feelings or the comfort of companionship. Equally, darker feelings may have been registered such as intense rivalry, brutality, betrayal or feeling unsafe in relationship, mistrusting of companionship. The progressed Moon in the 3rd can reflect light on the mystery of lost siblings. The 3rd is the first terrain of consciousness and as the Moon progresses through here, deep emotional or feeling life may be brought into consciousness. An emotional event, such as the birth, separation, initiation or rite of passage of a sibling, may have been registered by the Moon in its first passage through the 3rd house. As the Moon progresses through the 3rd house, for the first time we become aware of the feelings towards sibling/s and their impact on future relationships. Planets in the 3rd house and the patterns they suggest will be triggered as the Moon progresses through this sector. The natal pattern of the sibling relationship is consciously felt and recorded.

As the progressed Moon moves through the 3rd house in its second and adult cycle, the focus is turned back to the primary relationship with the sibling. I vividly remember attempting to amplify to a client the image of the progressed Moon's passage into the 3rd house. It had just entered this sphere of her horoscope. When I mentioned the sibling relationship, she exclaimed: 'I just heard from my brother last month and he is coming down to visit me next week.' Not particularly eventful for most, but for this woman, who had been estranged from her brother for over twenty years, it was momentous. This meeting was an attempt at reconciliation. The image that always remained with me was that the progressed Moon 'hit' the 3rd house cusp, and bells (literally, in this case the phone) went off. The second passage of the Moon through the 3rd house may revive incomplete sibling themes. As adults we are in a position to examine the early relationship more clearly and sometimes more objectively. The Moon also acts as a loosening agent as it progresses through the chart, breaking up the psychic complexes and resistances that defend this territory. As it progresses through the 3rd, it may catalyse some of our earlier memories of our sibling relationship. The psyche's propensity for dream images as a messenger to the ego's realm is important, as the sibling may appear in the dream to alert us to the shadow material that is being unearthed. This is lunar memory. This passage of adult life brings to light a more conscious understanding of our sibling dynamics. Instinctively we may find ourselves drawn to reconnect with our siblings, attempting to nurture the early relationships.

During this phase of adult life, when the Moon progresses through the 3rd, we may be drawn into the examination of our sibling relationships and their impact on our current relationships. We may now be ready to enter into adult relationship with our siblings. If this is not possible, we may recognize the need to relinquish it and mourn the loss. During the second passage we will recall whether we felt comfortable in or were able to feel that we belonged in the sibling system; we have more emotional latitude as to whether we are going to connect with our sib/s in a personal and individual way. With the Moon progressing through the 3rd, we are more able to discern the individuality of our sibs and not merely see them as members of a group, or keep them fixed in the role they played in our childhood.

The Moon is our emotional barometer and indicator of how best to vent our feelings. When the Moon progresses through the 3rd house in its third and final phase, we come to find peace and reconciliation in the sibling relationship. During this phase we are most likely drawn together because of an important transition in the family life cycle: the death of a parent or another family member, the birth of a grandchild, the rite of passage of one of our children, grandchildren or member of the extended family. This progression will also draw to the surface the feelings regarding our relationships with our partners and friends, the sibling substitutes of our lives. Lunar memory will recall much of the relationship with the sibling over the lifespan. With its third movement through this house, the progressed Moon consciously addresses our sense of communal belonging and whether this applies to our siblings. As it moves through the 3rd house towards the IC in this phase, consciousness is turned towards the 'end of life', providing a nest and a sense of security for the latter years. This may or may not include the sibling.

While the progressed Moon's passage through the 7th or 11th house may not speak directly of the sibling relationship, this is often highlighted because these spheres connect us back to our earlier sibling relationships. It is during the first cycle that these links are probably more visible, when our forays into relating are often witnessed and shared by the sibling. The progression of the Moon through the 7th house focuses on the adult relationship, while the progression through the 11th focuses on our social circles of friends and colleagues. The shadow of the sibling is ready to be constellated in these situations, whether they are personified as the other in the triangle with our partner or appear as the rival other in our professional life. The connection between our adult relationship and the sibling is apparent when the progressed Moon crosses the Descendant in its second cycle. Here the psyche is sensitive to relational issues and is beginning to recognize the patterns in our adult relationships. Quite often I have seen that the sibling other becomes important again at this time, as a representative of the primal sense of comfort in relationship. The Moon progressing through the 7th will reflect light on the relational pattern in one's life and often brings the incomplete aspects of the sibling relationship into the present one.

Similarly, when the progressed Moon passes through the Water houses the emotional focus is on family relationships. With the Moon progressing through the 4th house the family foundation stones are excavated and turned over. During this first passage of the progressed Moon through the 4th, many of the family scripts and patterns are experienced, deeply felt and reacted to. The relationship with the mother is highlighted as is the mother herself. For the duration of this phase the sensitivity to the mother is heightened and her moods and emotional changes affect our sense of security.

During the second cycle of the progressed Moon through the 4th house, many childhood memories are stirred up and reactivated. It is often during this phase that the familial past encounters the present so that more light might be shone on the family legacy and its impact on our adult relationships. A client, who had Pluto and Uranus in his 4th house opposing Saturn and Chiron in the 10th, came for a consultation when the progressed Moon had just crossed the IC and entered his 4th house. He wanted to explore why he was feeling so anxious. During the consultation I asked John what happened 27-28 years ago when the progressed Moon would have first passed through his 4th house. Quite astonished by the question, he answered, 'My mother died.'

We explored her death, and his loss and grief, but John's rational side could not connect his present-day anxiety with the loss that he experienced when he was a young boy. However, psyche's timing is always quite impeccable so I continued listening to hear any hints of family time. I asked about his career and family life, remaining focused on themes of the 4th and 10th houses. Two significant events had recently occurred: a female colleague had just left the workplace after their close association of five years, and his dog that he had loved for five years had been struck by a car and had to be euthanized.

Synchronously, the convergence of his colleague's departure and his dog's death, both after five years of knowing them, echoed the loss of his mother when he was five, a loss well protected in psyche's vault. The progressed Moon through the 4th helped him to remember and in this adult phase of the cycle the memory also evoked the loss he could now mourn more fully. The progressed Moon entering his 4th house had begun to loosen some of John's interred feeling life that was too painful to experience during the first round as a young child. The progressed Moon was in Virgo and it was through the loss of his pet that other feelings of loss and grief were unfastened. This is the cumulative nature of grief: when we grieve it reminds us of the other sorrows of our lives.

By the time the Moon progresses through the 4th house in its third cycle, we have participated in both the families of our youth and the families we have chosen. We gather together the threads of our familial experiences to reconstruct and shape the emotional foundations for the next phase of life. During each passage of the progressed Moon through the 4th house, the structures of family life are reshaped as members join or leave. This progression is often synchronous with important passages in the family that become touchstones and milestones in the family history. The Moon's progression through the 8th and 12th houses in each of its cycles also brings the relationships, legacies and patterns of the family to consciousness.

The Progression of the Inner Planets

The secondary progression of the other inner planets may also inform us of evolving familial and sibling relationship. The progressed Sun is often active at the birth of a younger sibling because the arrival of a sibling is a jolt to consciousness and for an elder child this may be the first sense of being separate. This coming to consciousness through the facility of the sibling or the sibling image could also be reflected in the adult progressions of the Sun. The progressed Sun is a symbol of the development of conscious life, the growing sense of self and identity in the world. As the Sun progresses, we expand our tolerance and awareness of differences to accommodate and include other ways of being. With the birth of a sibling we need to be more tolerant and are initiated into our own sense of individuality. This developing sense of individuality and difference is constantly tested in the sibling system, as it is in all our relationships. I see the progressed Sun as an important indicator of our growing awareness of self in our relationships with others: siblings, partners and friends.

The solar progression is also an important symbol for the developing psychic image of father. As a child it is a potent indicator of the relationship with father and how his being impacted upon our identity. It is also synchronous with the growing ability to feel more centred in ourselves and the development of a strong ego container. This allows us to move through narcissistic stages and be more conscious of the need to tolerate differences in others. The progressed Sun is the creation of the capacity to begin to tolerate shadow and foreign aspects in others and is often synchronous with important turning points in relationship.

Progressions of the Sun to the other inner planets may signal sibling themes. I have found that the progressed Sun's aspects to Mercury, Venus and Mars are the most significant for identifying sibling issues or themes. The progressed Sun in aspect to natal Mars could trigger the awareness of rivalry, competition, an intruder in the environs, aggressive feelings, as well as a sense of independence and separateness. With this progression we may become more aware of our individuality and how we express this sense of independence and energy. This may be intimately tied to the experience of a sibling who may have been the original catalyst for this sense of individuality.

The Sun's progressed aspects to Venus signal a growing consciousness of our self-esteem, sense of value and personal tastes, as well as our comfort: relating and feeling equal and attractive to others. An emphasis on our sense of body image, sensuality, creativity and sexuality may come to light. These are components of the earlier sibling relationship which now could be released into consciousness. If Venus is later in zodiacal longitude than the Sun, we will experience the progressed Sun conjunct Venus at some point in the first half of life (maximum age approximately 48). This is an important progression as it is the herald of a deeper relationship, recalling the earliest layers of the parental or sibling relationship. In contemporary astrology, this is more an image of the inner marriage, a consciousness of valuing the self or the love of the self. However, this 'marriage' may also stir up the image of the parental marriage or the archetype of the brother-sister marriage, awakening earlier images of love and sexuality in the family. It is an image of union but often I have seen the progressed Sun in aspect to Venus as reconciliation with the sister. Ultimately, it is the consciousness of our own internal sister and feminine figure.

The progressed Sun's aspects to Mercury will speak most directly of the sibling pattern and the astrological combination may speak of the necessity of clarity, understanding and reconciliation in our sibling relationships. It may also signal the conscious need to separate and claim equality in the system. Again, if Mercury is ahead of the Sun in zodiacal longitude, the Sun will progress to a conjunction within the first 28 years of life. In reference to the sibling, this progression suggests becoming conscious of the dynamic of the relationship and its impact on how we express ourselves and communicate effectively with our current partner.

Progressed Mercury is a symbol of the evolving relationship with our siblings. Its change of signs offers us greater tolerance and scope in our sibling relationships and its aspects to the other planets may bring about a greater understanding of the relationship dynamics.

When Mercury is retrograde, it is more intently focused on a specific area. If an individual has Mercury retrograde, then during the years spent at home with the sibs the progressed Mercury is focused on a specific zodiacal ground. This symbolizes the intensity of the relationship. Mercury retrograde may be symbolic of a much more deep and complex relationship to the sibling. The progressed change of Mercury's direction can also be significant in marking a distinct change in the sibling relationship. As it turns direct, the progression may signify a turning away from the intensity and focus on the sibling. As Mercury moves from a retrograde to a direct position, we may feel a greater sense of freedom within our sibling system, being more capable of accepting the complexity of the relationship. The planet aspected by the progression of Mercury would symbolize the sibling dynamic or theme that is ready to be seen in a different light.

Progressed Venus or Mars may be linked to the evolving relationship with either a sister or a brother. Both are important in their progressed aspects to the other planets in the horoscope, as well as the years when they may change direction. The progressions of Venus and Mars are often synchronous with the formation and sustaining of adult relationship, therefore there is a possible sibling undertow. Because a literal sister or brother often embodies these archetypes, the progressions may also parallel important turning points in the siblings' lives.

The Impact of the Outer Planets' Transits
Transits in our adult years may be helpful indicators of times when family and sibling dynamics are in focus and when reconciliation or separation may be more appropriate in our relationships. The prime indicators would be when the outer planets are transiting the luminaries and inner planets or the angles of the horoscope.

Transits to the Sun and Moon, as well as the MC-IC, suggest developmental changes in the parental relationship and family, as the images of hierarchy are being reshaped under the influence of the transiting planet. As the Sun, Moon or MC-IC is transited, the family system, which also contains the sibling system, is affected. The issues may be systemic, familial or generational. When Mercury, Venus, Mars or the Ascendant-Descendant axis is being transited, the sibling relationship is highlighted because these images correspond more to a horizontal or equal relationship.

Uranus's cycle in our adult life presents what has been relinquished. The transit of Uranus can bring the severed parts of our lives into consciousness – the separations, the unlived aspects, the untravelled roads. What was abandoned, split off or dismembered is met again as Uranus's cycle impacts upon our lives. What Uranus shatters is the fixity that the ego has employed to keep these aspects of self away from consciousness. With reference to familial relationships, the Uranus transit may offer an opportunity for reconnection and reconciliation or, conversely, it may break the symbiotic tie.

Neptune loosens the bonds that keep us blind to our larger potential. The planet's cycle is synchronous with the times of life when there is less certainty, clarity and direction. What is missing presents itself through yearnings, fantasies and dreams. In an adult context, the transits of Neptune help to formulate a spiritual perspective, as the ego is forced to confront the difference between what can be incarnate and what cannot. All the outer planets conspire to break down the ego defences and constructs encouraging the authenticity of self; however, Neptune's nature is more evasive and illusive. All boundaries of time, priority, identity and certainty are subtly shifted and rearranged until the ego feels lost. A sacrifice is demanded so the initiate may be able to move on. For families who are enmeshed and have been unable to untangle their symbiotic bond, this transit could help to dissolve the web of their relationship. The longing to bond with a parent or sibling who has been lost, sacrificed or unavailable may become heightened, encouraging more realistic expectations of what may be possible with this family member.

Pluto is a much more definite encounter with the underworld of the self. In an adult context, Pluto transits reveal unresolved loss, activating an encounter with grief. Pluto is synonymous with disclosure, revelation and remembering. The past returns so that we may let it go, and the shades ask to be properly buried so that life may be renewed. In the context of the sibling, there is now the necessity to mourn these losses, confront the secrets and strive for a more authentic and intimate bond. We may be ready to deal with what keeps us compulsively bound to a parental or sibling image, letting go of the residue of unexpressed feelings towards our earliest companions.

In context of the family, the outer planets' transits to the Moon restructure our relationship to the family but, in particular, they change the format of our relationship with mother and our inheritance from her. When Pluto transits the Moon the memories and images we hold of mother are challenged and transformed. Pluto is a confrontation with the truth and therefore something may be revealed, a secret disclosed or an incident remembered that allows our relationship with mother to become more authentic. This transit suggests letting go, whether that is a transition in the relationship, a step towards independence, a separation or something in the past being forgiven or relinquished. Ultimately, the inner image of mother, the outer relationship, as well as mother herself, are all undergoing a transforming transition which reverberates throughout the whole family. The family past is being unearthed and reformed.

Transiting Neptune to the Moon suggests that subtle shifts may be beginning in the family, especially in the personal relationship with mother and grandmother. While there may be a general sense of bewilderment or feelings may seem confused or desires blocked, there are bigger changes taking place in the family that are altering emotional patterning and familial roles. At these times we might expect entrances and exits in the family to stir up emotional alliances within the family. Our expectations and disappointments about the family are being challenged, but at the same time new dreams and ideals are coming into focus. The maternal bond is shifting, exposing vulnerability and dependency, ushering in a new phase of family life.

Uranus does not fit comfortably with the Moon; therefore its transits can jolt or abruptly bring something into the family's awareness that rearranges its structure. These transits stress the rigidity of the system and change the dynamics. Often something severed from the past may unexpectedly return to shake up the complacency of the family. These transits are also suggestive of separation, which might be natural initiations and independence but might also represent something out of the blue and unforeseen. However, upon reflection, what was not anticipated is often what the family has tried to suppress. During these transits our relationship with mother may be altered so that both parent and child feel freer in their being and in their relationship.

When the outer planets transit the Sun, the image of father and fatherhood is highlighted. Pluto's relationship to the Sun brings the polarity of light and dark and life and death into focus, which could manifest in a variety of ways. Both archetypes are uneasy counterparts, yet together they forge a deep sense of integrity and stability. However, the transmutation is confronting and revealing. Therefore, this transit might literally suggest father is going through a dark night of the soul or being challenged with the need to be honest and accountable. During this transit the individual may need to face up to their relationship with their father and question its impact and legacy. Grief for what one never received from father or the loss of the ideal relationship is stirred. Loss and bereavement become apparent in the relationship, but on a soulful level the self is strengthened and becomes more resilient.

Neptune is also the antithesis of the Sun. While the Sun urges us to shine, Neptune diffuses the light. Therefore during this transit what was once identified as the truth and upheld as being right may gradually dissolve, but what is left is more authentic and true to the self. Therefore, during this transit father's authority and values are questioned. The expectations that he had of his children are defused. Attempting to satisfy father's unlived life or seeking his approval may not be as important now as finding one's authentic purpose and spiritual identity. During this transit the legacy of father's creativity and spirituality may be brought to light. On a literal level, father may be undergoing his own metamorphosis which might include a sense of vulnerability or weakness, an encounter with illness or loss, allowing the child to become more aware of father's sensitive side. Idealization may be a defence against loss; under this transit the losses that come to light might break some of the illusionary spell about the father.

Uranus in transit to the Sun alters our perception of the father and our relationship to him. As a central symbol this might suggest that the core of who we are is being radically reshaped. Perhaps opportunities for advancement or sudden moves ignite new possibilities. The power balance is being rearranged and in the psyche the power of father may become more aligned with the true identity. Uranus often signals separation and this might suggest a literal or emotional separation at some level, whether this is from the literal or psychological father. This transit stimulates independence supporting the individual's urge to break free, take a risk or travel the road not taken. To do this often requires a challenge from the central authority; hence the image of father may arise.

The outer planets' transits to Mercury are a potential indicator of a shift in the sibling dynamic. Mercury symbolizes how we negotiated our place in the system, found our niche and were able to find our unique expression in the larger group. Mercury's role as a guide, the patron of travel and psychopomp is important as well. During a transit to Mercury, the sibling may guide us to another level of understanding. The transit may not always manifest as a literal sibling who embodies the role of guide or fellow traveller, but it will be a similar figure. Transiting Pluto to Mercury brings the underworld god into the sibling system, exposing the truth of the relationship. Perhaps the sibling needs to disclose a secret in order to heal the relationship. The death, or threat of the death, of one of the siblings may become an issue. Mercury was the guide into Pluto's domain; during this transit the sibling may be the guide into an unknown aspect of the past, an agent of revelation or the trickster who uncovers the darker aspects of the self. In our adult years this would bring an intensification of the relationship, and a need for honesty and integrity with the sibling. However, some of the resentment and powerful feeling towards the sib may first have to be expurgated. If we cannot do this, then we must face the fear of letting the relationship go.

Transiting Neptune to Mercury confronts our ideals of the sibling relationship, the illusions that we may have carried to defend a sense of feeling disappointed in the relationship. The dynamic as we knew it may be dissolving; there is a loosening of the bond and a potential new one emerging. Certainly this transit may synchronize with the image of the internal sibling appearing in dreams, memories, visions, reconnecting us to the image of the lost sibling. The individual may feel lost, directionless and unable to navigate using old maps and theories; however, the inner guide through this shifting landscape may be a figure inspired by the sibling.

Uranus to Mercury symbolizes separation from the sibling. This could be a conscious awareness of either a sibling or partner entering or leaving our space. If there is a crisis of accession, this may be accompanied by feelings of suffocation, a lack of space, and by feeling invaded. If this is a crisis of disengagement, the separation may constellate abandonment, accompanied by feelings of panic, anxiety or relief. Consciousness towards the sibling is heightened. In our adult years, Uranus reconnects what has been severed, so this may be an image of the reconnection to a sibling from whom we are separated.

Transits to Venus may awaken our relationship to the inner feminine, partially shaped by our relationship to sister, but also to mother. If we have a sister, then this may synchronize with the literal relationship to her. However, if we do not have a sister, this transit may awaken the sister archetype in our relationships. With Pluto transiting Venus, a woman may be aware of the need to deal with her dark feelings towards her 'sisters', now incarnate in a rival, an associate or acquaintance. This transit offers the confrontation with the darker feeling side, carried by a sisterly double or the sister herself. For a man, a powerful Eros is awoken which may confront the brother-sister taboo; he may be aware of a dangerous force making him face up to his feelings. Ultimately, the man's desires lead to a confrontation with intimacy and a sense of equality and fairness in his relationships. In adult years, this transit facilitates more comfort with the darker sides of his internal feminine, represented as the dark sister.

Neptune to Venus engages us with the creative power of the feminine and sister archetype. We may feel the need to relinquish a personal relationship to find creativity or spirituality. As an adult, this transit may suggest that we are able to negotiate more equality in our relationships and break the enmeshment or the victim role played out with the sister. We may be drawn to engaging with the sister archetype as creatrix and muse. This is a 'soulful' transit that stirs the longing for the other half, an image often carried by the sibling archetype.

Uranus's effect by transit is to shock, to jolt us into consciousness. When it transits Venus, we may be shocked to locate feelings we are disconnected from. Both sexes may be more capable of separating from the ancestral feminine images, confirmed through familial experiences. Uranus offers a radically different perspective: our severed sister relationship may present for reconciliation, or our symbiotic relationship with our sister may be shattered. A new perspective on the feminine is becoming conscious.

Similarly, transits to Mars may speak of the masculine or brother image being stirred, literally or psychologically. Fraternal themes range from rivalry to loyalty, fratricide to sacrifice. For sisters, mythic brothers were protective and heroic, but sometimes, like Apollo, too controlling. The mythic brother could also be a partner and spouse. Transits to Mars will awaken these themes. For a woman, her internal brother, her equal and partner, is constellated. For a man, the outer planets' transits to Mars awaken the brotherly themes of rivalry and competition, or challenge and support. As an adult, he may have to confront both the inner rival and the ally in order to forge a truce between the warring aspects of himself. This transit often presents a literal threat or challenge to the man, personified by a brother figure, which constellates his desire and urge to be independent.

Pluto transiting a woman's Mars may stir up powerful desires to be equal in relationship or to venture independently to claim her own desires and destiny, contacting the powerful figure of her own internal brother. For a man, this transit may awaken the incomplete feelings with his brother, healing archaic feelings of resentment and powerlessness. With Neptune transiting Mars, a woman may have to sacrifice her old way of being in relationship to the brother figure to find her new partner. This dissolution of the bond to the external brother may be necessary to facilitate the emergence of her heroic and independent animus image. A man may face disappointment with his brother, having idealized the relationship. Through this transit the complexity of the enmeshment with the brother or a brother figure becomes apparent for both sexes. Uranus to Mars stimulates the desire to challenge the brother, to separate from his dominance and be independent. The Uranus-Mars transit is a call to equality with the masculine and the opportunity to forge a unique and liberating relationship with the brother.

With the outer transits to Venus or Mars, the literal brother or sister may become a living symbol for dynamic internal changes that are taking place in our lives. These transits could also signify the urge to resolve the relationships with our siblings who are intricately part of our lives and whose influence contributed to shaping our relational patterns.

Into the 3rd and 4th Houses

Jupiter and Saturn will transit through the 3rd and 4th houses more than once in an average lifespan. Jupiter's nature by transit is to magnify what is inherently ready to be brought to consciousness. If nothing is ready to be dealt with, nothing happens: more of nothing *is* nothing. But if a dilemma is festering, Jupiter's tendency is to blow it up. In the 3rd, I take note of any unresolved issues around the siblings. Jupiter's gift is the ability to put the situation into a life context, endowing it with meaning and strengthening the facility to grapple with bigger issues.

Because Jupiter's cycle will return to the 3rd house every 12 years, there are opportunities over one's life to expand one's understanding in relation to the sibling. An only child may feel more able to relate to a wider system, as Jupiter transits the 3rd, while an elder may feel less inclined to be stuck in the role of the responsible one. The transit could also be lived out by one of our siblings who may go back to university, travel overseas or become affiliated with a new church: the sibling is the catalyst for our own inner change. As Jupiter moves through the 3rd, it is interesting to take note of the developments with our siblings, as these are indicators of what may be shifting inside us.

When Jupiter crosses the IC and moves into the 4th house, its focus for the coming year is on home and family. This is the area that Jupiter now seeks to amplify. Every 12 years Jupiter returns to this lowest point and brings new meaning, understanding and ideals to our family situation. At an outer level we might be ready to expand, whether that is the home or the family. This symbol of growth and extension is buoyed by an underlying hope and faith in the future that often comes through renewal. Jupiter's transit to planets in the 4th house suggests that there may be more understanding about the family patterns or more understanding is gleaned about the family situation.

Saturn will transit the 3rd house three times in an average life. Like the progressed Moon, the transits of Saturn divide the life into three phases. Saturn represents the building of ego structures through concentrated effort and dedication. Saturn's cycle leads us further into the world, and therefore is constantly suggesting separation from dependant structures, as its purpose is in establishing autonomy and self-regulation. Saturn is the formation of boundary, and as it passes through the family houses the unspoken rules, traditions and canons from our family of origin are questioned.

As Saturn passes through the 3rd, the work focuses on the sibling issues. Its transit of the 3rd house in our adult years may synchronize with establishing a more mature relationship with our siblings, engaging together as adults. It may be necessary to find an autonomous voice, learn to speak for ourselves and define more clearly the nature of the relationship. Saturn is about responsibility, and we may now be more inclined to say what we need to say to our siblings in order to commit ourselves to a more honest relationship. The reality of the Saturn transit may redefine our sibling responsibilities, re-examining our roles and coming to new arrangements and agreements about the management of familial tasks. The consequences of our relationship to siblings could become visible. We may feel alone and separate from our sibs, and take the responsibility for trying to bridge the distance. A new foundation for these relationships and relationship in general may be laid.

Saturn's transit to the IC signals a new chapter in family life. As it enters the 4th this might manifest as a parting or leave-taking, such as leaving home or moving. Or it could also represent new foundations being secured, perhaps symbolized by building a new home, family planning or restructuring the family situation. However this manifests, the transit through the 4th house is an initiation into the responsibilities of family life. When younger, this might mean that changes in the family situation brought new duties and roles. In later life this may suggest conscious decision-making around the family and home in order to activate the new chapter. As the home is such an outer symbol of our inner security, changes to the home are symbolic of deeper internal shifts. The 4th house is the family home so we might suspect a major restructure or change in this home. When planets are in the 4th house they play a role in our security systems and our familial relationships. When Saturn transits these planets our attitudes towards family traditions, rules and directives are highlighted, helping us to become more autonomous in this area. When these areas are too rigid or limiting, the Saturn transit motivates the individual to rework them in their favour.

An outer planet's transit of the 3rd or 4th houses may not happen in a lifetime but, if it does, the transit will last for a long period of time.

Sibling and family issues may be brought to the surface when these planets aspect other planets while they transit this sphere. Uranus, Neptune or Pluto transiting the 3rd house may stress our relational patterns, while in the 4th house they focus on the family legacy, patterns and issues. If these transits occur when we are younger, they may symbolize the lifelong imprint that the sibling and family relationship marks upon our adult relationships.

Outer planets rising across the Descendant may also bring sibling and family themes sharply into focus. This is especially significant when the transiting planet may be in the 3rd house natally. With the planet moving from the 3rd into the 7th, the larger area of relationship is examined and the primary influence of the sibling becomes of utmost importance. The planet crossing the Descendant may signal a sibling re-entering our lives, or the shadow of the sibling archetype rising up to conscious awareness. Similarly, when an outer planet is in the 4th and it rises above the Descendant, issues from the family of origin are brought out into the open, generally through the formation of relationships.

Transiting Uranus in our youth may symbolize what we split off from or cut out, but in our adult years the transit may bring back what was disenfranchised. What may have been necessary to separate from when we were younger may not be necessary now: the ego is stronger and the psyche demands a chance to integrate what has been disconnected. In this way the Uranus cycle is a powerful link back to what has been severed. Pluto transits in our adult years may be confronting, yet they help to heal the familial past. Neptune's transit across the Descendant might also be a call for reconciliation of sibling or family relationships.

Marian has Neptune in the 3rd house and has always described her relationship with her sister as difficult. She recognizes now how often she rescued her sister by taking the blame for her and suffering the parental punishment for something her sister was ultimately responsible for. When Neptune transited her Descendant, Marian's sister, Jennifer, came back into her life. Jennifer had escaped from an abusive relationship and moved in with Marian because she had nowhere else to go. As adult sisters they began to redefine their relationship on a more conscious and committed level. Their estrangement was being confronted and Marian felt she coped better with her sister and was more aware of her instinctive tendency to rescue her sibling. Their arguments were more honest and their feelings were now overt.

Family relationships are never static and are constantly being renewed and reworked throughout the phases and stages of adult life.

– CHAPTER 19 –
PLOTTING THE ANCESTORS
Genes, Genealogy and the Genogram

Cosmic Genetics

When Dr Michel Gauquelin, a psychologist and a statistician, turned his focus towards astrological research he was able to accurately correlate planets in certain sectors of the horoscope with professional achievement. Specific planetary archetypes resonated with individuals who were successful in certain fields of endeavour. Additionally, his research of over 25,000 parents and children suggested that there was a correspondence between certain planets in the sectors of parents' horoscopes with that of their children. In his own words, he stated:

> The total picture drawn from the data examined indicated a correlation between the cosmic conditions of the birth of parents with that of their children. This genetic effect was noticed with the Moon, Venus, Mars, Jupiter and Saturn.[135]

He also suggested that planetary genetics extended to siblings from the same family:

> We have been able to extend our observations of the planetary effect to children of the same families (6691 birth comparisons). Planetary similarities at the horizon and meridian are more frequent between siblings than between unrelated children.[136]

This exploration was furthered in his book *Planetary Hereditary*.

It is customary to refer to having inherited our parents' personalities and genes. Expressions such as 'you have your mother's eyes' or 'your father's temper', 'your mother's spirit' or 'your father's know-how' are common. Therefore it is reasonable to propose that we also inherit our parents' planets: perhaps 'your mother's Venus', 'your father's Mars', 'your grandmother's Sun' or 'your grandfather's Saturn/Moon' are passed down in a similar way. These are cosmic genetics, the inheritance of planetary influences through the familial line. Astrological genetics refer to the planetary arrangements that are carried by the family through time, rearranging and morphing with each new generation.

Our etymological roots of the word *genes* take us back to its early Greek connotation, which is similar to its modern meaning 'born of' or 'produced by' and is an aspect of many words used today that are connected to birth or beginnings, such as *genesis*. Genesis, the first book of the Old Testament, is the account of the creation of the world or the origin of the human race. This root is also part of *generation* or the idea of a group of descendants from one family or one period of time.[137] It is also the prefix for *genealogy*, the account of a person or family's line of descent. Darwin first used the word *genetic* in 1859 to refer to biological origins and natural growth. As astrologers we are informed by the time of an individual's genesis or birth. But for our purposes here, we are interested in the family genes and genealogy to help us understand the inheritance of familial traits, characteristic patterns of behaviour and inherited trans-generational trauma and complexes. Hence we will consider using a genogram, which is a map of our family lineage that outlines the family patterns passed through the system, in order to develop the images that have already been revealed through family horoscopes.

Genus in Latin refers to a kind or class of things and takes its roots from the Greek *génos* or race and *gónos* or birth. Interestingly, this word in Old English is *kin* which is connected to race and family, closely associated with our family kin, kinship and kind. Embedded within our genes are our origins, our unique cosmology and birth, as well as the ways the ancestors have contributed to our inheritance. These are visible through our physically inherited traits, but when looking through an astrological lens these genes become visible through the planetary arrangements within our horoscope. Like genes, planetary themes are passed through families and awareness of how the family is orientated to the planetary archetype helps to reveal both an individual's inheritance and the instinctual response to this archetypal energy.

While genes are usually thought of in terms of physical inheritance and the transmission of bodily characteristics, we might also think of 'emotional genes' or 'psychological genes', even 'spiritual genes'. These genes are passed on, not through DNA, but through familial traditions, values, the parental atmosphere, etc. They are carried through time and through generations, finding new life and expression. Much of these types of genes or the contents of their legacy is also passed down unseen through the waters of the unconscious; therefore it is difficult to often know what this legacy is. We might 'feel' it, 'intuit' it, or sense that something is there, but what is it? This is often what is behind the questions that clients ask of astrologers and therapists. Astrologers have the horoscope to guide them, which can be an exceptional map for delineating familial patterns. However, there is also another tool that can be employed to help view the unfolding pattern through family time. This tool is the genogram, and being aware of it is a marvellous addition to your astrological data. Consulting astrologers can learn to use a genogram effectively in their consultations, while students and apprentices can use it to explore and reflect on their own family patterns. The information gleaned from the genogram often personalizes or familiarizes the archetypal patterns provided by the horoscope.

What Is a Genogram?
The genogram is a diagram that outlines family ancestry and tabulates information about its members through time. It is a valuable tool that brings the present family together with their families of origin, establishing a continuous picture of the complete family. The genogram displays at least three generations of the first degree relatives, centred on the parents. By adding descriptive comments and astrological statistics, patterns of identification and modelling can be revealed. While a genogram is a graphic representation similar to the family tree, it differs in that it includes data that promotes the analysis of hereditary patterns as well as details of ancestors and their relationships.

The genogram has been widely used in family therapy and is usually constructed by the individual client with the guidance of their counsellor or therapist. Genograms are psychological tools that allow the therapist and their client to identify various patterns in the family history which may continue to influence the client's current state of mind. Relationships and characteristics that might not have shown up on a family tree help to crystallize family motifs. When reflecting and researching the family, genograms are a valuable assistant that can be modified for use by astrologers.

The idea of the genogram has its own roots in the family tree but the actual paternity of the genogram is unclear. The genogram was developed by Dr Murray Bowen to replace what was then known as a family diagram. This was a simple history-taking process for his family therapy practice. A similar, yet less extensive, process had been a routine part of family medicine practices to determine any inherited diseases. Salvador Minuchin in his book *Families and Family Therapy* (1974) outlined the symbols that he used for creating the genogram, and by the later part of the 1970s these symbols were becoming regulated. In the 1980s The National Society of Genetic Counselors created standardized symbols for use in genograms. However, it was through the publication of *Genograms in Family Assessment* by Monica McGoldrick and Randy Gerson (1985) that genograms became developed and popularized in clinical settings. Now genograms are used by a range of groups in a variety of fields such as medicine, psychology, social work, genealogy, genetic research and education. Monica McGoldrick went on to write many excellent books in the family therapy field, including *Genograms: Assessment and Intervention* as well as *The Genogram Journey: Reconnecting with your Family* (2011). She also collaborated with GenoPro in establishing their software symbols for creating genograms.

Genograms contain a wealth of information on the families represented. First, they contain basic data such as the name, gender, year of birth and year of death of each individual. Additional data may include education, occupation, major life events, chronic illnesses, social behaviours, nature of family relationships, emotional relationships and social relationships. Some genograms include information on disorders that are prevalent in the family, such as alcoholism, depression, diseases, alliances and living situations. Genograms can vary significantly because there are no limits on what type of data can be included.

Listed in the genogram might be other significant dates, such as the date of marriage or divorce, as well as other life-altering experiences. Astrologers can also add the date of birth as well as the place if they wish. Jotted notes typify family members' characteristics, such as nurturing, cold, stern, joyful, happy-go-lucky, generous or spendthrift, and illnesses such as depression, alcoholism, diabetes or other conditions such as hyperactivity and learning disorders. The emotional atmosphere of relationships might be highlighted, such as marital difficulty, domestic abuse or familial loyalty, or a note on the schisms, separations and reunions might be added. Astrologers can cross-reference these emotional milestones by researching dates and times. I like to think of a genogram as a constantly evolving piece of work and one where I feel open enough to sketch and write on it what I feel. As a holistic diagram, the genogram draws attention to familial patterns. Maggie Scarf articulates the genogram in this way:

> Overall, what the family genogram tends to document and highlight are the myriad (and sometimes uncanny) ways in which people tend to remain deeply loyal and internally committed to the extended family's existential blueprint for being – even when they neither want nor mean to be, and, in some instances, even when they believe they are no longer connected to their families of origin in any way at all.[138]

For astrologers, the genogram becomes a potent puzzle because laid out on a linear map are themes and patterns that recur through the family history. Often individuals are aware that their present concerns are rooted in their familial past. But when unrecognized patterns are pointed out, it becomes evident how past familial histories puncture the present-day atmosphere. This is not a new concept for astrologers and astrological students because we are familiar with seeing the patterns that repeat through similar planetary themes in the family. However, the genogram allows us to see the links more clearly and immediately once we have the family tree growing in front of us. The genogram records a great deal of family data, which may be a key to unlocking some current trauma or questions. For our purposes we will restrict the data-gathering to three generations in order to begin working with the genogram and to keep the information that is gathered manageable.

A genogram can be completed at differing times during the family life cycle to capture a transition in terms of family life. For instance, one of the first genograms to consider is the one constructed for the time of your birth, which freeze-frames the family system at this stage. You can then construct a genogram for other transitional times in your life such as when you left home, married or the death of a parent. These maps are informative schemas of the family and it is important to research the necessary information so the genogram can be completed as thoroughly as possible.

When constructing the genogram, it is important to note the ages of the family members at the time of its creation. When other genograms are put together for different times it is interesting to see how the family members move through the stages of their own life cycle and that of the family's. Family therapists have proposed when the important transitions of the family life cycle will occur; therefore, astrologers can complement this with their own understanding of the planetary cycles and transits. The genogram assists us to understand the multi-dimensional changes that are also taking place in the family, so it helps us to recognize that our personal transits and progressions are also systemic, i.e. that they also symbolize changes that may be occurring simultaneously with other family members.

Marriage, whether legal or de facto, and/or living together mark a transition to a new family and therefore the beginning of a new family genogram. However, it is the birth of the first child of the new couple that is the marker for the beginning of a new family dynamic. Each partner's familial background provides valuable information about the complexes and issues that are involved in shifting loyalties from their families of origin to their new family, as well as how new traditions and roles in the new family can be successfully implemented. However, it is when the first child is born that the family takes root. The birth of the first child becomes a hallmark and any perinatal disturbances and/or traumas may ignite a family pattern which may already be visible within the family genogram. As a counselling astrologer, it is helpful to have a way of thinking about the birth of the first child and any family pattern or disorder that may impinge upon the family at this time.

The genogram is also very helpful for deciphering recurrent patterns in the family as well as stressors which trigger family disturbances. On the scale of life-stressing events, gaining or losing a family member is seen as a major contributor to shock, anxiety and suffering. As discussed previously, these two nodal events in families were coined as a 'crisis of accession' when someone joined the family, or a 'crisis of dismemberment' when someone left the family or died. 'Crisis of accession' includes marriage, the birth of a sibling, an elderly grandparent or another family member moving into the family home or an adult child returning home. 'Crisis of dismemberment' includes children leaving home, divorce, the death of a parent or a parent leaving the family. These are critical phases of family life.

These transitions, major traumas and experiences in the family life cycle can be noted on the genogram. Become aware when there are arrivals or departures in the family. We have already explored the family timeline in a previous chapter and this helps us to become aware of the stressors in the system and nodal points in the family. Some of the pressures and traumas that affect the equilibrium of family life that are worthwhile bearing in mind and noting on the genogram are:

The Loss of a Child
The loss of a child in the family life cycle is out of time and out of place and alters the complete structure and dynamic of the family. Being out of time, the loss is especially shocking; those left behind are deprived of the relationship and all its possibilities, and often flooded with feelings of guilt, blame, remorse and 'if only'. The loss feels unfair, inappropriate and wrong. Parental grief may be so intense that the remaining children feel as if they have lost their parent as well. When a child dies, parental anxiety about the surviving children intensifies. The issue of a replacement child, one that is either living or one yet to be born, can also create a disturbance in the family atmosphere. Sibling loss may not be adequately dealt with, remaining a ghost that haunts adult relationships and/or the lives of the surviving siblings' children.

Adoption
The loss of a child through adoption is important to note as this often resurfaces in the next generation and intrudes upon both the relinquishing family and the adoptive one. When adoption or relinquishment occurs, this loss is woven into the family fabric and resurfaces each time a new child in the family is born. When a child is adopted there are three points of grief to which the relinquished child is exposed. One is the grief of the relinquishing parent/s, who lose the creative possibilities and potentials of this unique relationship. Secondly, the adoptive parents have often not worked through the grief that leads to their decision to adopt. Finally, the baby itself loses access to its genetic memory and

biological family in the nursery of childhood. An adopted child is at risk of absorbing the grief in the atmosphere of both the relinquishing and the adoptive families, as the grief of both families is often not sanctioned nor respected.

The Death of a Parent

When a parent dies, the family is irrevocably changed because it is a reminder of each family member's mortality. Each person on the family ladder moves up a notch and becomes an older generation. If the relationship with the parent has been complicated, distant or disappointing, there is greater potential for a problematic grieving process. If a parent's death is out of time in the family life cycle, their spirit still lives on for each member. The ghost of the parent is still present in the family atmosphere and most recognizable during a crisis of accession.

Loss of Home

The traumatic impact on the family due to immigration or expulsion is often underestimated. The loss of homeland and culture, a favoured home and neighbourhood, or the upheaval of moving across state and country creates a fault line that runs underneath the family. This fault line often quakes the solid ground of future generations when there is a major transition in their lives. Unexpressed grief and loss at the relinquishment of home is a potent pattern that is carried by future generations.

Blended and Step-families

Reconstructed families have their own set of complexities and relational dilemmas, and the genogram helps to ascertain where each one might find their niche in the modernized family unit. When systems are blended, the unattended feelings and grief from the collapse of each one's previous family is brought into the new system. Often the grief of the previous relationship breakdown or loss of access to a parent has not been fully addressed, provoking issues of trust and divided loyalties in the blended system.

Launching Children and Moving On

When children navigate their way through adolescence and then eventually leave home, the family changes. The partners at the centre on the family must find a new level of relationship so they can move into the new phase without the child. This might trigger a crisis of recession, trying to recapture what once was from a time that no longer exists. The parental marriage is challenged to find its new creativity. The adult children's choice of partners, as well as ways of parenting, often becomes an issue during this transition. As the adult child forms serious relationships, primary loyalties begin to shift from the family of origin to the family of choice. At this stage two systems are overlapping and becoming a third.

Families in Later Life
The transition from adult child to parent is synchronous with the transition from parent to grandparent. Mortality, ageing, life and death, youth and age come more into focus and the question about how to deal with the new roles and phase of life are at the forefront. New concerns, new roles, new topics of life become the centre of attention.

Divorce and remarriage can also be plotted. When the genogram shows the coming together of two separate families, it will indicate where each spouse is in their own family life cycle as well as giving clues about familial roles, the level of spousal attachment and the couple's relationship to other familial members. In the 21st century the composition of the family is multi-dimensional, given the amount of blended families, step-families, single-parent families, same-sex families, etc. Remarried families have a unique genogram. The next phase of building life with the new family is constructed from the loss of the previous one. The genogram includes the ambivalence around the loss of the old family and the joy of the new. It is also important to note the potential of triangles formed between the present and past family constellations. For instance, this triangle might be the two new partners and one of the previous spouses. Or perhaps the two partners and only the memory of the previous spouse form a triangle. The new relationship lives with the ghosts of the past relationships. When children are involved a triangle develops between the two partners and children from the previous marriages. Genograms are helpful to delineate potential triangles throughout all families.

John Bradshaw said, 'Learning to use the genogram was like finding the Rosetta stone', as it helped him to understand that 'many aspects of my life were part of my mutigenerational history rather than decisions based on my own thoughtful choices'.[139] This certainly was true for Helen, a long-term client, whose genogram revealed her strength and determination.

The Power of the Genogram: Helen's story

Helen has been a regular client for over 27 years. She was originally recommended to me by her psychoanalyst, as Helen had been unresponsive to any of the traditional forms of psychology and biomedicine that he had been suggesting. During her therapy he urged Helen to see me when she mentioned her interest in astrology. With traditional psychotherapeutics seemingly so ineffective in her case, he wondered what her chart might reveal about this. When she first came for a consultation Helen was 44, chronically depressed and had been on medication since she was 27. She admitted harbouring suicidal thoughts and suffered chronic fatigue as well as battling bulimia. During the first 8 years there was a series of revelations about her family; the most potent of these discoveries came when she was 49, during the year of her Chiron return, when her ailing mother told Helen that she was adopted.

Secrets in Helen's family background started to be unravelled. Her adoptive mother had given birth to a stillborn son and had also endured two miscarriages before she considered adoption as the only remaining option. Helen was fostered for seven months in a series of homes before she was legally adopted. It was Helen's understanding that the case doctor at the time was making sure that Helen was normal and healthy before releasing her to her adoptive parents.

Her mother's sister Dorothy committed suicide at the age of 13 by hanging herself in the garage of their family home. Bertha, her mother's mother, had also committed suicide; therefore Helen's mother had lost both her mother and only sister to suicide. Helen had not only been severed from her birth family and endured 7 months in foster care but had lost her aunt and grandmother in her adoptive family. Her adoptive father Ormond had only one sister, who had no children. Helen was the only child in the system.

When Helen's mother died she felt free from the indifference, unkindness and lack of concern that she had suffered at the hands of her adoptive mother. However, the transformation that took place in Helen was more directly linked to the exploration of the familial history and the powerful revelation that she had when she finished constructing the genogram of her adoptive mother. Her research led her to a powerful healing moment.

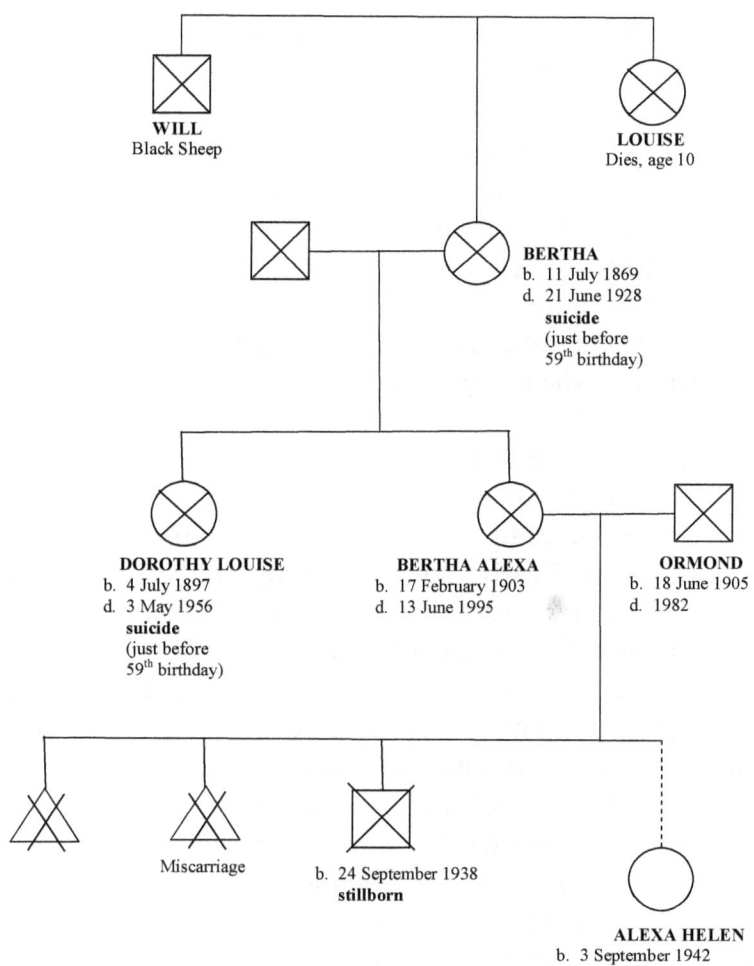

Having constructed the genogram Helen described her family tree as a 'dead tree'. With the number of suicides, stillbirths and adoptions that she had researched in the extended family, she said she could only describe it as a dead family. And now the family tree was at the end of its life. Once her aunt, her father's sister, died she would be the only surviving member. No one else would survive her as Helen has no children, her aunt has no children and no other members of the family had any surviving children.

But this helped Helen to realize her resilience. In discussing the genogram she had constructed, she said 'How strong I am to have survived the family. I was grafted onto a dead tree and I survived.' Helen saw herself as the surviving family member – not its victim, but a powerful woman who found the strength of her inner resources to cope with such a loss. Helen was now in a much better position to inherit the fortunes of the family, having recognized the shadow elements of her family fate. But she was also in a much better position to accept her true self in the wake of realizing the fate of the family system that she had grown up in.

How Do I Construct a Genogram?

When drawing a genogram there are many standardized symbols which represent the family members as well as the nature of their relationship. In the early family therapy movement, Salvador Minuchin in *Families and Family Therapy* (1974) suggested some standard symbols but, as mentioned previously, it was Monica McGoldrick and Randy Gerson's book *Genograms in Family Assessment* (1985) that help to standardize these symbols in the field. There are now many books and websites on the topic of genograms. Many websites are dedicated to teaching about their symbols and helping people to construct their own genogram. For instance, the website www.genopro.com helps the individual to both learn about genograms and to construct their own. Therefore, you can use the many tools the Internet has available to build a detailed genogram of your family; www.genopro.com/genogram is the section on the Genopro website that gives genogram examples and helps you construct your genogram.

However, for our purposes we will concentrate on the more commonly used symbols of the genogram and construct a three-generational genogram. First, collect as much of your own family's birth details as possible, spanning at least three generations that include your grandparents. If you are a parent then you will be able to extend this genogram later to four generations by including your children; if you are a grandparent, it might be possible to construct a five-generational genogram that includes your adult children and their children.

Use at least an A3 size paper when you begin to create your extended genogram as there will be lots of changes as you go along. Don't be concerned about the chaos or mess at the beginning. I often prefer to start on butcher's paper, realizing that my extended genogram will take many attempts before it is complete and presentable in the way I would like. I also prefer to draw the genogram by hand rather than use a computer program as this builds confidence to use the technique during consultations. Later, it is always possible to transfer the information onto a computer-generated genogram.

At the beginning it is often very revealing just to start focusing on a two-generational genogram that includes you and your parents and siblings, and then to extend this to include your grandparents, aunts, uncles and cousins.

Genogram Symbols

1. Male and Female Symbols

Men are signified by squares and women are represented by circles.

Male Symbol Next to the symbol add your name, year of birth and/or present age. Later you will be able to add descriptions, even astrological highlights, next to the symbol.

□

Female Symbol Next to the symbol add your name, year of birth and/or present age. Later you will be able to add descriptions, even astrological highlights, next to the symbol.

○

Pregnancy and Gender Unknown The symbol of the triangle is used when the gender of a child in the family history is not known and is in itself a family secret.

2. Deceased Family Member

Death   If a family member is dead, an X is drawn through the gender symbol and is annotated with the year of death.

Stillborn  If the male or female was stillborn, the X is extended through the gender symbol.

Miscarriage  For a miscarriage, the X is extended through the 'gender unknown' symbol.

3. Marriage and Divorce

The relationship between the male and female can be shown by joining them with specific lines. A bold unbroken line refers to marriage. The male is always shown on the left.

Married ——————— This line joins the male and female symbol; the date of marriage can be added.

De facto - - - - - - - - When the relationship is a de facto relationship, it can be shown as a broken line; add the date considered to be the start of the relationship.

Separation ——/—— When the people in the relationship have separated, a line is placed across the marriage or de facto line and the date of separation is added.

Divorce ——//—— When the couple is divorced, two lines cross the relationship line and the date of divorce is added.

4. Children

Biological children are shown by solid vertical lines that are drawn down from the marriage line. They are drawn from left to right according to their birth order; therefore the oldest sibling is on the left with the youngest on the right. Each child's year of birth as well as their current age can also be shown. If any siblings have died, their date of death is also shown. If a child is adopted, the line connecting them to the marriage line is a broken one. There are now symbols that can also represent a miscarriage, abortion or spontaneous abortion. Of course, many times in the family history these are unknown because they are a family secret.

5. Type of Relationships
Many types of relationship can be signified on the genogram. For instance, a conflicted relationship is drawn with a jagged line.

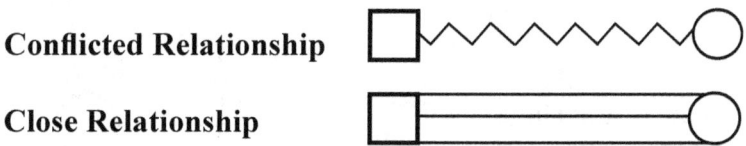

Conflicted Relationship

Close Relationship

A close relationship is shown by three parallel lines uniting the couple. It is important to differentiate a close relationship from an enmeshed relationship. A close relationship supports each partner's individuality and selfhood through flexible and healthy boundaries, whereas boundaries in an enmeshed relationship have collapsed, merging the partners in an unhealthy dynamic that does not tolerate separateness or support individuality.

Distant Relationship

A distant relationship is one where the boundaries between the couple are more like walls that isolate each one into their own disconnected lives.

Twins or triplets

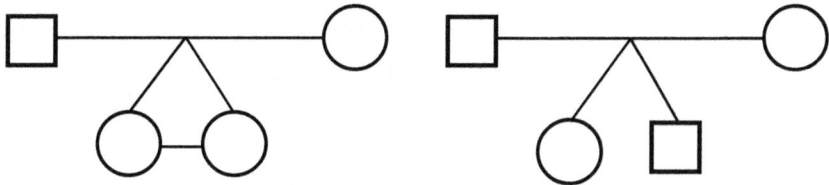

The lines descending from the marriage line start from the same point. If the twins are identical, a horizontal line connects the children. When they are fraternal twins, the children are not connected.

Genogram Notes
As mentioned previously, you can document important information on the genogram such as:

1. Date or year of birth
This is shown as b.1956

b.1956

2. Date or year of death
This is shown as d. 2012

b.1956
d.2012

3. Date or year of marriage
This is shown as m.1985 and
is placed above or below the connecting line between the couple

m.1985

4. Date or year of divorce
This is shown as dv. 2002
and is placed near the two slashes that break the marriage line

dv.2002

5. Age of the person
This is shown as (56)
and is generally placed   b.1956 (56)
after the year of birth

Genograms in the Astrological Consultation
Each astrologer develops their own method of consulting using the techniques that they feel are best suited to their practice. As a result, astrological consulting is varied and individualized. However, the genogram can be a tool used in any type of consultancy as it is shorthand for gathering important family details which are pertinent to the client's question or situation. They do not necessarily need to be used therapeutically as they are equally valid as a method of acquiring and remembering details. However, there is always a

bonus and that is the potential to perceive a trend or illuminate a pattern.

When doing a consultation I often quickly sketch the genogram for one or two generations. This is quite easy and not intrusive to the flow of the discussion. For instance, if the sibling relationship is important in the context of our session, I would ask how many siblings the client has, what sex they are and the order of their birth. I then quickly draw the sibling constellations and then I ask for each sibling's name and their current age. My experience is that the client is always appreciative of my asking these details. As the conversation continues I may add details and text to the genogram based on the client's implications and associations. This information is invaluable and can be referred to again in the current or subsequent sessions. In a short period of time much information has been gleaned about the nature of the relationships, the pattern of relating, roles and a sense of belonging, which are all highly significant in forming adult relationships. For instance, the following sketch is one I recently did in a consultation where the sibling relationship between the three sisters was important to consider.

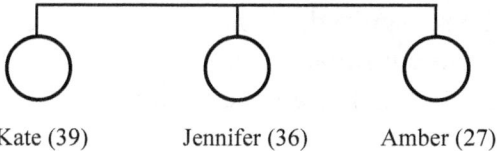

Kate (39)   Jennifer (36)   Amber (27)

If the client is talking about his or her children I quickly sketch a genogram for the parent, their spouse and their children. I do this for the present; however, while doing it I am mindful of the ages of the client and his or her partner, linking these to the ages of their parents as well as the ages of the children. When referring to the ages of the children, it is helpful to encourage the parents to reflect on how they felt at that age and what was occurring for them. In this way they are more able to be aware of their own internal dynamic and how that may be getting triggered at this time through their child.

This small outline facilitates a way of thinking systemically and through time. For instance, the quickly sketched genogram below helped the client to recognize the repetition of family time and to become more aware of her own process and the power of the family theme repeating. In this case the line connecting Frank and Beth is dropped below the couple – this is another way of drawing the marriage line to give more room for notes, etc.

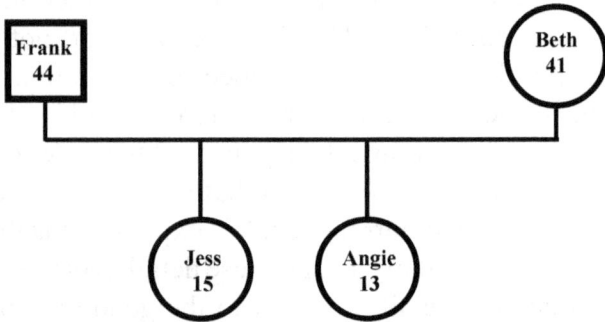

I try to gather the information as part of the consultation without inhibiting the flow or trust I am building with the client. When taking down the information I may write some characteristic keywords along with the aspect pattern or astrological symbols I feel are connected to the theme we are exploring. The instant genogram is very helpful for me to bring familial threads together, as this encourages themes and patterns to begin to coalesce into a form that can be recognized. However, the horoscope and any other pages I use during consultations are often messy and chaotic. After the consultation, I often redraw the genogram adding pertinent notes which not only benefit my own understanding but make the next consultation with the client easier and more intimate. For instance, being able to mention the children's names that have been recorded on the genogram is a signal that you want to build familiarity and trust and also that you have listened and taken note!

Resources

1 There are many versions of genograms and numerous symbols. On a website for students run by Dr Stanfield, he has a PDF called *Explaining Genograms* which includes symbols for income, immigration, cross-cultural families, etc. See http://stanfield.pbworks.com/f/explaining_genograms.pdf

2 As previously mentioned, there are many websites with information on constructing the genogram. Therefore, if you prefer, you can use the many tools the Internet has available to help build a detailed

genogram of your family. The website that I have found very useful is www.genopro.com This website helps you to both learn about genograms and to construct your own – the section on this website that gives genogram examples and helps you construct your genogram is www.genopro.com/genogram

3 Two books on genograms that I have found both fascinating and informative are:
McGoldrick, Monica, 2011. *The Genogram Journey: Reconnecting with Your Family.* New York: WW Norton & Company.

Carter, Betty and McGoldrick, Monica (eds.), 1989. *The Changing Family Life Cycle.* Boston: Allyn and Bacon.

– CHAPTER 20 –
A FAMILY PORTRAIT
Freud's Legacy

Identifying With a Myth
Sigmund Freud suggested that biographers are fixated on their subjects because they have felt a special affinity for the core character. Their choice, conscious or not, of their preferred hero is made for reasons in their own personal emotional life. To some extent a *participation mystique* occurs with our own mythological heroes, perhaps as Freud felt for Oedipus. Through his sympathy for Oedipus, Freud presented a new premise to psychology and this cornerstone code of belief resonated throughout 20th century psychoanalysis. Named after the central character in *Oedipus Rex*, the doctrine was christened the Oedipus complex.

> The Oedipus Rex is a tragedy of fate ... His fate moves us only because it might have been our own ... It may be that we were all destined to direct our first sexual impulses toward our mothers, and our first impulses of hatred and violence toward our fathers ... King Oedipus, who slew his father Laius and wedded his mother Jocasta, is nothing more or less than a wish-fulfilment – the fulfilment of the wish of our childhood.[140]

Sophocles, in his tragedy written in the 5th century BCE, left a literary legacy for Freud, who retold the archetypal tale from his own psychoanalytic point of view. This frequently told tragedy corresponded to Freud's own childhood fantasies and reveries that were summoned up during the period of his own self-analysis. Was it because of his own troubling identification with the storyline that he assumed it was everyone's childhood pattern? Or was it through an enmeshment with the myth that he became its narrator? No doubt Freud's Oedipal obsession was a great work of the imagination and a great example of archetypal patterning, but his understanding of the pattern seems to be born out of his family experience and atmosphere which are threaded through the tapestry of his horoscope.

The horoscope could be likened to a family portrait. Each horoscope image can be metaphoric of a family member or a symbol of a family characteristic or pattern. The combination of all of these images shapes the horoscope, just as the congregation of all the family members creates a family portrait. Researching family history in the context of astrological images can both amplify and illuminate the familial inheritance and patterns. In turn, this facilitates a deeper understanding that the impact of the familial inheritance impresses upon the soul.

Family stories are told and retold, embellished, mythologized and romanticized. However, always lying behind and underpinning the personal and familial narrative is the way in which the experience of a particular archetype has been shaped by our past. Although an archetypal pattern operates instinctually through us, by reflecting on our family portrait we are often better informed and therefore more conscious about how we might choose to respond to its command.

What follows is a partial portrait of Sigmund Freud, focusing on a few motifs. Besides my own personal interest in his history and biography I have chosen this case because his familial history and legacy so obviously affected his personal relationships and professional philosophy. Mythic motifs flow beneath the course of our everyday lives and when we are closely identified with their patterns, as Freud was with Oedipus, we serve as living voices for these myths. Perhaps the only choice we have is to become more conscious of the riddles presented in the family drama of our lives.

A Complex Family Portrait
Sigmund Freud was the eldest sibling with five sisters and one brother. Another brother had been born seventeen months after Freud, but died at seven months old. Freud was born into a complicated family situation as his father, who was twenty years older than his mother, had two sons from his first marriage who were closer to his mother's age.

The complexity of this family environment most definitely played a role in shaping Freud's psychological theories. Freud's Oedipal theory was inspired by Sophocles's classical tragedy *Oedipus Rex*. However, the protagonist Oedipus, although intellectually brilliant, is blind to his own familial fate. Quite unsuspectingly he marries his biological mother and has four children with her. These children are also his half-siblings because their mother is also his mother. Perhaps, without fully recognizing it, Freud strongly identified with the myth that resonated with his own familial story.[141] Ironically, he became professionally identified with the mythic figure who unconsciously replicated some of his own inner processes.

Sigmund Freud was the eldest child in his family of origin, the first-born son of his mother, Amalia, but the third son of his father, Jacob, who had two sons from his first marriage to Sally Kanner. This complicated family portrait meant that Freud had two adult half-brothers when he was born. Both his half-brothers were from his mother's generation: Emanuel was two years older than Sigmund's mother Amalia, while Philip was one year younger than her. Emanuel had one child at the time of Freud's birth; therefore Freud became an uncle at birth to John, aged one. A niece, Pauline, was born six months after Sigmund.[142]

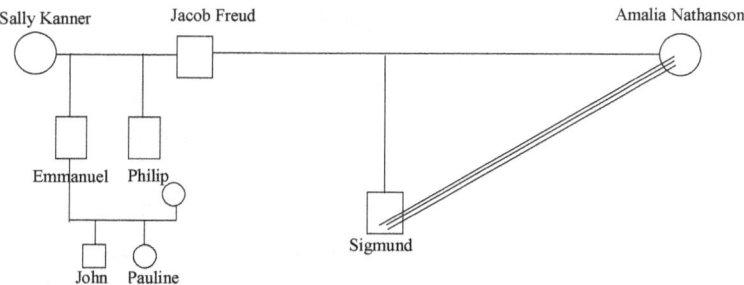

The confusing family picture placed Amalia, Sigmund's mother, in the same generation as his half-brothers and made him an uncle to a niece and nephew from his own generation. His mother was young and their bond became very strong. Jacob may also have remarried after leaving Sally; however this is uncertain. But what is certain is that his mother Amalia is much younger than his ageing father who has already had another family life. For Freud, the sign on the IC, the first imprint of the family of origin, is Aquarius, ruled by Uranus which is conjunct the Sun and Mercury, thereby offering images of an out-of-the-ordinary family atmosphere. It suggests that in Freud's inner world the familial foundation stones may have been split or cracked.

Sigmund Freud was born on 6 May 1856 at 6.30 p.m. in Freiberg, Moravia. His father, Jacob, recorded the event and his son's birth time in the family Bible, along with the details of his circumcision.[143]

Freud was named after his father's father who died only two and a half months before Sigmund was born. The name inscribed in the Bible was Sigismund Schlomo, Schlomo his grandfather's name.

An unconfirmed story about his birth tells of a shopkeeper's prophecy: upon hearing of the child born in a caul, he announced to Amalia that a great man had been brought into the world. With Scorpio rising and the ruler Pluto on the horizon of the horoscope, the imagery of death, mystery and prophecy surrounding the birth is not surprising. Pluto, regent of the underworld, is on the western horizon, the astrological threshold where setting planets descend into the unseen world. Planets on the horizon are often constellated at birth and met early in the family. Pluto also squares Chiron in the 3rd, which is significant in his relationships with his siblings and the development of his 'talking cure'. Pluto, lying just below the western horizon, is metaphoric of Freud's descent into the underworld of other peoples' psyches to excavate what was not yet consciously visible to them. However, it also was a herald of his dynamic inheritance of loss.

The family atmosphere that contained his parents' transgenerational marriage spawned fantasies for Freud of his mother having a relationship with his half-brother, Emanuel. The situation also fed fanciful fantasies of his half-brother as father, confusing the parental and sibling roles, a theme that would recur in many ways in Freud's life. As already mentioned, Aquarius is on the IC and is more an image of equality rather than hierarchy. Its ruler Uranus meets the ruler of the 10th, the Sun, in the 7th house, which also confuses the roles of the parent with the partner – a textbook Oedipal arrangement. The Moon in Gemini is square to Neptune in the 4th, blurring the boundaries between feminine roles in the family. The Moon in Gemini in the 8th is astute at responding to the depths of the psyche. However, it also suggests that the images of mother are more akin to those of sister and partner; the square to Neptune obscures these boundaries.

Role Confusion
In Freud's *The Psychopathology of Everyday Life*, the book that inspired the popular phrase 'Freudian slip', he illustrates how forgetting and making unconscious errors reveals deep complexes. Freud describes two errors that he found after his book *The*

Interpretation of Dreams was published. One of the errors was to incorrectly name Hannibal's father as Hasdrubal, who was in fact Hannibal's brother. Hence the brother was substituted for the father, fuelling the fantasy; as Freud says: 'how much pleasanter it would have been had I been the son of my brother instead of the son of my father!'[144] Here is another imprint of the Sun-Uranus conjunction. The other error was to name Zeus as the one who castrates Ouranus, virtually missing out one generation. How could this have happened when Freud, a classics scholar, consciously knew it was Chronus, Zeus's father, who castrated Ouranus? Freud explains that his half-brother had once admonished him in a way he never forgot. His brother had clearly pointed out that Freud belonged 'not to the second but really the third generation of [his] father'.[145]

The confusion between the roles of the father (authority) and the sibling (equality) was evident in his own family role as the surrogate authority figure to his sisters and younger brother. This influenced his affiliation to his friends and colleagues in adult life. The sphere of friendship and colleagueship, the 11th house, is also the arena where we will re-encounter incomplete psychic fragments from sibling relationships.

Having Mars here, Freud re-enacted the familial pattern of being in charge, becoming highly reactive when his control was challenged by others in his environment. In adult life he continued to be the authoritarian father towards his peers and colleagues, unable to fully embrace colleagueship and equality. Sibling rivalry was also re-enacted in his relationships and in his adult years this blend of control and rivalry led to many separations and conflicts with his peers. The blurred boundaries between his roles as a sibling and parent are suggested by the following statements in his horoscope:

- Capricorn (authority) on the cusp of the 3rd (sibling) with
- Saturn (authority), the ruler in Gemini (sibling)
- Aquarius (equality) is on the 4th house cusp (parent)
- The rulers of the parental axis, the IC-MC (hierarchy), are conjunct in the 7th (equality)

Freud's confusion was not just between the eldest brother and father but also extended to the eldest sister and mother. Freud analysed his own errors in the first category confusion of brother/father, but how would he analyse the error he made in swapping eldest sister for mother? In his 'Introductory Lectures on Psycho-Analysis', he quotes George Bernard Shaw:

> There is probably no nursery without violent conflicts between its inmates. The motives for these are rivalry for parental love, for common possessions, for living space. The hostile impulses are directed against older as well as against younger members of the family. It was, I believe, Bernard Shaw who remarked: 'As a rule there is only one person an English girl hates more than she hates her mother; and that's her eldest sister'.[146]

Shaw did use this line in *Man and Superman*. But Freud transposed the elder sister and mother, echoing the confusion in roles between the sibling and the parent; this was especially reflective of the Moon-Neptune square. In Shaw's play, his character Tanner says: 'As a rule there is only one person an English girl hates more than she hates her elder sister; and that's her mother!'[147] This confusion between parent and sibling was also part of the Oedipal drama: Oedipus's daughter Antigone was also his half-sister because his wife Jocasta was also his mother.

Sigmund Freud (chart opposite) has Venus at 26♈11 conjunct the North Node at 24♈19. Remarkably, at his birth the asteroid Antigone was at 24♈35, conjunct his Venus-North Node.[148] His daughter Anna, whom he referred to as his Anna-Antigone, had her Venus at 24♎29, conjunct his South Node and opposite his Venus-Antigone. Like Oedipus's daughter Antigone, who was her father's companion in older age, Anna had a similar fate. She also bore the same name as Freud's first-born sister; the sibling with whom Sigmund was the most conflicted.

Perhaps Freud's sister Anna was a more convenient hook for some of the hostility that Freud could not divert towards his mother. Anna was born on 31 December 1858.[149] This was eight months after their brother Julius had died, at only seven months old. Four more sisters followed, one nearly every year after that, and finally the youngest child, a brother, was born ten years after Freud. It has been postulated that Freud's idealization of his mother concealed his rage towards her.[150] Strong feelings like rage are often too intense

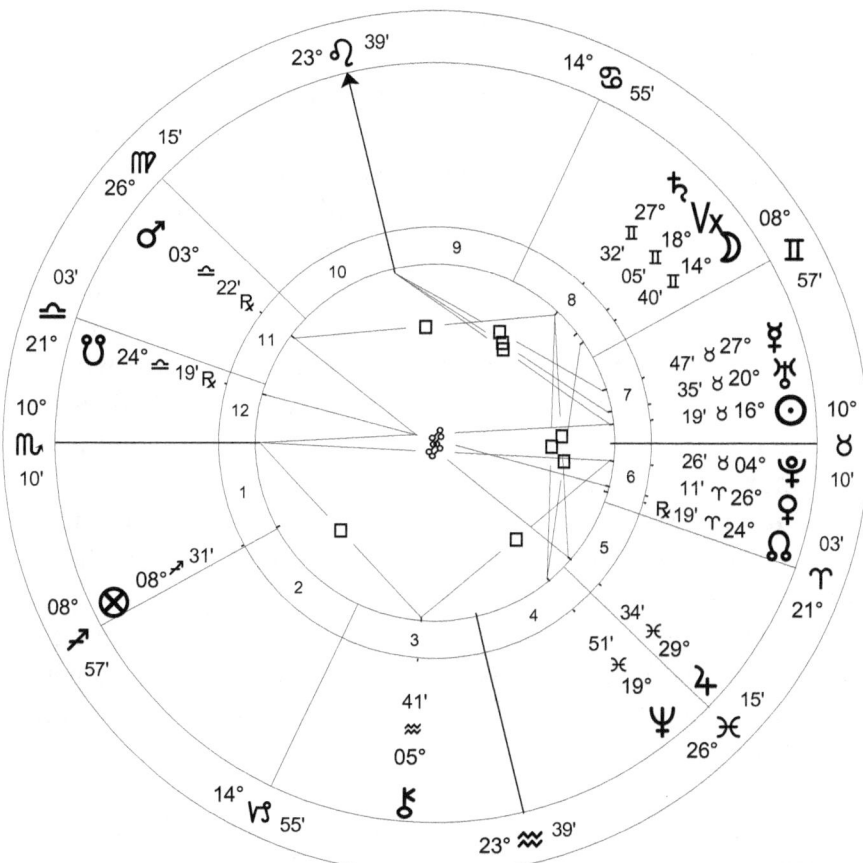

for a Moon-Neptune aspect; therefore spiritualizing these feelings by forgiving or forgetting are often a good defence against feeling them. These intense feelings may have stemmed from the loss of his mother to his sibling rivals, a changeover he often analysed in his later writings. Idealization often masks loss and this is evident in the astrological statement of the 8th house Moon squaring Neptune. The other feminine planet, Venus, is on the North Node conjunct Pluto, revealing the intensity of the sister/lover archetype that has been inherited. Pluto and Venus are placed in the 6th along with the North Node; therefore much of this confusion and intensity of feeling was met in his workplace as the hysteria of his female patients. Frequently for Freud, the archetype of the powerful feminine was met through his analytical relationships with female clients.

Arrivals, Departures and Rivalries

Freud often referred to the eldest child's violent reactions to a newborn. In a paper on femininity, Freud suggested that a young girl's motive for turning away from mother to her father is her grievance against the mother for this act of betrayal. The betrayal is the birth of a new child in the family, a sibling. He also described the elder child's feelings at the arrival of the intruder-sibling, suggesting it 'feels dethroned, despoiled, damaged in its rights, throws a jealous hatred upon the little sibling'.[151] These are powerful sentiments which have often been interpreted as Freud's own overwhelming feelings at the birth of his next sibling who will naturally displace or replace him in his mother's affections. These feelings will become even more challenging when the newborn dies.

Julius, his younger brother, was born seventeen months after Freud and died at seven months old.[152] Freud greeted the baby 'with rage and wicked death wishes'.[153] In 1897, when Freud was in the process of his self-analysis, he wrote to his colleague Fleiss mentioning his feelings of rivalry towards his younger brother and the guilt associated with his death. In a stream-of-consciousness writing style he explained:

> That I greeted my one-year younger brother (who died after a few months) with adverse wishes and genuine childhood jealousy; and that his death left the germ of (self-) reproaches in me ... This nephew and this younger brother have determined, then, what is neurotic, but also what is intense, in all my friendships.[154]

Freud's comments on sibling rivalry seem to stem from his relationship with his nephew, John, and his younger brother Julius. Fifty years after Julius's birth he wrote: 'the unwelcome arrival of a baby brother or sister is the oldest and most burning question that assails immature humanity'.[155] Freud also recognized the impact of his younger brother and elder nephew on his adult friendships. His struggle with close friends and colleagues could partially be linked to these earlier feelings of jealousy and rivalry. His nephew, John, was a surrogate older brother. Freud commented how this relationship 'determined all my later feelings in intercourse with persons my own age'.[156] As suggested, Mars retrograde in the 11th house symbolizes the themes of intensity, rivalry and jealousy that plagued many of Freud's friendships and colleagueships. It also symbolizes his research on sexuality and his theory of libido, the theory that created the most dissension and conflict amongst his psychoanalytic colleagues.

Many losses in the family coincided with the death of Freud's brother Julius on 15 April 1858. Freud's mother had also just lost her own brother, Julius, for whom the new baby had been named. Therefore Sigmund lost a brother and an uncle, both named Julius, at the same time. These losses were compounded by the synchronous failure of Freud's father's business. With the loss of a child, a black hole appears in the constellation of the family. The missing sibling holds a void of unlived potential.

Without adequate mourning, grief over the dead child and its lost potential creates a vacuum in the family system. The mother often feels unavailable, lost in her own depression. Her anxiety, provoked by the loss, is experienced by the surviving children, often quite intensely. The mother's ability to bond with the surviving children is threatened because she now fears their loss. At the time of Julius's death, Freud felt the loss of his mother and, as previously suggested, redirected his anger towards the next arrival, Anna. His sister Anna also arrived when Freud's nanny mysteriously disappeared; this nanny had been a surrogate mother to Freud. Once more, the Moon-Neptune square registers the disappearing feminine figure synchronous to the birth of his sister. Exits and entrances into the family at this time imply that the family atmosphere around Anna's birth was charged with grief and bewilderment.

Freud directed most of his hostility towards his sister, Anna, his least favourite sibling. Whether this was because of her challenge for their mother or because of his guilt reaction to an erotic bond can never be certain. However, the covert hostility between the two siblings remained throughout their adult years. Anna is described in Freud's interpretations of his earliest memories.[157] His father had allowed Sigmund, aged five at the time, and Anna, almost three, to rip up an illustrated book. Freud described tearing the book, leaf by leaf, like an artichoke. Paralleling this memory were fantasies of masturbation. Freud was to postulate later that these erotic fantasies felt guilt-laden and therefore were converted into hostility. Freud's Oedipal complex centred on the young boy's desire for the mother; yet sexual desire for the sister could be even more overwhelming owing to their closer proximity, equality and symmetry, again part of the Venus-Pluto constellation. Freud's own theory of the Oedipal stage of development was that the young boy turned to mother as his desired object, yet here Freud turns towards sister, a theme which would reveal itself later in his marriage.

It was Freud's younger brother Alexander who became his closest sibling and companion. Alexander was born ten years after Freud on 19 April 1866. At a family council, ten-year-old Sigmund suggested the name Alexander for his baby brother, after the military leader Alexander the Great whose power and leadership had made an impression upon him. Unconsciously he also chose a conquering hero who surpassed the glory of his father. Later, Freud was to name his children after significant men or women who were related to his friends. Anna, his youngest daughter who followed in his professional footsteps, bore the same name as her father's sister, but was named for the daughter of one of his intimate friends, *not* his sister.

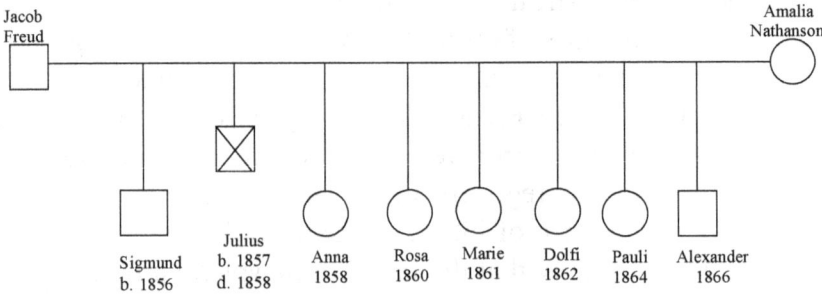

As a younger brother, Alexander became Sigmund's supportive follower, travel companion and suppliant ally and helper. Sigmund's fatherly role towards this brother is reminiscent of the confusion between the father-brother roles he experienced with his half-brother, Emanuel. This relationship may have been the pattern that Freud hoped to find with his younger colleagues, with them as compliant followers. Perhaps it was this model of a colleague that he referred to when writing to his younger associate and heir apparent, Carl Jung:

> Just rest easy, dear son Alexander. I will leave you more to conquer than I myself have managed, all psychiatry and the approval of the civilized world, which regards me as a savage.[158]

Now it is Jung whom Freud names Alexander, the brother who is to surpass the father. Referring to Jung as Alexander blurred the boundaries between Freud's role as an older sibling and a father figure. Alexander, Freud's youngest sibling, was the prototype for how Sigmund would deal with his younger male friends and colleagues. Freud's role as a surrogate father to his sibs also created a distortion with his younger colleagues – he often placed himself in the role of leader/father rather than equal/colleague. In a letter to Sabrina Speilring, Jung lamented: 'I want to be a friend on an equal footing while he [Sigmund Freud] wants to have me as a son.'[159] The split between hierarchy and equality, part of Freud's family portrait and horoscope, continued to complicate his adult relationships.

Sibling Marriages
An interesting enmeshment between the siblings continued into their adult lives. Anna and Sigmund married a sibling pair, Eli and Martha Bernays. Eli, the older brother of Martha Bernays, married Anna three years before Freud married Martha, even though Sigmund and Martha were the first couple to become engaged. Eli and Martha, unlike Sigmund and Anna, had a close sibling bond. This intimacy was threatening to Freud, especially when his fiancée would seek her brother's advice. For reasons never mentioned, Freud did not attend his sister's wedding! He transferred much of his hostility and rivalry to Eli, twice a brother-in-law. It is common that a sibling's marriage ignites the taboo feelings too dangerous to express to the sibling. Certainly, in opposite sex sibling pairs, the sibling's marriage partner is a prime target for unexpressed hostilities or feelings. Anna, writing about her brother in later years, criticized his dominance and favouritism in the family, resenting what she had to sacrifice for Sigmund and his education.

Another sibling triangle formed part of Freud's marriage. In November 1895, nine years after Sigmund and Martha married, Minna Bernays, his wife's sister, came 'for a stay of several months'.[160] In reality, she lived with her sister and brother-in-law for the rest of her life. This arrival occurred a few weeks before the sixth and last child, Anna, was born. The sisters shared the management of the household. Martha knew little of her husband's vocation or seemed little interested, but Minna was actively involved and supportive of his work.

Minna was intellectually aligned with Sigmund while Martha was more pragmatic, attending to the care of their children. Freud has referred to Minna as 'my closest confidante'.[161] Her presence was part of his daily life – he discussed his analytic practice with her, they spent evenings playing cards together and she accompanied him on his daily walk. In essence, Freud had two wives: his wife's sister became his spiritual wife. As we would imagine, this situation gave rise to rumours and speculation by biographers about an affair between Sigmund and Minna. The enmeshment of the sisters' relationship with Freud may have been partially fuelled by his earlier incestuous wishes towards his sister as well as his triangular relationship with his siblings and his mother. And it may have been easier for Freud to speak about the hostile feelings between siblings rather than the erotic ones.

How might this aspect of the family portrait be illustrated in Freud's horoscope? The 7th and 8th houses are of interest as this motif concerns marriage partners. The 3rd house is the sphere of the sibling; therefore, the sibling's partner would be the 7th house (partner) from the 3rd (sibling) or the 9th house. Likewise, the partner's sibling would be the 3rd from the 7th or the 9th house; therefore this house also draws our attention. In my experience, triangles often are constellated around the archetype of Venus and the territory of the 8th. I would also note Venus as the partner or sister and Mercury as a sibling story. I would begin with these ideas in mind to see if I could start to unravel this dynamic.

The Moon is conjunct the Vertex in Gemini in the 8th house. Gemini on the cusp of the 8th brings the image of the sibling into the underworld and intimate territory of the 8th. The Vertex is often an image of unseen complexes that lie beneath the surface of relationship attraction. The 7th house cusp might serve to reveal projective aspects of our self as well the qualities that we seek in a relationship; however, the Vertex is often an indicator of the more compelling unconscious bonds that are stirred through the alliance. For instance, in Freud's horoscope, Taurus is on the cusp of the 7th, reflecting the relational qualities of endurance, patience, steadfastness and stability; however, the Vertex in Gemini reveals restlessness around the question of commitment. And on a psychological level it brings the incomplete sibling relationship into the current one. The Moon-Vertex square to Neptune reveals the enmeshment and muddle that is brought from the sibling relationship into the marriage.

The ruler of the 3rd is Saturn and the ruler of the 9th is the Moon. Both ruling planets are in Gemini in the 8th house, again suggesting that the sibling and their partner are brought into the intimacy of the marriage. Certainly this was true for Minna but not so for Eli. Other astrological factors such as Mercury in the 7th could be interpreted as the sibling story entering the contemporary relationship. With Uranus conjoining both Mercury and the Sun in this house we would suspect an unconventional arrangement. Uranus as ruler of the 4th brings the familial patterns into the present marriage. We have also noted that the Venus-Pluto conjunction also might contribute to the intensity of the sister archetype being brought into the current union. Venus and Mars are also in mutual reception, which suggests that they displace each other, just as Eli displaced Sigmund at times. In myth, Venus and Mars were both siblings and partners and here their roles are becoming confused. Therefore there are many astrological threads that can be unravelled to gain insights into this pattern.

We know little of Freud's other sisters besides descriptions of family life given by Freud in his letters. Rosa was the second sister, born on 21 March 1860, and his favourite, followed by Marie, Adolfine (Dolfi) and Pauline. Freud was also fond of Dolfi, who never married and who lived with their mother and whom Freud helped to support. Freud was automatically the authority figure to whom his sisters and the extended family would turn for advice and resources. It was these four sisters Freud left behind when he emigrated to London in 1938. After his death, all four died at the hands of the Nazis.

The Last Child
As mentioned earlier, Anna Freud, the last of Sigmund Freud's six children, was born synchronous to a 'crisis of accession' in the family with the arrival of Freud's sister-in-law. As we already explored, this is this a potent time in the family life cycle for all its members. In Freud's case this meant the birth of a daughter and the arrival of his sister-in-law, 'a second wife'. Freud was in midlife, his fortieth year, and turned forty in May 1896. Shortly after his birthday his father became ill and died on 23 October 1896. This began Freud's descent into his own self-analysis.

The birth of the last child can also be a significant turning point in the family as the family settles into its arrangements and roles. This passage for Freud was multifaceted: the birth of the last child corresponded with growing acknowledgement that he also fathered a new psychological theory; the death of the father and his descent into his own analysis was parallel to his publication of a new book and his professorship. We can view the impact of the birth of the last child on Sigmund Freud by comparing Anna's horoscope with his. However, this will also reveal the larger movements in the family life, as his daughter's horoscope is also the transits of the period synchronous with her birth. Anna's time of birth has been taken from Freud's letters and her chart is placed around the outer rim of her father's horoscope. This is a snapshot of a moment in time in the family life cycle.

Their synastry is remarkable. Anna shares her father's Moon in Gemini, but hers sits atop her father's Saturn in the 8th. Anna is born

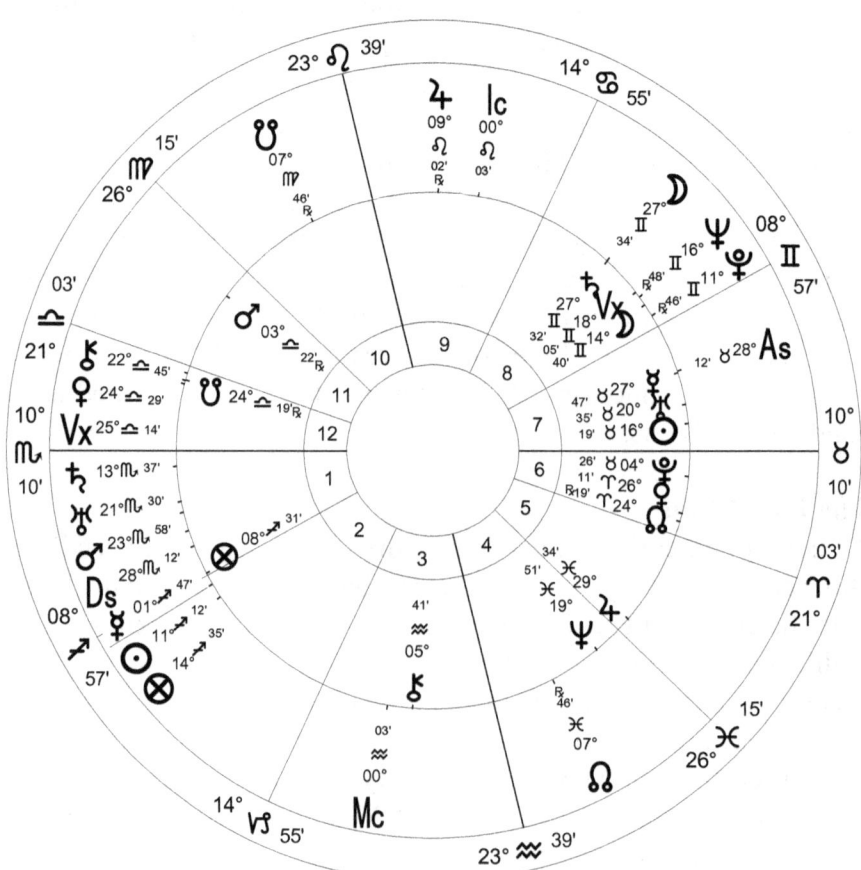

in the years following the rare Neptune-Pluto conjunction and the midpoint of these two planets is exactly conjunct Sigmund's Moon. The transit of Neptune conjunct his Moon is declining while the transit of Pluto to his Moon is gaining momentum. Approaching his forties also meant he was approaching his first Neptune square; therefore his potent natal aspect of the Moon-Neptune square will be astrologically highlighted over these next few years; the natal aspect is being reiterated by transit, always a priority when analysing transits. Representative of an important passage of time in his life, this transit points to the profound changes occurring in the depths of his psyche. In the system of the family it speaks of the changes taking place for the women in the system, especially mother, wife and sister (or sister-in-law).

I would also take note of the progressed Moon at this time, as this image is very revealing in the family life cycle. Freud's progressed Moon is 16♏23. This is exactly opposing his natal Sun and has been in his 1st house for the last six months, which includes Anna's gestation. The image of the awareness of new life and new relationships in the family and its members is certainly confirmed by this image. Freud's awareness of his new emerging identity is being reflected back to him during the progression of the Moon in opposition to his Sun, which parallels Anna's arrival.

Uranus is at the midpoint of its cycle. We have already noted Uranus as the ruler of the 4th, and the potent Sun-Uranus conjunction which brings the rulers of the 4th-10th axis together in the 7th house. The midlife crisis which brings the event of the death of father is culminating at this time. However, as we convert this aspect into a soulful reflection, it speaks about the image of the father in the psyche and the family undergoing a separation, liberation and a new direction. Freud died at his Uranus return and therefore this is literally its halfway marker. In terms of family life, a major Uranus transit might speak of a 'crisis of dismemberment'; however, this transition in the Freud family was heralded by Anna's birth.

Saturn is approaching Uranus in Scorpio, so the existing Saturn-Uranus cycle is in its final phase. The new cycle will begin directly opposite Freud's Mercury, which not only reveals the emergence of his intellectual and conceptual ideas but the changes in sibling relationships in the family. This is also Anna's Ascendant. At the time of Anna's birth, transiting Saturn is approaching the opposition to Freud's Sun, which will become exact three times in the following year. Something is being consolidated in himself and also in terms of the masculine principle within the family. Anna will always have her Saturn opposite her father's Sun, which will bind them together through mentorship and work. In retrospect this also foreshadows Anna's parental responsibilities to her father in later life. This is also replicated with her Moon conjunct his Saturn.

Chiron has just entered Freud's 12th and rests on his South Node. His understanding of the depth of his life work is beginning, as he excavates the unconscious and composes the healing narrative of psychoanalysis. Since Anna's Venus-Vertex conjunction also lies on her father's South Node, I would imagine this powerful relationship is a creative trigger to a deeper understanding of the psyche and its processes. On an ancestral level, this could also suggest that the awareness of a profound wound in the family is becoming conscious. Anna's Jupiter sits high in her father's 9th house, squaring his Ascendant-Descendant axis. All the social and outer planets are dramatic at this nodal point in Freud's life. This is not only a transition in his life but in the lives of those he is attached to in the family system.

The Freudian Legacy
Sigmund Freud is probably psychology's most famous figure. However, he is also credited with being one of the most influential and controversial thinkers of the last century. His legacy left its mark on the way we think about childhood, sexuality and memory. He introduced the public to dreams, therapy and the 'Freudian slip'. Generations of analysts, philosophers, therapists, counsellors, sociologists and many more have been influenced by his life work, perhaps without even knowing. Yet, curiously, Janine Burke begins her exceptional book on Freud by saying: 'Freud built the entire edifice of psychoanalysis on childhood memories: by the age of three the compass was set. When it came to telling the story of his own childhood, Freud created a fairy tale;'[162] a mythology motivated by his family portrait.

We might surmise that this was Freud's legacy: to continuously recreate our childhood in order that we ensoul our family story and our own. And in reflecting on our family story and our childhood we do begin to ensoul our lives through its living narrative. Freud inspires the subjective life, our inner examination of the past, which is always best to begin with the fairy tale opening, *once upon a time*.

From an astrological perspective the archetypes of our horoscope are better understood and deepened through the examination of the familial past and its relationships. Our family, its patterns and its fate are embedded within our chart. No doubt an examination of our parents' and siblings' horoscopes enhances our understanding of the family holistically; however, as astrologers who are aware of family dynamics, we can be effective family counsellors using only one horoscope. We can witness aspects of Sigmund Freud's chart that, while far from complete, reveal family patterns and complexes as well as how these helped to shape his life, his work and his legacy. In essence, our horoscope is our family legacy.

– IN CONCLUSION –

American funny man George Burns is quoted as saying something like 'happiness is having a large, loving, caring, close-knit family in another city'. We laugh because we all recognize that great need to belong, to be attached, bonded; yet at the same time we yearn for our separateness and singleness. But sometimes when we are free and independent we long for the shelter of family.

In English, we use the expression the 'family circle'. For, like a circle, the family has no beginning or end. It continuously evolves and returns. Like all organisms it has its life cycle; therefore the family experience comes full circle. The child becomes the adult who in turn becomes the elder. One family member dies, another is born and the circle of family life once again returns and renews itself. The exit of a family member creates an opening in the family matrix. The new member who enters and fills the space is influenced by the one who has left, even if they are a distant relative or have never met.

The life force of the family continues on in its mysterious ways through the legacies of the ancestors. The generations of the family that are now moving through their life cycle are impacted by those who have come before. In turn, those living will have a bearing on the generations of the future, those family members not yet born.

This cyclical nature of family life is naturally compatible with many planetary cycles, as each member is born at certain points in the unfolding of each astrological round. Their moment of birth is also the same moment of entry into the family matrix recorded by every horoscope. And as we look with an astrological eye, we can identify the commonality of threads and patterns passing through the family line. Identifying the synchronicity of these family designs evokes a sense of belonging to something much greater and more profound than we can ever know. Our astrological journey into family often allows us to become more aware of, and therefore more consciously participatory in, the energetic systems and legacies from our familial past.

Contemplating the birth chart in the context of the family is humbling, because the connection between the parents, siblings and other family members is evident in our own horoscope. Through the repetition and similarities of astrological signs and symbols, we clearly observe that we are part of the family system and a thread in the ancestral tapestry. The astrological DNA that is part of our family is also part of us.

– APPENDIX 2 –
Birth Data used in Text

Chart/Chapter	Birth Data	Source of Data
THE KENNEDYS **Chapter 2**		
Joseph	6 September 1888, 0706 EST, Boston, MA	Unverified birth time
Rose	22 July 1890, 1900 EST, Boston, MA	Unverified birth time
John	19 May 1917, 1500 EST, Brookline, MA	From mother's memory
Edward	22 February 1932, 0358 EST, Dorchester, MA	Birth certificate
Eunice	10 July 1921, 1100 EDT, Brookline, MA	From memory
THE ROYAL FAMILY Chapter 2		
Elizabeth, The Queen Mother	4 August 1900, 1200 GMT, London, UK	Unverified birth time (noon chart)
George VI	14 December 1895, 0305 GMT, Sandringham, UK	Biography
Elizabeth II	21 April 1926, 0240 GDT, London, UK	Official records
Princess Margaret	21 August 1930, 0922 GDT, Glamis Castle, Scotland, UK	Doctor's report
Charles, Prince of Wales	14 November 1948, 2114 GMT, London, UK	Official announcement

Diana, Princess of Wales	1 July 1961, 1945 GDT, Sandringham, UK	From mother's memory
Anne, Princess Royal	15 August 1950, 1150 GDT, London, UK	Official announcement
Andrew, Duke of York	19 February 1960, 1530 GMT, London, UK	Official announcement
Sarah, Duchess of York (Fergie)	15 October 1959, 0903 GMT, London, UK	From memory
William, Duke of Cambridge	21 June 1982, 2103 GDT, London, UK	Official announcement
WOMEN in FAMILY Chapters 15/17	All births in Australia except Lauren AEST = Australian Eastern Standard Time AEDT = Australian Eastern Daylight Time	
Margaret	30 January 1908, 1200 AEST, Bairnsdale, Victoria	No recorded time (noon chart)
Kaye	5 December 1944, 0055 AEST, Melbourne, Victoria	Birth record
Yvonne	19 August 1970 AEST, 1815, Melbourne, Victoria	Birth record
Lauren	17 March 1996, 1807 EST, Baltimore, USA	Birth record
Mae	29 June 1999, 2329 AEST, Melbourne, Victoria	Birth record
Elsie	23 June 2000 AEST, 1645, Chelsea, Victoria	Birth record
Trinity	14 November 2003 AEDT, 1133, Boronia, Victoria	Birth record
Grace	12 March 2013, 1909 AEDT, Narre Warren, Victoria	Birth record

WENDY **Chapter 17**		
Wendy	6 February 1945, 1620 CWT, Belle Plaine, IA, USA	Birth certificate
FREUD **Chapter 20**		
Sigmund	6 May 1856, 1830 LST, Freiberg, Moravia	Birth record
Anna	3 December 1895, 1515 MET, Vienna, Austria	From memory

– BIBLIOGRAPHY –

Adler, Alfred, trans. Colin Brett, *What Life Could Mean to You*, Oneworld Publications (Oxford: 1994).

Bank, Stephen and Kahn, Michael, *The Sibling Bond*, Basic Books (New York: 1992).

Bell, Lynn, *Planetary Threads*, Ibis Press (Lake Worth: 2013).

Bowlby, John, *A Secure Base: Parent-Child Attachment and Healthy Human Development*, Routledge (London: 1988).

Carter, Betty and McGoldrick, Monica (eds.), *The Changing Family Life Cycle*, Allyn and Bacon (Boston: 1989).

Cicirelli, Victor G, *Sibling Relationships Across the Lifespan*, Plenum Press (New York: 1995).

Clark, Brian, *Keys to Understanding Chiron*, Astro*Synthesis Series (Melbourne: 2008).

Clark, Brian, *Secondary Progressions*, Astro*Synthesis Series (Melbourne: 2012).

Clark, Brian, *The Zodiacal Imagination*, Astro*Synthesis Series (Melbourne: 2010).

Clark, Ronald W, *Freud: the Man and his Cause*, Jonathan Cape/ Weidenfeld & Nicolson (London: 1980).

Crago, Hugh, *A Circle Unbroken*, Allen & Unwin (Sydney: 1999).

Earnshaw, Averil, *Time Bombs in Families and How to Survive Them*, Spencer Publications (Sydney: 1998).

Edis, Freda, *The God Between*, Arkana (London: 1995).

Freud, Sigmund, trans. Strachey, James,. *The Standard Edition of the Complete Psychological Works of Sigmund Freud*, 24 volumes, Hogarth Press, London: 1953-75.

Gay, Peter, *Freud: A Life for Our Time*, WW Norton (New York: 1988).

Greene, Liz, *Relating: An Astrological Guide to Living with Others on a Small Planet*, Samuel Weiser (New York: 1980).

Greene, Liz, *The Astrology of Fate*, Allen & Unwin (London: 1984).

Greene, Liz and Sasportas, Howard, *The Development of the Personality*, Samuel Weiser (York Beach: 1987).

Greene, Liz and Sasportas, Howard, *The Inner Planets*, Samuel Weiser (York Beach: 1993).

Hillman, James, *Healing Fiction*, Station Hill Press (New York: 1983).

Hillman, James, *The Dream and the Underworld*, Harper & Row (New York: 1979).

Hillman, James, *The Myth of Analysis*, Harper & Row (New York: 1978).

Homer, trans. Charles Boer, *The Homeric Hymns*, Spring (Dallas: 1970).

Homer, trans. Richmond Lattimore, *The Iliad*, University of Chicago Press (Chicago: 1961).

Homer, trans. Richmond Lattimore, *The Odyssey*, Harper Perennial (New York: 1991).

Imber-Black, Evan (ed.), *Secrets in Families and Family Therapy*, WW Norton (New York: 1993).

Jung, CG, trans. RFC Hull et al, *The Collected Works of CG Jung*, 20 volumes, London: Routledge & Kegan Paul and Princeton: Princeton University Press, 1953-79.

Jung, CG, trans. R and C Wilson, *Memories, Dreams, Reflections*, Pantheon Books (New York: 1973).

McGoldrick, Monica, *The Genogram Journey: Reconnecting with Your Family*, WW Norton (New York: 2011).

Minuchin, Salvador, *Families and Family Therapy*, Tavistock/Routledge (London: 1991).

Moore, Thomas, *Care of the Soul*, Harper Perennial (New York: 1992).

Moore, Thomas, (ed.), *The Essential James Hillman: A Blue Fire*, Routledge (London: 1990).

O'Connor, Peter, *Facing the Fifties*, Allen & Unwin (Sydney: 2000).

Ovid, trans. Mary M Innes, *Metamorphoses*, Penguin (Harmondsworth: 1955).

Reinhart, Melanie, *Chiron and the Healing Journey*, Arkana (London: 1989).

Reinhart, Melanie, *To the Edge and Beyond*, Centre for Psychological Astrology (London: 1996).

Rudhyar, Dane, *The Astrological Houses*, Doubleday (Garden City: 1972).

Rudhyar, Dane, *The Pulse of Life: New Dynamics in Astrology*, Shambhala (Berkeley: 1970).

Sandmaier, Marian, *Original Kin: The Search for Connection among Adult Sisters and Brothers*, Dutton (New York: 1994).

Sasportas, Howard, *The Gods of Change*, Arkana (London: 1989).

Sasportas, Howard, *The Twelve Houses*, Aquarian (Wellingborough: 1985).

Satir, Virginia, *Conjoint Family Therapy*, Science and Behavior Books (Palo Alto: 1983).

Scarf, Maggie, *Intimate Partners: Patterns in Love and Marriage*, Random House (New York: 1987).

Sullivan, Erin, *Dynasty: The Astrology of Family Dynamics*, Arkana (London: 1996).

Sullivan, Erin, *Saturn in Transit*, Arkana (London: 1991).

Sulloway, Frank J, *Born to Rebel*, Pantheon Books (New York: 1996).

Sutton-Smith, Brian and Rosenburg, BG, *The Sibling*, Holt, Rinehart & Winston (New York: 1970).

Toman, Walter, *Family Constellation*, 4th ed., Springer (New York: 1991).

Winnicott, DW, *Home is Where We Start From*, Penguin (London: 1990).

– ENDNOTES –

[1] Thomas Moore, *Care of the Soul*, Harper Perennial (New York: 1992), 31.

[2] RS Sauber, et al, *The Dictionary of Family Psychology and Family Therapy*, 2nd ed., Sage Publications (Newbury Park: 1993), 142.

[3] Ptolemy, *Tetrabiblos*, trans. F E Robbins, Harvard University (Cambridge: 2001), III.4.

[4] For instance see Guido Bonatti, *Book of Astronomy, Volume II*, trans. Benjamin Dykes, The Cazimi Press (Golden Valley: 2007), 1235-44 for Bonatti's discussion on siblings and 1245-56 for his discourse on the parents.

[5] Liz Greene, *The Astrology of Fate,* Allen & Unwin (London: 1984), 94.

[6] For a thorough investigation of the family life cycle, see Betty Carter and Monica McGoldrick (eds.), *The Changing Family Life Cycle,* Allyn and Bacon (Boston: 1989).

[7] To explore the transits to an individual's horoscope and how this affects the gestalt of the whole family, see Erin Sullivan, *Dynasty: the Astrology of Family Dynamics*, Arkana (London: 1996), 195-223.

[8] The Greek Classical period is between the Archaic and Hellenistic periods from approximately 479-323 BCE and included the flourishing golden 5th century in Athens.

[9] The word comes from the roots *zoe* (life) and *diaklos* (wheel). The zodiac as the wheel of life is an ancient symbol for the eternal round, the circle of life.

[10] Robert Schmidt, Translator's Preface in Vettius Valens, *The Anthology: Book I*, Project Hindsight's Greek Track IV, Golden Hind Press (Berkeley Springs: 1993), vvi-xvii.

[11] See Brian Clark, *The Zodiacal Imagination*, Astro*Synthesis (Melbourne: 2010).

[12] See Nicholas Campion, *The Dawn of Astrology, A Cultural History of Western Astrology,* Continuum (London: 2008), 173-184.

[13] James Hillman, *The Dream and the Underworld*, Harper & Row (New York: 1979), 23.

[14] From an interview in *Neues Weiner Journal* with Carl Jung on 9 November 1932, translated by Ruth Horine. See *CG Jung Speaking*, Princeton University Press (Princeton: 1977), 58.

[15] Melanie Reinhart, *Saturn, Chiron and the Centaurs*, Starwalker Press (UK: 2011), 215.

[16] CJ Jung, *Psychology and Alchemy*, Volume 12n. 16, 30.

[17] For two excellent astrological examinations of fate, see Liz Greene, *The Astrology of Fate*, 1-14 and Robert Hand, 'Fate and Astrology, Some Ancient Insights', *The Mountain Astrologer*, Feb/Mar 2006. Fate has many synonyms, or words used in a similar context with a slightly different inference due to historical, cultural or religious perspectives. For instance, 'Heimarmene' might suggest the past, fate already ordained, while 'Nemesis' could refer to the future consequences of action or choice. Tyche was a Greek goddess who during the 5th century came to represent chance, fortune or the fateful present. 'Providence' could refer to the work of God while 'Karma' could refer to the inherent justice of the cosmos; hence 'Justice' or the distribution of what is due (*nomos* – law) is similar to fate, the laws that are written. 'Lot' is also fated, such as our lot in life, which is essentially the lot that we are born with.

[18] Hesiod, *Theogony*, trans. Dorothea Wender, Penguin (London: 1973). See lines 211 and following for the first description of the Fates born of Nyx and lines 900-5 for their individual names and birth as daughters of Themis.

[19] I recommend an excellent article by Liz Greene on the Kennedy family curse. Originally written for *Apollon* this article is now available on the Internet: http://www.astro.com/astrology/in_oracle_e.htm [Accessed 25 November 2015].

[20] I first became aware of this through Penny Thornton's book *Synastry*, The Aquarian Press (London: 1982), 149. However, since then, I have examined many cases of repetitive degrees in families.

[21] Early Greek literature and tragedy was masterful at depicting the family curse which was passed down generation after generation. The three best known classical playwrights during the 5th century BCE were Aeschylus, Sophocles and Euripides. Each one was fascinated by mythic family tragedies. Aeschylus's trilogy *The Oresteia* tells the tragic tale of the House of Atreus and the catastrophic family legacy that befalls Agamemnon and his son Orestes.

[22] Sophocles, *Antigone* from *The Three Theban Plays,* trans. Robert Fagles, Penguin (London: 1984), 103.

[23] Greene, *The Astrology of Fate*, 92.

[24] Jung, *Memories, Dreams, Reflections*, Pantheon Books (New York: 1973), 233.

[25] Erma Bombeck, *Family: The Ties that Bind ... and Gag!*, Random House (New York: 1988).

[26] Salvador Minuchin, *Families and Family Therapy*, Tavistock/Routledge (London: 1991), 47.

[27] Two different versions exist of Thetis's attempt to render Achilles immortal. One is his baptism by fire and the other is by water in the River Styx.

[28] The different versions of the twins' birth suggest both are Zeus's sons, or both are sons of Tyndareus. Fragments of Greek epic suggest Castor is mortal and Polydeuces immortal, indicating the dual parentage. No version ever suggested the reverse.

[29] 'Psychopomp' refers to the guide of the souls and often references Hermes's role as the conductor of souls both into and out of the underworld.

[30] For the various sources that describe the differing versions of the Dioscuri's afterlife, see Timothy Gantz, *Early Greek Myth*, John Hopkins University Press (Baltimore: 1993), Volume 1, 327.

[31] See RH Allen, *Star Names, Their Lore and Meaning* (Dover Publications: 1899), 224-5.

[32] See DW Winnicott, *Home Is Where We Start From*, WW Norton, (New York: 1990). TS Eliot's phrase was 'Home is where one starts from'. TS Eliot's *Four Quartets* can be accessed online at http://www.davidgorman.com/4Quartets/.

[33] Guido Bonatti, *The Book of Astronomy, Volume II*, trans. Benjamin Dykes, 1248.

[34] Ibid, 1355.

[35] Llewellyn George, *A to Z Horoscope Maker and Delineator*, Llewellyn Publications (St Paul: 1970), 34.

[36] Some texts and encyclopedias state the following:
Larousse Encyclopedia of Astrology, Plume (Canada: 1982)
– under *4th House*: 'Home and mother (sometimes father). Emotional foundations, parents' (page 149)
– under *10th House*: 'father (sometimes mother), authority figures' (page 150)

The Arkana Dictionary of Astrology, Penguin Books (London: 1985)
– under *mother*: 'The 4th house is sometimes called the House of the Mother' (page 328)

– under *father*: 'The House of the Father is a name given to the Tenth House' (page 190)

The Modern Textbook of Astrology, LN Fowler (Romford: 1978)
– under *4th House*: 'This house generally refers to the mother, though the connection is not as infallible as older books imply. The mother does not always connect herself solely with the home as in days of large families and little outer life for women' (page 93)
– under *10th House*: 'It used to be called "the house of the career and the father"' (page 95)

Astrology, A Cosmic Science, Fellowship House (Boston: 1978)
– under *4th House*: 'the least prominent parent in the life. Some say it rules the mother, others the father. Depends on which is boss (10th house)' (page 60)
– under *10th House*: 'His father' (page 62)

[37] Howard Sasportas, *The Twelve Houses*, Aquarian (Wellingborough: 1985), 89. (Reprinted edition, Flare, 2007.)

[38] Liz Greene, The Parental Marriage in the Horoscope in *The Development of the Personality*, Samuel Weiser (York Beach: 1987), 96.

[39] Vera von der Heydt, On the Father in Psychotherapy in *Fathers and Mothers*, Spring (Zurich: 1973), 133.

[40] Howard Sasportas uses this phrase in reference to the mother in the 10th in *The Twelve Houses*, 89.

[41] Carl Jung, *The Collected Works of CG Jung*, Volume 6: 307.

[42] Sullivan, *Dynasty: The Astrology of Family Dynamics*, 187.

[43] AT Mann in his book *Life Time Astrology*, George Allen and Unwin (London: 1984), 33-4, develops the idea of the 12th house as being the period 'seventeen weeks before birth until birth'.

[44] In Jungian terminology *participation mystique* is an archaic connection between the unconscious of an individual with objects or

people. Originally this was an anthropological term describing the participation in a tribal or collective unconscious.

[45] Minuchin, *Families and Family Therapy*, 59.

[46] Sophocles, *Oedipus Rex* in *The Three Theban Plays*, trans. Robert Fagles, Penguin (London: 1984).

[47] Carl Jung, Freud and Psychoanalysis in *The Collected Works*, Volume 4, trans. RFC Hull, Routledge & Kegan Paul (London: 1961), 347-8.

[48] For an astrological commentary on the psychoanalytic fathers and their sibling dynamics Brian Clark, *The Sibling Constellation*, Penguin (London: 1999).

[49] Victor G Cicirelli, *Sibling Relationships Across the Lifespan*, Plenum Press (New York: 1995), 2.

[50] Minuchin, *Families and Family Therapy*, 59.

[51] Sasportas, *The Twelve Houses*, 50.

[52] Houses 1-4 are the personal houses; houses 5-8, the interpersonal houses; and houses 9-12, the transpersonal houses. Each group contains four houses which correspond to the four elements:
Houses 1, 5 and 9 are the houses of life (Fire);
Houses 2, 6 and 10 are the houses of substance (Earth);
Houses 3, 7 and 11 are the houses of relationship (Air);
Houses 4, 8 and 12 are the houses of endings (Water).

[53] Monica McGoldrick, The Joining of Families through Marriage: the New Couple in *The Changing Family Life Cycle*, Betty Carter and Monica McGoldrick (eds.), 228.

[54] Walter Toman, *Family Constellation,* Springer Publishing (New York: 1976).

[55] In synastry analysis it is very helpful to make notes of each partner's birth order, sibling position and roles.

[56] Minuchin, *Families and Family Therapy*, 59.

[57] Adler, Alfred, *What Life Could Mean to You*, trans. Colin Brett, Oneworld Publications (Oxford: 1994), 124.

[58] See Demetra George, *Astrology and the Authentic Self*, Ibis Press (Lake Worth: 2008), 90-3.

[59] All quotes are from Dane Rudhyar, *The Astrological Houses*, Doubleday (Garden City: 1972), 74-5 and 117.

[60] Jung, *The Collected Works of CJ Jung*, Volume 2, 1007.

[61] Liz Greene, The Parental Marriage in the Horoscope in *The Development of the Personality*, 83-162.

[62] In the myth of Psyche and Eros, Psyche is told by her envious sisters that the man she is with is monstrous, whereas in reality he is Aphrodite's son Eros, the personification of love.

[63] Homer, The Second Hymn to Artemis in *The Homeric Hymns*, trans. Michael Crudden, Oxford University Press (Oxford: 2001), 87.

[64] JM Ashmand, Symbols and Signs in *Ptolemy's Tetrabiblos* (North Hollywood, CA: 1976), 124.

[65] Jung, Synchronicity: An Acausal Connecting Principle in *The Collected Works of CG Jung*, Volume 8, 869.

[66] C Kerenyi, *Zeus and Hera – Archetypal Images of Father, Husband and Wife,* trans. Christopher Holme, Princeton University Press (Princeton: 1975), 113.

[67] This is the tale from the island of Samos. The story is either that the wedding night lasted 300 years or the marriage was kept secret for 300 years. For amplification on this see C Kerenyi, *The Gods of the Greeks,*

Thames and Hudson (London: 1951), 95-99, as well as C Kerenyi, *Zeus and Hera, Archetypal Images of Father, Husband and Wife*, 91-113.

[68] Lynda Schmidt, The Brother-Sister Relationship in Marriage in *The Journal of Analytic Psychology*, Volume 25, No. 1, January 1980, 34.

[69] Thomas Moore (ed.), *The Essential James Hillman: A Blue Fire*, Routledge (London: 1990), 193.

[70] Liz Greene and Howard Sasportas, *The Luminaries*, Samuel Weiser. (York Beach: 1992), 51.

[71] Maggie Scarf, *Intimate Partners: Patterns in Love and Marriage*, Random House (New York: 1987), 78.

[72] John Bowlby, *A Secure Base: Parent-Child Attachment and Healthy Human Development*, Routledge (London: 1988). John Bowlby and Mary Ainsworth are the pioneers of delineating attachment styles.

[73] Jung, *The Collected Works of CJ Jung*, Volume 17: 217a.

[74] Greene, *The Astrology of Fate*, 93.

[75] Walter Toman, *Family Constellation*, Springer (New York: 1961).

[76] John Bradshaw, *The Family*, Health Communications (Deerfield Beach: 1988), 33-6, summarizes the fourfold approach to birth order based on the research done by Dr Jerome Bach at the University of Minnesota.

[77] Karl Konig, *Brothers and Sisters: The Order of Birth in the Family*, 4th edition, Floris Books (Edinburgh: 1984).

[78] DW Winnicott, *The Child, the Family and the Outside World*, Penguin (Harmondsworth: 1991), 133. Winnicott often speaks eloquently of the only child. He was a youngest with two older sisters but has suggested he grew up as 'an only child with multiple mothers' (see *Winnicott* by Adam Phillips, Harvard University Press (Cambridge: 1988).

[79] Marilyn Mason in her article 'Shame: Reservoir for Family Secrets' lists eight 'rules' that perpetuate shame in families. These are: 1 Control; 2 Perfection; 3 Blame; 4 Denial; 5 Unreliability; 6 Incompleteness; 7 No talk; and 8 Disqualification. Evan Imber-Black (ed.), *Secrets in Families and Family Therapy*, WW Norton (New York: 1993), 37-38.

[80] Lily Pincus and Christopher Dare, *Secrets in the Family*, Faber & Faber (London: 1978), 135.

[81] Ibid, 9.

[82] Evan Imber-Black (ed.), Secrets in Families and Family Therapy: An Overview in *Secrets in Families and Family Therapy*, 19. I would recommend this chapter in the book as an excellent introduction to the power of secrets in families.

[83] Pincus and Dare, *Secrets in the Family*, 16.

[84] Samuel Slipp, *The Freudian Mystique*, New York University Press (New York: 1993), 119.

[85] The first five lines of TS Eliot's *Four Quartets* poetically captures the conundrum of time.

[86] Hesiod describes the Golden Age in his *Works and Days*. This quote from the translation by Hugh G Evelyn-White, Harvard University Press (Cambridge: 2002), 11.

[87] James Hillman (ed.), Notes on Opportunism in *Puer Papers*, Spring (Dallas: 1994), 153.

[88] Averil Earnshaw, *Time Bombs in Families and How to Survive Them*, Spencer Publications, (Sydney: 1988), 17.

[89] Ibid, 32.

[90] For a thorough investigation of the family life cycle, see Betty Carter and Monica McGoldrick (eds.), *The Changing Family Life Cycle*.

[91] EM Duvall, *Marriage and Family Development*, Lippincott (Philadelphia: 1977).

[92] These statistics were from World Population Prospects, 2006 Revision published by the United Nations. For lists of life expectancy from other organizations see: https://en.wikipedia.org/wiki/List_of_countries_by_life_expectancy [Accessed 3 October 2015].

[93] For the timing of the aspects for each Chiron sign see *Keys to Understanding Chiron* by Brian Clark, Astro*Synthesis (Melbourne: 1999). See: www.astrosynthesis.com.au.

[94] Gail Sheehy has been a popular author in this regard. Her books *Passages: Predictive Crises of Adult Life* and *Pathfinders* were highly popular and she has written *New Passages* and *Understanding Men's Passages* in the same vein.

[95] Erik Erikson, *Identity and the Life Cycle*, International Universities Press (New York: 1959). Erikson's eight phases of the life cycle were described as:

	Ages approximated	Task	Unsuccessful Outcome	Successful Outcome
1	Infants, birth to 18 months	Trust	Mistrust	Hope
2	Toddlers, 18 months to 3 years	Autonomy	Doubt	Will Power
3	Preschool, 3 to 6 years	Initiative	Guilt	Purpose
4	Childhood, 6 to 12 years	Industry	Inferiority	Competence
5	Adolescence, 12 to 19 years	Identity	Role Confusion	Fidelity
6	Young Adults, 19 to 40 years	Intimacy	Isolation	Love
7	Middle Adulthood, 40 to 65 years	Generativity	Stagnation	Care

| 8 | Seniors, 65 years to death | Ego Integrity | Despair | Wisdom |

We might ponder these eight stages as we would the eight phases of the lunation cycle.

[96] For instance, Carter and McGoldrick (eds.) in *The Changing Family Life Cycle* comprehensively track the family through its life cycle.

[97] Joni Mitchell used the phrase 'the carousel of time' in the lyrics of her song 'The Circle Game'.

[98] William Wordsworth, *Ode to Intimations of Immortality from Recollections of Early Childhood* from *Treasury of Favorite Poems*, edited by Louis Untermeyer, Barnes & Noble (New York: 1996), lines 58-66.

[99] Ibid, lines 1-9.

[100] The Queen's Sun at 0♉12 is exactly conjunct her first born son's Moon 0♉25 and North Node 4♉57. Charles and his mother share the powerful Sun-Moon bond, a classic 'marriage' image and one I have witnessed many times between mothers and sons.

[101] Stephen Arroyo, *Astrology, Karma and Transformation*, CRCS Publications (Vancouver: 1978), 211.

[102] Howard Sasportas, The Stages of Childhood in *The Development of the Personality*, 32-6.

[103] Howard Sasportas refers to the 12th house as a pre-birth image: see The Stages of Childhood in *The Development of the Personality*. Interestingly, Sasportas says: 'if Saturn is in the twelfth, then Saturnian feelings pass from mother to developing embryo via the umbilical cord', 26.

[104] Gil Dwyer, *Weird, Unconventional and Shocking; A Uranus-Moon Tale*, Astro*Synthesis Diploma Thesis, 2012, 39-40. See www.astrosynthesis.com.au.

[105] Wordsworth, *Ode: Intimations of Immortality from Recollections of Early Childhood.*

[106] This is how Wordsworth described his sister in his famous poem 'Tintern Abbey'.

[107] Hugh Crago, *A Circle Unbroken*, Allen & Unwin (Sydney: 1999), 31.

[108] Liz Greene, *Barriers and Boundaries, The Horoscope and the Defences of the Personality*, CPA Press (London: 2002), 5-23.

[109] Jung, *The Collected Works of CG Jung*, Volume 2, 1013.

[110] Lyrics quoted from Paul McCartney and John Lennon, 'She's Leaving Home', from the Beatles' *Sgt Pepper's Lonely Hearts Club Band.*

[111] Words and music by John D Loudermilk, 1962.

[112] For amplification on this see Liz Greene and Juliet Sharman-Burke, *The Mythic Journey*, Eddison Sadd (London: 1999), 74-90.

[113] These four messages are inspired by the work of Jay Haley, *Leaving Home: The Therapy of Disturbed Young People, Second Edition*, Brunner/Mazel (New York: 1997).

[114] On family systems see Sullivan, *Dynasty*, 53-60 which explores the archetypes of Uranus and Neptune in light of the disengaged-enmeshed family system.

[115] See: https://www.poets.org/poetsorg/poem/inferno-canto-i [Accessed 3 October 2015].

[116] Jung, *The Collected Works of CG Jung*, Volume 12, 439.

[117] Jung, *Memories, Dreams, Reflections*, 172.

[118] Murray Stein, *In Midlife*, Spring Publications (Dallas: 1983), 25.

[119] Jung was from the Pluto in Taurus generation. Pluto moves the slowest through this sign and this generation actually received their first square in their eighties; however, when Jung at 38 described his descent, Pluto was semi-squaring natal Pluto.

[120] Peter O'Connor, *Facing the Fifties*, Allen & Unwin (Sydney: 2000).

[121] Jung, *The Collected Works of CG Jung*, Volume 8, 772.

[122] Melanie Reinhart, *Chiron and the Healing Journey*, Arkana (London: 1998), 268.

[123] Erica Jong, Pathfinder in *What We Know So Far*, ed. Beth Benatovich, St Martin's Press (New York, NY: 1995), 6.

[124] Many themes around Chiron point to its role as a 'bridge' between the world of form and the 'other' world. It was discovered on 1 November, the Celtic festival of Samhain when the belief is that there is a gap between the worlds. Astronomically, Chiron lies between Saturn and Uranus, the archetypes of form and spirit respectively.

[125] Recent statistics have suggested that the average lifespan for a woman in Australia is 82, which is synchronous with the third return of the progressed Moon.

[126] See Brian Clark, The Progressed Moon: Mnemosyne's Recollections in *Apollon*, The Centre for Psychological Astrology, Issue 4 (December 1999).

[127] Drusilla Modjesja, Life at 50, *The Age*, Melbourne (19 August 2000).

[128] Erin Sullivan, *Saturn in Transit*, London (Arkana: 1991), 85.

[129] Tina Turner quoted in the article Tina Turner Turns Sixty, Robin Egger, *Herald Sun Sunday Magazine*, Melbourne (14 November 1999). Lois Rodden's Astro-Databank lists her birth data as AA.

[130] Germaine Greer interviewed for Baby Love, *Herald Sun Sunday Magazine*, Melbourne (16 April 2000). Lois Rodden's Astro-Databank lists her birth data as A.

[131] May Sarton quoted in Life at 50, *The Age*.

[132] Marian Sandmaier, *Original Kin: The Search for Connection Among Adult Sisters and Brothers*, Dutton (New York: 1994).

[133] Laura M Markowitz, Shared Passages, *Family Therapy Networker* 18, No. 1 (January/February 1994), 69.

[134] When referring to progressions, I will be referring exclusively to secondary progressions which use the equation: 1 day = 1 year. This is my preferred system of progressions/directions, as it keeps the ratio of the planet's speed and its direction intact. see Brian Clark, *Secondary Progressions,* Astro*Synthesis (Melbourne: 2012). See www.astrosynthesis.com

[135] Dr Michel Gauquelin, *Cosmic Influences on Human Behaviour*, ASI Publishers (New York: 1978), 182.

[136] Ibid, 184.

[137] Robert K Barnhart, *The Dictionary of Etymology*, Harper Collins (New York: 1988), 313.

[138] Maggie Scarf, *Intimate Worlds: How Families Thrive and Why They Fail*, Random House (New York: 1995), 67.

[139] John Bradshaw, *Family Secrets*, Bantam Books (New York: 1995), 99-100. The Rosetta Stone was the key that helped to decipher Egyptian hieroglyphics, just as a genogram is a means of revealing some of the hidden patterns of family history.

[140] Sigmund Freud, *The Interpretation of Dreams*, trans. Dr AA Brill, The Modern Library (New York: 1994), 159-61.

[141] I highly recommend a very interesting and dynamic novel that weaves together the story of Oedipus and Freud: Sally Vickers, *Where Three Roads Meet*, Canongate (Edinburgh: 2007).

[142] For an in-depth case study of Freud using genograms throughout his life cycle refer to Carter and McGoldrick, *The Changing Family Life Cycle*, Chapter 8, 164-89.

[143] Ronald Clark, *Freud: The Man and his Cause*, Jonathan Cape (London: 1980), 8-9.

[144] Sigmund Freud, *The Psychopathology of Everyday Life*, trans. AA Brill and T Fisher, Unwin (London: 1928), 253.

[145] Ibid, 250-1.

[146] Sigmund Freud, Archaic Features and Infantilism of Dreams in *The Standard Edition of the Complete Psychological Works of Sigmund Freud (SE)*, Hogarth Press (London: 1953-75), Volume 15, 205.

[147] George Bernard Shaw, *Man and Superman* in *The Complete Plays of Bernard Shaw*, Hamlyn (London: 1965), 355.

[148] The use of the asteroids in astrological practice varies, but from my experience they are powerful images that so often confirm themes already apparent in the horoscope. See Brian Clark, *Asteroid Archetypes*, Astro*Synthesis (Melbourne: 2008). See: www.astrosynthesis.com.au.

[149] Differing December dates have been suggested. The date of 31 December is confirmed by Freud's biographers, Gay and Krull. Anna's Sun is conjunct Freud's 3rd house cusp, which is a constant reminder of the conscious intrusion by his sister.

[150] This is suggested by Lucy Freeman and Herbert Stream in *Freud and Women*, Frederick Unger (New York: 1981). Samuel Slipp in *The Freudian Mystique*, New York University Press (New York: 1995), 108: 'instead of individuating from his mother and establishing a separate identity, Freud seems to have remained fused and identified with her. He continued to use the internal defence mechanism of splitting, repressing

his hostility and consciously idealizing his mother.' This echoes his Moon-Neptune aspect.

[151] Peter Gay, *Freud: A Life for Our Time*, WW Norton (New York: 1988), 307.

[152] Gay in *Freud: A Life for Our Time*, 8, confirms the October 1857 date. Krull in *Freud and His Father*, 214, confirms this from records.

[153] Gay, *Freud: A Life for Our Time*, 507.

[154] Sigmund Freud, *The Origins of Psychoanalysis: Letters, Drafts and Notes to Wilhelm Fleiss*, Basic Books (New York: 1950), 219.

[155] Giovanni Costigan, *Sigmund Freud: A Short Biography*, Macmillan (New York: 1965), 4.

[156] Ibid, 4.

[157] Freeman and Stream, *Freud and Women*, 26.

[158] William McGuire (ed.), *The Freud/Jung Letters: The Correspondence Between Sigmund Freud and CG Jung*, Princeton University Press (Princeton: 1974), 300.

[159] Aldo Carotenuto, *A Secret Symmetry*, Pantheon Books (New York: 1984), 184.

[160] Jeffrey M Masson (trans. and ed.), *Complete Letters of Sigmund Freud to Wilhelm Fleiss*, Harvard University Press (Cambridge: 1985), 152.

[161] Ibid, 73.

[162] Janine Burke, *The Gods of Freud*, Knopf (London: 2006), 9.

Astro*Synthesis

Astro*Synthesis was founded in Melbourne in 1986 as an astrological education programme. Since that time Astro*Synthesis has consistently offered an in-depth training programme into the application of astrology from a psychological perspective. The foundation of the course has been constructed to utilize astrology as a tool for greater awareness of the self, others and the world at large.

From 1986 to 2010, Astro*Synthesis offered its dynamic four-year teaching program in the classroom. Astro*Synthesis now offers the complete program of 12 modules through distance learning.

For a detailed syllabus or more information on Astro*Synthesis E-Workbooks, E- Booklets or reports please visit our website:

www.astrosynthesis.com.au

www.ingramcontent.com/pod-product-compliance
Lightning Source LLC
Chambersburg PA
CBHW050849160426
43194CB00011B/2089